Political Authority

ANTHEM STUDIES IN WITTGENSTEIN

Anthem Studies in Wittgenstein publishes new and classic works on Wittgenstein and Wittgensteinian philosophy. This book series aims to bring Wittgenstein's thought into the mainstream by highlighting its relevance to 21st century concerns. Titles include original monographs, themed edited volumes, forgotten classics, biographical works and books intended to introduce Wittgenstein to the general public. The series is published in association with the British Wittgenstein Society.

Anthem Studies in Wittgenstein sets out to put in place whatever measures may emerge as necessary in order to carry out the editorial selection process purely on merit and to counter bias on the basis of gender, race, ethnicity, religion, sexual orientation and other characteristics protected by law. These measures include subscribing to the British Philosophical Association/Society for Women in Philosophy (UK) Good Practice Scheme.

Series Editor
Constantine Sandis – University of Hertfordshire, UK

Forthcoming Titles in the Series
Kripke's Wittgenstein: Meaning, Rules, and Scepticism
Nightmariners And Wideawakes: The Philosophy of Dreams
Wittgenstein and Popular Culture

Political Authority:
Contract and Critique

Peter Winch

Edited by
Lynette Reid and Michael Campbell

ANTHEM PRESS

Anthem Press
An imprint of Wimbledon Publishing Company
www.anthempress.com

This edition first published in UK and USA 2025
by ANTHEM PRESS
75–76 Blackfriars Road, London SE1 8HA, UK
or PO Box 9779, London SW19 7ZG, UK
and
244 Madison Ave #116, New York, NY 10016, USA

© 2025 Lynette Reid and Michael Campbell editorial matter and selection;
individual chapters © individual contributors

The moral right of the authors has been asserted.

All rights reserved. Without limiting the rights under copyright reserved above,
no part of this publication may be reproduced, stored or introduced into
a retrieval system, or transmitted, in any form or by any means
(electronic, mechanical, photocopying, recording or otherwise),
without the prior written permission of both the copyright
owner and the above publisher of this book.

British Library Cataloguing-in-Publication Data
A catalogue record for this book is available from the British Library.

Library of Congress Cataloging-in-Publication Data: 2025930022
A catalog record for this book has been requested.

ISBN-13: 978-1-83999-165-3 (Hbk)
ISBN-10: 1-83999-165-8 (Hbk)

Cover image Credit: Helen Campbell, Yohaku (*Birds at Sunset*) (2022)

This title is also available as an e-book.

CONTENTS

Notes on Contributors   vii
Acknowledgements   ix
Notes on the Text   xi
Editorial Introduction   xvii

Part 1: The London Era [c. 1964–1985]   1
1.1   The Image of Law: Laws of Thought and Forms of Life [1966]   3
1.2   Intercollegiate Lectures on Political Philosophy [1969–1970]   11
1.3   Authority, Society and the State [N.D.]   33
1.4   Four Lectures on Consent [1984]   41
1.5   Lectures on Locke on Property [N.D.]   53
1.6   Authority [Freedom and Servility] [N.D.]   61

Part 2: The Illinois Era [c. 1985–1997]   69
2.1   Philosophy of Law and the State [1992]   71
2.2   Illinois Seminar on Political Authority [1990]   125
2.3   Plato's *Gorgias* [1996]   131
2.4   Reason, Will and Representation in Rousseau [1993]   149

Part 3: The 'Last Book Outline' [c. 1995]   155
3.1   The Paradox of Authority   157
3.2   Empirical and Conceptual Questions   159
3.3   Socrates and Politics   165
3.4   Reasons and Causes   185
3.5   The Historicity of Political Philosophy   191
3.6   Consent and Rationality   203
3.7   The Role of Authority in our Lives   207

3.8	The Authority of Reason	209
3.9	The Habit of Obedience	215
3.10	Formation of the Concept of the State	219
Appendices		223
4.1	Authority, Consent and Practical Reason [1990]	225
4.2	Reasons for Action/Wittgenstein on Authority [N.D.]	229
4.3	Session 9 of Åbo Seminar on Political Authority [1993]	231
Bibliography		235
Index		241

NOTES ON CONTRIBUTORS

Peter Winch (1926–1997) was a British philosopher known for his contributions to the philosophy of social science, Wittgenstein scholarship, ethics, political philosophy and the philosophy of religion. His work includes *On the Idea of a Social Science and its Relation to Philosophy* (Routledge, 1958), *Simone Weil: The Just Balance* (Cambridge University Press, 1989) and numerous articles, the most important of which were reprinted in his collections *Ethics and Action* (Routledge, 1972) and *Trying to Make Sense* (Basil Blackwell, 1987). He was also translator of Wittgenstein's *Culture and Value* (University of Chicago Press, 1984) and co-editor of *The Political Responsibility of Intellectuals* (with Ian Maclean and Alan Montefiore, Cambridge University Press, 1990).

Lynette Reid is Associate Professor at Dalhousie University. She received her PhD from UIUC with a dissertation on the *Tractatus* completed under Winch's supervision. She attended his lectures and seminars on philosophy of law and the state and on political authority in the final years of his life. Her recent papers on Winch's use of Melville's novella (and Britten's opera) *Billy Budd* draw connections between Winch's political and moral philosophies ('Winch on Punishment: Contested Concepts, Justification, and Primitive Reactions' in *Ethics, Society and Politics: Themes from the Philosophy of Peter Winch* (with M. Campbell, Springer, 2020), and 'The Ethical and the Political in the Dilemma of Winch's Vere' in *Ethics in the Wake of Wittgenstein* (2019, eds. de Mesel and Kuusela)). She also works in public health ethics.

Michael Campbell is Junior Associate Professor in the Department of Ethics at Kyoto University. He is editor of *The Philosophy of Transformative Experience* (Routledge, 2025), co-editor of *Wittgenstein and Perception* (with M. O'Sullivan, Routledge, 2015), *Ethics, Society and Politics: Themes from the Philosophy of Peter Winch* (with L. Reid, Springer, 2020) and *Spinoza on Ethics and Understanding* by Peter Winch (with S. Tropper, Anthem, 2020). He wrote the preface for the new edition of Peter Winch's *Ethics and Action* (Routledge, 2020).

ACKNOWLEDGEMENTS

The editors would like to thank David Cockburn, Lars Hertzberg, Olli Lagerspetz, Mark Theunissen, and Chris Winch for their support and feedback during the compilation of this manuscript. We are particularly grateful to Chris Winch for permission to publish Peter Winch's writings and for his enthusiastic support for the project, which kept up our spirits at moments when they may otherwise have flagged.

We would also like to thank the participants of the conference 'Truth in Politics and Metaphysics: Celebrating the Work of Peter Winch', which Michael Campbell organized at King's College London in 2017.

Michael Campbell would like to record his personal debt to Raimond Gaita, from whom he learned, in years of supervision, to appreciate the depth and sophistication in Winch's philosophising.

We would both like to thank the anonymous reviewers from Anthem Press for their helpful feedback on the manuscript. We would also like to thank Constantine Sandis and the editorial team at Anthem Press, particularly Jebaslin Hephzibah, for their patience and professionalism over many years.

NOTES ON THE TEXT[1]

The materials are selected from the Peter Winch Archives (GB 0100 KCLCA K/PP171, King's College London), along with a small number of typescripts distributed to students in Illinois, USA, or Åbo, Finland.

In arranging these materials for publication, we have tried to strike a balance between readability on the one hand and preserving the distinctive character of the different media (lectures, TSS and handwritten notes) and the development of Winch's thought on the other. For the most part, we have taken a light editorial approach to the content. We have divided the material into three parts and an appendix, with the first two corresponding to Winch's time living and working in London and Illinois, and the third consisting of the final book outline which Winch produced in the 1990s. We have included as an appendix three shorter book outlines which were composed prior to this final outline. Within each section we have selected, from the hitherto unpublished material available to us, texts which we believe best represent his thought from the time, and we have presented them in an order which prioritises readability over chronology.

Due to the heterogenous nature of the source material, there was no consistent standard of referencing throughout. Some MSS contained full citations, which would typically be in-text but would sometimes be in footnotes. Others contained only indications of the relevant text. We have standardised these, moving references to notes and filling in Winch's references when his intentions were clearly recoverable. At one or two points, we were forced to speculate; where this is so, we indicate it in the note. We have placed our transcriptions of Winch's marginal notes and handwritten comments in notes at the relevant sections, and have indicated our own narrative footnotes with 'Eds:'.

Winch frequently included emphases in his writing. In handwritten and typescript texts, this was typically done with underlining, and occasionally with capitalisation. Once he had access to a computer, he would also use bold, and – in rare moments – he would use a combination of emboldening, italicising and underlining points. Following the publisher's conventions, we have replaced all of these with italicisation but have kept all of Winch's own emphasis points. (Doubtless, almost all would have been removed

---

1. In what follows, we use the following abbreviations: Manuscript (MS), Manuscripts (MSS), Typescript (TS), Typescripts (TSS).

had Winch himself prepared material in these texts for publication.) We have silently corrected punctuation errors in opening and closing quotes and parentheses but for the most part left his own punctuation style, which often omits commas, otherwise intact. We have regularised quotation styles (single or double) to the publisher standard; Winch himself switched from British to US style over the years. We have also regularised some possessives which he formed inconsistently (Hobbes's) and changed his early 'Hobbist' to his later, more standard, 'Hobbesist'. He routinely used square brackets instead of parentheses, but as that is confusing in relation to editorial conventions signifying editorial additions, we have changed these to round parentheses.

In preparing for his lecture courses, Winch produced detailed lecture outlines, often using full sentences and paragraphs but formatted as outlines, with nested numerical lists, e.g. I.A.1.a.(1). Despite the full sentences and paragraphs, these were frameworks for expanding on while lecturing and their style, though recognisable as Winch's, is different from that of his published papers. In a lecture or seminar presentation, 1–5 pp. of such text would be the basis of a 50– or 75–minute class, or a three-hour seminar. Discussion with students, more patient exegesis of the text under discussion, and broader, more detailed reflection on particular examples would have ultimately filled out such outlines.

Winch was an early and enthusiastic adopter of computers, and then of specialised academic word processing. For the most part, we have drastically simplified the hierarchical list structure of lecture materials that read well as a continuous narrative. Presumably, his computer 'floppy' disks (the technology of the time) contained much more material than the printouts in the archive, but these (as with many digital sources) were not included in the archives.

There are very few unpublished drafts of papers in the archive. We cannot rule out that he systematically destroyed drafts, or that he never printed them off; but the archival evidence is most consistent with someone developing his thinking in conversation, in teaching and in reflection, then setting them to paper or later to disk in a single go for a single purpose (a lecture, a talk, a paper for publication).

Part 1: The London Era

In the archives are eight green folders labelled Politics I–VIII. In these folders, diverse materials are filed: handwritten reading notes or lecture notes torn from bound notebooks; TSS of lectures or syllabi or reading lists; a draft of a book chapter on Simone Weil (a variation of the contents of his *Simone Weil: The Just Balance*). The contents of these folders appear to be roughly thematically grouped, though the materials in each file are mixed in terms of form and content. The themes can be summarised as follows:

I. Hobbes
II. Consent and force
III. Vico
IV. Hume and consent; Weil; Intercollegiate lectures on political philosophy
V. Hobbes and Rousseau

VI. Locke, including on property
VII. Authority; Weil
VII. Rousseau, Mill and Marx[2]

Material in these folders ranges in length from 100 to over 10,000 words. It is rarely possible to date these, though speculating based on the development of his handwriting and the age of the paper it seems that some may have come with him from Swansea or earlier. We think that they were all produced within the period 1967–1985.

Incorporated Material from the London Era

From these materials, we have selected a number that are cohesive in their treatment of a specific topic or in the overview they offer, that show a range of different approaches he is exploring to addressing the central puzzle of political authority and that are accessible for readers. The BBC lecture 'The Image of Law: Laws of Thought and Forms of Life' (1966) (Chapter 1.1) serves as an effective introduction to the way that Winch approaches interconnected philosophical concerns about logic and social life. The 'Intercollegiate Lectures on Political Philosophy' of 1969–1970 (Chapter 1.2) (given together with the Marxist analytic philosopher G. A. Cohen, the game theorist Lloyd Thomas and others) demonstrate a key element in Winch's approach to political philosophy as a philosopher influenced by Wittgenstein and Rush Rhees: mere description of the language game of politics would not treat the philosophical questions that make us puzzled about political life in the first place. Three shorter TSS, which are clearly notes for a short lecture series, represent different approaches to the same issue. The first investigates the role of intelligence in social affairs and shows the challenges Hobbes faces in giving a material account of concern with truth and truthfulness ('Authority Society and the State' (Chapter 1.3)). The second explores the nature and limits of express and tacit consent ('Four Lectures on Consent' (Chapter 1.4)). The third frames the question of authority in terms of freedom: 'Authority [Freedom and Servility]' (Chapter 1.6). We have also included our transcription of a selection of handwritten lecture notes on Locke on property (Chapter 1.5), since 'Locke on Property' appears in the last book outline (Chapter 3.9, n. 2) as a bullet point to be expanded on.

Part 2: The Illinois Era

The archives contain much material from his time in Illinois, including course syllabi, lecture notes, and MSS of published papers and books and related correspondence with publishers and conference organisers. The syllabi and lecture notes are for mixed

---

2. Peter Winch Archives (GB 0100 KCLCA K/PP171), King's College London. Most of the green Politics I–VIII folders are in Box 21; the exceptions are IV, which is in Box 7 and VIII, which is in Box 19.

undergraduate/graduate lecture series and for the introductory sessions of graduate seminars, after which students would have taken on presenting. These materials include lecture notes entitled: Philosophy of the Social Sciences, Wittgenstein and Logic, Philosophy of Religion, Ethics and Value Theory and Classical Ancient Philosophers. Especially relevant to our purposes, there are complete lecture notes for Philosophy of Law and the State from 1986, 1988 and 1992, a (lone) syllabus from 1994, and notes for his 1990 Illinois and 1993 Åbo Akademi seminars on Political Authority. A number of TSS (dot matrix printer, but some dated 1993) appear as TSS of papers – these almost entirely match or duplicate the last book outline.

Incorporated Material from the Illinois Era

Central to this section is a complete reproduction of Winch's 1992 lectures on 'Philosophy of Law and the State' (Chapter 2.1), which cover the debate between legal positivism and naturalism; the philosophical puzzle about the possibility of legitimacy; Hobbes: language, mind and covenant; Locke on leaving the state of nature; Hume and Locke on tacit consent; H. L. A. Hart and rules; public order and natural law; and punishment.

The 1994 syllabus (for which no printout of the lectures themselves was located) comes closer to the ordering of topics in what we call the 'Last Book Outline' (Part 3). We have not reproduced the 1993 Åbo Authority Seminar introductory sessions, as these are identical for large stretches to the last book outline. We have included the 1990 'Illinois Seminar on Political Authority' introductory sessions (Chapter 2.2) as they bring into focus a line of thought that he was exploring, namely that the philosophical depth of the problems of political authority could be *unsettling* (with reference to Wittgenstein's comments on Ramsey as a bourgeois thinker) and (with reference to Weil) that the difficulty of specifying content for the concept of legitimacy be essential to the way the concept engages individual commitment and judgement.

We also include here a number of sessions from his Ethics and Value Theory lectures (Chapter 3.3) on Socrates and the sophists. This provides more detailed exegesis and context for the bullet points in the last book outline (Chapter 3.3) where Plato and the 'authority' of Socrates come to the fore.

One TS distributed to students at the Åbo Authority Seminar, 'Reason, Will, and Representation in Rousseau' is included here as Chapter 2.4. Unlike other similar-looking TSS, it does not correspond to any part of the 'Last Book Outline' (Part 3).

Part 3: 'The Last Book Outline'

The archives contain a printout of a book MS outline. Although it is undated, given that it was produced using Nota Bene software and printed using a laser printer, and given also the relationship of its content to the Åbo Authority Seminar of 1993 (and to the 1992 lecture notes and 1994 syllabus), we believe that it was likely produced within the last two or three years of his life.

The contents of the printout are highly mixed. The text takes the form of a chapter-by-chapter outline, sometimes in bullet points and sometimes in continuous text but formatted as an outline. However, this was a work in progress, and as a result, certain chapters were much more thoroughly developed than others. It appears from the archives that his practice with the Weil book was to teach one or more graduate seminars from a draft MS of an entire book and then to revise substantially. Hence we might infer that the materials here were extremely preliminary. Had he lived longer he might have developed the full book MS, taught from it, and then substantially revised.

There are seven TSS (five in the archive and two in Olli Lagerspetz's personal collection) that either follow the outline of the chapter or are the same as the continuous text in the corresponding chapter (but not formatted as an outline: 'The Limits of Argument', 'Action, Reason and Will', 'Generality and Particularity', 'Authority of Reason', 'Reasons and Causes', 'Habit of Obedience', and 'Reason, Will and Representation in Rousseau'. Two of these TSS ('Authority of Reason' and 'Reason, Will and Representation in Rousseau') were distributed to students at the 1993 Åbo Authority Seminar,[3] one of which ('Authority of Reason') follows the outline of a chapter. Similarly, some of his lecture notes for the 1993 Åbo Authority Seminar (which are mostly continuous sentences and paragraphs but in outline formatting) either follow the outline in the 'Last Book Outline' TS, or are identical to the 'Last Book Outline' TS or the corresponding TSS, and accordingly, we have used these resources to reconstruct the content indicated by the 'Last Book Outline' where these seemed directly relevant. We cannot however conclude that these materials were in their final intended format. Some of the TSS appear to fill out the outline, but sometimes (e.g. 'Habit of Obedience'), there is reason to think the Outline may have been written after the TS because suggestions made in an aside in the TS are carried out in the Outline.

In the 'Last Book Outline' TS, most of Chapters 3.1, 3.2 and 3.8 have content that is in full sentences and paragraphs, but formatted as an outline. We have removed the outlining from these parts to improve their readability, as we did with lecture notes. Presumably, he had intended to expand on the matters discussed, as he did with the similarly formatted lecture notes. For those chapters that take the form of a true bullet point outline consisting mostly of sentence fragments (most of Chapters 3.3, 3.5, 3.6, 3.7, 3.9 and 3.10), we have created reconstructions using TSS. For some of these chapters, TSS in the archives or distributed to participants in a seminar at Åbo Akademi match the progress of topics and examples given in the bullet point outline. Where this is the case, we have replaced the bullet point outline with continuous text from a corresponding TS, and we have indicated the corresponding outline number and heading in square brackets. However, no chapter that takes this form is complete. Thus, we retain the bare outline material where there is no replacement from the TSS and supplement it

---

3. Olli Lagerspetz, 'Peter Winch on Political Authority and Political Culture', *Philosophical Investigations* 35, nos. 3–4 (2012): 277–302.

xvi · POLITICAL AUTHORITY

with footnotes indicating similar or relevant discussions either in the archive materials reproduced in this book, or Winch's published writings.[4]

Correspondence Between the 'Last Book Outline' and Other Materials

The Åbo Akademi Seminar materials in the archives contain TSS and also Winch's own notes for his presentation. Winch also distributed two TSS to participants in the seminar, which Olli Lagerspetz has provided. We have notes corresponding to each of 10 sessions of the Åbo seminar (hereafter ASN*x*, with *x* representing the session week), together with six TSS from the archives and one of the TSS distributed to participants.[5] The relation of these with chapters in the Book MS is detailed in the list below. For the most part, this correspondence is direct, suggesting that he copied and pasted the text from the seminar into the book outline, or vice versa. Where there is content in the Åbo Seminar that is missing from the book outline, we provide that content in footnotes. As the book outline is undated, we have no way to know whether the differences reflect materials added or removed.

Chapter 3.1: ASN1
Chapter 3.2: ASN2, ASN3
Chapter 3.3: ASN4, ASN5, 'Action, Reason and Will' TS and 'Limits of Argument' TS
Chapter 3.4: ASN6 'Reasons and Causes' TS
Chapter 3.5: ASN7, ASN8, 'Generality and Particularity' TS
Chapter 3.6: ASN7, ASN8, 'Generality and Particularity' TS
Chapter 3.7: Brief bullet outline with no comparable lecture or TS sources
Chapter 3.8: ASN 10, 'Authority of Reason' TS
Chapter 3.9: 'Habit of Obedience' TS
Chapter 3.10: 'Habit of Obedience' TS

Appendices

The notes for Session 9 of the Åbo Seminar are in themselves akin to a book outline. He takes stock of what has been discussed to that point in the first eight sessions and sketches out where he will take it. We have published it as an outline in its own right as an appendix (Chapter 4.3), along with two further short outlines. One of these is dated 12 February 1990 (Chapter 4.1), and the other is undated (Chapter 4.2).

---

4. Chapter 3.4 posed a unique challenge. It consists of five major sections (I–V). Section I seems to present an outline in bullet form of what follows in II–V. However, in II–V, not everything outlined in I is present, and the material that is present is not introduced in the same order as that indicated in I. Therefore, we have decided to reconstruct the chapter by taking the sentences and paragraphs of II–V out of outline form and preserving their order (contrary to what was planned in I), with the interpolation of the bullet points from I that indicate discussions missing from II–V.
5. One of the TSS distributed at Åbo does not fit into the outline and is reproduced here as Chapter 2.4 ('Reason, Will and Representation in Rousseau').

EDITORIAL INTRODUCTION

Overview

Peter Winch (1926–1997) was a British philosopher known for his contributions to the philosophy of social science, Wittgenstein scholarship, ethics, political philosophy and the philosophy of religion. He was a lecturer in philosophy at Swansea University from 1951 until 1964. In 1964, he moved to Birkbeck College, University of London, before becoming Professor of Philosophy at King's College London in 1967. In 1985, Winch moved to the United States to become Professor at the University of Illinois at Urbana-Champaign. He served as president of the Aristotelian Society from 1980 to 1981 and was serving his term as Past President of the Central Division of the American Philosophical Association at the time of his death in 1997.

This volume collects together, for the first time, Winch's unpublished work on political philosophy. We have drawn the majority of our source material from the Peter Winch Archives at King's College London, supplemented by material from students. Winch returned to topics in and around political philosophy throughout his career and left papers that vary widely in format, including unpublished talks, typescripts for seminars, lecture course outlines, handwritten notes for his own reference and a draft of a book outline. Since it is not possible to publish all of this material, we have selected a range of indicative texts which bring out the contours of Winch's thoughts on political philosophy, their development over time, and their most recent developments when he passed away.

Political philosophy was very much a work in progress for Winch (who would perhaps have agreed with the sentiment that philosophy is always a work in progress), and had he lived to bring these writings to publication we are in no doubt that much would have been changed, both in form and content. This is a 'what-if' question that must, alas, remain unanswered. Our hope in presenting this material is not to provide a definitive record of Winch's work on the topic, but only to help fill out this particular, and peculiarly neglected, dimension of his thought.

Winch emphasised the practice of doing philosophy in conversation – in graduate supervision, in discussion of papers and in reading groups, including his Sunday afternoon, paragraph-by-paragraph reading group in Illinois on the *Philosophical Investigations* and the late volumes on the philosophy of psychology. His ideas were developed in this medium. Unlike in his lectures, he was not, in these contexts, presenting a sustained line of thought, but responding to the question of the moment and the thought of his interlocutor. However, certain themes would recur in these settings, gradually take on significance and eventually appear in his publications.

Taken as a whole, Winch's published writings have an overlapping character, with thoughts, examples and thinkers threaded through his essays. In 'Text and Context',[6] he observed that the meaning of a text or work of art has reference to the context in which it appears and that new dimensions can be revealed by juxtaposition: one thing 'casts light' on another, revealing internal features and relations. Following Wittgenstein's injunction to collect 'reminders', Winch worked and reworked ideas and passages, making subtle modifications to emphasis and placement as he went along. In his work on political philosophy, this tendency is apparent. The development of his thought is not the work of a theorist adding detail and complexity into a fixed framework – rather, through interrogation and juxtaposition, images of the political are brought into clearer focus. Progress in political philosophy for Winch involved showing how difficult it is to provide any definitive shape to the realm of the political; paraphrasing Ludwig Wittgenstein, how far, in discussing political life, we must already use political language 'full blown'. Thus, the political sphere is interdependent with and inseparable from the social, political, ethical and moral spheres of human affairs. Fluency in political critique means being able to recognise the inherent contestability of any distinction between the political and extra-political – and also to be able to participate in such contestation, where doing so is necessary to overcome a practical or intellectual difficulty.

A central preoccupation of Winch's was the nature of political authority and the source of the legitimacy of the state, in particular, the puzzle of how rational agency can be consistent with obedience to legitimate authority. He was suspicious of reductive and foundationalist tendencies in political philosophy, doubting both that the authority of the state could be understood as an instance of a more general category of obedience to the dictates of reason, and that the concept of the political could be built up from more primitive materials, such as contracts made between self-interested individuals. In the opening of his 'Last Book Outline' (Chapter 3.1), he put this point in a striking way: 'If we think that reason must be the source of authority we must ask *what is the authority of reason?*' Yet, having reached this insight, how exactly Winch was going to develop this thought to his satisfaction is what is left incomplete: the pivotal chapter (Chapter 3.7) is the most truncated.

As with Wittgenstein before him, Winch's philosophical difficulties had a personal character, being questions that arise within, and draw their animus from, the lives of the people who ask them. Transposed to the political context, this means the political theorist must work to have a keen eye for the way that political forces shape the contexts in which political agency appears. This includes the institutional and social contexts in which we work, the form that our defences of and challenges to these contexts take, and the shifting conditions under which such defences or challenges are,

---

6. Peter Winch, 'Text and Context', in *Trying to Make Sense* (Oxford: Basil Blackwell, 1987), 18–32.

or are not, found wanting. This approach gave him a deep concern for questions about the nature of justice and social oppression, reflected in his engagement with Simone Weil in the 1970s and 1980s.[7] As he put it at the end of his (unpublished) TS, 'Simone Weil on Other People': 'The language which I use to describe myself (as 'object') is a language expressive of the hierarchical structure of the societies whose language it is'.[8] His manuscripts from this period show him circling around a view of the recognition of legitimacy or justice in a given political order as a matter of taking a personal stance towards it – one which is revealed in the details of daily life and action.[9] Abstract principles, if adopted, have what sense they do insofar as they are expressed in action and the texture of daily life. In other words, the authority of reason stands in relation to the authority of a life lived in accordance with reason. For an example of this form of the 'authority of reason', he turned to Plato's portrait of Socrates (Chapter 2.4 and Chapter 3.3).[10]

Winch's emphasis on the embeddedness of thought should not be taken to suggest that he was chary of idealisation *per se*. In fact, he was sympathetic to a strand of thinking in Rousseau and Weil that without an ideal of justice not to be found in the world, there could be neither such a thing as relations among citizens, nor relations of citizens to the state. He expresses this point forcefully in the conclusion to 'Man and Society in Hobbes and Rousseau':

> The relation between citizen and sovereign cannot be understood simply in *quantitative* terms (Hobbes's 'strengths united') but requires a certain *quality* of life shared by the citizens. What it requires is a life in which the citizens can exercise judgement and in which they do apply that judgement to questions about the justice of social arrangements. It is at this point that the various strands in Rousseau's thought […] come together. As he emphasizes in both the *Discourse on Inequality* and *Émile*, men are born and grow up in societies which are all riddled with injustices of various sorts. This must be taken as a datum in any discussion of the possibility of political arrangements which will embody conceptions of justice, permit of liberty in the relations between citizens and state, and thereby allow us to think of the state as legitimate. […] Conceptions of justice are only developed through discussions of

---

7. In addition to his book *Simone Weil: 'The Just Balance'* (Cambridge: Cambridge University Press, 1989), he and his students translated and published relevant texts by Weil, in particular Simone Weil, 'The Legitimacy of the Provisional Government' (trans. Peter Winch, *Philosophical Investigations* 10, no. 2 (1987): 87–98) and 'Are We Struggling for Justice?' (trans. Marina Barabas, *Philosophical Investigations* 10, no. 1 (1987): 1–10). Winch also references Weil's 'Essay on the Notion of Reading' (trans. Rebecca Fine Rose and Timothy Tessin, *Philosophical Investigations* 13, no. 4 (1990): 297–303) in the context of politics.
8. Peter Winch, 'Other People' (1977). Typescript; book chapter draft; 19 pp., Peter Winch Archives (GB 0100 KCLCA K/PP171, Folder 'Politics IV', Box 7), King's College London.
9. For discussion of Winch's interpretation of Simone Weil, see Levy, 'What is *la force* in Simone Weil's Iliad?' *Philosophical Investigations* 43, nos. 1–2 (2020): 19–39.
10 A paper that Winch would frequently refer to in this connection is Marina Barabas, 'The Strangeness of Socrates', *Philosophical Investigations* 9, no. 2 (1986): 89–110.

injustices. Men capable of becoming citizens must then receive an education which enables them to understand what those injustices are, an education which consists not merely in inculcating a 'science' of what human relationships necessarily are, but rather in creating human beings of a sort who will be capable of discerning qualitative distinctions between different types of human relationship and who will therefore be capable of entering into such relationships.[11]

Throughout his thinking on politics, Hobbes is returned to as a constant foil, since Hobbes both perceived the necessity of explaining the formation of both state and subject alike, and yet provided an account of rational agency which left no room for the conceptual step-change involved in coming to see one's actions in the light of moral-cum-political concepts like justice.[12] This thought links his political thought directly to a number of themes in his many papers on ethics. His lectures on the state's justification for punishment (Chapter 2.2, Lectures 27–29) develop in social and institutional directions a concept whose ethical dimension was a preoccupation of his.[13] Furthermore, many of his ethical papers involve consideration of dilemmas that people face in fulfilling their duties as functionaries of the state.[14] In his late paper 'The Expression of Belief', this connection is made explicit in his juxtaposition of Herman Melville's Captain Vere (from the novel *Billy Budd*) with Hobbes's theory of practical rationality.[15]

In his last years in Illinois, as the religious right gained political power and Pat Buchanan declared the 'culture wars', Winch began to rethink the relation between the spheres of religion and science which in his 'Darwin, Genesis and Contradiction',[16] he had held to be logically separate. He continued to hold that it was a mistake to think that religion and science contradict one another in what they assert, but he came to

---

11. Peter Winch, 'Man and Society in Hobbes and Rousseau', in *Ethics and Action* (London: Routledge and Kegan Paul, 1972): 90–109.
12. At one point, he considers using his 'Wittgenstein's Treatment of the Will' (in *Ethics and Action* [London: Routledge and Kegan Paul, 1972], 110–129) as the approach he will take to critique the 'solipsism' of atomic agency in contact theory (Chapter 4.2).
13. See 'Ethical reward and punishment' and 'Can a Good Man Be Harmed?' in *Ethics and Action* (London: Routledge and Kegan Paul, 1972), 210–228 and 193–209 respectively, and 'He's to Blame!' in *Wittgenstein: Attention to Particulars: Essays in Honour of Rush Rhees*, eds. D. Z. Phillips and Peter Winch (Palgrave Macmillan, 1989), 151–164. See Lynette Reid, 'Winch on Punishment: Contested Concepts, Justification, and Primitive Reactions' in *Ethics, Society and Politics: Themes from the Philosophy of Peter Winch*, eds. Michael Campell and Lynette Reid (Cham: Springer International Publishing, 2020), 57–83.
14. Peter Winch, 'The Universalizability of Moral Judgement', in *Ethics and Action* (London: Routledge and Kegan Paul, 1972), 151–170 and 'Particularity and Morals' in *Trying to Make Sense* (Oxford: Basil Blackwell, 1987), 167–180.
15. Peter Winch, 'The Expression of Belief', *Proceedings and Addresses of the American Philosophical Association* 70, no. 2 (1996): 7–23.
16. Peter Winch, 'Darwin, Genesis, and Contradiction', in *Trying to Make Sense* (Oxford: Basil Blackwell, 1987), 132–139.

think that certain forms of religious belief did require of their adherents a conception of 'commitment to truth' which is at odds with the attitude towards truth – as a spirit of open inquiry – required by the scientific method. (In such cases, he felt this to be to the detriment of religion.) This was closely connected with his reflections in conversation at the time on Primo Levi's account of science as a refuge from and resistance to fascism, and Václav Havel's portrayal of the way that the Eastern bloc authoritarian states based their power on corrupting citizens' relation to the truth.[17]

Winch's forays into political philosophy can be seen as developments of his critique of 'positivist' social sciences.[18] He contrasts sociological accounts of power (roughly linked to legal positivism) with philosophical concerns about the nature of authority.[19] One prominent philosopher of law who saw the relevance of Winch's early work was H. L. A. Hart, who took up Winch's work on rules (Chapter 2.2, Lectures 22–23). The contrast between rules and causes survives in Winch's lectures and book drafts all the way until the 'Last Book Outline' draft of the mid-1990s (Chapter 3.4). His critique of supposed universal standards for rationality in 'Understanding a Primitive Society'[20] is recalled in the 1993 Authority Seminar (Chapter 2.3). If reason is the touchstone for the legitimacy of the state, then we cannot avoid the question, *whose* reason? As he put it in another early paper:

> What we can ascribe to human nature does not determine what we can and what we cannot make sense of; rather, what we can and what we cannot make sense of determines what we can ascribe to human nature. It is indeed precisely for this reason that the concept of human nature is not the concept of something fixed and given; i.e. the reason for this is a philosophical, not a sociological, one.[21]

---

17. Lynette Reid, personal communication. See Primo Levi, 'The Periodic Table' (in *The Complete Works of Primo Levi*, ed. and trans. Ann Goldstein [W. W. Norton and Company, 2015], 2:761–966); and Vaclav Havel, 'The Power of the Powerless', in *Living in the Truth*, ed. Jan Vladislav (London: Faber and Faber, 1987), 36–122. See also Diamond 'Truth: Defenders, Debunkers, Despisers', in *Commitment in Reflection: Essays in Literature and Moral Philosophy*, ed. L. Toker (London: Routledge, 1993), 195–222, and Raimond Gaita, *A Common Humanity, Thinking About Love and Truth and Justice* (Abingdon: Routledge, 2000), Chapter 10.
18. Peter Winch, *The Idea of a Social Science and Its Relation to Philosophy*, 2nd Edition (London: Routledge, 1990 [1958]).
19. Lest it seem that Winch's criticisms rest on a conflation of positivism, legal positivism, and sociology, he was careful in distinguishing (e.g.) Hobbes and Austin (Chapter 2.2, Lectures 2–4) and treated Hart – as a contemporary expositor of positivism – with detailed care. He also maintained a close engagement with sociology and with critical social theory; see Peter Winch, 'Apel's "Transcendental Pragmatics"', in *Philosophical Disputes in the Social Sciences*, ed. S. C. Brown (Sussex: Harvester Press, 1979), 51–73.
20. Peter Winch, 'Understanding a Primitive Society', in *Ethics and Action* (London: Routledge and Kegan Paul, 1972), 8–49.
21. Peter Winch, 'Human Nature', in *Ethics and Action* (London: Routledge and Kegan Paul, 1972), 73–89 (84).

Winch is not generally known as a philosopher of politics. Nevertheless, the political dimensions of his work have generated some noteworthy research. John Horton produced an influential critical account of his early papers on authority.[22] Lars Hertzberg – whose discussions with Winch were influential in the development of the latter's account of political philosophy – has written several papers drawing out the political dimensions of Winch's approach to philosophical problems.[23] Olli Lagerspetz has provided an in-depth survey of Winch's political thought from the perspective of a student who engaged deeply with him in this domain, drawing on his own lecture notes and materials that Winch shared with students.[24] Phil Hutchinson, Rupert Read and Wes Sharrock have provided a book-length treatment of Winch's approach to social science which emphasises its critical potential.[25] And most recently, Alice Crary has written an article connecting Wittgensteinian political philosophy and critical theory, drawing in part on Winch's writings.[26]

In the context of this background scholarship, we believe that the following volume will provide a stimulating resource for further work to engage with, and expand upon, the orienting methods and concerns of Winch's political philosophy. In many ways, Winch's critical engagement with the contract tradition anticipated later feminist and political realist critiques of ideal theory. Throughout, he held together a serious engagement with, and respect for, the abstractive tendencies of theory construction with an emphasis on the embodied dimensions of political concepts. In an era of growing instability with multiple crises of political legitimacy, we believe that Winch's humanising approach to the conceptualisation of such notions as community and collective authority may serve as a valuable resource and touchstone.

Winch's Published Papers on Political Philosophy

Winch believed in the interdependence of philosophical issues and would therefore find any separation of his corpus into different philosophical subject matters to be arbitrary and potentially misleading. Nevertheless, certain of his published papers include

---

22. John Horton, 'Peter Winch and Political Authority', *Philosophical Investigations* 28, no. 3 (2005): 235–252.
23. See Lars Hertzberg, 'Legitimacy and the Political Community', in *Legitimacy: The Treasure of Politics*, eds. Kurtén and Hertzberg (Frankfurt am Main: Peter Lang, 2011) and '"What Justifies the Justifications?" Winch on Punishment and Justice', in *Ethics, Society and Politics: Themes From the Philosophy of Peter Winch*, eds. Campbell and Reid (Cham: Springer International Publishing, 2020), 41–55.
24. Lagerspetz, 'Legitimacy and Trust', *Philosophical Investigations* 15, no. 1 (1992): 1-21; 'Peter Winch on Political Authority and Political Culture', *Philosophical Investigations* 35, nos. 3-4 (2012): 277–302; and 'Political Philosophy and the Primacy of Agency', in *Ethics, Society and Politics: Themes From the Philosophy of Peter Winch*, eds. Campbell and Reid (Cham: Springer International Publishing, 2020), 85–102.
25. Hutchinson, Read and Sharrock. *There Is No Such Thing as a Social Science: In Defence of Peter Winch* (Aldershot: Ashgate, 2008).
26. Alice Crary, 'Wittgenstein Goes to Frankfurt (and Finds Something Useful to Say)', *Nordic Wittgenstein Review* 7, no. 1 (2018): 7–41.

material with direct affinity to the topics broached in this volume, which the reader is encouraged to consult:

1. Peters, R. S., Peter Winch and A. E. Duncan-Jones. 'Symposium: Authority'. *Proceedings of the Aristotelian Society* Supplementary Volume 32 (1958): 207–260. Reprinted (Peters and Winch) in *Political Philosophy*, edited by A. Quinton, 97–111. Oxford: Oxford University Press, 1967.
2. Winch, P. 'Man and Society in Hobbes and Rousseau'. In *Hobbes and Rousseau: A Collection of Critical Essays*, edited by M. Cranston and R. Peters, 233–253. New York: Doubleday, 1972. Reprinted in *Ethics and Action*, 90–109. London: Routledge and Kegan Paul, 1972.
3. Winch, P. 'Authority and Rationality'. *The Human World* 8 (1972): 11–21.
4. Winch, P. 'Certainty and Authority'. *Philosophy* 28 (Supplement) (1990): 223–237. Reprinted in *Wittgenstein Centenary Essays*, edited by A. Phillips Griffiths, 223–238. Cambridge: Cambridge University Press, 1991.
5. Winch, P. 'Introduction'. In *The Political Responsibility of Intellectuals*, edited by I. Maclean, A. Montefiore and P. Winch, 1–16. Cambridge: Cambridge University Press, 1990.
6. Winch, P. 'How is Political Authority Possible?' ed. D. Z. Phillips. *Philosophical Investigations* 25, no. 1 (2002): 20–32.

Part 1

THE LONDON ERA [C. 1964–1985]

1.1
THE IMAGE OF LAW: LAWS OF THOUGHT AND FORMS OF LIFE [1966][1]

An anecdote of John Wisdom's will set my scene. 'It is, I believe, [he writes] extremely difficult to breed lions. But there was at one time at the Dublin zoo a keeper by the name of Mr. Flood who bred many lions without losing one. Asked the secret of his success, Mr. Flood replied, "Understanding lions". Asked in what consists the understanding of lions, he replied, "Every lion is different". It is not to be thought that Mr. Flood, in seeking to understand an individual lion, did not bring to bear his great experience with other lions. Only he remained free to see each lion for itself.'

This story neatly illustrates an enduring central concern of philosophers: how to distinguish between sophistry and sound thinking. It shows too some of the difficulties, which surround this distinction, arising out of an obscurity about the way in which our

---

1. Eds: 'Laws of thought and forms of life' is a handwritten addition; a previous subtitle is crossed out: 'Law, generalization, and sophistry'. Typescript; lecture notes; 14 pp., Peter Winch Archives (GB 0100 KCLCA K/PP171, Box 5), King's College London. Winch was invited to contribute to a BBC Third Programme series called 'The Image of Law' in 1966. As an indication of the notorious erudition of the BBC Third Programme, perhaps, Winch replied in a letter to the invitation musing about the trajectory of his philosophical thought for the decades to come:

    ...this logical background [Aristotle's treatment generality and the syllogism] has, I think, been influential in determining the course which discussion has taken all sorts of fields: in the philosophy of science, e.g., we have Hume's insistence that the concept of causality involves generalizations, which make possible inferences from one particular matter of fact to another; in moral philosophy we have recurring attempts to produce ethical systems in which very general moral principles provided foundation for reasoning about particular moral issues—this comes out, e.g., in Kant's emphasis on the universality of the categorical imperative and also in J.S. Mill's utilitarianism, where the very general principle of utility is the basis of all particular moral inferences; and in the philosophy of law we have attempts, in history of of Austinian legal positivism, to do justice to the generality of laws conceived as a command of the sovereign—the issues here are very well brought out in Hart's *The Concept of Law*.

   Winch also gave a talk based on this paper at an October, 1967 colloquium on the theme '*Probleme der Wissenschaftstheorie*' in Germany put on by the *Studienstiftung des Deutschen Volkes* (a graduate scholarship foundation) to which Apel facilitated his invitation. Apel, Habermas and Luckmann were among the speakers. The editors thank Mark Theunissen for identifying this second version of the 'Image of Law' TS.

experience of general patterns of behaviour, which may be formulated in the form of laws, is related to our understanding of particular individual cases.

Let me spell this out a bit. If anyone wanted an enlightening comment on a particular lion, he would clearly be better advised to go to Mr. Flood than to, say, me. Unlike me, Mr. Flood has made an intensive study of the characteristics and behaviour of lions and is in a position to make many well-founded general observations about what lions are like and how they behave. In some sense, this is the foundation of his ability to talk sense about any particular lion. If I tried to do that, I should very quickly be reduced to uttering sophistries, simply because I don't have the general knowledge and experience to support what I say. This remark has a quite general application. In thinking about, or enquiring into, anything whatever, men draw on their past experience; they use concepts of great generality, in terms of which they see analogies between what confronts them now and what has confronted them – and other men – on past occasions; on the basis of the repeated patterns of regularity they have observed, they formulate laws which they will use in subsequent investigations; they follow rules of thinking which they have learnt from other men and which have a long tradition behind them. Moreover, it doesn't just *happen* to be the case that investigations are carried out in this way: these are features of a man's behaviour which we look for if we want to determine whether what he is doing is indeed investigating or thinking about something; they belong to what we mean when we say that he is. It would be a case of sophistry if someone claimed to be conducting an investigation and did not act in this kind of way.

And yet, as Mr. Flood said, 'every lion is different'. Anyone who doesn't take account of this is liable to a different kind of sophistry: that of relying too slavishly on the thinking and observing which he and others have done in the past; trotting out glib generalisations without enquiring how far these apply to the case at hand. The very system of practices and reliances – without which there couldn't be any understanding at all – this is at the same time and by virtue of the same characteristics one of the biggest obstacles in the way of understanding. We often come a cropper by expecting a situation to develop in just the way similar situations have developed in the past; analogies can be misleading and lead us to overlook what is special about the instances before us; reliance on traditional modes of thought can lead us into scholasticism and failure to see that sometimes a radically new approach is needed; and so on.

The sort of dilemma I've tried to sketch is one which has always deeply concerned philosophers, working in all sorts of fields. They have reacted to it in a particular way[2] – a way which marks off the sort of interest *philosophers* have in the distinction between sophistry and sound thinking, from the sort of interest that any serious thinker will have: because I certainly don't want to claim that only the philosopher is interested in detecting and avoiding sophistry. No, what distinguishes the philosopher is that he takes the dilemma as a point of departure for an enquiry into the nature of enquiry, for thought about the very nature of thought. Now such an enquiry – and I'm thinking of it here particularly in connection with the relations between the general and the

---

2. Eds: From this point to the end of the sentence is omitted from the *Studienstiftung* version of the paper. The following sentence begins: 'The Philosopher takes the dilemma [...]'.

particular in thinking and reasoning – very soon runs into a fundamental difficulty. Wisdom, you remember, said: 'It is not to be thought that Mr. Flood, in seeking to understand an individual lion, did not bring to bear his great experience with other lions. Only he remained free to see each lion for itself.' The point is that 'seeing each lion for itself' is internally, necessarily, connected with having great experience with lions in general. But if we ask *how* precisely the two terms are connected, it becomes difficult to see any real distinction between them at all. For however much we try to specify what is peculiar to *this* lion, we must do so in terms of concepts which are general in their application: we 'must' do so, I say, because that is part of what is *meant* by 'specifying what is peculiar to something'. Anyone who tried to dispense with general terms would find himself unable to say anything at all. If he paid no attention to the 'laws' about lions, he wouldn't be able to say anything about the individual lion.

Such a line of thought has suggested to many philosophers that the generality involved in any use of language must always stand between men and the reality of the individual case. It seems to reflect nothing more than a system of conventions which people follow in their dealings with each other. What men *call* 'reality' is itself a human convention and 'man is the measure of all things'. The existence of the conventions and habits involved in language makes it possible for people to influence and elicit responses from each other, but it must be an illusion to think that there could be any sort of cooperative *enquiry*, for this would presuppose that man's responses involved a genuine grasp of some independent reality; and this the very nature of language seems to preclude.

Now the enquiry which led to this conclusion arose from an attempt to draw some sort of distinction between sophistry and sound reasoning: between ways of thinking directed towards a genuine grasp of the way things really are and ways of thinking which are not. But now it seems as if this distinction must itself be illusory. If sophistry consists simply in the attempt to elicit the reactions that suit us – from others or from ourselves – without regard to any truth, our conclusion seems to be that all thought and discourse is nothing more than that. This is in fact the sort of conclusion, and the sort of argument which led to it, which the original Greek sophists came to. Socrates, Plato and Aristotle were all, in their different ways, anxious to undermine this sophistical position. I want now to say something about the form of Aristotle's attempt to do this – not because I think it was the best-conceived, but because I think it has probably been the most influential and because the difficulties involved in it can be used to highlight important points in recent thought about these matters.

One of Aristotle's major achievements was the construction of a *system* of logic. Within it, forms of valid inference were exhibited, and the rationale was given for the distinction between them and invalid forms. Now, the system leant heavily on the kind of distinction I've been talking about – between statements asserting general relationships and statements asserting particular matters of fact. The element of generality, essential to all reasoning, is introduced by Aristotle in the form of explicit generalisations. Between these and statements of particular fact, systematic relationships were then explored. Now in the subsequent history of philosophy, this account led to difficulties of two sorts. On the one hand, forms of inference came to be detected which certainly seemed to be valid but which could not, apparently, be fitted into the Aristotelian system.[3] On the other hand, difficulties emerged concerning the interpretation to be given to Aristotle's system and its relation to the world, [namely] what guarantee was there that reasoning conducted according to its principles would be well-adapted to arriving at the truth about the real world?

These latter doubts about Aristotle's logic had an answer within the metaphysical system that went along with it. Aristotle thought of reality as divided into natural kinds; and of the class concepts out of which his system of logic is constructed as corresponding to these natural kinds. So the metaphysical structure of real classes and of the relations between them mirrors the logical structure of the propositions in which our thought is expressed, and of the inferences by which we move from one proposition to another. However, since there is at least as much of a problem concerning the relation of this metaphysical system and the real world as there is about the relation of any other mode of thought to the real world, it is clear that the difficulty cannot really be resolved in this way.

But there were all sorts of *extra*-philosophical reasons why, particularly in the seventeenth and eighteenth centuries, this Aristotelian account came to look less and less satisfactory. Most important was the revolution in the natural sciences, involving new ways of thinking, and new methods of investigation, which it was very hard to interpret on the Aristotelian model. And this brings me to the other sort of difficulty which the Aristotelian account of the relation between thought and reality came up against, which I mentioned: the difficulty of accounting for the sort of mathematical reasoning which became so fundamental in the development of science from the seventeenth century onwards. Kant was struck by two characteristics of simple mathematical propositions like '7 + 5 = 12'. On the one hand, they seemed to be as 'necessarily' true as any principle of logic; but on the other hand, it seemed impossible to account for this necessity in straightforward Aristotelian terms. It doesn't seem right to say that the numeral '12' stands for a class which is included in the class designated by '7 + 5'. Kant called propositions like '7 + 5 = 12' 'synthetic *a priori*' – 'synthetic' because they didn't seem merely to analyse the meanings of their subject terms; '*a priori*', because their verification did not, all the same, seem to depend on observation and experiment. He thought that other propositions fundamental to science – such as that every event has a cause – were similarly synthetic *a priori*.

Now Kant recognised that such propositions could only be accounted for in terms of a completely new understanding of the way *any* proposition is related to the reality it expresses. And in making the peculiarities of synthetic *a priori* propositions play a central part in this account, he seems to me to have been hinting at a conception which has played an enormously important part in recent philosophical thinking about this question: the conception of a *paradigm*, about which I will say more later.

---

3. Eds: '– in particular, inferences based on the use of mathematics in modern science' is added in the *Studienstiftung* version of the talk.

Since Kant, logic and mathematics have been brought into a much clearer relationship, and mathematical techniques have been applied to logic itself. With this development has grown a new grasp of how concepts are formed and interrelated. The traditional view was that concepts were formed by 'abstracting' properties from complex experienced wholes and thus came to form hierarchies of genera and species according as they included fewer or more ranges of thus abstracted properties. But a large part of what is involved in coming to understand mathematical concepts is grasping their position in a series, rather than grasping the 'abstracted properties' they cover. Thus, in understanding what '5' means, I understand its position in the series of natural numbers, rather than any property of 'fiveness' which I have abstracted from the different groups of five objects. This is more easily seen with large numbers. Have I abstracted the property of 2,364-ness from groups of 2,364 objects? Of course not. As far as I know, I have never come across such a group. But I know *how to get to* the number 2,364 from other numbers by applying a certain rule of progression. From this viewpoint, it begins to look just inappropriate to follow Kant in asking of the proposition '7 + 5 = 12': is the concept of the predicate contained in that of the subject? – The necessity of the proposition is better understood in terms of the necessity with which the series of natural numbers is generated by the rule of progression by which we proceed from one number to another.

But what sort of necessity is that? This question runs in an almost obsessional way through Wittgenstein's work on logic. Put differently, what is a man doing when he follows a rule? And in particular: if someone starts on an arithmetical series – say '3, 6, 9, 12 … ' how is [it] that he *knows* he can continue, even though he certainly can't have *thought* of every subsequent step (since the series could be continued indefinitely)? It won't help to refer to a *formula* (n + 3), because exactly the same question can be asked about how he knows he will be able to *apply* the formula in cases he has not yet thought about. Thus, we seem to have here a very fundamental sort of connection in human thinking, the nature of which can't be displayed by reference to any explicitly formulated laws. And this is brought out in Wittgenstein's treatment of the matter: instead of trying to provide a direct answer to the question 'How does a man following the rules know how to go on?' – instead of offering an *explanation* – he *describes* in detail a wide variety of different examples exhibiting related phenomena; he constructs a picture of the human, social contexts in which we should certainly (and correctly) say that a man knew how to continue the series, and contrasts these with other contexts in which we should not correctly say this. In this way, he builds up a representation of the concept 'knowing how to go on': he doesn't *tell* us, he *shows* us, what it consists in.

The reference to a social context in Wittgenstein's discussion is of great importance. It is necessary because the notion of doing something in accordance with a rule involves the distinction between a correct and an incorrect application of the rule; and this distinction requires the existence of procedures that are followed in detecting and correcting mistakes. Correctness or incorrectness doesn't essentially depend on what any one person says: the distinction is established in the language that is being spoken, and anyone who speaks it can in principle apply the distinction for himself. Now the relation between a man capable of this kind of behaviour and a social context is not that of one who observes what other people are doing and who formulates generalisations and laws to describe and explain it. It *cannot* be this insofar as we are discussing here what is involved in a mastery of concepts which has to exist if there is to *be* any describing or explaining. Perhaps I can put the matter like this: the notion of *generality* is needed for describing the behaviour of someone who follows a rule; but it is not the generality explicitly involved in laws and generalisations, not a generality in what he thinks *about* the behaviour of those with whom he has social relations: it is a generality which is a feature *of* the social relations themselves.

This has a bearing on the procedure of, for example, social anthropologists, who often face the problem of understanding the life and thoughts of people with very different cultures from our own. Anthropologists often proceed by connecting primitive thought – magical or religious for instance – with the social institutions that go along with it. They often speak as if this were an *alternative* to investigating the intrinsic meaning of the thought itself. But I don't think it is. Men's social life and their conceptions of reality are two sides of the same coin.

Now forms of social life are infinitely varied; and so, for the same reasons, are possible ways of understanding the world. Explaining phenomena in terms of laws they exhibit is just one way in which phenomena can be seen in relation to each other. It has, of course, been developed into a very powerful instrument in the natural sciences. Partly for that reason, it is fatally easy to take that kind of understanding as a paradigm of what it must be to understand anything at all; and this tendency may be encouraged by difficulties about what logic is and how it is related to the real world, of the sort I've alluded to. Perhaps, too, there is much in Max Weber's suggestion that the modern tendency to equate 'understanding in terms of general laws' with 'understanding' *sans phrase*, is connected with the bureaucratic and hierarchical structures of modern industrial societies. But, whatever the explanation, it is a tendency that encourages sophistry, in that it represents one particular way of looking at things, which can certainly lead to greater understanding, as the only possible way of understanding anything. The philosopher has a particular responsibility to draw attention to the wide-open variety of possible forms of life and modes of understanding – to 'connect', in E. M. Forster's phrase, in many different ways.

I wish, in conclusion, to guard against a possible misinterpretation of Wittgenstein's thought which may be encouraged by what I have said so far. It might be thought that Wittgenstein's emphasis on 'forms of life' simply results in a sophisticated version of the old sceptical position – that he is saying that what we *call* 'understanding how things are' is really no more than a way of reacting to each other in accordance with certain conventions, which must forever fail to make contact with the real nature of things. But this interpretation really misses the most important point of all. Conceptions like 'how things really are', 'the real nature of things', themselves belong to our language; their substance derives from their place in human forms of life. And they will have to be understood in different ways according to the particular form of life under consideration.

Wittgenstein's discussion of the role played in our thought by *paradigms* is important here. For example: I spoke earlier of the place of a numerical concept like '5' in a series generated by a rule of progression. But of course numbers are not just related to other numbers; they have, as Wittgenstein put it, a 'civil life' – in connection with things like bank-notes, marbles, areas, apples and so on. Procedures like counting, weighing and measuring are just as important as a part of a man's understanding of numbers as the procedures of purely symbolic manipulation. Wittgenstein would have said that *both* these kinds of procedure belong to the grammar of a numerical expression. As he said in another connection: 'It is part of the grammar of the word "chair" that *this* is what I call sitting in a chair.' Now these two kinds of rule – the syntactical and the semantic – are intimately interrelated. Suppose I order some plates: 500 from one supplier, 400 from another. I count the whole lot on delivery and get 901 as a result. I do *not* then say that the arithmetical proposition '500 + 400 = 900' isn't true or doesn't apply here; I say I have miscounted or there was a mistake in the delivery, or something of the sort. The truth of the arithmetical proposition, taken as strictly 'beyond question' is being used as a paradigm against which I measure whether things have been correctly counted, how many things there are. Wittgenstein said of such paradigms that they belong both to the language and the world about which something can be said; and thus a proposition, to use an earlier phrase of his, 'reaches right up to reality' and can say something about reality.

I believe that the light which Wittgenstein's discussion of these matters throws on the nature of human thinking can with great advantage be directed at the kind of problem which faces investigators like social anthropologists. For example, the African Azande have the practice of consulting oracles about the future.[4] Now *we* are inclined to say: 'Of course an oracle can tell us nothing about the future'. But before saying this, we should ask ourselves what the Azande *mean* when they say the oracle reveals the future. And to answer this, we must understand what are their paradigms for determining whether the future has been correctly foretold. We must beware of assuming that these will have more than a perhaps quite distant family resemblance to the paradigms *we* employ to determine whether a prediction has turned out correctly or not. Anthropologists these days are of course much more cautious in these matters than was once common. But I think, there is still at least a vestigial tendency among some, when faced with problems like this, to suppose that the question I have to ask is: 'how can such an obviously mistaken set of beliefs have maintained itself for so long?' They then start talking about the 'social function' of those beliefs. Now the role played by beliefs in the life of a society is indeed a matter of great importance, as I have been trying to bring out. But it is important, first of all, for our understanding of what those beliefs *are*: and this is the aspect of the matter which may too easily be lost sight of, if we are not clear about what is involved in thinking anything at all and about the dependence of the human ability to connect one thing with another on particular forms of social life.

There is a kinship between Wittgenstein's notion of a paradigm and Plato's doctrine of the Forms. Whereas Aristotle placed the Forms *in* the world to be abstracted by the intelligent observer, both Plato and Wittgenstein thought in terms of, as it were,

---

4. Eds: Peter Winch. 'Understanding a Primitive Society', *American Philosophical Quarterly* 1, no. 4 (1964): 307–324. Reprinted in *Ethics and Action* (London: Routledge and Kegan Paul, 1972), 8–49.

yard-sticks, applied to observed situations from outside. Correspondingly, Plato and Wittgenstein both differ fundamentally from Aristotle in their conception of human potentialities in relation to social life. Whereas for Aristotle, the potentialities of individual men are part of their original nature, though they may be furthered or stunted by the social environment; for Plato and Wittgenstein, *new potentialities* can be created in men by contact with outside influences – with eternal forms, for Plato; by being caught up in new forms of social life, for Wittgenstein. Wittgenstein wanted to emphasise that the very *conception* of the most important human potentialities would be impossible apart from the existence of these forms of life.[5] And these forms, when they flourish, are forever creating new possibilities, throwing up new paradigms, in terms of which the world can be seen in quite new ways. I believe that the working out of such ideas would lead to important new insights for instance in the fields of ethics, social philosophy and philosophy of religion. But these would be subjects for different talks.

---

5. Eds: In the *Studienstiftung* version, a series of examples are given: 'We couldn't even say, for example, that a man was a mathematical genius if there were no such activity as the pursuit of mathematics; we could not speak of someone as a religious mystic apart from a religious tradition. Forms of life constitute the space within which individuals having such qualities can exist and be conceived'.

1.2

INTERCOLLEGIATE LECTURES ON POLITICAL PHILOSOPHY [1969–1970][1]

Six Introductory Lectures

Main topic of course: relations of domination and subordination in human society – generally, but with special emphasis on the political.

Two preliminary questions: (a) Why is there a special problem about the political? (b) What has philosophy to say about such matters?

1. Political authority is said not to be 'natural'. (But what does this mean?)
2. Political authority is not *obviously* acceded to voluntarily.

1. and 2. together have been thought to give rise to a special problem, which we can take as a starting point from which other problems radiate.

Questions about what is natural in human affairs are very involved: 'natural' occurs as one term in many different contrasts: e.g. with 'conventional', with 'artificial', [with] 'what would be true of social life considered in abstraction from the political', 'corrupt', 'primitive' (equals 'pre-social'). These distinctions overlap but they often need to be distinguished and have not always been so adequately.

A pervasive theme in political philosophy is that political authority is not just a *de facto* relation but involves the idea of *legitimacy*. The significance of this can be brought out by considering the point of view of the subject. He may submit because he feels he cannot do otherwise – the consequences of doing so would be too adverse. Or he may submit because he thinks he ought to – i.e. apart from the question of whether he is constrained. (But the relations between constraint and obligation are tangled, especially in political contexts.) Here he will appeal to the nature of the authority which is making demands on him.

A major question is: What is the relation between what we can say about the nature of the authority and the subject's acknowledgement of it? Does the authority have a nature independently of this acknowledgement? There is a pervasive and persuasive argument – taking many different forms – that it does not and cannot. Hence the importance of contract theories.

---

1. Eds: Typescript; lecture notes; 16 pp., Peter Winch Archives (GB 0100 KCLCA K/PP171, Folder 'Politics IV', Box 7), King's College London.

What is the relation between questions about the nature, justification and origins of political authority?

The main authors I shall refer to will be Rousseau (*Émile, Discourse on Inequality, Social Contract*) and Hobbes (*Leviathan*).

Also, possibly, Max Weber (*Theory of Social and Economic Organization*) and Simone Weil (*Oppression and Liberty, The Need for Roots*).

Lecture Notes: Political Philosophy 1[2]

Questions about what is involved in a philosophical treatment of political life.

Periodic rash of concern by philosophers about the nature (and even possibility) of their subject. Not necessarily neurotic self-indulgence.

During the 50s (especially): many writers preoccupied with the nature of political theories. Physics? (Hobbes), Poetry (?)/(Cameron), Ideology? (Marx, Mosca, Pareto, etc.). A common reaction: stop worrying about the nature of (political) philosophy and get on with investigating particular questions. *Something* in this. But if we leave it there we shall miss something important.

Philosophy: 'the relation between thought and reality'. This at least includes 'the relation between philosophical thought and reality'. And this implies that the very questions the philosopher wants to ask are philosophically problematic. Not *obvious* what his questions are nor (what amounts to same thing) what would count as an answer to them. I.e. a philosopher is characteristically puzzled by something but finds it difficult to see clearly what the nature of his puzzlement is. This not necessarily a sign of professional incompetence. On the contrary: one of the most difficult but necessary things is to get a student not to take the things philosophers say too much for granted. ('The existence of the external world'. 'Our knowledge of other minds'. 'The nature of political obligation'.)

Two things which should catch our attention here:

(1) How very naturally it comes to us (some of us) to ask questions (or apparent questions) of a certain sort.
(2) How difficult it is to see what these questions amount to, to be clear about exactly what it is that's bothering us. (Cf. Plato's argument (in *The Meno*) that unless one already knew what one was looking for one would not know when one had found it: but if one does know what one is looking for why should it be necessary – how should it be possible even – to look for it?)

Why (1) is important. – Otherwise we may be too impatient with philosophical questions and think they can be eliminated in one clean sweep (*Language, Truth and Logic*[3]). It is

---

2. Eds: Each of these lectures concludes with Winch's signature and the date, as follows. We include these as notes at the start of the corresponding lecture. This one is: P.W. 14.10.69.
3. Eds: A. J. Ayer, *Language, Truth and Logic* (London: Gollancz, 1946).

an *important* feature of philosophical questions that they tend to survive such attempts at purges. (Kant on the 'transcendental illusion'. Corrected with 'philosophy as an activity'.[4]) Suggests there is something inherently and endemically problematic about human thinking. Why it is important to discuss (2):

(a) An obvious point – if one is hazy about what one is asking, natural to expect that one's attempts at answering it will also result in something hazy. But this point may seem to have nothing especially to do with anything that is peculiar to philosophy.
(b) This does have more to do with the special character of philosophical questions.

Trying to be clear about what philosophical questions amount to may lead us to compare those questions with other questions which don't (on the surface) seem problematic in the same way. (Comparing 'Does the material world exist?' with 'Is there water beneath the surface of the Sahara?'. Comparing 'Why should I (not) show allegiance to the State?' with 'Why should I (not) show allegiance to the Stormont Government?'.)

This begins to show why there need (ought) to be no antithesis between being concerned with the nature of philosophical questions and getting on with work on the answers to philosophical questions. For concern with the nature of philosophical questions leads us directly on to concern with the nature of other sorts of question, and it was precisely worry about the nature and possibility of these other sorts of question which gave rise to our philosophical difficulties in the first place.

But now it may well seem to someone that I am arguing in an intolerably vicious circle, trying to justify a constant philosophical concern with the nature of philosophical questions, and I seem to be doing this by arguing that in this way, we can be led back to asking the original 'first order' philosophical questions that one started with, and with the nature of which I said we should be puzzled. So, you may say, why not shortcut this diversion and just get on with the first-order philosophical questions straightaway. But I think I can meet this objection.

Approaching the matter in the way I've described can help in the following (extremely important) ways:

(i) Concentrates the philosopher's attention on the actual form which questions and enquiries of various sorts actually do take. Instead of trying to answer straight off and in a large way the question 'What is the nature of our knowledge of the external world?', our attention will be concentrated on the actual and very various ways in which we do outside philosophy as a matter of fact carry on investigations into the existence and nature of objects of different sorts. I.e. we may be induced to see (what is not easy to see) that what seemed to us one big question has many diverse facets.

---

4. Eds: Ludwig Wittgenstein, *Tractatus Logico-Philosophicus*, trans. David Pears and Brian McGuinness (London: Routledge and Kegan Paul, 1961), 4.112.

(ii) But it is also important that we should have been tempted to ask one big question. For now our enquiry into the nature of the myriad particular questions that arise will seek (amongst other things) an answer to the question: 'What is it about all these diverse questions which subjected us to that temptation?'. And if we do not have *this* question in our minds, there is a danger that our analysis of particularities will run into the sand.

What is at issue here is the unity of philosophy. More generally: how do unity and diversity enter into human thinking. (Plato: the one and the many. Wittgenstein: 'the craving for generality'. Cohen: 'the craving for particularity'.[5])

The difference between Wittgenstein and [J. L.] Austin.[6]

Apply all this more specifically to questions about political philosophy. Many people have been struck by the curious character of the things political philosophers say. Contracts which the parties have never made with each other at any particular time, which they may be quite unaware of, and which, on any obvious interpretation, they had not choice but to make. A general will which is not the will of any particular person, not even a summation of the wills of particular persons (≠ the 'will of all'), and which is said to belong to a person whether or not he's aware of it and even if it is directly contrary to what he thinks he wills. Etc.

If we are interested in the relations between thought and reality (i.e. if we are interested in philosophy) we must be interested in what reality these theoretical constructions are related to (if any) and what is the nature of their relation to it.

It is necessary, but not sufficient, to notice that these terms are not used as they are in other contexts. So we must look at how they are used in other contexts. And we must try to see if there is any relation between those contexts and the sort of thing the philosopher is talking about. – This won't be a quick or easy job.

Not sufficient, because we must also understand the nature of the problems which made the philosopher talk like this in the first place. Let's now make a start on this.

It would be dangerous to assume that there is any one problem which all political philosophers have been concerned with. Even if one uses a formula which could be thought to cover the enquiries and difficulties of many different philosophers, there is the real possibility that different men have been troubled about the problem in different ways and hence have had different kinds of requirement about what would constitute a satisfactory solution.

This being said, I am going to ignore the danger for the time being and talk about what I do think is in a way the fundamental problem in political philosophy.

---

5. Eds: This is a reference to the analytic Marxist G. A. Cohen, who was part of this Intercollegiate lecture series.

6. Handwritten: cf. *Without Answers*, p. 133 ff. Eds: Rush Rhees, 'Art and Philosophy', *Without Answers* (London: Routledge and Kegan Paul, 1969), 133–154. In the opening section of these comments (133–135), Rhees situates philosophical questions about art through a discussion of the difference between 'linguistic confusions' and the kinds of confusion about language that lead to philosophical problems.

Hume said that the fundamental question is how so many come to be ruled by so few. (A rough paraphrase.)[7] There can be all sorts of questions which could be put in that form. Historical, social psychological and sociological. (Though I do not mean we should take it as obvious what these various kinds of enquiry will actually amount to.) But many of the accounts offered within these disciplines would be of no (at least direct) interest to a philosopher – by which I don't want to deny that these enquiries may often provide the philosopher with interesting material.

Rousseau: discusses what is sometimes called 'the right of the stronger' in a way which provides us with a clue, though what he says must be handled carefully.

> The stronger is never strong enough to stay permanently in control, unless he converts his strength into right, and obedience into duty. Hence the right of the stronger; a right apparently so called ironically and yet really established in principle. But will no one ever explain this expression for us? Strength is physical power; I do not see what morality can ever result from its effects. To yield to force is an act of necessity, not of will; at the most it is an act of prudence. In what sense can this be a duty?[8]

Lecture Notes: Political Philosophy 2[9]

What is it about the existence of the state which gives rise to a philosophical problem?

In the state there is a distinction between those who *rule* and those who are ruled. We are interested in *what it is* to rule or to be ruled. But what exactly are we asking here and why should it be philosophically puzzling?

The relation of ruler and ruled seems undeniably to be a case of domination and subordination: the ruler commands, the ruled obeys. But [it is] only [one] case of [it]. I.e. there are other human relations which we should call subordination and domination which we should not yet call cases of ruling: e.g. the relation of father to child (in the good old days); of teacher to pupil (in the even better old days); of employer to employee; of gunman to the man he is robbing; etc.

Now certainly a philosophical treatment of ruling may well (probably will) involve careful discussion of the relations between these and other different types of domination: discussion of the analogies and disanalogies. And this discussion is not likely to be easy.

But to leave the matter there is to miss out something important. We might ask: why bother? Of course a philosopher, as we know, is one who does take an interest in questions like this and he might well want to get clear about such questions without requiring any special impetus. Still, if we look at the writings of men like Plato, Hobbes, Locke, Rousseau and Marx, we ought to be struck by the fact that there is something behind the desire to get clear about these things.

---

7. Eds: David Hume, 'Of the First Principles of Government', in *Political Essays*, ed. Charles W. Handel (Bobbs Merrill, The Library of Liberal Arts 1953), 24–27 (24).
8. *Social Contract*, Book I, Chapter ii[i].
9. P.W. 20.10.69.

No doubt there is more than one thing behind it: for instance a desire to make a contribution to particular political issues at the time of writing. (Plato and the upheavals in the Greek world; Hobbes and the English Civil War; Locke and the Revolution of 1688; Marx and the evils of nineteenth-century industrialism.) It would be silly to try to discount the importance which such direct political involvement has had in influencing the direction which the writings of different political philosophers have had, as well as in stimulating them to write on political philosophy in the first place. Nevertheless, plenty of men get politically involved and write on the political issues of their time without our feeling inclined to say that their writings have much of a philosophical dimension. So we are still left with our question what gives political writings a philosophical dimension. If we go back to the comparisons made earlier between ruling and other forms of domination and look at the way some of those comparisons have entered into the writings of certain political philosophers, we find an important clue. There has been a very strong tendency to assimilate, reduce ruling to one or other (or more than one) of the other forms of domination-relation. E.g. Filmer: political authority explained as a form of paternal authority (cf. Locke's criticisms in the *First and Second Treatises on Civil Government*); Hobbes: political authority as compounded out of elements of being forced by superior power and of having agreed to obey; Locke: political authority as something consented to (as, e.g., I might consent to let a certain person make the decisions in a joint enterprise); Marx: political authority as a form which economic domination takes (Mr. Cohen will be talking about this); Rousseau: political authority ('true'[10] political authority) as not really a form of being dominated by another at all, but as a case of following one's own will.

All this ought to look familiar. Cf. explaining physical objects in terms of sensations; reducing induction to deduction; reducing deduction to induction; reducing moral obligation to self-interest.

Why do philosophers attempt such 'reductions'? Because there is something *puzzling* about the term they try to reduce. Because it looks as though it *cannot* amount to what it appears to amount to. (The example of deduction and induction, where reduction attempts have been made in both directions, shows that (as one could anyway expect) different things can seem puzzling according to the direction from which one approaches them.)

From what point of view then does political authority look puzzling; seem that it really cannot be what it makes itself out to be?

Let me return to the quotation from Rousseau's *Social Contract* ([Book] I, [Chapter] ii[i]) with which I concluded the last lecture (see notes).

The passage is a complex one. Rousseau starts it by apparently raising a sociological issue: what technique does someone who is stronger have to employ in order to make his domination of the weaker permanent. The assumption here is that mere strength is a variable factor and one who bases his domination merely on this will never be in

---

10. That this addition is sometimes natural is important. I may come back to it.

a safe position. Let us just accept this. This technique consists in 'converting strength into right', and it is here that Rousseau raises the philosophical difficulty: what can we understand by such a 'conversion'? To talk of the 'right of the stronger', he says, would ordinarily be taken ironically, since right is something that does not necessarily (perhaps we could even say usually) go along with strength and certainly does not *follow* from strength. We might put this by saying that talk about right and talk about strength seem to belong to different universes of discourse, so that to talk of 'the right *of* the stronger', as if his right were somehow a derivative of his strength or even to be identified with it, would be to commit what some philosophers would want (or would once have wanted) to call a category mistake.

Yet, Rousseau notes, a phrase which one might expect to have only an ironic use, seems to correspond with something that is 'really established in principle'.

Now Rousseau, I think, would have wanted to say that this really is only appearance: that what he has described is an impossibility and that the description simply serves the purpose of hoodwinking the citizen and preventing him from seeing the unpleasant facts of his situation. He would have wanted to say, that is, that societies with state institutions based on force are not really political societies as he understood them at all. He would not, perhaps, have been dismayed by the natural rejoinder that what he calls a 'political society' or 'body politic' is something that has no real existence and never has had any. For he himself wrote of what he called the 'state of nature' – the state of man living without any organised political society – that 'it exists no longer, it has perhaps never existed, it probably never will exist' and yet 'it is necessary to have correct ideas about it in order to judge properly of our actual present state' (*Discourse on the Origins of Inequality*). He might have said (and did in fact, I believe, think) something similar of the notion of a body politic properly so called.

This not necessarily as daft as it sounds. (The relation between geometry and the figures we draw.)

Cf. Rousseau in *Émile* (Book V): he first instructs Émile on what is involved in citizenship of the sovereignty in a civil society properly so called (= one constructed on the principles of the *Social Contract*); but he then points out that Émile will not find such a society anywhere in his travels. But he still thinks that it is necessary to understand those principles in order to be able to live in a manner approximating to free citizenship in states as they do exist.

I return to the original quotation from *Social Contract* [Book] I, [Chapter] ii[i]. I said in my concluding remarks last week that we need to be on our guard about the precise purport of the distinction Rousseau draws between right and force. It may seem (and no doubt did much of the time seem to Rousseau) as if the task he has undertaken is that of justifying a particular form of society to us, his readers.

This is certainly something which he, along with most other political philosophers, attempts. But there is something else in what he is doing, which ought to be distinguished and which is what I want to emphasise here.

He is asking not merely: 'What kind of State (should) can we recognize as legitimate?' but also: 'What is it to recognize a state as legitimate?' This second question is obviously closely bound up with our original question: 'What is ruling?'

I don't suggest that it is easy to keep these two sorts of question apart or even that in certain contexts they can be kept apart. But I do think it important to recognise the distinction. The distinction comes out, e.g. in circumstances where I would say of a state: 'It is not a society in which I should want to acknowledge the political power being exercised as legitimate: however it is clear that its members so acknowledge it and that the relation between citizen and government is not just one of force'. (The situation in Rhodesia?) *One* question which, I think, has always been involved in political philosophy is: 'What is it to recognize a government as legitimate?' (Cf. Hare's contribution to the Third Series Laslett and Runciman volume[11]; and also, for those who read French, an extremely searching article by Simone Weil in her *Écrits de Londres*, called '*La légitimité du gouvernement provisoire*'.[12])

(E.g. it may well be that there are limits to what we can recognise as cases of 'recognizing a government as legitimate' which stem from the limits to what we can recognise as legitimate. But I do not believe that the limits are so narrow as to prevent us from recognising a distinction here.)

Lecture Notes: Political Philosophy 3[13]

'Recognizing a government, a regime as legitimate'. This must be in Rousseau's phrase 'an act of will', not of necessity. Thus, questions about the nature of the relation between government and subject are intertwined with questions about the nature of the will. The reason why *freedom* is a concept which plays such a large part in political and philosophical discussions. Not merely as something valued, but also as something which has to be taken account of if *political* power is to be understood at all. There is a sense in which, except in the context of a relation between free men, political power doesn't exist at all. (Of course, this is not to say that in actual states we have to do simply with relations between free men.)

This freedom, act of will, comes in with the *recognition* of a regime as legitimate. (Questions here about [the] relation of will and *understanding*. Cf. Kant's characterisation of will as 'practical reason'.) I may be almost entirely passive in relation to the regime's edicts: taxes are exacted from me which I'd rather not pay, my house is compulsorily purchased, I'm conscripted into the army, etc. On the other hand, I don't actually wait for them to come and take the money out of my pocket at gunpoint or wait till I am marched off to the military induction centre between a posse of military policemen. It isn't even clear that I do this in a concealed way, by calculating what the long-term effects are going to be of not acquiescing. (Again, this may come into it; but it's not the whole story. And could the behaviour of *everyone* in a given state be explained like this?) Cf. Socrates in the *Crito* and the *Phaedo*.

---

11. R. M. Hare, 'Lawful Government', in *Philosophy, Politics and Society, Third Series: A Collection*, ed. Laslett and Runciman (Oxford: Blackwell, 1967), 90–108.
12. Eds: Winch eventually published a translation of this paper: Simone Weil, 'The Legitimacy of the Provisional Government', *Philosophical Investigations* 10 (1987): 87–98.
13. P.W. 28.10.69.

I can now re-phrase my main question. What room is there for freedom in the relationship between government and subject? – The importance of the idea that, in some sense, the state is an organisation I have joined *voluntarily* (Hobbes, but Hobson's choice: Locke: consent, explicit and tacit; Rousseau: the sovereign's will is really my will – N.B. Hobbes too says something like this and the similarities and differences between him and Rousseau in this regard are very instructive). If I have joined, say, a club for a particular purpose, I may have to submit to pushing about by the officers of that club in the interests of that purpose and do things against my immediate will but I can say that my will is active in the situation in respects: (a) I will the purpose of the club to which these constraints on my immediate freedom are a means; (b) I chose to join in the first place; (c) if I find it intolerable, I can get out. None of these conditions is *obviously* satisfied in the political case. Much effort has gone into showing that one or more of the conditions really is (are) satisfied, contrary to all the appearances.

> Should it be said that, by living under the dominion of a prince which one might leave, every individual has given a tacit consent to his authority and promised him obedience it may be answered that such an implied consent can only have place where a man imagines that the matter depends on his choice. But where he thinks (as all mankind do who are born under established governments) that, by his birth he owes allegiance to a certain prince or certain form of government, it would be absurd to infer a consent or choice which he expressly in this case renounces and disclaims.
>
> Can we seriously say that a poor peasant or artisan has a free choice to leave his country when he knows no foreign language or manners and lives from day to day by the small wages which he acquires? We may as well assert that a man, by remaining in a vessel, freely consents to the dominion of the master; though he was carried on board while asleep and must leap into the ocean and perish the moment he leaves her.[14]

The force of the last sentence here should not be taken positively. I.e. Hume is not asserting that the relation of a subject to his sovereign is like that of the press-ganged sailor. Only that we cannot elucidate the difference between the two cases in terms of the *consent* of the citizen. If we want to leave a place for the exercise of the citizen's will in relation to the state authority, it has got to be in some different way. I shall come back to this in a later lecture.

Let me consider this question in a slightly more formal way, by considering something from Hobbes. Hobbes spends a good deal of time distinguishing what he calls 'command' and 'counsel'. This distinction is vital to his attempt to explain what sovereignty is and to locate it unambiguously in one will. One difficulty here is that in any complex state, there is a very large number of officers who 'exercise the sovereign power', but who are not sovereign. With regard to them, it must be clear when what they say is to be taken as expressing the sovereign's will, when not. There is a need for clarity at the other end too. The sovereign will need expert advice on matters of state which

---

14. David Hume, 'Of the Original Contract', in *Social Contract: Essays by Locke, Hume and Rousseau, with an Introduction by Sir Ernest Barker* (Oxford: Oxford University Press, 1948/1967), 147–168 (155–156).

are too diverse and complex for him to master them all. He may have to rely entirely on a minister's advice on many matters. Why then should we not say that the will that is being exercised is not the sovereign's at all, but the minister's, and that the sovereign is merely his mouthpiece?

> COMMAND is, where a man saith, *do this*, or *do not this* without expecting other reason than the will of him that says it. From this it follows manifestly, that he that commandeth, pretendeth thereby his own benefit: for the reason of his command is his own will only, and the proper object of every man's will, is some good to himself.
> COUNSEL, is where a man saith, *do*, or *do not this*, and deduceth his reasons from the benefit that arriveth by it to him to whom, he saith it. And from this it is evident, that he that giveth counsel, pretendeth only, whatsoever he intendeth, the good of him, to whom he giveth it.
> Therefore between counsel and command, one great difference is, that command is directed to a man's own benefit; and counsel to the benefit of another man. And from this ariseth another difference, that a man may be obliged to do what he is commanded; as when he hath convenanted to obey: but he cannot be obliged to do as he is counselled, because the hurt of not following it, is his own; or if he should covenant to follow it, then is the counsel turned into the nature of a command. A third difference between them is, that no man can pretend a right to be of another's counsel; because he is not to pretend benefit by it to himself: but to demand right to counsel another, argues a will to know his designs, or to gain some other good to himself: which, as I said before, is of every man's will the proper object'.[15]

Now I suggested in my first lecture[16] that Hobbes makes a mistake here, in supposing that one who commands does so for the sake of some good to himself rather than (possibly) for the sake of some good to the one commanded (or to some third party; or for the good of no one at all). This mistake goes with a more general thesis about the nature of human action and about the relation between the will and the notion of the good of the agent – an issue which is still of course very controversial in the philosophy of mind and of morals. But we can get somewhere by ignoring this mistake for the moment. Let us ask: if Hobbes is right in what he says about the relation between will and the good of the agent, is what he says about command coherent?

If 'the proper object of every man's own will, is some good to himself', then the proper object of the will of one who obeys a command must be some good to himself. But, if this is so, it seems that the one who commands must be under an illusion when he gives the command 'without expecting other reason than' his own will to be the reason why the one commanded does what he is told. For the latter will act only if he sees (or thinks he sees) some good for himself. So the reason why he does what X tells him to do is not simply that X has told him to do it, but rather that he expects some good for himself (or some avoidance of evil for himself) in doing what X tells him to do. (Connected

---

15. Hobbes, *Leviathan*, Part 2, Chapter XXV.
16. Eds: This comment suggests that the note 'Hobbes/physics' was filled out verbally in lecture by a discussion of the role of analogies to physics in Hobbes's views of reason and action.

with Hobbes' insistence that 'the bonds of words are too weak to bridle men's ambition, avarice, anger, and other passions, without fear of some coercive power' – *Leviathan*, Part 1, Chapter XIV. The expression of the commander's will is, for the commandee, just words; they have no reality for him unless he can find some ulterior reason why he should take notice of them.) Rousseau's words seem to characterise the situation exactly: 'at the most it is an act of prudence'.

But I am not sure that the difficulty is one which springs solely from what I called the mistaken doctrine about the relation between the agent's will and his good. It is a difficulty connected with the question, how is the notion of the subject's will possible at all. How can obedience to the will of a political authority ever be more than an act of 'prudence' or of 'necessity'? If an act of mine is to be an expression of my will, rather than something forced on me in one way or the other, it must be an act which I have performed according to my judgement of what is best. But obedience to an authority seems to involve delegating the judgement of what is best to someone else – which we must distinguish from the case where I myself judge that the best thing will be to let someone else judge (because I think him wiser, more powerful, or whatever). But such 'delegation' seems to be a metaphysical impossibility. (This is in fact the kind of argument Rousseau relies on when he says that sovereignty (which he equates in a queer way with the will of any citizen) 'cannot' be delegated. He means it makes no sense to speak of delegating it.) We might say: in so far as my action does not issue from my will, it is not my action at all.

> I maintain, therefore, that sovereignty, being no more than the exercise of the general will, can never be alienated, and that the sovereign, who is a collective being only, can be represented by no one but himself. Power can be transmitted, but not will.
>
> If, therefore, the People undertake simply and solely to obey, they, by that very act, dissolve the social bond, and so lose their character as a People. Once the Master appears upon the scene, the sovereign vanishes, and the body politic suffers destruction.[17]

Rousseau's point here is interestingly like Hobbes's, but also interestingly different. 'Power can be transmitted, but not will'. A ruler may delegate his power to a minister, in the sense that the operations necessary to getting the measure in question carried out, even the actual decision to carry out that measure, are taken entirely by the minister. But insofar as the minister's actions are taken to be legitimate exercises of political authority, they are taken to be not expressions of *his* will but expressions of the will of the state (of the sovereign). We can't speak of *that* being delegated, without entirely losing the conception of measures as being state measures. This, so far, is much the same point that Hobbes is making in his distinction between command and counsel.

Yet Rousseau sees this very point as refuting a Hobbesian account of the relation between citizen and state: a point which Hobbes had taken as confirming that account. Who is in the right here?

---

17. Rousseau, *Social Contract*, Book II, Chapter 1 (Barker, 269 and 270).

Rousseau's claim is that an undertaking 'simply and solely to obey' yields a relation which is not a political relation, but one which is antithetical to a political relation. My acquiescence in a state edict must be on the grounds that it is the exercise of a power which I recognise as legitimate; that is, I lend my support to what is decreed simply because it is the state (recognised by me as legitimate) that has decreed it. The difficulty we are faced with here is that of understanding the force of that 'because'.

Rousseau's objection to Hobbes is that an undertaking simply and solely to obey leaves no free space in which I can continue to exercise my judgement that a given decree really is the exercise of legitimate state power. Hobbes wants questions about legitimacy to be, as it were, settled once and for all in the original 'covenant': the sovereign has got to be the sole judge of what is legitimate and what is not, otherwise he is not sovereign. Rousseau agrees with this last point, but argues, in effect against Hobbes, that this can only be intelligible in so far as the citizen is himself in some sense the *continuing* source of the state's legitimacy. In this I think Rousseau is in a sense right. But in what sense and how can Hobbes's counter-argument be refuted?

Lecture Notes: Political Philosophy 4[18]

Rousseau: 'power can be transmitted, but not will', This is advanced as a *criticism* of a Hobbesist conception of the relation between subject and sovereign (or at least as an attempted refutation of the contention that this relation is a political one).

Does Hobbes dispute Rousseau's remark? We can look for the answer in Hobbes's account of the way in which sovereignty is established, which is in terms of men's unilateral renunciation of their 'right of nature' in favour of a sovereign. Now we might expect that the renunciation of a right would be something like a 'transmission of will'. In fact Hobbes does so treat it in one context, viz. his discussion 'Of Persons, Authors, and Things Personated':

> A PERSON, is he *whose words or actions are considered, either as his own, or as representing the words or actions of another man, or of any other thing, to whom they are attributed, whether truly or by fiction.* When they are considered as his own, then is he called a *natural person*: and when they are considered as representing the words and actions of another, then is he a *feigned* or *artificial person*.[19]

It is plainly such an 'artificial person' who is set up by Hobbes's covenant. The point of the notion is that the acts of an artificial person who acts for others are taken ('deeded') to be the acts of the person represented. *But this is a fiction*. Which is as much to say that 'will' cannot *really* be transmitted.

What Hobbes does think to be really transmitted to the sovereign in the covenant is power. For the 'right of nature' 'is the liberty each man hath, to use his own power, as he will himself, for the preservation of his own nature'; and this liberty simply consists

---

18. P.W. 5.11.69.
19. Hobbes, *Leviathan*. Part 1, Chapter XVI.

in 'the absence of external impediments' (Chapter XIV). And to 'renounce' a right, of which transferring a right (e.g. to the sovereign) is a special case, is 'to divest himself of the *liberty*, of hindering another of the benefit of his own right to the same. For he that renounceth, or passeth away his right, giveth not to any man a right which he had not before; because there is nothing to which every man had not right by nature: but only standeth out of his way, that he may enjoy his own natural right, without hindrance from him; not without hindrance from another. So that the effect which redoundeth to one man, by another man's defect of right, is but so much diminution of impediments to his own right original'. (Ibid.)

On the other hand, it is really essential to Hobbes to be able to talk about the relation of subject to sovereign in the legalistic way apparently provided by his talk about 'representation'. An important question in this connection is the sense in which one can speak of a body politic forming a unity. This is clearly important, in particular for Hobbes, in determining over what people sovereignty is exercised. But it is important in a wider context too. For all political philosophers have perceived that there is a sense in which the legitimacy of a regime depends on the relation this regime has to the special character of a particular society. Hobbes's account of this is unequivocal:

> A multitude of men, are made *one* person, when they are by one man, or one person, represented; so that it be done with the consent of every one of that multitude in particular. For it is the *unity* of the representer, not the *unity* of the represented, that maketh the person *one*. And it is the representer that beareth the person, and but one person: and *unity*, cannot otherwise be understood in multitude.[20]

Some very important Hobbesist contentions hang on this point. For instance, the impossibility of supposing any covenant to exist between sovereign and subject. (Which is *one* way in which some writers have tried to understand the dimension of freedom that exists between ruler and ruled in the political relation.) One of the reasons this is impossible for Hobbes: there cannot be a contract between sovereign and society, because no unitary society exists in the absence of the sovereign. (N.B. that this too is Rousseau's doctrine, though of course transmuted by his different conception of sovereignty.) Whereas a contract between subject individually and the sovereign will not work: because 'sovereign' and 'subject' are categories created by the original covenant; there are none such prior to it; but the relation could not be created by a number of individual contracts, since the sovereign is sovereign over the body politic and the notion of a body politic presupposes in some sense a unitary will. Now once the sovereign has been instituted by the covenant we can (perhaps: though there are other difficulties) think of a unitary will via Hobbes's conception of 'representation'. The difficulty comes in seeing how there can be any idea of such a unitary will in the original setting up of the sovereign. Yet, this is somehow necessary; otherwise there is no body politic for anyone to be sovereign over.

---

20. Ibid.

The peculiar form of Hobbes's covenant is an attempt to solve this difficulty:

> ...as if every man should say to every man, *I authorize and give up my right of governing myself to this man, or to this assembly of men, on this condition, that thou give up thy right to him, and authorize all his actions in like manner.*[21]

What is important about this form is the way in which it tries to provide, simultaneously, universal mutuality and a focus. This is clear from the way Hobbes defines a commonwealth in terms of the covenant:

> ...the essence of the commonwealth; which (to define it) is o*ne person, of whose acts a great multitude, by mutual covenants one with another, have made themselves everyone the author, to the end he may use the strength and means of them all, as he shall think expedient, for their peace and common defense.*[22]

The snag here is that the way in which Hobbes conceives the 'each one' in the state of nature which precedes the covenant makes it difficult to see how there can be any 'mutuality'. In other words, what is the nature of the passage from 'each one' to 'them all'?

This is of course a way of expressing the familiar difficulty about Hobbes: how can a covenant create a settled society, since we can only conceive a covenant to be possible within a settled society? (I imagine that Mr. Lloyd Thomas[23] will be discussing how some of these difficulties might be overcome in his excursus into games theory.)

I have been trying to emphasise, by approaching the difficulty in this way, that the difficulties go far beyond internal technical troubles in Hobbes's own theory: they point towards difficulties we must all face in understanding the relations between 'power' and 'will' in political relationships. One more word about Hobbes before I pass on to these more general questions. I noticed earlier the split between two radically different ways of speaking we find in Hobbes: on the one hand, what we might call the 'sociological' strand (though Hobbes is more inclined to use military analogies: I mean that Hobbes's talk about 'the sword' reappears in the thought of contemporary sociologists in the form of the idea that some external force is necessary in order to maintain the cohesion of a political unit, that the 'will' of the citizens is insufficient here); and, on the other hand, the 'legalistic' strand, which we see in his talk about 'representation'. What Hobbes seems to forget here is that all this talk about 'feigning' and 'deeming' has a place within a settled legal system only, whereas he is talking of a situation which preceded any such system. Or, if this temporal way of talking is unacceptable, let us say that he is confusing different levels of analysis: the analysis of the internal structure of a legal system with

---

21. Ibid., Part 2, Chapter XVII.
22. Ibid.
23. Eds: Another lecturer in the Intercollegiate Series, D. A. (David) Lloyd Thomas at Bedford College. See D. A. Lloyd Thomas, 'Political Decision Procedures', *Proceedings of the Aristotelian Society* 70 (1969–1970): 141–158. At 141n, he thanks Peter Winch for his comments on a draft.

the analysis of the conditions which make a legal system possible at all (cf. Hobbes's refusal to distinguish questions of justice from questions of legality). I said at the end of last week's lecture that I would consider the objection Hobbes might make to Rousseau's attempt to conceive the citizen as in some sense the *continuing* source of the regime's legitimacy. Hobbes's contention is that talk about legitimacy can only be made sense of *within* the framework provided by the dictates of the sovereign will. So that, once the sovereign has been established, no further questions can be raised about his legitimacy. (But, we might ask, how can we talk about the 'establishment' of a sovereign unless the act of establishment is the establishment of a rule which commits people to future acts? This cannot apparently be provided by the sovereign's *power*, since what we are asking is what warrant we have for speaking of a continuing sovereign who is regarded as *entitled* to exercise that power. Cf. Hart's discussion of the distinction between rules and habits in *The Concept of Law*.[24])

Hobbes's objection to a Rousseauist conception might be put in this way – The unity of the body politic can only be thought of in terms of a certain relationship between the members of that body politic to sovereignty; yet we cannot speak of sovereignty, Rousseau alleges, except by reference to a body politic.

In lectures at King's last year Rush Rhees spoke of the unity of the body politic in terms of the idea that its members are all 'facing in a certain direction'. Hobbes's question is *what* direction? – He would claim that a direction is only provided given that there *is* a sovereign towards whom they can face.

The point is connected with one that Hume is making in a passage from the essay quoted last week,[25] in which he argues against the idea that the legitimacy of government can be derived from the consent of the governed: 'they consent; because they apprehend him to be already by birth, their lawful sovereign'. The point does not depend purely on the characteristics of hereditary monarchy. It is rather that, supposing we can speak of 'consent' at all here, it would have to be a kind of consent which already involved the conception of legitimacy: the notion of legitimacy cannot be derived from an independent notion of consent; not any old consent will be a consent to the exercise of sovereignty.

What Rousseau wants to emphasise is that the conception of legitimacy involved in sovereignty can only be understood in terms of an active relationship between citizen and government, i.e. an activity on the part of the citizen. At this point I have to bring out a distinction that I have not so far made clearly enough. In the passage quoted at the end of the first set of lecture notes Rousseau talks about what is necessary if 'the stronger' is to be able to remain *permanently* in control. As I said subsequently, this suggestion is misleading. For it fails to take account of the fact – one which it is important for Rousseau to emphasise – that the mere fact that a government is in the saddle does

---

24. Eds: H. L. A. Hart, *The Concept of Law* (Oxford: Oxford University Press, 1961), 55–58. Hart cites Winch's *Idea of a Social Science* in this and another section.
25. Winch frequently quotes this passage from Hume; in the notes for Lecture 3 above, he has quoted the paragraph before the two paragraphs he quotes from here.

not make it legitimate. (Though of course Hobbes has to argue that it does.) Otherwise, Rousseau could not say: 'Man is born free; but everywhere he is in chains'.

Cf. Simone Weil: '*La légitimité du gouvernement provisoire*':

> After 1937, the government (of France) did not only *de facto* abandon the forms of legality – that would not matter much, for the British government did likewise, and yet there was never a British Prime Minister who was more legitimate than Winston Churchill – but the feeling for legitimacy was gradually extinguished. Almost no Frenchman approved of Daladier's usurpations. Almost no Frenchman got indignant about them. It is the feeling for legitimacy which makes one indignant about usurpations.
>
> People simply began to say in a depressed way: 'What does it matter what happens. We have nothing to lose.' They didn't merely say it. They thought it. They showed as much in June 1940 and during the weeks that followed.
>
> June 1940 was not a conspiracy of a treacherous elite. It was a failure, an abdication on the part of the whole nation.
>
> In July there took place at Vichy the black comedy which ended the 3rd Republic; and the abolition of the regime caused no shadow of regret, of sadness or of anger in the hearts of Frenchmen, outside the tiny coteries of those who were professionally attached to the institutions which had been destroyed.
>
> No one was interested anymore in succession. People were totally indifferent. Later on the Pétain legend took on a bit of life.
>
> So legitimacy is not a jewel which was stolen from the French nation, either by the enemy or by an internally organised conspiracy. The French people as a whole, from the elites to the labouring masses, opened its hand and let the jewel fall to the ground, without even looking down to see where it had rolled. Passers-by kicked it with their feet.[26]

Lecture Notes: Political Philosophy 5[27]

End of last lecture: distinction between what is required to keep a government in control and what is required to make a government legitimate.

The quotation from Simone Weil. A case in which while a regime is in a sense 'accepted', the people concerned, both those in the government and those subjected to it, have lost all sense of 'legitimacy'.

This is important in connection with the question of the relation between legitimacy and power and with the question of the relation between both of these and the 'will' and the 'power' of the people. When, e.g. Rousseau speaks of the people as the necessarily continuing source of sovereignty, he is speaking of will and of legitimacy, not just of power; he is speaking of what is lacking in the situation described by Weil.

The kinds of thing Weil mentions as necessary to legitimacy: the existence of free and spontaneous discussions of issues concerning justice, freedom, etc.: discussions which draw in men from all walks of life in society and which, in particular, draw in both ordinary citizens and members of the regime. What this suggests is that we must

---

26. Weil, *Écrits de Londres [et dernières lettres* (Paris: Gallimard, 1957)], 60–61.
27. P.W. 10.11.69.

see the relation between citizen and government as mediated by the ideas of what is just and right which grow out of such discussions. I.e. we must not see these ideas as just a bit of salad dressing ('ideology', 'opium of the people') which accompanies the 'real' relation of subject and state, but as genuinely constitutive of that relation. Of course, in any actual situation such ideas may be no more than salad dressing; but such situations will be those in which the conception of legitimacy has been lost (though nobody need have noticed this).

But though there is a distinction here it is not an easy one to apply. Three related complications:

1. It may well be that, at least characteristically, the question of legitimacy only arises vis-a-vis a body of men who exercise the power of the state. (This is a view suggested, e.g. by Hume's discussion.) This doesn't *always* have to be the case: cf. recognition of legitimacy in a government in exile and withholding of such recognition from the regime actually in power. But perhaps this case is only conceivable against the background of our understanding of the normal case in which the question of legitimacy only arises concerning the regime actually in power.

   Simone Weil is considering this sort of special case in her discussion of the relation of de Gaulle to legitimacy in France, while in exile in England. She suggests a further distinction here: that we shouldn't regard de Gaulle as actually the legitimate state authority, but as the temporary 'custodian' of French legitimacy during a period when it was not possible for anyone actually to exercise legitimate authority.

2. Conversely, it may also be that we cannot understand the concept of 'the power of the state' except by presupposing the concept of legitimacy, i.e. to understand the special sort of power, characteristic of the state, we have to understand what people mean when they think of 'the state' and *that* is a concept [the] elucidation of which will have to bring in the concept of legitimacy somewhere along the line. This point is connected with Rousseau's insistence that even though there may be no actually existing case of the exercise of legitimate sovereignty, still we have to understand what *would* be involved in such an exercise, if we are to grasp how men do stand in relation to actually existing regimes.

3. Parallel to the contention that the legitimacy of a regime must spring from the will of the people is the contention, also often met with, that the power of a regime must somehow derive from the society over which it is exercised. I.e. a regime, it might be said, can only continue in existence as long as the people are prepared to 'go along with it' in some sense. But, as Rousseau points out, this going along may be no more than necessity or prudence. But obviously, there is a connection between the question of what is necessary to keep a regime in power at all and the question of what is necessary to make it legitimate and these questions will not always be easy to distinguish. (Importance of Marx here: attempts to show how power can be concentrated owing to facts of social (especially economic: but not necessary to emphasise this in connection with the general point) organisation, which have come to be independently of the wills of any individuals or groups of individuals. Habermas was getting at something similar in his distinction between 'pure' and

'deformed' communication situations:[28] he wanted to suggest that all deviations from a situation where all participants have an equal right to speak their minds, have an equal concern with reaching the truth, and are accorded equal rights to respect, are due to concentrations of power in particular sectors of society. There is something important here; but whether we should accept this way of putting it depends on the view we take of the relation between the actual and the ideal. Can we have any understanding of a 'pure communication situation' independently of our understanding of particular social settings, furnishing the possibility of particular kinds of social relationship and roles. To put this differently, can we make sense of the notions of freedom, etc. *outside* the contexts of particular power structures? To put it differently again, can we make sense of the notion of freedom independently of contrasts with particular forms of oppression. Though in putting it in this last way, I should want to resist the suggestion that someone might derive from it: that the mere fact that there are particular power structures is necessarily incompatible with a free society. Cf. Simone Weil's discussion of legitimacy in relation to certain forms of monarchy in *The Need for Roots*.)

'The relation between the actual and the ideal'. To take this further, I must raise some more general questions about the relations between the lives which individuals lead and the societies in which they live their lives. It will be useful to take Hobbes as a stalking horse once more.

Lecture Notes: Political Philosophy 6[29]

The Hobbesist picture of the relation between man and society:

A man has a certain nature and he is placed in a world which he discovers to have certain features. In considering his relation to that world the most important aspects of man's nature for us to understand are his wants and needs and the means he has of satisfying those wants and needs. It may be recognised that he may acquire new wants and needs as a result of his interaction with his environment, but this development is seen in quasi-causal terms. (I use this way of speaking to express the negative fact that it is not seen in terms of a man's coming to stand in internal relations to the institutions of the society he finds himself confronted with. On the Hobbesist view we must always think of a man as 'confronted with' society; if he cooperates with it, it can only be because of the influence of some external force ('the sword') which forces him or makes it worth his while to do so.) An important part of man's ability to satisfy his wants will be his understanding of the causal processes which he comes to distinguish in the world

---

28. Eds: Habermas was not yet translated to English in 1969. Winch spoke at a 1967 Colloquium in Germany that also had Habermas on the schedule. Habermas engages with Winch's *Idea of a Social Science* in his 1967 *On the Logic of the Social Sciences* (first translated 1970). Habermas published on systematically distorted communication in 'Towards a Theory of Communicative Competence', *Inquiry* 13 (1970): 205–218.
29. P.W. 14.11.69.

around him and of the extent to which he is in a position to intervene in the operation of those processes and divert them towards his own satisfaction. One of the most important features of his environment is the existence of other men; correspondingly, amongst the most important causal processes which he will do well to understand are the principles upon which other men will act. He will try to achieve this understanding both by careful observation of the ways in which other men behave and also by attention to the principles upon which he himself acts, which he will then extrapolate to explain the actions of others. For this Hobbesist individual the world consists of instruments for furthering his desires or obstacles in the way of such furtherance; and other men similarly are either such instruments or such obstacles. He will understand that he, similarly, is such an instrument or such an obstacle in the eyes of other men too; so he will realise that one way in which he can't intervene and influence the actions of other men in his own interests will be by using his own instrumental or counter-instrumental status for them as a bargaining counter. Hence the origin of the covenant.

One of the most vital points (probably the most vital point) on which Rousseau differs from Hobbes is in his account of the relation between the individual and society. When Jean-Jacques, in *Émile*, comes to prepare his pupil to enter the world of human society, he says that the consideration which must be made central in acquainting Émile with the ideas and beliefs current in society is whether those beliefs are true or false. The evil which Rousseau wants to guard against here is the evil of governing one's actions in order to flatter the beliefs and expectations of other men without considering whether those beliefs and expectations are justified. A point he makes in this connection is that any 'power' which depends on the support of other men is illusory in that it can only be gained by putting oneself in *their* power (by flattering their expectations) in the first place. His point is that such a posture is incompatible with a genuinely independent and critical point of view in that it smothers any possible consideration of what is really the best way to live under consideration of (to put it crudely) what one can get away with in a world full of watchful eyes.

The point of view which Rousseau is rejecting here is in fact Hobbes's point of view. (I do not mean that Rousseau must have had Hobbes specifically in mind.) For Hobbes, if we are concerned with those 'beliefs' men have about the best ways of living in various contexts, there *is no question* to be raised about whether those beliefs are correct or not. 'For these words of good, evil and contemptible, are ever used with relation to the person that useth them: there being nothing simply and absolutely so; nor any common rule of good and evil, to be taken from the nature of the objects themselves; but from the person of the man, where there is no commonwealth; or, in a commonwealth, from the person that representeth it; or from an arbitrator or judge, whom men disagreeing shall by consent set up, and make his sentence the rule thereof'.[30] What is noteworthy here is the directness with which Hobbes moves from the premise that there is no possible discussion of the real merits or demerits of any policy proposal (except as it relates to an individual's own 'desires and aversions') to the conclusion that, if there is to be any sort

---

30. *Leviathan*, Part 1, Chapter VI.

of organised social life at all, [then] any claim to independent criticism of such proposals on the part of individuals must be given up to an all-powerful sovereign. Rousseau could hardly have found a better advocate for his own views about the true nature of 'power'.

The Hobbesist view about the nature of good and evil goes along with the Hobbesist view about the nature of language as consisting of a public representation of ideas originating in the mind of the individual. It is a view which ignores the fact that ideas are impossible without a grammar. I argued more fully elsewhere that a grammar is only conceivable in a society in which men recognise common concerns and appeal to common standards of argument.[31] The point can be driven a little farther home by considering another point at which there is a crucial gap in Hobbes's scheme of thought. It is of the utmost importance to the picture he paints that we should be able to speak of a man as coming to understand his own nature independently of his coming to understand the world of men around him. But in fact a man comes to understand his own nature (I might almost say that he comes to have a specifiable nature) only in relation to problems and difficulties which he finds himself confronted with. Those problems and difficulties, and the ways in which he meets them, spring from the social world in which he lives, the kinds of activity and of personal relation which it makes available to him.

Social institutions and traditions furnish a grammar within which there can be certain discussions of problems (problems which are formulated in the same grammar); the formulation of policies and ideals. These ideals may point beyond any state of society which we, or anyone, have actually come across. What we can understand as a possible mode of intelligible human conduct is not confined to kinds of conduct which we have actually experienced; but it is limited by the grammar which we have learned to apply to actually observed cases of human action (Cf. my objections to MacIntyre in 'Understanding [a] Primitive Society'.) An analogy: suppose I learn the word 'table' with reference to four-legged tables; the tables I have observed in learning this word do function as a sort of paradigm in the subsequent use I make of the word; but I can and do use the word also to apply to articles differing quite radically (e.g. number of legs) from tables which I have ever met. Also, more importantly for us, my understanding of what a table is ('based' on my observation of actual tables, but not simply 'abstracted' from those cases), enables me to understand what might count as an *improvement* in the method of constructing tables.

Apply this to the word 'state'. I learn what the state is by reference to actually existing or past states; but at the same time, I learn a language in which I can criticise political arrangements. This is partly because I do not learn the meaning of this word in a vacuum;

---

31. See *The Idea of a Social Science [and its Relation to Philosophy* (London: Routledge and Kegan Paul, 1958)]; 'Nature and Convention' [*Proceedings of the Aristotelian Society* 60, no. 1 (1959–1960): 231–252] and 'Understanding a Primitive Society' in *Religion and Understanding*, edited by D. Z. Phillips [and earlier in *American Philosophical Quarterly* 1, no. 4 (1964): 307–324. Both papers are reprinted in Peter Winch, *Ethics and Action* (London: Routledge and Kegan Paul, 1972)].

I learn it in the context of becoming initiated into various kinds of discussion into which other concepts enter. E.g. the concepts Simone Weil emphasises in connection with her discussion of legitimacy: concepts like justice, freedom (which also receive substance from their application to fairly concrete issues).

This is why I can (*pace* Hobbes) discuss the justice and other merits or demerits of a particular state's actions; my understanding of this particular institution as 'a state' depends on my understanding that there are other possibilities of institutions which I would also want to call 'states' and these different possibilities may be compared from the point of view, e.g. of their different relations to justice and liberty.

What is more important in relation to Hobbes: without my understanding of these further possibilities, it would no longer *be* 'a state' for me.

Relation to patriotism as 'my country right or wrong'. 'My country' is not exhausted by any particular set of facts. In growing up in a country I inherit a tradition within which I can grasp the possibility of certain ideals and of ways in which particular regimes may fall short of, or even attack and damage, those ideals. Hence it would be possible for someone to claim without absurdity that he is acting patriotically in opposing – even to the limits of his powers – the aims and policies of his country at a given time. Cf. those Germans who wished for, and worked for, the defeat of Germany in 1945.

1.3

AUTHORITY, SOCIETY AND THE STATE [N.D.][1]

In this course I shall be concerned with central and familiar questions raised by philosophers of politics in the 'classical lexicon': e.g. Hobbes, Locke, Rousseau.

My aim will not be exegesis of these authors as such, though it will in fact prove desirable to do a certain amount of exegesis from a particular point of view. But the order of my argument will not be that of any particular author; I shall follow the logical order suggested to me by the questions I shall raise and the subsidiary problems that will come up in the treatment of these.

What questions are these? Here is a sample:

– What is a human society?
– How do human beings have to be related to each other if we are to be able to say of them that they belong to a human society?
– What is the relation between society and its members?
– What is the relation between the last-mentioned relation and the previous one?
– Is our concept of a human being independent of that of a human society? What is the relation between a human society and the various kinds of institutions which may exist within it?
– What is it for a man to be a participant in a social institution?
– What is the relation between the concept of participating in an institution and that of being a member of a human society?
– What is the difference between *a* human society and just human society?
– What is the role of the state in a human society?
– Is it just one institution amongst others or is its role quite special?
– Can there be a human society in the absence of the state?
– What is authority? Are there different forms of authority? If so, how is political authority related to other forms?
– Where does authority fit into our answers to the other questions I've raised?

---

1. Eds: Typescript; lecture notes; 7 pp., Peter Winch Archives (GB 0100 KCLCA K/PP171, Folder 'Politics IV', Box 7; plus 1 p. in Box 1), King's College London. The TS references Rhees's paper 'Wittgenstein's Builders' and Winch's paper 'Nature and Convention' (anthologised in *Ethics and Action*, 1972), both of which were read at the Aristotelian Society, in March and May, respectively (*Proceedings of the Aristotelian Society* 60 (1969-1970): 171–186 and 231–252, respectively).

These are a lot of questions. Some of them run into each other and can hardly be considered separately. Obviously, I shan't be able to treat them all explicitly. Some of them I shall hardly be able to treat even by implication. But it was worth mentioning them, to give some idea of the complexity of the subject and of the way issues are interconnected.

What sort of questions are these? Are they indeed all of the same sort? And why should a *philosopher* ask them?

Some of them, as formulated, do look like philosophical questions. E.g. we are on familiar sounding enough ground with 'Is our concept of a human being independent of that of a human society?' and with 'How do human beings have to be related to each other if we are to be able to say of them that they belong to a human society?' and with 'What is the difference between human society and a human society?'[2]

These wear their 'conceptual' character pretty well on their sleeves. But what of 'Can there be a human society in the absence of the state?' That looks more as though it raises empirical issues. Cf. 'Can there be such and such a chemical reaction in the absence of such and such a catalyst?'

And I do not want to deny that there are empirical questions which can be raised in this form. But I shall argue that all of my questions do raise philosophical, i.e. conceptual, issues.

But I shall argue also for more than this. Not merely that there are conceptual questions connected with politics which are formally similar to questions raised elsewhere in philosophy and which are therefore treatable by similar methods. But that there is continuity and mutual dependence between the questions themselves – in their substance.

Now I think a proper understanding of this is of some importance; not merely in order to be clear about the nature of political philosophy, but in order to retain some sense of the unity of philosophy as a whole.

It is a view which, quite a short time ago, it was fashionable to deny. It used to be said, e.g. that the epistemological and metaphysical parts of Hobbes's philosophy really had no internal logical connection with his theory of politics. I suppose the most extreme statement of this sort of thesis was Weldon's *The Vocabulary of Politics*.[3] Of course it was connected with various other philosophical positions fashionable at the same time – with versions, e.g. of the emotive theory of ethics, and with the idea that on the one hand you had empirical statements – establishable only by observational and experimental methods, and on the other hand linguistic muddles, which might stand in the way of genuine scientific understanding, but the resolution of which could not in itself lead to any positive advance in understanding.

---

2. Handwritten marginal note: Cf. language/a language (Rush Rhees 'W[ittgenstein]'s Builders'). Eds: The distinction is not exactly drawn in these words in the paper Winch references; in that paper, Rhees famously probes problems around Wittgenstein's claims that any of the given simple language game he describes could be a complete language in itself, and wards off the idea we might take from Wittgenstein that language is simply the sum total (assemblage) of language games.

All of this seems to me misconceived, though no doubt, like other misconceptions, it contained some elements of truth – or at least derived from some genuine differences between philosophical questions and empirical or evaluative questions.

The thread which connects the sort of question I have raised with questions, e.g. in epistemology and philosophy of mind, is that of the nature of human reason and intelligence. One is raising questions about the role of intelligence in human affairs and in the life of society and of social institutions; with questions about the connection between the fact that men are 'rational beings' and the nature of human society; with questions about the dependence of rationality on the existence of social life and certain kinds of institution; with questions about whether rational intercourse between men is, as it were, self-supporting, or whether a background of brute force is required to make it possible.

And it is because I think questions like this central to political philosophy – and indeed a condition of the existence of political *philosophy* – that I want to start by considering Hobbes – who raises such questions, makes them central to his enquiry and, indeed, sees the fact of their interconnection very clearly. I think he is almost completely wrong about the account we are to give of their interconnections, but wrong in a way which is of great help in arriving at what seems to me to be the right view.

I shall ask about the relations between the following elements in Hobbes's philosophy: his materialism; his account of human nature and in particular: of the relation between reason and passion; his account of morality; his account of social life and of the role of the state in social life.

Hobbes

Materialism: combination of philosophical with more common sense notion of 'substance' – the only thing real is matter and the motion of matter (Cartesianism minus *res cogitans*).

So *man* has to be accounted for in these terms too – what will distinguish him from other material bodies is not something non-material (which can't be) but certain peculiarities in the way he moves. Hence Hobbes's account of the passions. Basic concept is *endeavour* (= motion towards or away from something: *desire* and *aversion*).

Or rather endeavour is 'the small beginnings of motion' towards or from. – Physiology.

What we call desire and aversion is really a process in the nervous system (cf. Smart's identity theory).[4]

Similarly with perception and imagination and memory. (Trace theory.) Notion of 'phantasms' – Hobbes starts with a metaphysics and never really comes to terms with the epistemological difficulties it raises. This [is] a difficulty which runs *right through* his philosophy [and is] connected, e.g. with the incoherencies in his notion of the 'covenant', as I shall try to show.

---

3. T. D. Weldon, *The Vocabulary of Politics* (Harmondsworth: Penguin Books, 1953).
4. Eds: J. J. C. Smart, 'Sensations and Brain Processes', *Philosophical Review*, 68 (1959): 141–156.

Practical reasoning (I shall not discuss his account of theoretical reasoning, through lack of time). A train of phantasms organised under the leadership of a dominant desire or aversion. Leads to a knowledge of causes and the possibility of foresight and hence *prudence*.

(Though, curiously, he does touch on the interestingly parallel difficulties that arise in his account of morals, and indeed, exploits them.)

Deliberations [are] exposure to conflicting forces (forces which can also contain, via knowledge of causes and prudence, an idea of the future). Will = last desire. No freedom (bogus etymology).

This gives us most of the basic material which Hobbes uses in his account of society and the state. In order to understand what he tries to do with it and what's wrong with what he tries to do with it, we will first explore some of the basic incoherencies.[5]

1. The tendency to solipsism. Hobbes's account of the grammar of good:

 > For these words of good, evil, and contemptible are ever used with relation to the person that useth them: there being nothing simply and absolutely so; nor any common rule of good and evil.[6]

 If we note that Hobbes's reasons for saying this are just a special case of a much more general epistemological position, we can raise the question whether the same must not be true for him regarding *any* use of language. – Must not these all relate to one individual's phantasms? – Problem of other minds.

2. Does this matter? Well, yes. – Given that men have no common conceptions of mutual obligations prior to the covenant, and given the difficulties this creates for the *notion* of the covenant, [it] might still appear that the matter could be patched up in terms of some recognition of a common *interest*.

 But any such recognition presupposes a going system of communication – and it is hard to see that Hobbes can give a coherent account of what this could be. He glides over the matter rather rapidly in *Leviathan* (see pp. 18 and 19 [Chapter IV]).

 Relevance of Wittgenstein here – general rules, something established, [therefore] a certain sort of mutual *trust* – cf. my 'Nature and Convention' article.[7]

3. *Leviathan*. p. 86 [Chapter XIV] ('injustice' and 'absurdity')
4. [No content]

---

5. Handwritten marginal note: Connections with causal theories of meaning. Cf. Russell's 'Limits of Empiricism' [*Proceedings of the Aristotelian Society* 36 (1935–1936): 131–150]. Russell [attempted] to distinguish between a right and a wrong way of using an expression [illegible word] into a good and a bad reason. 'To weigh'. Reason as calculation/naturalism/contradiction. (Names of sentences: Rousseau).
6. Hobbes, *Leviathan*, Chapter VI.
7. Peter Winch, 'Nature and Convention', *Ethics and Action* (London: Routledge and Kegan Paul, 1972), 231–252.

Last time: I argued that the difficulties Hobbes gets into with regard to the covenant are symptomatic of more general difficulties involved in his account of language and rationality. And that this is important in that he shows a tendency to overcome the more special difficulties by reference to general considerations concerning language and rationality, without seeing that the same kinds of obstacle stand in his way here too.

I then started to argue (on the lines of 'Nature and Convention') that if we investigate the kind of condition that has to be satisfied if there is to be language and the sort of rationality that goes along with the existence of a language, we find that these include certain relations of a moral sort, such that Hobbes's conception of a *bellum omnium contra omnes* is exposed as incoherent.

I started this by noting the necessity that for the most part what people say should be taken as *true*. But this is not enough – [there is] nothing moral involved so far – [since] I am not being truthful every time I say something true.[8] It might be argued, on Hobbesian lines, that people will see that for the most part, it is to their interest to say what is true – or at least that it is not contrary to their interest to say what is true: so that there would be no point in lying except in special sorts of circumstances. – And of course this is by and large so.

But of course when we put the matter like that, we are *assuming* a going system of communication. And the point we are interested in is: what is involved in the idea of a going system of communication.

So now, let us look at what is the case with regard to *truthfulness* – or, to make the discussion as wide as possible, with *sincerity* or *meaning what one says*.

Remember that Hobbes says that force and *fraud* are characteristic of the state of nature – i.e. I suppose that the rational thing to expect in a state of nature is that other people are going to *deceive* you i.e. that insincerity will be the rule.

Could this be? What do I do when I try to deceive someone? I try to take advantage of what I expect to be the *standard reaction* of someone being spoken to as I am speaking to him. So before there can be a question of deceit, there must *be* a standard reaction.[9]

This rather obvious point has ramifications of the utmost importance.

1. Could there be this standard reaction if the general rule were an intention to deceive? Yes, *in particular cases*. But generally? How then are we to describe the reaction? Not a *psychological* matter, this characterisation of the reaction is intrinsically related to that of which it is a reaction *to*. Cf. Obedience.[10]
2. Wittgenstein's account of what is involved in learning a rule. – 'Going on in the same way' – i.e. going on in what is generally recognised as *counting* as 'the same way'. It is just a *fact* that most people agree on what is to so count. It might not have been so. Then there would have been no language.

---

8. Eds: This echoes Holland's response to Winch's 'Nature and Convention', which Winch cites in his Introduction to *Ethics and Action*. See R. F. Holland, 'Is Goodness a Mystery?', *The University of Leeds Review* 13, no. 1 (May 1970). The paper was reprinted in Holland, *Against Empiricism* (1980).
9. Handwritten: Not same as expecting to be true.
10. Eds: (1) was overwritten as (2) and this handwritten note was made (1).

3. Contrast my emphasis on certain natural relations and reactions between people as essential to the possibility of ascribing rationality with what Hobbes says about the contrast between men and other 'social' animals (*Leviathan*, Part 2, Chapter XVII). Reason as a characteristic of individuals which divides him from his fellows. Of course, reason can be divisive: but this does not mean that it is divisive of its nature. (Strychnine can be a curative medicine in small quantities. Cf. also Wittgenstein's remark that friction is necessary if one is to walk.[11])
4. But what is 'moral' about all this? Am I not just making assertions about the way men do behave towards each other, not about how they think they ought to behave?

Hobbes's 'laws of nature' – 'theorems' or 'commands'?

Wittgenstein: 'My attitude towards him is an attitude towards a soul; I am not of the opinion that he has a soul'.[12]
Austin: 'inadvertently' stepping on the baby's head.[13][14]
In sum: Hobbes's views about the relation between individuals, society, social institutions, the state and authority.

(a) In the absence of the state, there can be no other social institutions, no civilised life. So the state is certainly not just one institution amongst others: it is logically prior – a condition of others. – Hobbes draws the conclusion that there is no *authority* involved in other social institutions which can compete with the authority of the state.
I think he might say: insofar as such competition takes place, the other institution is in effect making a bid to *be* the state (religion and universities) (compare Rousseau on 'sinister interests').[15]
(b) A corollary of (a) is that, considered in abstraction from their relation to the state, individuals living together can constitute no genuine unity. (*Leviathan*, Part 2, Chapter XVIII): Nominalism + materialism. Contrast Rousseau. The political difference between Hobbes and Rousseau which follows from this metaphysical difference is that while they agree on the relation between individual and sovereign in respect of subjection to authority, they disagree about the nature of that authority and about its proper exercise. Rousseau's 'two capacities':[16] Hobbes would have regarded this

---

11. Ludwig Wittgenstein, *Philosophical Investigations*, eds. G. E. M. Anscombe and Rush Rhees, trans. G. E. M. Anscombe (Oxford: Basil Blackwell, 1953), §107.
12. Wittgenstein, *Philosophical Investigations*, Part 2, Section iv. Eds: See Winch's later paper, '*Eine Einstellung zur Seele*' in *Trying to Make Sense* (Oxford: Basil Blackwell, 1987), 140–153.
13. Eds: 'We may plead that we trod on the snail inadvertently: but not on a baby – you ought to look where you're putting your great feet.' J. L. Austin, 'A Plea for Excuses: The Presidential Address', *Proceedings of the Aristotelian Society* 57 (1956–1957), 1–30 (20).
14. Handwritten notes:
Connection with Anderson; [?] over-use of 'ought'
'To act in any other way would be unthinkable.' – 'My eyes are closed' (Solipsism.) (Moral necessity.)
15. Handwritten note: cf. de Juvenal – On Power [Bernard de Juvenal, *On Power: Its Nature and the History of its Growth* (New York: Viking Press, 1948)].
16. Rousseau, *Of the Social Contract*, Chapter 7: capacity as an individual and capacity as with others constituting a unity, the sovereign.

as no more than a legalistic fiction: he didn't mind using these himself, but also tried to reveal, as it were, what he regarded as the sociological reality (of force and counter-force) beneath them.

(c) 'Authority' (as distinct from power) is accounted for thus legalistically. Derived from 'author' – Peters follows this.[17] So (i) the state has the only genuine authority: all other is as it were delegated and can always be overruled. (ii) At the same time, the source of the state's authority is the individual's power to act (which he alienates). N.B. that it must be an all-or-nothing alienation [with] no reservations: cf. Rousseau; also no distinction between 'natural rights': just one 'right of nature' which is seen as following from the very nature of human action. – Locke regarded this as *incompatible* with civil authority – cf. his differentiation of natural rights.

But for Hobbes, there is one limit on the state's authority, deriving from the same source – i.e. the state cannot compel me to submit to my own death. I think Hobbes would say, it doesn't make sense to suppose that it could. Or rather, of course it can compel me, but it can't take away my right to resist. The point here surely is really that talk about 'rights' just becomes inappropriate at this point.

(d) Following from foregoing: no covenant *with* sovereign: (a) can't be with individual, because covenants presuppose an *external* power to compel compliance; (b) can't be with 'society' because [there is] no such thing in absence of sovereign.

Hence [the] only limits on a sovereign's power are prudential ones. [The] Sovereign [is] in state of nature vis-a-vis subjects; but in his interests to do what they want of him. Not, as in Rousseau, an *identity* of interests, but a *balancing* of interests.

Optimistic? Cf. Rousseau, p. 7; Locke, p. 78 and p. 74.

Cf. Simone Weil, *Need for Roots* on conditional and unconditional loyalty.[18]

Hobbes might have said: a conditional loyalty is a contradiction in terms. Is it?[19]

Simone Weil on patriotism and loyalty to the State.[20]

The paradox – the State seems to demand an *unconditional* loyalty; yet the State can do and be evil.

1. The Conditionality:
   ◦ State seems to act on behalf of the whole society in a way that other institutions don't
   ◦ State responsible for protection of society's way of social life
     • Regulation of employment
     • Education
     • Weakening of family
     • Welfare services

---

17. Eds: R. S. Peters, Winch's co-symposiast at the Aristotelian Society session on Authority. 'Symposium: Authority', *Proceedings of the Aristotelian Society* Supplementary Volume 32 (1958): 207–260.
18. Eds: Simone Weil, *The Need for Roots: Prelude to a Declaration of Duties Toward Mankind*, trans. Arthur Wills (New York: G. P. Putnam's Sons, 1952).
19. Ibid., 115. Cf. Plato. Oakeshott or Hobbes's magnanimous man.
20. The following text comes from a page headed 'A, S and S – 7', consistent in format with the preceding text, found amongst other papers in Folder 'Politics IV', Box 7.

- Even religion sometimes
- Etc.
  ◦ (not here a question of whether we *approve* of this)
2. Loyalty, if I am asking whether I should bestow it, must be regarded as something *good*; can it be though, unless it is *towards* something good. But no fact, no existing state of affairs, institution, can of itself necessarily be good (a grammatical statement – related to Moore's 'Naturalistic Fallacy': we can ask of anything 'Is it good?' – but N.B. I am not hereby endorsing any particular analysis of ethical utterances or everything Moore says about naturalism).

This suggests the idea that there is an incoherence in the idea of an unconditional loyalty to any actual person or institution (at least to any institution in any condition it happens to be in). Yet it might also be argued that if my loyalty is conditional it is hardly loyalty at all. Since it now appears that my ultimate attachment is not to that towards which I am supposed to show loyalty. Cf. 'fair-weather friends'.

But we must now ask whether there are not distinctions between the kinds of object to which I can be ultimately attached, which are relevant here. Fair-weather friend's ultimate attachment is to *himself*.

But this is not the only possibility. I can also be attached to values which I regard as transcending myself *as well as* other persons and institutions. Is this sort of attachment necessarily inimical to loyalty? To answer this we must ask how my loyalty will express itself in cases where the object of my loyalty is responsible for some assault on values that I hold dear. If, e.g., my friend commits a murder. Certainly I should feel I must 'stand by him'. Does this mean I must let him think, and persuade myself, that what he has done is perfectly all right? Of course not. But I can still think I owe him a kind of consideration and help which I would not owe to someone who wasn't my friend. (I certainly don't want to say, though, that there can't be ultimate conflicts here. But I don't think the possibility of this is confined to situations involving loyalty to individuals (though it may be characteristically true of these) – it is a possibility which runs right through morality.

Why[21] cannot something similar be true of my loyalty to the state? (We must remember here – it makes it easier – that the state can itself become hostile to those features of my country's social life which I value and which I take the state to be there to protect and nurture.) E.g. Suez, Vietnam.

But we still have to go deeper. Simone Weil's conception of a 'particular vital medium'.[22] A vital medium for what? – Values. Relevance to relativism and to 'natural law'. A common form.

Time to introduce a direct discussion of the notion of 'authority' in this context.

Is there a certain incoherence in the idea that my loyalty to the state might be absolute? (Loyalty incomprehensible except in context of other values.)[23]

---

21. Eds: The remainder is a loose TS page found in Box 1 (marked as A, S and S 8, consistent with the pagination and format of the preceding text).
22. Ibid., 161, 162.
23. Handwritten: (Socrates: 'unity of virtues').

1.4

FOUR LECTURES ON CONSENT [1984][1]

I. The roots of the problem of legitimacy in the philosophy of mind.
II. Consent as the source of political authority. Locke.
III. Criticism of II.
IV. Hume: 'They consent because they perceive him to be by birth their lawful sovereign.' Simone Weil.

Suggested Reading

John Locke
Second Treatise on Civil Government
David Hume
Political Essays:
    'Of the Original Contract'
    'That Politics May be Reduced to a Science'
    'Of the First Principles of Government'
    'Of the Origin of Justice and Property'
    'Of the Origin of Government'
John Plamenatz
Consent, Freedom and Political Obligation
Man and Society (see index for 'consent')
Simone Weil
'Are We Struggling for Justice'
'On the Legitimacy of the Provisional Government'
G. E. M. Anscombe
'On the Source of the Authority of the State' in *Collected Philosophical Papers*, Vol. III

Lecture 1: The Roots of the Problem

Hume begins his essay 'Of the First Principles of Government' with a famous remark which will serve to introduce the problem I want to consider in these lectures.

---

1. Eds: Dated 'Michaelmas Term 1984'. Computer printout (dot matrix); lecture notes; 24 pp., Peter Winch Archives (GB 0100 KCLCA K/PP171, Box 35), King's College London.

> Nothing appears more surprising to those who consider human affairs with a philosophical eye than the easiness with which the many are governed by the few and the implicit submission with which men resign their own sentiments and passions to those of their rulers.[2]

This remark *sounds* superficially as though it introduced a kind of causal question: what is the mechanism by which a certain result is brought about? As one might ask; how is it possible for a man to lift a 10-ton weight, using a suitable combination of pulleys, when he would not be able to move it by his own strength otherwise? Hume probably did think he was asking a question of this sort, thinking of himself as he did, as applying Newtonian methods of inquiry and explanation to human affairs. And of course, questions of that sort can be asked here. But reflection on the question – even reflection on the course which Hume's own discussion takes after this introduction – will show that there are issues of a different sort involved here, issues which undoubtedly belong to philosophy, rather than to what are called the 'behavioural sciences'.

Consider for instance the phrase 'the implicit submission with which men resign their own sentiments and passions to those of their rulers'. Before we investigate *why* people do this, we had better understand *what* it is we take them to be doing. (In philosophy, we often find that what actually puzzles us is not just, or perhaps even mainly, why things are as they are, but what these things are.) Hume does not simply speak of some people submitting to others in respect of what they do, he speaks of their submitting to 'resign their own sentiments and passions to those of their rulers'. We might put the point (or at least a closely similar point) in this way. In the context of the state, those who are ruled do not just do what they are told, they recognise some sort of *right* to command in those who tell them what to do. Moreover, the right which is acknowledged is a right of a peculiar sort, of the sort, namely, exercised by a 'ruler'.

Professor Anscombe compares the power overseen by the state with that exercised by gangsters; the Mafia, say.[3] That is a way of bringing out the point. The word 'legitimacy' is often used in this connection. The inquiry on which we are embarking could be characterised as an inquiry into the nature of this legitimacy ascribed to the state.

Here we need to make an important distinction. Sometimes, for instance at times of civil war or revolution, opposing factions offer competing regimes. Each perhaps claims legitimacy; and questions may then be asked about which, if either, of them constitutes the 'legitimate government'. (Simone Weil raises an analogous, though not quite identical, question concerning the Free French Provisional Government in London, after the defeat of France in 1940, and the Vichy regime. See her essay:

---

2. Eds: David Hume, 'Of the First Principles of Government', in *Political Essays*, ed. Charles W. Handel (Bobbs Merrill, The Library of Liberal Arts 1953), 24–27 (24).
3. Eds: G. E. M. Anscombe, 'On the Source of the Authority of the State', in *Ethics, Religion and Politics: Collected Philosophical Papers*, Vol. III (Oxford: Basil Blackwell, 1981), 130–155.

'*La légitimité du gouvernement provisoire*' in *Écrits de Londres*.[4]) Or again, questions may be raised about whether a regime constitutes a 'legitimate government' under special circumstances even when there is no alternative in sight. Such questions are sometimes asked, e.g. about the Soviet-backed regime in Afghanistan or, for rather different sorts of reason, about the current regime in South Africa.

If we ask such questions we are, of course, taking the concept of 'legitimacy' for granted. If someone thinks that the regime in Afghanistan is *not* a legitimate one, that will be by way of contrast with what he will think, say, about the regime in power in the United States. Such contrasts are essential to the point he wants to make; and they are contrasts which involve the application of the concept of legitimacy.

I would not call such questions 'philosophical' questions, though of course philosophical issues can be raised concerning them.

But a different sort of question may be raised. Suppose that someone, taking up Anscombe's contrast between the government of a state and the bosses of the Mafia, were to question whether the former is really legitimate, whether, that is, there is really *that* sort of distinction between the Mafia and the state. It cannot be denied that there is indeed, in one sense, a distinction: namely, that those who are subject to the power of the state do indeed characteristically *think* of it as exercising genuine authority, i.e. as having legitimacy, whereas those who are subject to the power of the Mafia do not. But it may be claimed that the former are under an illusion, that there is no distinction of the sort they suppose between the state and the Mafia. – This is claimed, of course, by anarchists; but not only by them; there are others who, while agreeing that the idea of legitimacy is an illusion, think that it is a salutary illusion and one that should be fostered.

Now in order to evaluate such claims we should of course have to be clear about what it is they are denying. We cannot determine whether or not the notion of 'legitimacy' is an illusion unless we understand what it is supposed to be.

However, I shall not tackle this question head on. Instead, I want to try to express what seems to me the deepest, the most fundamental, philosophical difficulty there is in the way of accepting such a notion. This difficulty has its roots in the philosophy of mind, in the notion of *acting for a reason*. We can get at it by considering something Hobbes says in *Leviathan* in a chapter concerned with the difference between *commanding* and *counselling* (or *advising*).

> COMMAND is, where a man saith, *do this*, or *do not this*, without expecting other reason than the will of him that says it. From this it followeth manifestly, that he that commandeth, pretendeth thereby his own benefit: for the reason of his command is his own will only, and the proper object of every man's will, is some good to himself.
>
> COUNSEL, is where a man saith, *do*, or *do not this*, and deduceth his reasons from the benefit that arriveth by it to him to whom he saith it. And from this it is evident, that he that giveth counsel, pretendeth only, whatsoever he intendeth, the good of him, to whom he giveth it.[5]

---

4. Eds: Simone Weil, 'The Legitimacy of the Provisional Government', trans. Peter Winch, *Philosophical Investigations* 10, no. 2 (1987): 87–98.
5. Hobbes, *Leviathan*, Part 2, Chapter XXV.

I am not concerned here with the question how accurate an account this is of the distinction between command and advice as ordinarily understood. What interests me rather is the distinction between the appeal to a person's reason in the two cases distinguished by Hobbes. Let me call the speaker 'S' and the hearer 'H'. Then in each case what S says may be thought of as providing H with a reason for doing something. In the case called 'counsel' by Hobbes, it is in a way irrelevant to S's reason for acting that H has said what he has. Suppose S has advised me to invest my money in oil stock; if I then do this, I do it because I think this will be a good investment. Of course, the fact that S has advised me to do it may be a factor which has helped to convince me that it will be a good investment (because I'm aware of his past record of sound advice on such matters). But it is the judgement that this will be a good investment that is decisive for my action; and I might in principle have arrived at this judgement without S having said anything at all.

In the case of what Hobbes calls 'command', however, the situation is different. If what I do is done in obedience to S's command, then it is done *because S said it was to be done*. Suppose, for instance S has *ordered* me to invest my money in oil stock. (Let us not ask any questions about what might have put him in a position to do this.) To obey him is to invest the money in oil stock because he has told me to. S may have told me to because he thinks it will be a good investment for me; and I too may think that it will be a good investment for me. However, in so far as I make the investment for that reason, I am not acting in obedience to S.

Lecture 2: Consent as the Source of Political Authority

At the end of last week's lecture, I discussed Hobbes's way of distinguishing between 'command' and 'counsel' and tried to make something like the distinction he is getting at without using his suspect (indeed false) assumption that 'the proper object of every man's will is some good *to himself*'. This assumption does of course play a crucial role in the development of Hobbes's own philosophy, but we are not directly concerned with that here. The important phrase from our point of view is: 'without expecting other reason than the will of him that says it'. The relation of will to action is unproblematic in the case of the man who acts *on advice*: it is unambiguously he who decides what to do and he who evaluates (or rather, is responsible for evaluating) the reasons for doing it. But the position of one who acts in obedience to someone else is more obscure. It is the will of the commander that is decisive for what he does. And yet his, H's, own will plays an essential part. It is still his action. And H's will is not merely a *cause* of his doing what he does, it is his *reason* for so doing.

The question is how such a thing is conceivable.

There is no difficulty if H's reason for acting is the threat with which S backs his command. Because then his reason is *not* really H's will so much as the desire to avoid the unwelcome consequences of not doing what S says. This we may take to be the situation of the man who does what he is told by the Mafia. His reason ultimately is not that the Mafia has ordered it, but the consequences of his not doing what the Mafia ordered. (It is interesting that when Hobbes is discussing the 'covenant' which he thinks of as the source of the sovereign's authority, he himself emphasises that the expression of a promise, considered by itself, has no power to 'bind' the will of the one who promises at some later time, being nothing but 'breath'. This is a crucial step in his argument, since on it depends his conclusion that the sovereign must have the power of the 'sword': i.e. the power to *enforce* the covenant. And in this case, the will that is in question is at least the promiser's own will. In the case of command, the will by which the one commanded is to be bound is the will of *someone else*; one would have thought it should be even more difficult in this case to see how that could be possible: even more necessary to see that he is really bound by something else, namely, the threat of sanctions in the event of his non-compliance. And that, much of the time, seems to be quite clearly Hobbes's actual view.)

But the case we are trying to understand is one in which the order is given by someone (or some institution) which H acknowledges as having the right to command, and where H acts because that someone has so commanded, it is difficult to state the situation in a way which does not make H look like just an extension of S's body. S executes his will through the movements of H's rather than of his own body. But since a man who obeys a command does not cease to exercise his will and since, connectedly, he can *still* be said to be acting for a reason (if a peculiar one), it looks as though in this case S is executing his will not just through H's body but *'through H's will'*. And it is unclear what this can possibly mean.

Incidentally, the problem crops up again in Hobbes in his chapter 'Of Persons, Authors, and Things Personated' (*Leviathan*, Part 1, Chapter XVI). This is equally central to his account of the state since the sovereign is essentially the author of the subject's actions. And Hobbes really does seem to want to take the responsibility for the action away from the subject and give it to the sovereign. The *only* responsibility to the subject is to obey; nothing else. But is this possible? Hobbes himself seems to doubt it, for he speaks of 'feigning' in this connection: i.e. the idea that the one 'personated' is the true author of the action is, in his view, a sort of 'fiction'.

Let us look at the main root of our problem again. When someone is said to act in compliance with somebody else's authority, two 'wills' seem to be involved: that of the one who exercises authority and that of the one over whom it is exercised. The question is how the action of the latter can be thought of as genuinely *his* action if the former is its ultimate 'author'. I believe, incidentally, that this is the problem at the root of Rousseau's insistence that 'sovereignty is indivisible'. Sovereignty, for him, is essentially will: 'the general will'. And the notion of will precisely concerns the ultimate authorship of action: the ultimate bearer of responsibility for action. It is for the sake of being able to determine this that Hobbes, indeed, raises the question of how command is to be distinguished from counsel. In a state, many contribute to the formation of policy; the question in which both Hobbes and Rousseau are interested and which seems to them paramount, is: who is ultimately responsible for its adoption? This question seems to need an answer if we are to determine what it is that *makes* a given policy *state policy*.

In plenty of cases the difficulty of seeing how the acceptance of somebody else's authority over one is reconcilable with one's own agency can apparently be resolved fairly easily by distinguishing a long-term and a short-term perspective on this situation. Suppose, for instance, that half a dozen of us go rock-climbing. On such an expedition there are many occasions when decisions have to be made affecting the actions of the whole party and they are decisions which can be made only if one member of the party has the authority to make them on behalf of everyone. In that case we may all agree – consent – to confer this authority on one of our number. That is to say each of us has exercised his or her will in giving that person a special status, a status of authority. If he or she subsequently tells me to do something that lies within the limits of the authority that has been conferred (and it is an important point that it is implicit in the situation that there will be such limits), then, in doing so, I just carry out the commitment to which I previously consented, or which as we might say, I previously willed. My earlier expression of my will extends over my present action.

This way of looking at things helps to make clear what the division of responsibility is for what happens. If I voted for X as leader, I am responsible for that. If I didn't but accepted the majority decision I am responsible for having done that. If serious grounds have since developed for doubting X's competence or good will, I am responsible for not having spoken up or even rescinded my earlier consent to his authority. On the other hand he is responsible for the particular decisions that are made, etc.

There are of course countless kinds of human situation which can be understood according to such a model. Sometimes these involve quite short-term arrangements (as in my example); sometimes the arrangements are very long-standing and the conferment of authority more or less permanent. It is very tempting to try to construe the authority of the state along these general lines; and many people have of course done so. Locke is one of the most important of these.

In my very simple example the authority of the expedition's leader sprang from a definite act performed by the members of the party on some earlier occasion. And I supposed that all the members of the party participated: so that *each one's* subjection to the leader's authority derived from a definite act of his will. This is required by the form of the problem we set ourselves to which this example was to help provide the answer. For the problem has to do with the relation between the will of each individual citizen and the 'will' of the state.

Lecture 3[6]

I said at the end of last week's lecture that we were going to consider whether the model of a voluntary association in which each man conferred on someone or on some body of people the authority to make decisions on his behalf could serve as a model for the authority of the state over its citizens. Now Locke of course does start his account of the 'original' or source of the state's authority by supposing such a collective act of submission to have taken place: 'collective', that is, in the sense that each person over whom the states authority extends is to be thought of as having voluntarily submitted. As I emphasised last time, this has to be an essential ingredient of this account. (Recall that Hobbes says that those who do not participate in the conferment of sovereignty remain in a state of nature vis-a-vis the rest and vis-a-vis the sovereign too.)

---

6. Eds: Subtitle: 'Criticism of II' is missing in the printout.

I do not want here to get entangled in a lot of questions about how far what Locke said is to be understood historically or about how much that matters. There are, however, certain questions relating to this that are important for my purposes. One such question, which Locke himself takes very seriously, is the fact that we are dealing with a structure that persists over many generations of human beings. What we are interested in is the relation we, the present generation, have to the state; if the answer is in terms of something done by our forefathers, long before we were born, the question has to be raised what relevance that has for us. It is important to remember that the problem that concerns us is about the relation between our, the present subjects', will and that of those who exercise political authority over us. We seem to be merely complicating matters if we now bring in the will of someone else entirely who did something long ago before any of us even existed.

This consideration is, incidentally, especially weighty for Locke. Prior to developing his own positive account of the state's authority he had attacked a rival idea which, in support of the thesis that kings had a 'divine right' to rule, attempted to derive that right from the patriarchal right of a father to rule over his children. The right of kings was traced from a supposed right of Adam, the father of the human race, to rule over his children. Such a theory had been put forward by Sir Robert Filmer, whom Locke attacked in his *First Treatise on Civil Government*. Certain elements of the attack are reiterated in the *Second Treatise*. Part of Locke's attack was precisely that, whatever may have been the relation between Adam and his children; and whatever may have been the relation of contemporary kings to Adam, the rights of the latter could not be derived from the rights of the former. So, it was clearly not open to Locke in the context of his account to make a similar derivation of the authority of contemporary states over their subjects from an authority which involved quite different people long ago.

That point is only of limited historical interest. But there is a more substantial philosophical point involved which I would like to discuss very briefly. In conceding that a contract made by our forefathers cannot explain how *we* can be bound, Locke seems to argue that one man cannot at all be bound by the act of another. And it is relevant for us to ask whether this is in fact so and if it is, in what sense.

This is a complicated question and for the sake of brevity I will only consider it in political contexts and only in broad outline. Now it seems quite clear that we (at least many of us) *do* think of ourselves as bound by decisions made by earlier generations. Take the constitution of the United States of America. That represented a compromise between many conflicting interests at the time of the Declaration of Independence. Certain safeguards were written into the constitution in order to allay the fears of some (certain of the states, for instance) who were afraid of having their interests trampled on. In that respect the constitution can be regarded as a sort of promise, to those who feared for their interests from those who might find themselves in a position to damage those interests, that they would not do so without formal consultation on a revision of the original undertakings. (I mean the provisions for constitutional amendment.) Those who laid down the original constitution are of course long dead; but certainly most Americans would regard themselves as bound by those original promises, unless these had subsequently been rescinded or modified in the agreed way. So, it does not seem to be true, certainly not *obviously* true, that a later generation cannot be bound by the undertakings of an earlier generation.

However, I don't think that this, as it stands, can properly be treated as a counterexample to Locke's thesis. He is speaking of people in a state of nature, i.e. in a state which is supposed to be prior to, or at least innocent of, any commitment to a political bond. Whereas, I think he would say, those who have reached the stage of seriously debating a political constitution, with detailed provisions, must have *already* consented to be bound together in one 'body politic' in the way it is his purpose to explain. In other words, if I am, say, a citizen of the United States, then I am bound by the promises enshrined in the constitution of the United States. Locke's question is, however, what is it that can make such a 'citizen' in the first place.

His idea of someone in a state of nature *is* precisely the idea of someone who is sovereign over his own actions, who is himself finally responsible for what he does: someone who is a quite untrammelled agent, from whose command over himself nothing has so far been subtracted. His question then is: what is it that *can* 'subtract' anything from this? And his answer is: nothing external can do this; it can only be voluntarily conceded by the agent himself. Of course, someone's status as an agent can be impaired or destroyed by external circumstances. But we are not talking about that. We are talking about someone who remains fully an agent, but whose responsibility for his own actions nevertheless rests, at least in part, with someone else. And that *sounds* like a contradiction.

For this reason then Locke needs to be able to point to something in each contemporary citizen's situation which can reasonably be thought of as expressing a conceding to the state of a certain authority over his own will. We are dealing with fully rational adults here, because Locke recognises only these as unqualified agents.

Of course there could be something like a formal and expressed conceding of authority to the state on the part of every citizen on reaching his majority. But the account cannot be made to depend on that since, for the most part, there is no such institution and we should be left without any account of the authority exercised in states where it is lacking.

For this reason Locke has to introduce a notion of 'tacit consent', i.e. the idea that there may be something about the citizen's relation to the state which signifies his voluntary concession to it of authority without the necessity for any explicit statement to this effect. This essential part of Locke's account has attracted a great deal of criticism. As will become clear, I believe that *some* of this criticism is well founded. But if we are not careful about exactly what is and what is not a valid criticism here, we shall miss points of great importance.

People sometimes write and talk as though the whole notion of tacit consent were a confusion, as though there could only be genuine consent where there is an explicit expression of what is being consented to. (Plamenatz sometimes reads as though he would like to say this, though perhaps he does not actually go quite so far – ???[7]) The motive behind this is probably admirable: i.e. not to give those who claim authority too

---

7. Eds: John Plamenatz, *Consent, Freedom and Political Obligation* (Oxford: Oxford University Press, 1968).

much room for potentially dishonest manoeuvre. But pretty plainly it is not a position that can be sustained. Human relationships abound in situations in which people's habitual behaviour shows clearly that they are consenting to actions on the part of others which would otherwise be inadmissible. It is hard to see how life would be possible, or at least tolerable, if this were not so. Consider, for example, what the consequences would be for relations between friends, lovers. Of course, this so far does not show that there is anything comparable in the relations between citizen and state.

It is in general important for our concept of consent that we do have conventional forms in which it is explicitly expressed. Furthermore, particular forms of expression, when very firmly rooted in the life of a community, can take on a deep significance (a 'symbolic' significance, if you like; I'm thinking here of Simone Weil's marvellous analogy of the significance of a wedding ring may have in a woman's conception of her marriage). But the observance of such forms is not *sufficient* to show that consent has truly been given, because there are countless possibilities of corruption and coercion (different forms of bribery and blackmail, for instance), some obvious, others very much less so which we should think of as nullifying consent at least in any morally significant sense. What these possibilities are will depend on the nature of the context within which we are deploying the notion of consent: they will for instance, be different in a political context from what they will be in an intimate personal relationship. Again, the observance of such forms will not always be *necessary* to the giving of consent. (Here, Simone Weil's remarks about the contrast between the legitimacy of Churchill's wartime government and that of Daladier's at the outset of the war are worth reflecting on.)[8]

Lecture 4[9]

I made some remarks at the end of last week's lecture about the complexity of the relation between consent and its conventional forms of expression. It is pretty obvious in the light of these considerations that the question whether consent can or cannot be thought of as having been truly given in any political context is likely to be an extremely complex and controversial one. It is highly unlikely that any useful, short, generally applicable criterion could be given. *One* important criticism that Locke's account is certainly vulnerable to stems from the fact that it *does* attempt to formulate such a criterion. He is forced in the end to say that the mere presence of someone, almost, within the confines of the territory over which a state exercises power is sufficient to signify his consent to its authority to do so. It is fairly evident that this is going to make the notion of consent quite useless for what should have been its main purpose: namely to distinguish those cases where the state's exercise of power is legitimate from those in which it is not.

---

8. Eds: See 'Intercollegiate lectures', above, Chapter 1.2, and Simone Weil, 'The Legitimacy of the Provisional Government', trans. Peter Winch, *Philosophical Investigations* 10, no. 2 (1987): 87–98.
9. Eds: Subtitle in the outline ('Hume: "They consent because they perceive him to be by birth their lawful sovereign." Simone Weil.') is missing in the printout.

This criticism is connected with another one, consideration of which will perhaps take us deeper. Recall the context of argument in which I introduced the notion of consent and the problem it was supposed to help with. We were faced with the difficulty about how a person's *will* could be understood as subservient to that of another in the way apparently implied by saying that he accepts the other as having (legitimate) authority over him. The solution to the problem was supposed to lie in the idea that this authority itself derived from an act of will on the part of the one over whom it was exercised, so that, accepting the authority of the other, he was really, contrary to appearances, following only *his own will*. But obviously this will only work if the giving of consent can itself be seen as a genuinely voluntary act. And the trouble with Locke's lax criterion of tacit consent is that it provides no guarantee of this, nor even any likelihood of it. Most people can't help being within the territory of a given state; even less can they help being within the territory of *some* state. As Hume graphically puts it in his important essay, 'Of the Original Contract':

> Should it be said that, by living under the dominion of a prince which one might leave, every individual has given a *tacit* consent to his authority and promised him obedience, it may be answered that such an implied consent can only have place where a man imagines that the matter depends on his choice. But where he thinks – as all mankind do who are born under established governments – that by his birth he owes allegiance to a certain prince or certain form of government, it would be absurd to infer a consent or choice which he expressly in this case renounces and disclaims.
>
> Can we seriously say that a poor peasant or artisan has a free choice to leave his country when he knows no foreign language or manners and lives from day to day by the small wages which he acquires? We may as well assert that a man, by remaining in a vessel, freely consents to the dominion of the master, though he was carried on board while asleep and must leap into the ocean and perish the moment he leaves her.[10]

Hume is making *three* points here, two negative, one positive. First, he is making the point I had made: that it is unreal to say that mere presence in a state's territory signifies consent to the state's authority. But second, he is making the wider negative point that in any case a person who lives under a government does not suppose that his allegiance to that government depends on his own choice. That of course cuts the ground from under the question that had led to the search for a criterion of tacit consent in the first place. Third, he is making a positive suggestion: that, characteristically at any rate, such a man thinks 'that *by his birth* he owes allegiance to a certain prince or certain form of government...' That seems to mean that Hume thinks it misguided to argue in the way I have in introducing these problems: that a man or woman cannot be said to owe allegiance to anyone else unless by his own choice. Unless, of course, he were to claim that people's thoughts about this are confused and that, although they think that they owe allegiance by birth, this cannot in reality be the case. But Hume does not in fact argue thus.

---

10. David Hume, 'Of the Original Contract', in *Political Essays*, ed. Charles W. Handel (Bobbs Merrill, The Library of Liberal Arts, 1953), 43–63 (51).

He does, a little bit later in the essay, say something that contains an interesting suggestion which I find I am unfortunately not going to have time to take up, but which I will mention. He suggests that a people who acclaim the return of the prince they regard as legitimate after the ousting of a usurper, though they

> willingly acquiesce in his authority, they never imagined that their consent made him sovereign. They consent because they apprehend him to be already by birth their lawful sovereign.[11]

What I find interesting in that (though it is only one sentence on which perhaps I should not rest too much weight) is that though Hume is denying that these people regard their ruler's authority as *deriving* from their consent, he still gives the notion of consent a place in his description of this situation. There is a very complicated tangle of issues underlying this point; I will have to content myself with a very general comment. What Hume is (as it seems to me, rightly) rejecting is the idea that the authority of the state *derives from*, has its *source* in, the consent of the governed, in the way in which your right to use my car has its source in my consent for you to do so. This does however leave open the possibility that there is room for the exercise and withholding of consent within the limits set by the concept of the state's authority. In a similar way, my consent for you to use my car is exercised within the limits set by concepts such as that of property. And similarly if you, wanting to use my car, decide to ask for my consent or, alternatively decide to take it anyway, that is a decision only intelligible within a context in which the concept of property applies. What counts as the giving and withholding of consent; when it is regarded as necessary to seek someone's consent; when that obligation may be thought to be overridden by another consideration (war, emergency, 'national interest'); [these] are all questions the sense of which is in part determined by the fact that it is someone's *property* that is in question (and, of course what sort of property it is). *Mutatis mutandis* we can say something similar of the concept of the state. The question whether a given state is legitimate or not may indeed depend on the consent of the citizens of that state. But that does not mean that the very authority of 'the state' depends on anyone's consent. Indeed, apart from the concept of the state's authority, we should hardly know what the word 'consent' amounted to here.

All of this is closely connected with the point Durkheim was making in an aphorism: 'not everything about a contract is contractual.'[12]

I must leave this matter in that rather unsatisfactory state in order to say a little about Hume's reasons for rejecting the line of argument which had led to the derivation of authority from consent in the first place. These are to be found in his presentation of what he calls a 'more regular, at least a more philosophical, refutation of this principle of original contract or popular consent'.[13]

---

11. Ibid., 53.
12. Eds: Émile Durkheim, *The Division of Labour*, trans. George Simpson (Glencoe Illinois: Free Press, 1933), 211. (This translation differs from Winch's.)
13. Hume, 'Of the Original Contract', 54.

The argument is roughly this. The problem was: how can a person's will be bound by the will of another. The answer was: that person's having bound his or her *own* will by some past undertaking. But, Hume argues, if there is a difficulty here there must be *exactly the same form of difficulty* concerning how a man's *present* will can be bound by his own *past* will.

> The obligation to allegiance being of like force and authority with the obligation to fidelity, we gain nothing by resolving the one into the other. The general interests or necessities of society are sufficient to establish both.[14]

The cogency of this reasoning plainly depends on the assumption that there is no relevant difference between my present relation to a past expression of will of my own and my present relation to the expression of will of *another person*. No doubt Hume is the more prone to make this assumption because of his peculiar views about personal identity, as developed in the *Treatise of Human Nature*. Since he thinks (at least part of the time) that personal identity is a fiction and that all we have is a succession of separate and disparate psychological states, it is open to him to suppose that the relation between a past and a present psychological state (i.e. to 'willings') of 'myself' has no special status which differentiates it from the relation between the psychological state of 'someone else' and one of my own.

It may well be that we cannot accept Hume's presuppositions about personal identity. Indeed, one good reason for not accepting them may be precisely that we want to maintain that there is a difference between my relation to my own past acts and my relation to those of someone else. But then Hume's arguments will at least have pointed to an important connection, which we might otherwise overlook, between this question about the roots of political allegiance and questions about the nature of personal identity.

And there I must unfortunately leave things, just as they are getting interesting!

---

14. Ibid., 56.

1.5

LECTURES ON LOCKE ON PROPERTY [N.D.][1]

Lecture 17

We were discussing Locke's views on 'natural rights'. – The force of calling them 'natural' etc. and some comments on liberty and equality.

Property

– Independent of other two; not usually made a 'natural' right.
– One of the most distinctive features of Locke's theory: N.B. Locke himself considers a special justification necessary.
– Section 25: 'I shall endeavour to show how men might come to have a property in several parts of that which God gave to mankind in common and that without any express compact of all the commoners.'[2]

Connected with 1688 revolution. – Whig land-owning aristocracy the most important political class: protection of their economic interests.
   But it is paradoxical that the form of argument which Locke used to justify this protection was later taken over by Marx precisely to *attack* the interests of seated property.

– Locke's theory that property is 'based' in labour, became the 'labour theory of value', reading Marx via Ricardo (?).
– The theory that all of the value a thing held derived from the labour it embodied and that therefore anyone who derives benefit from an object without having expended labour was 'exploiting'/'robbing' the worker of his rightful due.

What sort of an undertaking is a 'justification of property'?
   Suppose you see me in possession of a motorcar which you thought to be the property of the Principal: you might require me to 'justify' my possession of it. I might do so by

---

1. Eds: Handwritten; lecture notes; 18 pp., Peter Winch Archives (GB 0100 KCLCA K/PP171, Folder 'Politics VI', Box 21), King's College London. These are handwritten pages torn from a bound notebook in which the pages were numbered 76–133, and the lectures were numbered 15 to 21. The following excerpt is Lectures 17 and 18, pp. 89–107.
2. Handwritten marginal note: (N.B.: an alternative definition of Locke's natural right might almost be: 'a claim rightfully maintainable against others without their *consent* being necessary in any form'!).

telling you that the Principal had given it to me. This, if true, would be a perfectly good justification. But what sort of justification is it? It is not a 'justification of property' (in general), but a justification of my possession of a particular object by pointing out the fact that it *is* my property, and this is done by referring to certain procedures, which we use as criteria for deciding what is my property and what isn't.

It is very important to notice what an extremely complex notion 'property' is, – complex in many different directions. E.g.:

A. In respect of objects – land, moveable goods, money, *'choses* in action'[3]
   Does my ownership of shares in an industrial undertaking come to the same thing as my ownership of a fountain pen?
B. In respect of (within a given property system)
   – leasehold, trusteeship, freehold
   – all forms of 'property', yet all carrying importantly different rights.
C. In respect of different social systems – e.g. U.K. and U.S.S.R. and [illegible].

A thorough examination of the notion of property would reveal an almost incredible complexity both in these and in many other directions.

This terrific complexity/generality raises a number of difficulties regarding any philosophical theory like Locke's:

The fact that the notion of property is absolutely fundamental to our whole way of living and thinking makes it a matter of extreme difficulty to 'step outside' the notion, as it were, and criticise it impersonally. It's relatively easy to criticise particular ways in which the institution is operated in particular contexts: e.g. to say that it would be better if a *bona fide* finder were to become *ipso facto* owner of the object found rather than to retain the present role of 'stealing by finding', but this is criticism *within* the very wide boundaries set by the general notion of property.

The distinction between this and the criticism of property as such has often been overlooked. I.e. philosophers have often made sweeping generalisations about 'property', as if they were attacking/justifying the whole idea, when they have really been doing nothing of the sort. E.g.:

[α] Proudhon said that 'property is theft': this is nonsense if interpreted in the general way intended, as the idea of 'property' is presupposed by the idea of 'theft'. It only makes sense if interpreted as an attack on the existing arrangements for administering property rights in terms of some other 'ideal' arrangement. But the *idea* of property is presupposed by such a criticism.

Similarly when Marx, influenced by the labour theory of value, says that the capitalist robs the worker of his rightful due, he is saying that existing property relations are bad

---

3. Eds: Legal term for objects not in possession but for which the person has rights of possession (e.g. a debt); more broadly, rights of possession in incorporeal things.

as contrasted with some ideal – not that property in itself is something immoral. Here, it is difficult to conceive what the latter could mean.

[β] See Locke's argument:

> And will anyone say [he had no right to those acorns or apples he thus appropriated, because he had not the consent of all mankind to make them his? Was it a robbery thus to assume to himself what belonged to all in common? If such a consent as that was necessary, man had starved, notwithstanding the plenty God had] given him. (Section 28, p. 25)

This is a characteristically sophistical argument in 'justification' of property. It purports to show that *without* 'property' it would be impossible to maintain life.

1. But all it really shows is that there must be *some* means by which people can obtain their subsistence. Private property is not the only possible means: why shouldn't people be permitted to draw from a common pool without what they draw being regarded as their private property? (PTO)[4]
2. Even if it did prove that property of *some* sort is a practical necessity, it doesn't follow what sort: it isn't very informative.

To talk about 'Property' in the abstract like this, unless it is made clear precisely what *kind* of rights it carries with it, and their extent. Cf. Hume:

> Tho' the establishment [of the rule, concerning the stability of possession, be not only useful, but even absolutely necessary to human society, it can never serve to any purpose, while it remains in such general terms. Some method must be shewn, by which we may distinguish what particular goods are to be assign'd to each particular person, while the rest of mankind are excluded from their possession] and enjoyment.[5]

Hume also uses this as an argument against regarding property as a 'natural' right at all.

> Those rules, by which properties, rights, and obligations are determined, have in them no marks of a natural origin, but many of artifice and contrivance. They are too numerous to have proceeded from nature; they are changeable by human laws. And have all of them a direct and evident tendency to public good, and the support of civil society.[6]

---

4. Handwritten note on the reverse: Also, notice that Locke makes use of the notion of property in the *premises* of his argument – 'was it a robbery thus to assume to himself what *belonged* to all in common'. This is to beg the whole question regarding whether it makes sense to talk of anything like 'belonging to' anyone in a 'state of nature': i.e. where there are no agreed conventions governing the way people are supposed to behave.
5. *Treatise [of Human Nature]*, Book III, Part II, Section III, p. 501.
6. Hume, *Treatise*, [Book] III, [Part] II, [Section] VI. 528.

(N.B. All of Hume's remarks on Justice and Property in the *Treatise* [Book] III, [Part] II are worthy of study.)

Question – when can we say that a change in the particular rules by which property is administered becomes so great that the whole meaning of the idea of 'property' becomes altered?

There are several different points to consider here.

1. The idea of 'public property' – what does it mean to say that the railways are 'my property'?
2. On the continent, only *material things* (not *'choses'* in action') can constitute property. Cf. K-F's introduction to Rousseau.[7] I hope to say more of this later.

[γ] Locke's justification is based on examples drawn from a very limited field, namely, the acquisition of land in a state of society where there is much ownerless land and plenty for everyone. (He has the newly discovered [sic] continent of North America in mind as a model.)

His arguments do have a certain amount of solidity in such a state – though no necessity attaches to any one set of arrangement at the expense of any other.

But he does not seem to realise that in a country like England, where conditions are radically different, the whole argument breaks down. He seems to think that only a modification of *details* is required. Cf. Section 35 [of Locke's *Second Treatise*].

Even if we confine ourselves to land tenure, the Enclosure Movement, which was already a problem in Locke's time, introduces considerations far transcending Locke's simpleminded arguments. I.e. it is not true that (Section 35) 'condition of human life, which requires labour and materials to work on, necessarily introduces private possessions'.

Cf. Tawney: Religion and the rise of capitalism[8]

And when we explicitly introduce considerations relevant to a *money* economy, the whole situation is transformed.

Lecture 18

Detailed Consideration of Locke's Theory of Property
See [*Second*] *Treatise* [Book] II, Chapter V; *The Philosophical Review*, October 1952 – article by Leo Strauss.[9]
Property in the state of nature.
Governed by law of nature

---

7. Eds: We are not sure what book Winch is referring to here.
8. Eds: R. H. Tawney, *Religion and the Rise of Capitalism* (New York: Harcourt, Brace and Company, 1926).
9. Eds: Leo Strauss, 'On Locke's Doctrine of Natural Right', *The Philosophical Review* 61, no. 4 (1952): 475–502.

– (combination of utilitarian system and Christian ethics. But mainly the former, etc. Strauss.)

We start with a state in which there is *no property at all*.

– Locke puts this by saying that 'God has given the earth to all men *in common*', which is rather different. – *Common* ownership is not the same thing as the *absence* of ownership. But he does make a distinction between common ownership in a state of nature and common ownership based on compact/the law of the land.[10]

How can *private* property arise in such a state in the absence of artificial *conventions*?
Only because there is already a 'natural' prototype of private property in existence even here, viz. every man's 'property in his own person', which carries with it the idea that what a man *does* with his own person is also his private property.

'Therefore', material things which become impregnated ('mixed') into this private property become equally private property.

> Though the earth [, and all inferior creatures be common to all men yet every man has a property in his own person. This no body has any right to but himself. The labour of his body and the work of his hands, we may say, are properly his. Whatsoever then he removes out of the state that nature hath provided, and left it in, he hath mixed his labour with, and joyned to it something that is his own, and thereby]....makes it his property. (Section 27, p. 24)

There is a serious equivocation here which is fully responsible for such a plausibility as the argument has.
The sense in which one's body/labour 'belongs' to one is different from that in which external things 'belong' to one.
What exactly it does [it] mean to say that my body is 'mine' is not easy to explain. [Cf. Marcel in Vol. I of his Gifford Lectures on 'The Mystery of Being'.[11]]
But it is certain that it does not express the *same* ideas as those expressed by the quasi-*legal* notion of property, namely, the right to enjoy the benefits of what one owns. Of course, one might plausibly hold this *in addition*, but to say of a certain piece of labour that it is 'x's' is simply a way of *describing who did it*.
One might say: the *logic* of the words 'labour' (and 'human body') *requires* that they should be 'owned' by someone. – It doesn't make sense to talk of labour (in the appropriate sense) which is no-one's/done by no-one. Similarly with 'body' (at least, 'living body').
This is not true of the 'external *things*' in which Locke is ultimately interested. To say that *they* belong to someone is to say both more and less than to say that a piece of work/body 'belongs to someone'.

---

10. Eds: Locke, *Second Treatise*, Section 35.
11. Eds: Gabriel Marcel, *The Mystery of Being, Vol. 1, Reflection and Mystery* (London: The Harvill Press, 1951).

'*More*' – in that it ascribes certain *rights*.
'*Less*' – in that there is not the same 'internal' connection.

This central argument is supported by subsidiaries:

1. There is a difference between something which belongs to someone and something which doesn't. What makes this difference? Where to draw the line?

   > He that is nourished... [by the acorns he pickt up under an oak or the apples he gathered from the trees in the wood has certainly appropriated them to himself. No body can deny but the nourishment is his. I ask then, When did they begin to be his? When he digested? Or when he ate? Or when he boiled? Or when he brought them home? Or when he pickt them up? And 'tis plain, if the first gathering made them not his, nothing else could. That labour put a distinction between them and common. That added something to them more than nature, the common mother of all, had done; and so they became his] private right. (Section 28)

This assumes that there must be some one *criterion* by which to decide. But as Hume points out, it is the very '*artificiality*' of the notion of property (having as its corollary the necessity for firm lines of demarcation), which raises this problem in the first place, and it's a mistake to expect a clear line of argument from the vague and shifting distinctions involved in 'natural' distinctions to these. I.e. it's a mistake to think that the 'artificial' notion of property can coincide tidily with the shifting lines of demarcation (arising from the 'imagination') characterising distinctions of 'natural' kinds, etc.

2. The argument that utility (in the shape of survival) makes appropriation essential and urgent, and this cannot wait upon the uncertain issue of negotiation, which must precede the making of any *convention* governing this issue.

   > If such a consent as that was necessary, man had starved, notwithstanding the plenty God had given him. (Section 28)

But this again proves only that the means of subsistence must not be hindered by any sort of behaviour: it does not prove that the means of subsistence must be made private by any *one* form of behaviour rather than any other.

3. The derivation of *property* from labour is supported by the argument that all *value* is derived from labour.

   > Nor is it so strange.... [as perhaps before consideration it may appear, that the property of labour should be able to over-balance the community of land For 'tis labour indeed that puts the difference of value on every thing; and let any one consider, what the difference is between an acre of land planted with tobacco, or sugar, sown with wheat or barley; and an acre of the same land lying in common, without any husbandry upon it, and he will find, that the improvement of labour makes the far greater part] of the value. (Section 40)

This is the form of the theory developed by Marx. It is connected with the justification/ attack on property by the argument:

[α] What makes value is labour.
[β] Therefore, he who expends the labour *ought* to have the benefit.

The labour theory of value is, of course, false. Locke himself unwittingly admits this when he says (§45) that the use of money and increase of population 'has made land scarce and so of some value.'

The only limitation on the right of acquiring property set by the law of nature is that a man should not take more than he can use without allowing it to spoil. (PTO)[12]

This limitation is in effect nullified by the use of durable, *conventional* standards of value – i.e. *money*, which can be accumulated by anyone to any extent at all, since it cannot spoil.

N.B. when Locke starts talking about money, he has left the bounds of the state of nature, since the use of money implies the acceptance of artificial conventions, and this in turn implies a state of civil society, since the regulation of behaviour by means of *'conventional'* as opposed to *'natural'* standards is the distinguishing mark of civil society.

The status of property *within* civil society raises a number of fundamental difficulties and Locke's theory, which must now be considered.

1. How can Locke justify the rather mechanical (and seemingly sophistical) erosion of the 'law of nature' forbidding excessive accumulation, by means of the adoption of an artificial convention describing value to something non-perishable?

The force of this difficulty is brought out if we emphasise the utilitarian element in his conception of the law of nature.

(Strauss argues that the *whole* of Locke's conception of the law of nature is utilitarian, but this is probably going too far. Certainly we can argue that Locke *ought* to have held a purely utilitarian conception in view of his theories about the necessary connection between definability of moral notions in terms of the production of pleasure and pain. But Locke is not always consistent, and he doesn't in fact stick firmly to this.)

Nevertheless, the utilitarian element in his argument is pronounced enough to raise a serious difficulty. – Cf.:

> Nor was this appropriation of any parcel of land, by improving it, any prejudice to any other man, since there was still enough and as good left, and more than the yet unprovided could use. (Section 33)

The difficulty is that in civil society the utilitarian justification for this as the sole limitation vanishes, since, as Locke himself insists, things there become scarce, so that

---

12. Handwritten note on the reverse: Section 31 'As much as anyone can make use of to any advantage of life before it spoils, so much he may by his labour fix a property in.'

if I appropriate a great deal this *will* have the effect of depriving other people of what they need. (PTO)[13]

2. This is perhaps only an aspect of an even more fundamental difficulty, viz. that the argument that there is a 'natural right' to property *outside* civil society does not *ipso facto* provide a justification that the property rights of private citizens *inside* civil society are sacrosanct as far as the government and legislature are concerned, since the right to property within society is fundamentally different, being based on *consent* and the particular regulations agreed upon by the legislature. Cf.:

> ...the son cannot ordinarily enjoy the possessions of his father, *but under the same terms his father did, by becoming a member of society*;[14] whereby he puts himself presently under the government he finds there established, as much as any other subject of that Commonwealth. (Section 117)

This means that there must be some further argument to justify the sacredness of private property within society.

Strauss claims to detect this further argument, still based on the 'fact' that it is only *labour* which makes anything *worth* having (gives it *value*).

---

13. Eds: There is no text on the reverse of this MS page.
14. Eds: Winch's emphasis.

1.6

AUTHORITY [FREEDOM AND SERVILITY] [N.D.][1]

1. Philosophical interest in concept of authority to be distinguished from other kinds of interest (political, psychological, sociological, etc.)
   Philosophy is interested in the question: What makes authority possible? Or: How is authority possible (if at all)?
2. This question arises because, although we are very familiar with the exercise of, and recognition of, authority, we run into difficulties when we try to give an account of it which will be compatible with the accounts we want to give of certain other concepts: especially practical rationality, autonomous human action (and also justice).
3. Practical rationality and autonomy as deciding on one's own course of action in the light of one's own values and wants and by reference to one's own estimate of the relevant features of one's environment.

   'One's environment' includes the existence and dispositions of other human beings. These may often be seen as instruments for, or obstacles to, the realisation of one's wants and values; in this connection, other men's *power* vis-a-vis oneself is important. The exercise of such power can be thought of as imposing restrictions on (or as increasing the range of) what one can achieve by one's own actions, but as still leaving one the power to decide what those actions shall be. I.e. it can be seen as part of the environment in which such decisions are made. It may sometimes be that the space left for such decision is minimal, but this can be seen as the effects of *force majeure* which, though an affliction, does not touch the agent's essential dignity as a rational human agent.
4. However, to acknowledge that another man has authority over oneself and to cede to him the right to decide how one shall act seems to involve a more fundamental threat to rational autonomy. The following analogy suggests itself as marking the contrast with the previous case: It's the difference between a man driving a car who finds himself so hemmed in by traffic that he can hardly move and the man who leaves the driving seat and hands over to someone else. Only in the case we are interested in of course the 'car' is himself. This picture is encouraged by accounts of authority (like

---

1. Eds: Typescript; 6 pp, Peter Winch Archives (GB 0100 KCLCA K/PP171, Folder 'Politics VII', Box 21), King's College London. Other materials in this folder belong to the early to mid-1970s.

Hobbes's and Peters's)[2] which emphasise the notion of 'authorship' of actions – when I act under someone else's authority I am not the author of my own actions.

5. Looked at in this light, submission to authority (in so far as it is thought of as involving more than bowing to *force majeure*) seems to involve difficulties of both a moral and a metaphysical kind. A further complicating factor is that the moral and the metaphysical difficulties are hard to distinguish from each other. (Their running together is very evident, e.g. in Rousseau's writings.) Anarchists often exploit this merging of morals and metaphysics: they tend to argue that as long as a man remains a man he *cannot* escape responsibility for his actions (i.e. it makes no sense to speak thus); and that *therefore* it is morally reprehensible for anyone to try to do this by submitting to authority. But such an argument is puzzling. If it makes no sense to speak of a man as 'doing x', then it's not clear that it makes sense to speak of him as 'trying to do x' either. (If someone says he is trying to square the circle, we do not say that he won't be able to manage it; we say he is confused and has no clear idea *what* he is up to.) Of course, it is open to the anarchist to say that this confusion is itself a sign of moral turpitude, but I think as a matter of fact that his argument does rely on a thought which is itself confused: that the state of submitting to someone else's authority is both impossible and morally reprehensible; for the force of the condemnation of someone who *tries* to do this derives from the supposed viciousness of what he is trying to achieve. But if we cannot coherently describe what he is trying to achieve, how can we recognise it as something vicious? (Sartre's conception of 'bad faith' runs into closely parallel difficulties.)

6. The moral condemnation of submission to authority is in terms of *servility* and is closely connected with Kant's third formulation of the categorical imperative in terms of treating men never merely as means but also as ends in themselves. Here the accusation is that one is turning *oneself* into a mere instrument and thereby affronting one's essential human dignity. (N.B. that it's not merely a question of making one's *body* an instrument of another's purposes; but one's 'self': and certainly it's hard to see how this can be a coherent notion.)

   Alternatively, and perhaps more promisingly, it may be argued that since a man cannot intelligibly deny his responsibility for his own acts as long as he retains his rational and volitional faculties, and since submission to authority seems to involve such a denial of responsibility, it can only be a pretence made in bad faith.

   The charges of servility and of bad faith are distinct in themselves, but they may run together.

7. The following features of the foregoing arguments are worth noting, because they are characteristic of a large class of philosophical arguments. The features are mutually dependent.

   (a) Their starting point is not an examination of situations in which we actually do use the notion of authority, but a highly general and *a priori* 'analysis' of the notion

---

2. Eds: R. S. Peters. 'Symposium: Authority', *Proceedings of the Aristotelian Society* Supplementary Volume 32 (1958): 207–224. Winch was a Symposiast responding to Peters.

in terms of very large concepts (like 'will' and 'reason' and 'responsibility'). These concepts used in the *analysans* are again taken for granted and not examined in their concrete applications.

(b) The outcome of the arguments is to represent as impossible something that we all know to be perfectly possible. (Compare the denial that material objects can exist unperceived, that we can know the thoughts and feelings of others.) We in practice have no difficulty in principle in distinguishing situations in which someone is acting under someone else's authority from situations where he is not; and we can again distinguish such situations from those in which someone is merely subject to someone's power. It is true that we may sometimes find it difficult [to know/decide] what to say of a particular case; but there could be no such difficulty as this if we were *never* in a position to make such distinctions.

(c) Again, the effect of the arguments is to obliterate a large number of important distinctions. Take servility. Certainly there *are* servile attitudes to authority; but in order to be clear what these are, we have got to be able to distinguish them from attitudes to authority which are not. *Sometimes*, no doubt, the only non-servile posture will be complete resistance to someone's claims to exercise authority; but at other times such a complete resistance would be merely foolish. Important issues like these could not even be discussed if there were a[n] *a priori* identification between servility and submission to authority.

Similar remarks would apply to charges of bad faith in attempting to escape responsibility for one's own actions. Sometimes it is legitimate to claim that one was acting on someone else's authority. (E.g. an *aide de camp* who, on the general's authority, gives an order to retreat.) Sometimes it is not. (E.g. an SS man who appeals to superior orders when accused of murdering Jews.) Such distinctions are of course, again, often extremely difficult to make. But the result of accepting the previous arguments would be to make it appear that there were no such particular issues to discuss.

8. One might diagnose the source of the difficulties we've been considering as the peculiar combination of activity and passivity which recognition of authority seems to involve. On the one hand the exerciser of authority appears as the initiator and the one over whom it is exercised as the passive instrument. But on the other hand, there is an indispensable element of activity in the latter as well.

9. In the first place, as I said earlier, in a relationship of authority the instrument of the superior's will is not simply his inferior's body: it is he himself. The inferior carries out what the superior wills; and he may of course have to exercise considerable intelligence, practical resource and even firmness of will in doing so. His relationship with the exercise of authority is *not* like that of a machine to its operator.[3]

---

3. Eds: See Winch's discussions of someone acting under command ('Particularity and Morals', in *Trying to Make Sense* (Oxford, Basil Blackwell: 1987), 167–181) or as agents of the state (Captain Vere in implementing military justice in Melville's novella *Billy Budd*) in 'The Universalizability of Moral Judgement', *Ethics and Action* (London: Routledge and Kegan Paul, 1972), 151–170.

10. But there is a more fundamental respect in which the inferior is active, which is difficult to express unexceptionably. I will first express it in a way which is *not* unexceptionable. The relation between the superior and inferior in the exercise of authority is one of *reciprocity*: a right to command is presupposed which is recognised by both. The reason why this formulation won't quite do as it stands is that there are of course cases where the inferior does not recognise such a right but where others would still want to say that the superior *is* nevertheless in a position of legitimate authority over the other. I shall return to this sort of case presently. Where the authority is acknowledged by both parties to the relationship, we can say that the inferior acts as he does in response to the superior's command 'because' he acknowledges his authority in the matter.

11. We have to be careful in relying on this point to distinguish the exercise of authority from the exercise of power. For, in the latter case too, it may sometimes be the case that the inferior does what he is told because he recognises the superior's power (as the case of blackmail). What, I think, distinguishes the exercise of authority is that, in this case, the inferior's willingness to be commanded goes beyond the limits set by his recognition of consequences unwelcome to himself likely to follow on his not acquiescing. I do not pretend there is a sharp dividing line here. There will be many instances which are 'mixed' cases and many which we are uncertain about. But this doesn't affect the importance of the distinction.[4]

12. This reciprocity implies a certain 'active' posture in the inferior. The natural way to characterise this posture is to say that it is one of 'consent' and I don't think we can dispense with some such notion as this.[5] It has to be seen with great caution however, partly because of the contractarian tradition of thought which exhibits a tendency to misapply the notion of 'consent' or at least to conceive it too narrowly. Contractarians have tended to take as their paradigm cases in which a superior's authority *derives* from the consent of the inferiors. Of course there are such cases. Consider a group of friends who go on a walking tour with no question of any one of them having any authority over the others. However, they come into dangerous country and judge that they will only come through safely if they act as a united body with one of their number taking the important decisions. They decide among themselves that one of them shall have the authority to take such decisions. We could certainly say, in such a case, that his authority derives from the consent of those over whom it is exercised. He has the authority because they gave it to him. Contrast this with the authority of a patriarch; he possesses the authority by virtue of his patriarchal position, which he has acquired, not by having it conferred on him, but by virtue of his birth and the position he has come to occupy in the clan as a result mainly perhaps of purely 'natural' causes. His position in the clan can be distinguished from one involving merely the exercise of naked power by the

---

4. Handwritten marginal note: Connection with Justice. Simone Weil.
5. Eds: Note the change from the discussion in the third of the 'Four Lectures on Consent' above (Chapter 1.4), where Winch is concerned to maintain the reality of tacit consent, without yet suggesting that the idea is essential to understanding political life.

fact that its members willingly accept his authority – they do his bidding without particular thought to the consequences to themselves of not so doing. In this sense they consent to his authority; but they do not think of that authority as having been conferred on the patriarch by them; he has it by virtue of being the patriarch – and they did not *make* him the patriarch.

13. It may be said in objection that it is only in the context of the clan's institutions that the patriarch occupies the position he does; and that the existence of such institutions implies the general support of them by the clan's members. I think this would be true. But this posture of 'support of the institutions' is very different from the sort of 'consent' spoken of in the context of the example of the friends who chose a leader. The institutions do not come into being because anyone has decided that they shall; members of the clan grow into them and accept them: they accept them, we might say, because they are *there*, because they are the institutions they have grown up with. (I do not mean that this is *their reason* for accepting them: they may have no such reason – they just do accept them; the 'because' belongs to an explanation someone might give of why they accept them, not to any justification of their accepting them. There may be no such justification – and *cannot* be in *all* cases. 'Justifications come to an end' – Wittgenstein.[6] 'They consent, because they perceive him to be by birth their lawful sovereign' – Hume.[7])

We may, if we wish, speak of 'tacit consent' here. But if we do, we must recognise that the addition of the word 'tacit' carries with it a change in the grammar of the word 'consent': as the addition of the word 'unconscious' changes the grammar of the word 'intention' and as the addition of the word 'unperceived' does *not* change the grammar of the word 'table'.

14. Another way of bringing out the active element in the posture of one who acts under the authority of another would be to say that it involves the spontaneity which is a feature of any exercise of a concept. The concept of authority and also (what is important) the concept of a particular relevant kind of authority is applied in the lives of both inferior and superior. Each of them recognises what it makes legitimate and what it doesn't. For this reason I think it is essential to the notion of authority that it is subject to limits – I mean limits to its *legitimate* exercise, for everything, including power, is subject to natural limits. There are things you can and things you cannot do: and these are conceptual, not physical, modalities. Just as, in the context of speaking language there are things you can and things you cannot say; this doesn't mean that there is any force preventing me from talking nonsense. But if I *do* 'say' what I 'can't' say, – well, I haven't said anything. And if I do 'exercise' or 'submit to' authority in ways which the relevant concept of authority doesn't allow, well, whatever I have done, it wasn't exercising or submitting to authority. (Cf. Rousseau on the incoherence in the notion of 'absolutely unlimited authority'.)

---

6. Eds: Ludwig Wittgenstein, *On Certainty*, ed. G. E. M. Anscombe and G. H. von Wright; trans. Denis Paul and G. E. M. Anscombe (Oxford: Basil Blackwell, 1969), §204.
7. Eds: David Hume, 'Of the Original Contract', in *Political Essays*, ed. Charles W. Handel (Bobbs Merrill, The Library of Liberal Arts, 1953), 43–63 (53).

15. I should now like to put together the point made in 13. with an issue touched on in 3. In 3. I traced as one of the premises in the argument which leads to philosophical scepticism about authority the proposition that, speaking metaphorically, a man as it were carries his rational faculty within himself and applies it to his environment in the light of his own desires and ideals. I also remarked that this argument is likely to treat other human beings as simply additional features of the environment, to be treated in general according to the same principles as anything else in the environment. In 13., on the other hand, I spoke of men growing up into a human institutional environment; and what I said about an individual's relation to *that* aspect of his environment is sharply in conflict with the picture painted in 3. I claimed in effect that the institutions into which one grows up – something one could also express in terms of the relations with other men that one comes to enter into as one grows up – are not *merely* seen as data on which one exercises one's independent rational powers (I *don't* say they are *never* this), but are also in large part responsible for *forming* one's rational powers. I.e. it is in one's intercourse with other men that one comes to form a conception of what considerations count as reasons for and against actions of various kinds. One comes to accept, without question, ways of going about various activities; and unless much of this sort *were* accepted without question, there would be no foothold on which one could stand in raising questions and difficulties, nothing to which one could appeal as a reason for doing one thing rather than another. For instance, one can see that when two identical products are for sale at different prices, the lower price of the one is a reason for choosing it: but only in so far as one uses money in the way it *is* used – and this is not something for which one has any reason, but something one simply comes to do as the result of one's training. 'One's training' is constituted of interactions with other men; in responding to such training one does not decide to do this or that for reasons (cf. learning to count), one simply *does* respond in a certain way and thereby acquires the capacity to see that there are reasons for and against doing certain other things.
16. A digression. Nobody does treat other men as items of the environment like any other. You do not behave in the same way when another person is present as you do when alone: your whole demeanour is different. Of course *some* of these differences one can find reasons for (e.g. it is in my interest to impress a certain person favourably). But not all. It is just what Wittgenstein called 'part of the natural history of mankind' that men behave like this in each other's presence. What is more (though I shan't develop this) the very conception of 'a human being' rests on these differences of reaction as a substratum. (Wittgenstein – 'My attitude towards him is an attitude towards a soul. I am not of the opinion that he has a soul.'[8]) (Cf. wincing when I see another person in danger, or hurt.)
17. Such considerations are relevant to the concept of authority. In the first place, the response of a person (e.g. a child) undergoing training to those who are training

---

8. Eds: Ludwig Wittgenstein, *Philosophical Investigations,* eds. G. E. M. Anscombe and Rush Rhees, trans. G. E. M. Anscombe (Oxford: Basil Blackwell, 1953), Part 2, Section iv.

him is itself analogous to, or has a family resemblance with, the recognition by one person of another's authority. Sometimes such a recognition is quite explicitly involved in the response, though not always. (I am here expressing a point I made in my early article on 'Authority', though more cautiously.[9]) If it is wrong to say, as I once said, that a recognition of authority actually is as such involved in any such relation, I should still contend that it has a close relation to it and that recognition of authority can naturally be conceived of growing out of such 'primitive' relationships. The importance of recognising this is that it sees a much more internal relationship between the notions of authority and rationality and thus helps to undermine philosophical scepticism about the possibility of authority or of reconciling it with human rationality.

18. We might compare this account with what Locke says about the state of nature ('free and equal' – i.e. no 'natural authority' of one adult over another) in relation to what he says about the authority of parents over children. For Locke parental authority has a purely protective role: it enables a child to survive, so that its rational faculties can mature independently. He does not see that adults have a much more positive role in making possible the growth of rational faculties in children and that something like a recognition of authority is bound up with the whole concept of teaching. Of course this doesn't mean that men remain perpetually *in statu pupillari*. But it does imply that the existence of rational faculties as we understand them in men presupposes a background of *established* institutions and practices and makes it possible to see how a recognition of authority may be a feature *of* those institutions: i.e. a feature of what makes the exercise of rational faculties conceivable at all; therefore not something which is of its nature antithetical to the exercise of rational faculties.

19. None of this implies that no established authority can be questioned. Of course it can. But the issue concerns not the acceptability of this or that established authority; it has to do with the acceptability of authority as such, with whether it is a concept which can have any place in our understanding of men and of rational human behaviour. To assess a *particular* kind of claim to authority is to look at it in the light of the field of human activities, relationships or institutions within which it is claimed that it should be exercised. I have been arguing in effect that such claims only make sense when some such context is presupposed. And I have also suggested ('argued' would be too strong a word) that our whole understanding of human activities, relationships and institutions (and *therefore* of human rationality) involves at various points the recognition by one man of another's authority in certain areas.

---

9. Eds: Peter Winch, 'Symposium: Authority', *Proceedings of the Aristotelian Society* Supplementary Volume 32 (1958): 225–240.

Part 2

THE ILLINOIS ERA [C. 1985–1997]

2.1
PHILOSOPHY OF LAW AND THE STATE [1992][1]

Lecture 1

Two broadly different approaches possible to this investigation:

1. As an exploration of philosophical questions arising out of legal and judicial practice. Here, one might say, the philosophical issues spring from inside.
2. As an exploration of problems which arise when we contemplate law 'from the outside', as an institution or as a concept.[2]

I don't want to suggest this is a cut-and-dried distinction, but, with that qualification, my approach will be the latter; from the direction of philosophy, rather than of the law. So I shall lay much emphasis on the relation between questions in philosophy of law and politics to issues which arise elsewhere in philosophy. Furthermore, questions about the relation between the concept (institution) of law and that of the state will be central throughout.

---

1. Eds: These are transcribed from computer printouts of a lecture course that Winch gave in 1986, 1988 and 1992; some sections are repeated verbatim from year to year, while some sections are re-arranged, reworded or reframed. We have primarily worked from the 1992 version, but have supplemented this at points with the 1988 version, which has handwritten marginalia. Sources: Peter Winch, 1992 'Philosophy of Law and the State'. Computer printout; lecture notes; 61 pp., Peter Winch Archives (GB 0100 KCLCA K/PP171, Box 16), King's College London and 1988 'Philosophy of Law and the State'. Computer printout; lecture notes; 130 pp., Peter Winch Archives (GB 0100 KCLCA K/PP171, Box 6), King's College London. There is a syllabus but not notes from his final (1994) version of the course, also in Box 16. In that syllabus, he passes from legal positivism directly to Plato's *Gorgias* as grounding a discussion of reasons for action, as he does in the 'Last Book Outline' (Part 3, below); he also interpolates a discussion of Rousseau and the general will after the discussion of Locke and Hume and before the discussion of Hart, and proposes to centre the discussion of public order and justice around Simone Weil. (The discussions of Rousseau and of Simone Weil were also in the 1992 syllabus, but do not appear in the lecture notes.)
2. 'Inside' and 'outside' are, of course, spatial images. They can be useful; but also dangerous. There are important problems too about the relation between law 'as an institution' and 'as a concept'; and I shall certainly want to say more about these questions later.

'Issues which arise elsewhere in philosophy.' There is one notion, which is the locus of many, many problems in different branches of philosophy, on which a great deal of my discussion is going to hinge: that of 'a reason for acting'.[3] Let me say a bit about this by way of preliminary.

Lecture 2

I said I wanted to approach the question 'What is law?' from the point of view of the question: In what sense does an appeal to the law provide one with a *reason for acting*? I said this is closely connected with the question: What is the nature of the law's *authority*.

It's important to recognise that there's an enormous variety of different cases; that doing something because it's the law can't always be construed in the same way, and that many cases undoubtedly can be understood somewhat on the model sketched. And the model does bring out something important: the powerful apparatus of coercion that goes with a legal system, at least in modern, centrally organised societies.[4] But if someone were to suggest that all cases are at least something like that, then we may feel something important has been left out: the 'authority' of the law. The objection isn't so much (or not just, or mainly) that we are, as it were, short-changing the law; rather, we're failing to see how the case differs from others where the law is not involved. As e.g. when we do something because the rules imposed by the local Mafia demand it.

So clearly much more has to be said about the wider social context of law, its 'function' in society, the reasons people may have for supporting such a coercive system, and so on. What is not so clear is the relation between appealing to the fact of the law itself as one's reason, and these further reasons (on the one hand one's natural desire to avoid unpleasant consequences and on the other hand the wider social aims which one thinks of the law, perhaps, as furthering). Does the 'authority' of the law as it were collapse into one or other, or perhaps both, of these? Or does it also involve something else, something *sui generis*?

To make a first stab at relating all this to the reading in Feinberg and Gross.[5] Broadly speaking, to explain the nature and force of law in terms of its being an expression of the coercive power of the state is the aim of 'legal positivism'. This has undoubtedly been the dominant philosophical tradition in modern times – and especially in legal circles themselves. (I shall be saying much more about this subsequently.)

But now let's take a preliminary look at the opposing tradition: 'natural law'. In what I've said so far there's been no reference to content. And this may look very reasonable, if you look at the really enormous variety of laws, ranging from parking regulations, through law of contract and tort to serious criminal matters like murder and robbery; to say nothing of constitutional law... It would pretty obviously be hopeless to try to define

---

3. Optional reading: You might want to take a look at *The Idea of a Social Science [and Its Relation to Philosophy* (London: Routledge and Kegan Paul, 1990 [1958])] III, Sections 3 and 4.
4. Important to make this qualification. Law in primitive societies. International law.
5. Eds: *Philosophy of Law*, eds. Joel Feinberg and Hyman Gross (Encino, Calif.: Dickenson Publishing Company, 1975).

'law' by reference to content: even if (most unlikely) a formula could be found to cover all cases it would be so extraordinarily general as to be useless.

But there's clearly much more to be said about this and I'll be coming back to it.

Legal Positivism

Insisting that the law can be identified empirically. Keep moral considerations out of this. (Not 'scientific'.) Distinguish law as institution and law as concept. Contrast Austin and Hobbes in this respect. Hobbes is interested in the concept. And though, like Austin, he wants to make sure that the law is unambiguously identifiable and should not be subject to the whims of individuals' moral opinions, he, unlike Austin, does think that the law must have a sort of 'moral' basis. He doesn't want to make it a matter of *mere* coercion. Rather of coercion with a moral basis.

Austin is interested in the law as an institution. He proposes a definition which will enable one to identify law empirically:

> The superiority which is styled sovereignty, and the dependent political society which sovereignty implies, is distinguished from other superiority, and from other society, by the following marks or characters: – 1. The *bulk* of the given society are in a *habit* of obedience or submission to a determinate and *common* superior: let that common superior be a certain individual person or a certain body or aggregate of individual persons. 2. That certain individual, or that certain body of individuals, is *not* in a habit of obedience to a determinate human superior.[6]

A simple picture. But how is it to be applied?

Problem with 'separation of powers'. Perhaps leading to idea of 'sovereign people'. But now the picture is going to need a lot of interpretation. Perhaps most damagingly: notions like 'command', 'obedience', 'superior', 'inferior' must now be interpreted in legal, constitutional terms. Thus the legal system is already presupposed. It is an illusion to suppose that we have independent, external criteria for identifying it.

Lecture 3

Austin of course realises that some account of 'command and obedience' [is] necessary: some means of distinguishing them. The account he offers is in line with his overall empiricist, positivist, project. 'Command' [is] distinguished by the ability of the initiator to back his will with sanctions.

Note that we are close here to introducing a conception of the reason why the 'inferior' obeys. Austin does not say, I think, that we only have obedience where compliance is for the sake of avoiding sanctions. On the other hand, it is obvious that he understands the reference to sanctions here only in terms of our understanding that they provide a certain sort of reason for compliance.

---

6. Excerpted in *Philosophy of Law*, ed. Feinberg and Gross, from John Austin, *The Province of Jurisprudence Determined*, Chapter VI.

Let's have a preliminary look at this. On Austin's side, the ability to enforce one's will clearly does, in some cases, make it appropriate to speak of 'command', where otherwise it would be ludicrous. E.g. if I'm accosted by a weedy, unarmed individual who says: 'Give me your wallet', is that a command?

Again, it's obviously the case that, typically at least, what we call 'laws' are backed by the threat of sanctions by the state, which has the power to impose them. (This is not to say that this is the only reason why laws are obeyed. But, as I said, Austin does not need this.)

Lecture 4[7]

But against Austin, it looks as though there could be cases which meet Austin's conditions and where we should not want to speak of 'law' and 'sovereignty'. And remember that Austin intends his account to explain how it is that:

> The superiority which is styled sovereignty, and the independent political society which sovereignty implies, is distinguished from other superiority, and from other society....[8]

E.g. a city, even a country, run by the Mafia; again, the relation between the bandits and the village in the film 'The Magnificent Seven'.

The distinction between 'power' and 'authority'. In order to understand this, we have to look more closely at the notion of 'reasons for acting' and to consider different sorts of case.

If I make new financial arrangements because of a new tax law, I am responding to the authority of the law. If I recognise that I must act differently because my country is at war I am responding to the authority of the state. This notion of authority is, again, closely connected with that of a right. In this respect these cases are markedly different from those of the Mafia or of the Mexican bandits. I recognise that the Internal Revenue Service (IRS)[9] has a right to demand disclosure of my income; it derives that right from the authority of the law. Again, I recognise that the military have a right to do certain things by virtue of the President's authority which he exercised in declaring war and which he in turn possesses because he occupies a certain position established by the US Constitution.

A qualification has to be made here. It won't be the case that everyone thinks of this 'right' in the same way or even that everyone recognises it. (Anarchists; oppressed classes like the Blacks in South Africa, or like Serbs living in Croatia, or like Croats in relation to the Jugoslav Federal government.) If there is a very great deal of dispute

---

7. Eds: much of this is contained in Lecture 3 in the printout and then repeated in Lecture 4, presumably reflecting that the in-class course of the lecture involved much more detail and discussion than is reflected in the notes.
8. Austin, *The Province of Jurisprudence Determined*, 193.
9. Eds: The agency that collects taxes in the US.

about this, we may have doubts about the 'legitimacy' of the regime in question. So we have to make room for the distinction between legitimate and illegitimate authority; and I hope I can say more on this difficult subject later. For the moment I want to content myself with the suggestion that there would be nothing we should want to call a 'state', where there is no substantial recognition of right at all. – Even if some of you are doubtful about that, I think it is at least undeniable that, in virtually all instances where we recognise the existence of states, even where there is very much naked oppression, there is also substantial recognition of right.

The distinction between power and authority is closely connected with that between 'being obliged to do something' (i.e. being subject to coercion) and 'being under an obligation to do something' (i.e. having a duty). Austin characteristically conflates these.[10] Incidentally Hobbes does so too, but with less excuse. As I said, unlike Austin, he *does* want to allow for something that is more than *bare* coercion.

I will resist the temptation to run down Hobbes now. I shall be coming to him shortly. But let me just mention that Hobbes does find it necessary to give an account of 'command', and distinguish it from other forms of influence or control, in terms of agent's reasons for doing what he does. Not that he carries this far enough.

> COMMAND is, where a man saith, *do this*, or *do not this* without expecting other reason than the will of him that says it. From this it follows manifestly, that he that commandeth, pretendeth thereby his own benefit: for the reason of his command is his own will only, and the proper object of every man's will, is some good to himself.
>
> COUNSEL, is where a man saith, *do*, or *do not this*, and deduceth his reasons from the benefit that arriveth by it to him to whom, he saith it. And from this it is evident, that he that giveth counsel, pretendeth only, whatsoever he intendeth, the good of him to whom he giveth it.[11]

One point from last week: I spoke of the difficulty of applying Austin's definition of sovereignty in complex modern societies. We should ask: why do people insist then? And I think the answer is to be found, roughly, in the fact that they think that something like this structure is required if we are to be able to give a plausible account of legal obligation. This motivation probably manifests itself more clearly in the work of Hobbes.

Obviously, there are a great many sources of power, and of authority too, in a society like ours. On the one hand we need, then, to be able to *differentiate* the authority of the law from that of, say, a church or of a university. Furthermore it seems plausible to say that the authority of the law is at least closely connected with the *power* which promulgates it and enforces it.

---

10. Note that on Austin's view the authority of the law derives from that of the State. Often yes, but cf. the complaint to King John that he had broken the laws of England.
11. *Leviathan*, Part 2, Chapter XXV.

I speak of 'it'. And this expresses the sense we have that there is such a thing as '*the* law' (in a sense that is not incompatible with there being a diversity of different particular legal measures or precepts). And again, we have a sense that the authority of the law is paramount; and yet again that this paramountcy is connected with, perhaps dependent on, the overriding power of the institution that enforces the law. All this together suggests the sort of structure that, differently interpreted, we find in both Austin and Hobbes.

Lecture 5

Now let me take up another strand in the argument. – I mean Hobbes's attempt to explain the authority of the law in terms of the citizen's *reason* for obeying it. This requires that we look more generally at some of the complexities in the notion of *reason* in this context.

Let's first make some important general distinctions. We use the word 'reason' very promiscuously. Some examples:

A. What is the reason why my car won't start? (Perhaps the fuel line is frozen.)
B. What is the reason why she has not come to the lecture today? (Perhaps she is unconscious as a result of a traffic accident.)
C. Or perhaps she feels a bit feverish and thinks she had better stay at home and rest.

A. concerns an inanimate object, B. a human being. But A. and B. are similar in form when contrasted with C., which we can re-express: 'her reason for not coming...' This, in the present context, is one of the most important distinctions we have to keep our eye on.

We must not suppose though that we can always apply it quite mechanically. Consider e.g. someone who betrays his friends under torture. There are cases where 'we' (careful!) would probably want to say that 'his reason for …. etc.' – was to avoid further torture. That implies that he 'had a choice' (careful!). But in some cases we may think he 'had no choice'. We may think the disclosure was 'wrung', 'forced' from him. (As water may be wrung out of a wet cloth.) Such judgements (expressions) are disputable, and some may object to them. It's important for us to note and pay attention to such disputes. Their existence shows something about the character of the concepts being employed. (We should try to avoid precipitate judgements about the 'right' way to speak about such things. I don't say 'right' is meaningless here; but its sense is certainly not clear.)

I don't want to get farther into those issues at present. (They are almost certain to come up again.) What I do want is to notice that they are closely connected with issues that are central for us. Let us now concentrate on cases that clearly are cases of 'acting for a reason'. Can one say anything in general about the form of such reasons? Many have certainly thought so. E.g. Hobbes.

We were looking, earlier, at Hobbes's definition of 'command' and 'counsel'. We noticed the big difference between the direction he is pointing in and that suggested by Austin's definition of 'law' in terms of a habit of obedience. Hobbes's concern with definition here is a means to a wider end. He is not interested in the fact that a majority of people does habitually obey someone identified as sovereign. He is interested in their reasons for obeying; and again, not simply as a matter of detached theoretical interest. – He wants to *give us reasons* for obeying. (He cannot, therefore, take 'a habit of obedience' as a datum.) That is the aim of his political philosophy. It comes out clearly in this quotation from *Behemoth* (a work in which Hobbes described the chaos of the English Civil War which he saw as a product of people having lost sight of the overwhelming reasons in favour of obeying).

> You may perhaps think a man has need of nothing else to know the duty he owes his governor, and what right he has to order him, but a good natural wit; but it is otherwise. For it is a science, and built upon sure and deep principles, and to be learned by deep and careful study, or from masters that have deeply studied it. And who was there in the Parliament or in the nation, that could find out those evident principles, and derive from them the necessary rules of justice, and the necessary connection of justice and peace?[12]

Lecture 6

I want to raise two connected questions about [the quote from *Behemoth* with which I ended the last lecture]:

1. What sorts of 'reason' is he looking for?
2. Who, precisely, is the argument directed at?

As we saw last week, Hobbes thought that reasons for acting had to be in terms of some good expected by and for the agent: 'the proper object of every man's will, is some good to himself'. Hobbes is not the only one who has thought this: e.g. Socrates, as portrayed by Plato. (See, e.g., *Gorgias*.) What is the case for this? It usually hangs on a thesis about the meaning of the word 'good' and its relation to a person's wants. There is such a thesis in Hobbes, *Leviathan*, Chapter VI, in his idea that human action springs from what he calls 'endeavour', either in the form of desire or of aversion. These are tendencies towards or away from things, situations. Although all people have desire and aversions (since these in a sense constitute life), people differ as to *what* they desire, shun:

> But whatsoever is the object of any man's appetite or desire, that is it which he for his part calleth *good*; and the object of his hate and aversion, *evil*; and of his contempt, *vile* and *inconsiderable*. For these words of good, evil and contemptible, are ever used with relation to the person that useth them: there being nothing simply and absolutely so; nor any common rule of good and evil, to be taken from the nature of the objects themselves; but from the person of the man, where there is no commonwealth; or, in a commonwealth, from the person that representeth it; or from an arbitrator or judge, whom men disagreeing shall by consent set up, and make his sentence the rule thereof.[13]

---

12. Hobbes, *Behemoth*, Dialogue IV.
13. Hobbes, *Leviathan*, Part 1, Chapter VI.

Lecture 7

We were discussing, very much at large, two theses:

1. That the object of all wants is some good to the one who wants;
2. That all actions are done on account of wanting something.

But I want now to get back to Hobbes [repeats the quote above]. There are two elements of truth in this. First, people do differ in their desires and aversions. And second, people do call different things good and evil in ways corresponding to a large extent to the differences in their wants.

It seems an exaggeration to say there is no common rule of good and evil. But it is hard to evaluate Hobbes's claim, since he is not talking of *our* uses of these words; but of how they would be used by people in their 'natural condition', i.e. if there were no state power. But maybe this exaggeration doesn't matter too much. Hobbes's purpose is to investigate what gives rise to the state, and he might well argue that there is sufficient diversity and dispute in what people think good to give rise to a state of turmoil sufficient for us to be able to see the state as a desirable development. Anyway, I'm not going to contest this bit of Hobbes's thesis, at least for the time being.

(But another aspect of his thesis does seem to require correction. He interprets 'good' as 'some good to himself'. This interpretation is not peculiar to him; it crops up again and again and is still with us. Cf. Riches: 'an act from which there is no practical advantage vis-a-vis some other is impossible' (*The Anthropology of Violence*, p. 7).[14] This is surely a confusion. It is one thing (whether true or not) to say: I call 'good' what I desire; quite another to say: I desire (and hence call 'good') only what I see as beneficial to myself. Let's amend Hobbes's theory slightly, dropping this unnecessary claim: the core of his view is that we must explicate the reasons for a human action in terms of the agent's desires and aversions and his beliefs about how the objects of those desires can be obtained and of those aversions be avoided.)

So, looking back at the project described in *Behemoth*, we can say that Hobbes needs to show us what good we can expect from obedience; i.e. how the projects we have will be furthered by doing so. At least that is part of what he needs to show. But remember that, in the quotation, he speaks of 'the duty he owes his governor, and what right he has to order him'. And the big question is how an argument of Hobbes's form can arrive at this.

This brings me to a point about which I said something earlier: To whom is the argument addressed?

It's important to remember, first, that 'we' in this context means each one of us. The question is: what reasons for allegiance does anyone have. And, second, it's important to notice that *we* are not, in the first instance, being addressed as citizens or subjects. This is a status which presupposes allegiance. So each of us is being *addressed as an individual human being with interests that can be appealed to which do not depend on membership of civil society*.

---

14. Eds: *The Anthropology of Violence*, ed. David Riches (Oxford: Basil Blackwell, 1986), 7.

This is where the concept of 'the natural condition of mankind' (in Locke: 'the state of nature') becomes important. (Cf. Rawls's 'original position'.)

Of course, the crucial question here is: how much, and what kinds of difference are we to think of this non-political status as making? I want next to consider Hobbes's treatment of this.

How does one determine what properties and capacities one can ascribe to human beings in this state? What are the criteria?

Let me start, with Hobbes, by working backwards. Let's consider what he needs, tries, to demonstrate and what assumptions he allows himself for the demonstration. The outline of the demonstration is as follows:[15]

(1) An argument to show that the nature of human beings is such that 'during the time men live without a common power to keep them all in awe, they are in that condition which is called war; and such a war is of every man against every man.'
(2) This condition is an intolerable one.

> In such condition, there is no place for industry; because the fruit thereof is uncertain: and consequently no culture of the earth; no navigation, nor use of the commodities that may be imported by sea; no commodious building; no instruments of moving, and removing, such things as require much force; no knowledge of the face of the earth; no account of time; no arts; no letters; no society; and which is worst of all, continual fear, and danger of violent death; and the life of man, solitary, poor, nasty, brutish, and short.[16]

(3) An account of how the condition can be changed; i.e. of how a 'common power' can be established and maintained.

It's obvious, but important to note, that (3) may not make use of any materials inconsistent with (1) and (2). Note that each stage of the argument rests on claims about dependencies. 'Without this, not that.' Two types of such claim are particularly important:

(i) Without sovereign power no genuine society;
(ii) Without society, such and such concepts inapplicable to individual human beings.

But these claims are not independent of each other. The case for (i) rests on an application of (ii).

> Where there is no common power, there is no law: where no law, no injustice. Force and fraud, are in war the two cardinal virtues. *Justice, and injustice are none of the faculties neither of the body, nor mind. If they were, they might be in a man that were alone in the world, as well as his senses, and passions. They are qualities that relate to men in society, not in solitude.* It is consequent also to the same condition, that there be no propriety, no dominion, no *mine* and *thine* distinct, but only that to be every man's, that he can get: and for so long as he can keep it.[17]

---

15. *Leviathan*, Part 1, Chapter XIII.
16. Ibid.
17. Ibid. [The emphases are Winch's.]

Note, though this is not the main point I want to concentrate on, that there is something amiss with the argument here. Let's allow that justice and injustice are inapplicable to a man 'in solitude'. Still, a condition of war is not exactly one of solitude! Again, allow that notions of property involve those of justice and injustice; and hence that where these latter are inapplicable, we cannot speak of property. It's still misleading to call the resulting situation as one where 'that to be every man's, that he can get: and for so long as he can keep it'. That suggests there must be constant struggle; and while there may be, it isn't obvious there must be.[18]

Lecture 8

I was discussing Hobbes's claims about what cannot be said of human beings in 'natural conditions'. (Especially, justice and injustice.) But more important are the assumptions Hobbes is making about what can be attributed to human beings who do not live together 'in society'. These assumptions play a major (and I think indispensable) role throughout the argument. (And this situation is not peculiar to Hobbes. It is a major crux in discussion of issues like this.) In the quoted passage it is implied that 'the faculties of the body and mind', and in particular, 'the senses, and passions', *can* be ascribed to human beings in solitude. And these in fact, along with 'reason', are very prominent throughout Hobbes's argument.

It is at this point that what I may call the 'metaphysical' assumptions in Hobbes's thinking play a real role. For this, the opening Chapters of *Leviathan* are important. Hobbes's 'materialism'. Human beings are, like everything else, bodies in motion. Their characteristic motions include the behaviour everyone can observe and also motions too small to be observed within the body. Obviously, he has particularly in mind here what we should call events in the brain or nervous system. Though, obviously, the state of physiological knowledge was in the seventeenth century far behind the twentieth, Hobbes's general philosophical, metaphysical picture isn't so very different from views widely current now.

This is not the proper context in which to discuss these questions in the detail they really deserve. (That's a purely institutional use of 'proper', as it were; we cannot fit such a discussion into the present course; but I do think these issues are urgently relevant to the issues we are discussing.) I will try to bring out, though, how these issues impinge on the problems in political philosophy that concern us.

Hobbes's general picture of human life is this: a human being is a body in interaction with other bodies in the environment. This body has certain internal principles of motion; but the way it behaves is obviously modified by the other bodies with which it comes in contact. It tends to maintain its own internal economy of motion in the face of such outside influences. (See beginning of Chapter VI.)

---

18. N.B. no covenant with Sovereign because (a) it would make no sense (b) it would limit the sovereign power and bring back chaos. Hobbes's particular notion of 'right' in 'natural right'.

This tendency is what Hobbes calls *'endeavour'*. This was a concept very much in the air at the time. Cf. Hobbes's great contemporary and fellow spirit, Spinoza.[19] But they took it from earlier writers. However, we don't really need thus to historicise it. It's a concept that, in other forms is always with us and is clearly important to our thinking. Hobbes doesn't give it here as much explicit emphasis as its role in his thinking deserves.

> These small beginnings of motion, within the body of man, before they appear in walking, speaking, striking, and other visible actions, are commonly called ENDEAVOUR.[20]

It's important to remember, in the context of Hobbes's development of his account, that this endeavour is, as it were of necessity, directed at the preservation and well-being of its possessor. 'Of necessity' because, in a way, endeavour is precisely the expression of its possessor's fundamental being. We have to remember though, as Spinoza does, but perhaps Hobbes doesn't, that a being's conception of itself and of its preservation may take *prima facie* surprising turns. (Self-sacrifice.)

Lecture 9

Amongst the motions originating from external influences, especially important are the physiological modifications produced through the sense organs. These modifications leave traces which, organised in one way, constitute memory, in another imagination. Corresponding to these physiological states and changes are what Hobbes calls 'phantasms'. He means what others have called 'images' etc. Precisely what the status of these phantasms is Hobbes does not make at all clear; and indeed I think this is a major locus of confusion in his thinking. (The same can probably be said about more modern views about 'mental states' etc., so fundamental in cognitive psychology.) But, roughly, a phantasm is the manner in which a physiological state/change appears 'from the inside'. (In that phrase all the confusion is condensed.)

The ways in which the motions thus set up in a human body develop depend, obviously, on their interaction with the inherent, internal dynamic tendencies of the body. Especially important here, as well as and in conjunction with, memory and imagination, is *reason*. This consists in the organisation of phantasms in such a way as to predict future occurrences and adjust its behaviour accordingly, as fits its peculiar 'endeavour'. Obviously, here too a whole lot of important and difficult issues are being glossed over – by me, I mean principally; though Hobbes does his own share of glossing too.

Especially important to us here now are two connected features of this picture of the relation between a human individual, me for instance, and my environment. I face the objects in that environment as elements capable of helping me or hindering me in my endeavour. I will be interested in discovering how these various objects work: what are their own internal principles of motion, in order to make the best possible use of them;

---

19. Eds: For further discussion see Winch, *Spinoza on Ethics and Understanding*, eds. Michael Campbell and Sarah Tropper (Anthem, 2021).
20. Hobbes, *Leviathan*, Part 1, Chapter VI.

or at least in order to counteract any adverse effect they may have on my own projects. This is how I find out about them; how I come to understand the kinds of thing they are. The ability to do all this is, as it were, congenital. It is something which I *apply to*, and perhaps *develop through* the practice of such application to the things around me; it is not *derived from* my interaction with them.

Perhaps it will be obvious from the way I have highlighted these assumptions that I regard them as mistaken. I think as a matter of fact they are the source of the deepest difficulties Hobbes's whole political theory faces. I will try to bring out what I regard as erroneous and confused as I go along.

So far I have spoken promiscuously about 'objects in the environment'. Amongst these objects, and perhaps the most important, are other human beings. My relations with these will of course be of the same general pattern as my relations with everything else. I will find out what they are and how they behave by observation and systematic thought about the results of that observation. My whole interest in them will be their relation, good or ill, to my own endeavour. I shall want to discover the principles on which they act so as (a) to influence their behaviour in my own interest and (b) to adjust my own behaviour to theirs in my own interests. In this inquiry I shall have to rely on my observation of their behaviour on the one hand and, on the other, my own privileged awareness of the principles on which I act. Hobbes assumes that I shall have good reason to expect others to behave according to the same general principles (= motives). Now: my own overriding motive is to promote my own interests and use others for that purpose. I shall, therefore, assume that others have similar motives. Hence, I shall concentrate on finding out what their own projects are and how they go about promoting them; this will enable me to predict their behaviour and adjust my own to it in my best interests; it will also enable me to do things which will modify others' behaviour: either by putting obstacles in their way or offering them inducements.

Furthermore, I shall know that others are looking at me with exactly the same beady eye. What is being described here is the struggle for power which Hobbes regards as the most pervasive feature of human life in its 'natural condition'.

How does language fit into this picture?[21] It's obviously necessary, as an important part of the mechanism which generates the struggle for power (the *bellum omnium contra omnes*). This comes out in various places. But see especially the passage in Part 2, Chapter XVII, in which Hobbes contrasts men with bees and ants:

> First, that men are continually in competition for honor and dignity, which these creatures are not; and consequently amongst men there ariseth on that ground, envy and hatred, and finally war; but amongst these not so.
>
> Secondly, that amongst these creatures, the common good suffereth not from the private... But man, whose joy consisteth in comparing himself with other men, can relish nothing but what is eminent.
>
> Thirdly, that these creatures, having not, as man the use of reason, do not see, nor think they see, any fault, in the administration of their common business; whereas amongst men, there are very many, that think themselves wiser, and abler to govern the public, better

---

21. Eds: The 1988 lectures skip straight from introduction of the state of nature to this lecture on language, without the discussion of endeavour.

than the rest; and these strive to reform and innovate, one this way, another that way; and thereby bring it into distraction and civil war.

Fourthly, that these creatures, though they have some use of voice, in making known to one another their desires, and other affections; yet they want that art of words, by which some men can represent to others, that which is good, in the likeness of evil; and evil, in the likeness of good; and augment, or diminish the apparent greatness of good and evil... etc.[22]

Hobbes does go out of his way to emphasise the importance of speech to the human condition, seeing it (surely rightly) as an essential condition of characteristically human reason and understanding. 'And therefore if speech be peculiar to man, as for aught I know it is, then is understanding peculiar to him also.'[23] Even more obviously, speech is needed for the ending of that struggle; since this requires a very carefully worded covenant. It must therefore clearly be possible prior to the peaceful civil society which the covenant brings into being. I.e. (trying to put it non-temporally) we must be able to think of human beings as language users even if they are not in civil society if we are going to be able to see language use as one of the human capacities which makes civil society both necessary (or at least desirable) and possible.

But the most noble and profitable invention of all other, was that of SPEECH, consisting of *names* or *appelations*, and their connexion; whereby men register their thoughts; recall them when they are past; and also declare them to one another for mutual utility and conversation; without which there had been amongst men, neither commonwealth, nor society, nor contract, nor peace, no more than amongst lions, bears and wolves.[24]

Hobbes does give an account of language which certainly presents it in that light. But it is hopeless – and it is important to see this.[25]

The general use of speech, is to transfer our mental discourse, into verbal; or the train of our thoughts, into a train of words... So that the first use of names is to serve for *marks*, or *notes* of remembrance. Another is, very many use the same words, to signify by their connexion and order, one to another, what they conceive, or think of each matter; and also what they desire, fear, or have any other passion for.[26]

---

22. Hobbes, *Leviathan*, Part 2, Chapter XVII.
23. Part 1, Chapter V.
24. Part 1, Chapter IV.
25. *Pace* Fodor. See *Leviathan*. [Winch is presumably referring here to Jerry Fodor, e.g. his *Language of Thought* (Cambridge, MA: Harvard University Press, 1975).]
26. Cf. Wittgenstein's comment on Augustine in *Philosophical Investigations* [eds. G. E. M. Anscombe and Rush Rhees, trans. G. E. M. Anscombe (Oxford: Basil Blackwell, 1953)], §32:

Augustine describes the learning of human language as if the child came into a strange country and did not understand the language of the country; that is, as if it already had a language, only not this one. Or again as if the child could already think, only not yet speak. And 'think' would here mean something like 'talk to itself'.

'Hobbes' could, perhaps with more justice, be substituted for 'Augustine' in that remark.

Lecture 10

I was discussing Hobbes's account of language with a view, in particular to the questions:

A. What role does language play in Hobbes's account of the natural condition of mankind and of the genesis of the Commonwealth?
B. Does he succeed in showing that a language capable of filling this role can be attributed to people in their natural condition?

I quoted: 'Another use of language is, when many use the same words, to signify by their connexion and order, one to another, what they conceive, or think of each matter; and also what they desire, fear, or have any other passion for.'

The question here is of course, how am I supposed to know *what* thought you are referring to by a given sound or mark? Don't say: well, you can tell me! This is a hard enough question on its own. It becomes, if that's possible, even more pressing, given that, in the state of war we are supposed to be confined to here, Hobbes insists that the principal devices in dealings between human beings will be force *and fraud!*[27]

What becomes increasingly clear[28] is that a form of 'social' life, i.e. a life in which there are common practices, customs, established interrelations (everything that Hobbes thinks impossible in a natural condition)[29] is presupposed by thinking of human beings as having the kind of language-dependent rationality required by Hobbes's account of the genesis of the state of war and the creation of civil society.

I'll come to the consequences of this for the development of Hobbes's account shortly. But setting the difficulties aside for the time being, let's look briefly at how he does develop his account. It is the exercise of 'reason' on the part of each individual that has generated the state of war. But people, by exercising their reason, will also be able to see that such a condition is contrary to the interest of everyone (i.e. of each one) and that therefore it is 'rational' to seek a means of bringing the state of war to an end.[30] But it's by no means so obvious. Someone might perfectly reasonably calculate that he or she

---

27. See 'Nature and Convention' in my *Ethics and Action* [(London: Routledge and Kegan Paul, 1972), 231–252].
28. The philosopher who, at least in modern times, but probably altogether (*überhaupt*), has best shown this formally is Wittgenstein in *Philosophical Investigations*; see also my own *The Idea of a Social Science* [(London: Routledge and Kegan Paul, 1990 [1958])], Chapter 1 for a sketch of Wittgenstein's argument from this point of view.
29. So there's an appropriate logical irony in the fact that it's precisely the absence of these features in the 'natural condition of mankind' that both motivates people (as Hobbes argues) to make the covenant that creates the state and (as he does not of course see) makes such a move impossible for them.
30. For Hobbes's argument to be convincing at this point – 'as long as this natural right of every one endureth, there can be no security to any man, how strong or wise soever he be, of living out the time, which nature ordinarily alloweth men to live' (Part 1, Chapter XIV) – this has got to be particularly obvious, since everyone has to be able to see it: i.e. it's one thing on which people must be able to agree.

is likely to do best in a state of war. My point here is not to consider whether such a one would be right; the question is rather whether there might not be a pretty good case for such a view such that someone might reasonably accept [it].

Hence the first 'law of nature':[31]

> A law of nature, lex naturalis, is a precept or general rule, found out by reason, by which a man is forbidden to do that, which is destructive of his life, or taketh away the means of preserving the same; and to omit that, by which he thinketh it may be best preserved.[32]

And the first such 'law': 'that every man, ought to endeavor peace, as far as he has hope of attaining it; and when he cannot obtain it, that he may seek, and use, all helps, and advantages of war.'

The means of achieving this, it seems obvious, must be an agreement to forego the mode of behaviour which is responsible for war: viz. everyone's unlimited right to decide for him/herself what is in the interest of self-preservation. Now the chief obstacle to any such agreement, clearly, must be that it is in no individual's interest (and therefore irrational) to divest him/herself of the means of defence without assurance that others are going to do the same thing. And how can anyone have such assurance, given that the natural condition is one in which force and fraud are the primary, rational, instruments of interaction between people? (Note that it's no use to suggest Hobbes ought to drop this last point; it's a conclusion from assumptions to which he is deeply committed.)

> If a covenant be made, wherein neither of the parties perform presently, but trust one another; in the condition of mere nature, which is a condition of war of every man against every man, upon any reasonable suspicion it is void...

Again: 'A covenant not to defend myself from force, by force, is always void'.

Hence, conditions have to be created which will make it rational to make, and keep, such an agreement. The difficulty here is that the agreement itself has got to create the conditions. After all, it is precisely the absence of such conditions which the agreement is supposed to put right.

> The force of words being, as I have formerly noted, too weak to hold men to the performance of their covenants; there are in men's nature, but two imaginable helps to strengthen it. And those are either a fear of the consequence of breaking their word; or a glory, or pride in appearing not to need to break it.[33]

---

31. Eds: Winch lists two 'first' laws of nature here. The first one Winch gives (as the first law of nature) states as quoted that self-preservation is the law of nature (i.e. a law found out by reason), and it reflects the right of nature Hobbes has set out in the opening paragraph of Chapter XIV (a requirement to do whatever it takes to preserve oneself, including doing whatever ones sees need to do to other persons). Hobbes goes on to say the first precept of reason (which Winch next quotes) reflects two 'fundamental' laws of nature, the first of which is to law to seek peace, which Winch quotes next.
32. *Leviathan*, Part 1, Chapter XIV [Winch's emphasis].
33. Ibid.

It is on the first of these that Hobbes concentrates. His solution is ingenious. People must:

> (C)onfer all their power and strength upon one man, or on one assembly of men, that may reduce all their wills, by plurality of voices, unto one will: which is as much as to say, to appoint one man, or assembly of men, to bear their person; and every one to own, and acknowledge himself to be the author of whatsoever he that beareth their person, shall act, or cause to be acted, in those things that concern the common peace and safety; and therein to submit their wills, every one to his will, and their judgments, to his judgment. This is more than consent, or concord; it is a real unity of them all, in one and the same person, made by covenant of every man with every man, in such manner, as if every man should say to every man, *I authorize and give up my right of governing myself, to this man, or to this assembly of men, on this condition, that thou give up thy right to him, and authorize all his actions in like manner.*[34]

Lecture 11

The idea of a public power, authority. The idea of 'representation': of another acting on my behalf; so that his actions count as mine. (Very important to citizenship.) This is really the crux. It brings us back to the question how a subject's/citizen's will is involved in the acts of the sovereign.

Hobbes has a very specific, interesting and curious explanation of this. A person has two sorts of reasons for acceding to what the sovereign does. The fear of insecurity which led to the making of the covenant is sufficient to motivate someone's keeping it subsequently. This, however, will not serve to create a representative relationship; to make the subject the 'author' of the sovereign's acts. But the covenant itself has the power to 'bind' its participants' wills in a different way.

In making a covenant one transfers a right; in doing so:

> [H]e is said to be OBLIGED, or BOUND, not to hinder those, to whom such right is granted, or abandoned, from the benefit of it: and that he *ought*, and it is his DUTY, not to make void that voluntary act of his own: and that such hindrance is INJUSTICE, and INJURY, as being *sine jure*; the right being before renounced, or transferred. So that *injury*, or *injustice*, in the controversies of the world, is somewhat like to that, which in the disputations of scholars, called *absurdity*. For as it is there called an absurdity, to contradict what one maintained in the beginning: so in the world, it is called injustice, and injury, voluntarily to undo what, which from the beginning he had voluntarily done.[35]

Hobbes here sees an analogy between the bindingness of a promise and the commitment to the truth of something one says. But perhaps the point should be put more strongly. The former is a special case of being committed by what one says. I noticed that a promise makes sense only in the context of a prior notion of an obligation. Hobbes himself says that covenants without the sword are just 'breath', 'air'.

---

34. Part 2, Chapter XVIII [Winch's emphasis].
35. Hobbes, *Leviathan*, Part 1, Chapter XIV.

This looks as though he is *reducing* the obligation of a promise to 'being obliged' (by force). In fact, he does not want to do that. This is clear from his discussion of the distinction between '*in foro interno*' and '*in foro externo*':

> The laws of nature oblige *in foro interno*; that, to say, they bind to a desire they should take place: but *in foro externo* that is, to the putting them in act, not always. For he that should be modest, and tractable, and perform all he promises, in such time, and place, where no man should desire to do so, should but make himself a prey to others, and procure his own certain ruin, contrary to the ground of all laws of nature, which tend to nature's preservation.[36]

This clearly, in a sense, bolsters up the previous defence. What I called the deeper difficulty lies in the words 'oblige' and 'bind' here. Remember Hobbes's equivocation about the status of the laws of nature: are they mere 'theorems' or genuine laws. Now the importance of this point at this precise juncture is the difficulty there is in making sense of what it could be for anyone to make a 'covenant' in the 'natural condition' of mankind. I don't now mean the difficulty of inducing anyone to do it; but the difficulty in understanding what a covenant would be, what the term 'covenant' could mean in this context.

Covenants create obligations that did not exist before. Hobbes certainly cannot mean that it is a mere 'theorem' that it is in one's best interest to do what one has said one would. A promise would then be no more than an expression of intention. The notion of an obligation has to pre-exist the making of a promise; someone who did not know that a promise created an obligation would hardly know what 'I promise' meant. Hobbes's covenant is no ordinary promise: it is to create the very notion of an obligation (and of justice).

But as a matter of fact it's not clear that it could amount even to that. Just as there can be no 'binding' promise without an antecedent understanding that a promise commits one, so, more generally, there can be such a thing as 'maintaining' (asserting) something only in a context where one is understood to be committed in the future by what one says now.

And notice that Hobbes's account of language makes no provision for this. There can be such an institution as a 'Commonwealth' – even as understood by Hobbes – only given that human life is independently understood as involving a stability in human relationships such that people can understand each other, and themselves, as subject to certain mutual commitments.

Consider:

> A multitude of men, are made *one* person, when they are by one man, or one person, represented; so that it be done *with the consent of every one of that multitude in particular*. For it is the *unity* of the representer, not the *unity* of the represented, that maketh the person *one*. And it is the representer that beareth the person, and but one person: and *unity*, cannot otherwise

---

36. Hobbes, *Leviathan*, Part 1, Chapter XV.

be understood in multitude. And because the multitude naturally is not *one*, but *many*; they cannot be understood for one; but many authorize everything their representative saith, or doth in their name; every man giving their common represener, authority from himself in particular ....[37]

What I am saying is that there has to be another sort of 'unity', before the 'consent' of each one in particular can be understood: that consent is not an act that can be performed by the individual in isolation from others: because its force is to commit him or her with others.

Lecture 12

Let's now, after this long, long excursus, return to the central question of legal positivism.

There are two difficulties about the covenant: a (relatively superficial) 'sociological' difficulty and a (deeper) 'conceptual' difficulty. I said something about the former.

Two more words about that before I pass on to the other.

Since Hobbes is not talking history, it's perfectly possible for him to allow the possibility of a *de facto* seizure of power by an individual which is then legitimised by a covenant. And this he does:

> A commonwealth by *acquisition*, is that, where the sovereign power is acquired by force.... And this kind of dominion, or sovereignty, differeth from sovereignty by institution, only in this, that men who choose their sovereign, do it for fear of one another, and not of him whom they institute: but in this case, they subject themselves to him they are afraid of. In both cases they do it for fear: which is to be noted by them, that hold all such covenants, as proceed from fear of death or violence, void: which, if it were true, no man, in any kind of commonwealth, could be obliged to obedience.[38]

This will probably go against the democratic grain. But it is realistic: not in a servile sense; but in the sense that regimes originally imposed by force of arms do indeed acquire legitimacy by a historical process. (Think of the Norman Conquest of England.)

In fact, I would go further. Take a paradigm case of 'sovereignty by institution': the Declaration of Independence of the United States. Though in one sense the Founding Fathers started from scratch, in another sense they did not. They inherited, as it were, the sense of legitimacy: this came to them through history and presupposed the existence of prior states which had certainly not been instituted in any such way. (They even inherited the Norman Conquest, one might say.)

---

37. Part 1, Chapter XVI [Winch's emphases].
38. Part 2, Chapter XX.

But I am now heading in a rather un-Hobbesian direction: he of course does think of sovereignty as an original invention, creation, rather than a historically developed phenomenon, a natural growth. (Like language.)

Perhaps Hobbes shouldn't be allowed to get away with his argument quite as it stands. There is surely an important difference between making a covenant to support a sovereign because I am afraid of the dangers of anarchy and making it under threats from *him*.

Consideration of Hobbes's second point which might be used in his defence will take me on to what I called the deeper (conceptual) difficulty in his account: his distinction between *in foro intemo* and *in foro externo*. To remind you:

> The laws of nature oblige *in foro interno*; that, to say, they bind to a desire they should take place: but *in foro externo* that is, to the putting them in act, not always. For he that should be modest, and tractable, and perform all he promises, in such time, and place, where no man should desire to do so, should but make himself a prey to others, and procure his own certain ruin, contrary to the ground of all laws of nature, which tend to nature's preservation.[39]

This clearly, in a sense, bolsters up the previous defence. What I called the deeper difficulty lies in the words 'oblige' and 'bind' here. Remember Hobbes's equivocation about the status of the laws of nature: are they mere 'theorems' or genuine laws. Now the importance of this point at this precise juncture is the difficulty there is in making sense of what it could be for anyone to make a 'covenant' in the 'natural condition' of mankind. I don't now mean the difficulty of inducing anyone to do it; but the difficulty in understanding what a covenant would be, what the term 'covenant' could mean in this context.[40]

That is the problem as it arises on the side, so to speak, of the philosophy of mind. But it has its counterpart squarely within political theory/philosophy in relation to the question: who is it that exercises the authority of the state? This is precisely why Hobbes had thought it necessary to draw a clear distinction between 'command' and 'counsel'.

Lecture 13

I want now to move on to Locke. I shall use the discussion of Locke to explore further problems about the relation between the 'will' of the one who exercises authority and that of the person *under* that authority. I am going now to raise a question that didn't seem to particularly exercise Hobbes, though perhaps it should have. How can the 'subject' be regarded as acting genuinely rationally and responsibly?

---

39. Part 1, Chapter XV.
40. Eds: In addition to repeating the quote from the previous lecture, he has repeated his commentary on the quote.

The theoretical question here is: what is it that makes a given policy, or act of policy, state policy? That question in political philosophy, I am suggesting, is the counterpart of, or at least closely connected with, the question in the philosophy of mind: how is the will of the citizen related to that of the sovereign whose legitimate authority he accepts? I've suggested that this question is particularly acute when we are dealing with political contexts. The notion of someone else acting with authority does of course apply elsewhere. If it doesn't raise the same problems elsewhere, perhaps we can use these contexts as a source of leverage for dealing with the political case.

Consider the following case. A party of us go on a sailing expedition. Sailing is an activity in which the actions of all participants have to be coordinated and in which this can only be done if decisions are made by a single person and accepted and carried out by others. Let us suppose that, before we set sail, we meet and agree together to accept the authority in sailing matters – for the duration of the trip – of a particular member of the party. (It will probably be the one thought to be most expert in sailing; but that's an aspect of it we won't concern ourselves with, at least at present.) [If] I am a party to such an agreement, then, in situations in which the captain gives an order I am committed to acting on his assessment of the situation, rather than my own.

Now in this sort of context we probably won't feel that this creates a genuine problem concerning responsibility or will. We can distinguish the short-term from the long-term context of my action. In the short-term I do indeed abdicate my immediate responsibility for decision. Indeed, it may well happen that I find myself committed to a course of action by the captain's order which I would have rejected had the decision been my own. But this short-term abdication is part of a longer-term strategy which I have freely chosen as the best way of achieving my projects (having a successful sailing trip). The same may be said of all members of the party. Each one has freely consented to the authority of the captain. And the authority of the captain derives from that consent of those over whom it is exercised. Here is a case in which Hobbes's talk about 'representation' seems to have a useful application.

Incidentally, another important feature of the authority thus created is its limited character: both in respect of its duration and its range of application. The person chosen is captain only for the extent of this voyage; and he has the right to command only in matters which concern the safe and efficient management of the vessel. There is also the possibility (though this is not necessary) that there is a built-in proviso that his authority may be revoked by a decision of the participants arrived at according to previously agreed procedures. – All these features have been exploited by writers on the character of political authority.

In such a case then if I carry out an order given by the captain and lying within the scope of the authority he or she has been agreed by me and all the others to exercise, then I can be said to be carrying out my own will, as expressed in that earlier commitment. (Of course, there is still a philosophical question – and this will become important later – about the nature of that commitment, and the sense in which I can commit myself to subsequent decisions in advance. But I will leave that question aside for the present.)

This way of looking at things also helps to make clear the division of responsibility for what happens on the voyage. If I voted for X as captain I am responsible for that.

If I didn't vote for him, but agreed to abide by the majority decision, I am responsible for that. (I didn't after all have to take part in the trip – a very important feature of this situation, for obvious reasons which I will later discuss.) If, in the course of the voyage, serious grounds develop for doubting X's competence or goodwill I am responsible for not having (or for having) voiced my misgivings. And I am responsible for having, or for not having, insisted on the possibility of rescinding X's authority in appropriate circumstances at the time of the original agreement. On the other hand, the captain is responsible for having accepted this position of authority, against the background of his assessment of his own competence and of the acceptability of the terms of the agreement; and he is responsible for the general conduct of the voyage and the particular decisions he makes in the course of it.

There are undoubtedly countless human situations which can be enlighteningly thought of in terms of such a model. Sometimes these involve quite short-term arrangements, as in my example. Sometimes the arrangements are very long-term and the conferment of authority approaching the permanent. Consider various sorts of private association, club, etc. Of course, in many such cases certain features of the model will have to be modified. One very important aspect in which this is likely to be so is that of the way in which the 'consent' of the participants is thought to be expressed. In my example, there was a deliberate, datable and explicit act of consenting. But this is not always thought to be necessary. A relationship of authority may grow up between people as an outcome of habitual intercourse without any express agreement. And often enough we regard that as quite adequately expressing the consent of the parties. And on the other hand, the fact that explicit forms are observed is not always a sure criterion of consent having been freely given. (Different kinds of case: blackmail (explicit and concealed); deception; bribery; etc.) Our question now is: Can the authority of the state be adequately accounted in terms of some such model (given of course the necessary qualifications in such dimensions as I have been suggesting)?

One of the most powerful traditions in political philosophy (and one that is today in the ascendant probably) claims that it can. Locke's *Second Treatise on Civil Government* is one of the classical statements of such a view. Hume's 'Of the Original Contract'[41] contains one of the most powerful criticisms of it. This is what we shall turn to next week.

Lecture 14

Last time we considered some non-political forms of association which involve the conferment of authority on particular individuals in a way which seems not to create the problems about the will which threaten our understanding of the political case. They are cases in which the surrender of the power to decide on action in particular circumstances flows from a free decision to adopt a policy of doing that in the service

---

41. Eds: David Hume, 'Of the Original Contract', in *Political Essays*, ed. Charles W. Handel (Indianapolis: Bobbs Merrill, The Library of Liberal Arts, 1953), 43–63.

of the agent's own long-term ends. We now have to consider whether political authority can also be understood in that way.

There is a long tradition that it can. Not the first to state such a position, but one of the classical exponents of it, was John Locke in the late seventeenth century. Of course, Hobbes has one foot inside this tradition too. His account, however, raises difficulties of other sorts (which I have already discussed) which would stand in the way of taking his as our paradigmatic statement of the case for present purposes. However, it remains possible that the difficulties Hobbes faces have only been swept under the carpet by Locke. That is a possibility we shall have to consider, because it points to certain deep features of the whole problem which don't altogether emerge in Locke's own account.

One big difference between Hobbes and Locke is this: Hobbes equates the question of the basis of the state with that of the basis of settled social life altogether. For him the alternative to the state is no society at all. ('For it is the unity of the representer, not the unity of the represented, that maketh the person one. *And unity is not otherwise to be understood in multitude.*' (Emphasis mine)) Of course this is just what creates problems for Hobbes's account of that basis, since the notion of a covenant on which the account depends seems applicable only in the context of a settled communal life involving means of communication, some degree of mutual trust, etc. But the question remains: whether the difficulties in Hobbes's philosophy are really of his own creating, or whether they spring from the fact that his theory tries to confront problems which Locke, amongst others, just ignores.

The point is that for Locke there is society before there is the State. And, interestingly, he argues for this within a version of the natural law tradition. The state of nature, he claims, 'has a law of nature to govern it'. And by this he means more than the rational pursuit of individual self-interest which Hobbes means by 'law of nature'. Locke's natural men have mutual rights and obligations; and this of course, if allowed, at once removes one of the major obstacles to accepting the possibility of an agreement ('covenant') between them.[42] Interestingly, the genesis of his most famous work, *Essay Concerning the Human Understanding*, a treatment of fundamental issues in the theory of knowledge, arose directly out of his attempts to show that there could be a human knowledge of 'laws of nature' as he understood them: i.e. considered as standards of behaviour binding on the individual. But I shan't go into Locke's treatment of these questions in the present context.

Historically, Locke comes between Hobbes and Hume. Hume, without accepting Hobbes's picture of a natural condition which is a war of every man against every man (because of the role of 'sympathy' between men) does argue that Locke fails to see that there are difficulties in his idea of a contract which are identical in form with the difficulties in the idea of allegiance to the state.

---

42. Locke did indeed write a series of essays on the law of nature which is published as a separate book. [John Locke, *Essays on the Law of Nature*, ed. W. von Leyden (Oxford: Oxford University Press, 1954.)]

Lecture 15

Let us now consider what Locke actually says. I want to consider mainly three matters.

1. The contract by which people leave their natural state and put themselves into 'civil society', which involves being subject to the authority of government. (Though not, so far, to that of a particular government: an important difference between Locke and Hobbes.)
2. The relation between 1. and the acceptance of majority rule.
3. The notion of tacit consent (about which I have already said something, but there will be a bit more to be said in relation to Hume's critique of Locke).

There are perhaps three questions at issue here. Viz.:

(a) What is the difference between being in a state of nature and being in civil society?
(b) How is the transition from the one to the other to be understood?
(c) Why should people make (accept) such a transition?

The characteristics of the state of nature are that in it all people are 'free, equal, and independent'. There is really no plurality of criteria here; all three come to much the same thing seen from a slightly different angle. Freedom is to be understood as not being subject to anyone else's authority; it is freedom to manage one's own affairs as one thinks fit. Equality, similarly, is equality in respect of being free to manage one's own affairs; no one has a greater right to command than anyone else. That means that no one has a ('natural') right to command. Independence, again, is independence from the authority of any other person; it is the condition of owing no ('natural') allegiance to any other human agency.

In fact, as you can see, this conception is precisely the conception of primitive practical rationality which is the implicit framework of this whole investigation. This being the case, since we start with the idea that, in the first instance, the only authority for what any person shall do is that person's own authority, or will, it follows that if there is a transformation from that situation to one in which one person is subject to the authority of another person's will, that can only be the result of an exercise of his own will. There is nothing else from which it could result; anything else has been ruled out by the terms of the description of the original state.

I think our present intellectual and political climate is such that most people would naturally tend to accept something like Locke's starting point. That state of affairs no doubt owes much to the success of ideas like Locke's in the Western political tradition in the intervening years. Of course, this starting point was by no means an orthodoxy in Locke's day. He in fact spends quite a bit of energy in trying to refute a defender of what once had been an orthodoxy: the doctrine of 'the divine right of kings'.

That isn't a doctrine that is likely to have much political mileage nowadays, but there are features of the doctrine which are nevertheless worth considering, because they raise issues which are still relevant. A near-contemporary of Locke's, Sir Robert Filmer, had attempted to derive the right of kings to rule over their subjects from the right of Adam to command his children. Locke has two responses to that.

Firstly, whatever may have been Adam's relations with his children; and whatever may have been the relation of contemporary kings to Adam, the right of the latter could not have been derived from the right of the former. Adam's rights, whatever they were, derived from the situation he was then in vis-a-vis his children (and God of course); and any rights contemporary rulers may have over their subjects must in turn be derived from their contemporary situation relative (*inter alia*) to their subjects. The thought here is that history provides no justification for contemporary rights and obligations.

Secondly, the authority of parents over children lasts only during the children's minority: i.e. until they have developed rational faculties to the extent required for them to be capable of running their own lives. This authority derives from the parent's obligation to protect children from harm as long as they are not so capable. Hence this authority cannot be used to justify the authority of a ruler over (adult) subjects.

There are important points of general interest raised by both the foregoing arguments. The first argument of course has a more general application than to Filmer or to divine right. It rests on the thought that no succeeding generation can be bound by what was the case for a preceding generation. But is this true? It is an issue on which what we are inclined to think when it is put to us in general terms is liable to conflict with what we seem to think in particular cases. (Many philosophical issues are like this.) I will only touch on it here by considering an example.

In many cases people clearly do regard themselves as bound by the decisions of earlier generations. Take the Constitution of the United States of America. That represented a compromise between many different interests at the time of the Declaration of Independence. Safeguards were written into it to allay the fears of some (certain of the states for instance) of having their interests trampled on by an overall majority. In that respect the Constitution could be regarded as a sort of promise to those who feared for their interests from those who might find themselves in a position to damage those interests, that they would not do so without formal consultation on a revision of the original undertakings (I mean the provisions for constitutional amendment). The Founding Fathers are long dead; but would not most Americans, on reflection, regard themselves as bound by the original promises, unless these had been rescinded or modified in the agreed way?

Perhaps the example rests too much on the fact that there is machinery for enforcing the original Constitution. (A Hobbesist consideration.) In reply someone might point to the treaties between white Americans and Indians, which interested parties have certainly often not scrupled to ignore when they could get away with it. That, however, is not to the point – it would be perhaps to the point if the argument were with Hobbes, but not with Locke: and therein lies the difference between them. Locke is interested in the right of the matter. And can we not say that those latter-day Americans who broke their ancestors' treaties with Indians did the latter wrong? And again it is not exactly to the point whether someone does want to say it or not. The point is: it can be said, and intelligibly said.

The question of 'onus'. If the inclination to say the above conflicts with an idea we have of what practical rationality must consist in, which is to give way? Some philosophers (R. M. Hare, for instance) will often say that what we are inclined to say in the particular case has no particular authority, though it may perhaps deserve to occasion a pause for reflection. What really counts, they will say, is what we can determine on purely rational grounds. – But then questions can be raised about where we tend to find rationality. Others talk about a 'balanced equilibrium'[43] between the demands of 'theory', and our 'intuitions' (a word I dislike). My own inclination is to suppose that it is 'theory' that is most likely to be wrong in such matters. Just look at the history of philosophy! But I expect that is an unbalanced opinion! I will leave it to you. The most important thing, I believe, is that you recognise it as a genuine issue.

The second point I raised concerned the relation between the exercise of authority (e.g. by parents over their children) and rationality. Locke, as we saw, regards it as having a purely protective function: enabling the child to grow up in safety while his rational faculties spontaneously mature.

I believe that is an impoverished conception. It does not do justice either to the positive role of education in the development of rational faculties (Rousseau is good on that),[44] or to the role of authority in the process of education itself. By 'the role of authority in the process of education' I mean the kind of authority exercised when a child is taught the correct way to do things. 'The correct way' usually, or at least often, means the accepted way: something on which the teacher is an authority. I say some things about this, though not very well, in an old paper called 'Authority', reprinted in A. Quinton: *Political Philosophy* (Oxford University Paperback) [97–111].

Lecture 16

I turn now to a different question I raised in my last lecture: why should someone in a state of nature want to submit himself to civil authority? As we have seen, Hobbes has a clear answer to this, whether we accept it or not. Locke may give the impression of speaking from both sides of his mouth. On the one hand, he claims that the state of nature is not a state of war; because people in it have and recognise reciprocal rights and duties. On the other hand, he thinks that, left to itself, the state of nature easily degenerates into a state of war. The reason for this is that there is, by definition, no one in the state of nature with the authority to settle disputes that arise about rights etc. or to enforce any settlement. So each man is policeman and judge in his own cause; because of the natural partiality of individuals to him or herself peace will be fragile and impermanent.

It may look as though there is not all that much difference between Hobbes and Locke. And if we look at it from what I earlier called the 'sociological' perspective (i.e. roughly, in terms of what is likely to happen) perhaps there isn't. But there is a

---

43. Eds: Presumably a reference to reflective equilibrium in Rawls.
44. Eds: See Peter Winch, 'Man and Society in Hobbes and Rousseau', in *Ethics and Action* (London: Routledge and Kegan Paul, 1972), 90–109.

big philosophical difference; i.e. in respect of what each thinks it makes sense to say, what concepts are applicable, for people living in a state of nature. As far as Locke is concerned, however depraved people are, they have the means of recognising their depravity – because they have within them the law of nature by which to judge.

Incidentally there is often dispute about whether Hobbes thought of his 'natural' men as wicked and depraved. He himself denied this, saying that the desires and inclinations of people 'are no sin' 'unless there be a law' to judge them; which there is not in the absence of the state. It is not so entirely clear that this argument succeeds. Some might argue that the inability even to recognise (and perhaps feel remorse for) the harm one is doing adds an extra dimension of wickedness. But I will not pursue that. Perhaps it doesn't much matter.

What about Locke's remarks about majority rule?[45] Notice first the distinction he makes between the unanimity required for the original agreement and the acceptance of rule by the majority subsequently to it. Unanimity is required originally, of course, because a route has to be found to the will of each individual in order to establish legitimate authority over him. It can't be in any sense imposed upon any individual. The original terms of the problem make that impossible.

Lecture 17

I think it's important to recognise that the argument by which Locke seeks to establish majority rule as the only legitimate method of government for a civil society is completely fallacious. It's important for the following reason. Contemporary accepted Western political ideology tends to agree with Locke's conclusion. I have nothing to say about that – not at least in the present context. Maybe majority rule is the best method of government and maybe there are good arguments for it. But they are not arguments which can be drawn from the nature of government as such: at least Locke's attempt to do this fails.

N.B. *The above is a completely wrong interpretation of Locke! Though the general point holds.*[46]

---

45. Eds: Winch references a handout ('in the second of the excerpts I copied for you'). This is presumably the famous passage Section 96 of the *Second Treatise*:

    For when any number of Men have, by the consent of every individual, made a Community, they have thereby made that Community one Body, with a Power to Act as one Body, which is only by the will and determination of the majority. For that which acts any Community, being only the consent of the individuals of it, and it being necessary to that which is one body to move one way; it is necessary the Body should move that way whither the greater force carries it, which is the consent of the majority: or else it is impossible it should act or continue one Body, one Community, which the consent of every individual that united into it, agreed that it should; and so every one is bound by that consent to be concluded by the majority.

46. Eds: Winch is presumably referring to an argument he made in lecturing, as the notes do not make clear what argument he ascribed to Locke for majority rule.

What he is justified in saying is that, for there to be a genuine agreement to form a civil society, there must be general acceptance of some method of making public decisions. But that is all. Nothing so far follows concerning the necessity of one particular method rather than others. (Property qualifications, e.g. – as certainly in Locke's own day; mandarinism; lot (ancient Athens); hereditary aristocracy, etc.). This is not (N.B.) an argument to the effect that no one method is better than any other. All that's at issue is the compatibility of many, many diverse methods with the nature of civil society.

Lecture 18

Now let's come back to the notion of 'tacit consent', which is the subject of the last quotation from Locke on the handout and also of Hume's 'Of the Original Contract' (of which also you have excerpts). Let's make explicit the obvious fact that Locke's purpose, in speaking of the origin of state authority as lying in the consent of the citizens, was not as it were to design a blueprint for some ideal future society. He wanted to make clear the nature and foundation of authority in civil society as we know it. That is clear from the opening sentences of the *Second Treatise*.

But now it is clear that Locke is in a dilemma. On the one hand it would clearly have been useless to pretend that civil authority depends on some explicit act of consent on the part of the citizen. It would be immediately obvious that this would have no application to actual states (most of them at least, including, most importantly, Hanoverian Britain). But on the other hand, the whole theory would clearly be equally useless if it did not make possible some discrimination between those powers exercising, and those not exercising, legitimate authority. The theory is supposed to be of use to a person asking himself whether he owes anyone allegiance, and if so to whom; so it must allow him to discriminate from cases where he does and cases where he does not, owe such allegiance. The answer Locke gives is that he owes allegiance to what he has consented to give allegiance. So now the citizen needs to know to whom or what he has and has not so consented. He needs criteria.

The final passage in my selection from Locke shows him struggling with this dilemma; and, you might say, seems to show him giving up the struggle:

> Section 119. Every man being, as has been shewed, naturally free, and nothing being able to put him into subjection to any earthly power, but only his own consent; it is to be considered, what shall be understood to be a sufficient declaration of a man's consent, to make him subject to the laws of any government. There is a common distinction of an express and a tacit consent, which will concern our present case. No body doubts but an express consent, of any man entering into any society, makes him a perfect member of that society, a subject of that government. The difficulty is, what ought to be looked upon as a tacit consent, and how far it binds, i.e. how far any one shall be looked on to have consented, and thereby submitted to any government, where he has made no expressions of it at all. And to this I say, that every man, that hath any possessions, or enjoyment, of any part of the dominions of any government, doth thereby give his tacit consent, and is as far forth obliged to obedience to the laws of that government, during such enjoyment,

as any one under it; whether this his possession be of land, to him and his heirs for ever, or a lodging only for a week; or whether it be barely travelling freely on the highway; and in effect, it reaches as far as the very being of any one within the territories of that government.

The final sentence starts with a criterion which does indeed discriminate ('every man that has any possessions or enjoyment of any part of the dominions of any government'). But this will clearly not cover all those whom Locke wants covered. So it is rapidly weakened, through having 'a lodging only for a week' and 'barely traveling freely on the highway' until at last 'it reaches as far as the very being of anyone within the territories of that government'.

This at least provides the occasion for some innocent polemical fun on the part of Hume, for which we must be grateful. I needn't linger on Hume's decisive lampooning (I like especially the comparison with the press-ganged mariner).

There is, however, a point about Locke's 'argument' which Hume does not make explicitly (though his essay shows him well aware of the issue) and which is important enough to be worth noticing. We may want to agree that someone who is within the territories of a given state is, in normal circumstances, subject to the laws and the political authorities of that state for as long as he is there. And whether you want to agree or not, that is certainly the view that will be taken by the civil authorities and enforced by the domestic legal agencies. But this of course presupposes that it is already possible to recognise where legitimate legal and political authority lies within the territories in question. I.e. given the existence of a legitimate authority, then I am bound to defer to it if I am within the boundaries of its legitimate exercise.

But this is really no use for Locke, who is trying to give an account of what makes the exercise of power and command a case of legitimate authority. Now it might be said that if I find myself on alien territory then I can recognise where authority lies through the behaviour of the local inhabitants. And it might even be claimed that, in normal circumstances, I do have an obligation to respect the authority which the local inhabitants respect.

Lecture 19

I have been asked to say something about Macpherson's Introduction to Locke's *Second Treatise*,[47] since some of you are apparently puzzled by the difference between his treatment and mine. I will do that,[48] but not quite yet. I want to finish my train of thought first.

I was discussing tacit consent, as allegedly evidenced by simple territorial presence. Locke himself insists that *in the first instance* there has to be *unanimity* on the part of the people who are to become citizens. The point, in terms of my own discussion, is that

---

47. Eds: C. B. Macpherson, 'Introduction', to John Locke, *Second Treatise of Government* (Harmondsworth: Penguin Books, 1966), vii–xii.
48. Eds: See Lecture 20.

the original source of any genuine authority over an individual has to be the will of that individual. So no individual can, as it were, get from anyone else information about where authority lies. It isn't for Locke a question of 'getting information'; it is a question of a personal *commitment*. Clearly this is why he tries to interpolate 'tacit consent' between physical presence and duty to obey.

I have stated this narrowly, as a problem for Locke, as indeed it is. But it's actually a problem for anyone. What is involved here is a very fundamental and difficult set of questions about the nature of an individual's membership of a human community. All the difficulties we have encountered seem to spring from regarding that as simply a relation 'to an environment' – I mean in the sense of a stage on which the individual is placed and on which there are other things and people the behaviour of which he has to take account of. But it's becoming clear that this image does not adequately render what we understand by 'living in a human community'. Some further reflections on the notion of tacit consent may help to take us deeper into this issue.

One last point. Locke's excesses have (*inter alia*) led some people to reject the notion of 'tacit consent' altogether as a fiction. An example is John Plamenatz in *Consent, Freedom and Political Obligation*.[49] His view was repeated, and somewhat modified – though I don't think substantially changed – in later works.

This seems to me a bad mistake. Examples.

Explicit consent actually presupposes the existence of relation[s] of 'tacit consent' like the above. My criticisms of Hobbes's account of covenant turned on a closely analogous point.

> I may now ask on what foundation the prince's title stands? Not on popular consent surely; for though the people willingly acquiesce in his authority, they never imagine that their consent made him sovereign. They consent because they apprehend him to be already, by birth, their lawful sovereign. And as to tacit consent, which may now be inferred from their living under his dominion, this is no more than what they formerly gave to the tyrant and usurper.[50]

Hume seems to me to keep his balance beautifully here between opposing pressures. On the one hand he recognises the difference between the attitude of the people towards the usurper and towards the prince recognised as lawful. He expresses this difference by retaining the notion of consent (in the sentence I emphasised). But that consent is only intelligible as long as we place it within the context of institutions, practices and ways of thinking which involve a distinction between the 'lawful' and the 'unlawful'. That distinction does not spring from consent. It is a feature of the institutions which belong to the lives these people live. But of course it is important that they do live these lives: and it is important that their lives, in general, exhibit a certain quality.

---

49. Eds: Oxford, Oxford University Press, 1968.
50. David Hume, 'Of the Original Contract', 53.

These are matters which are beautifully brought out in some of the writings of Simone Weil. See '*Luttons-nous pour la justice?*' and '*La légitimité du gouvernement provisoire*', both from the volume of *Écrits de Londres*.[51]

If now we hold both these points together in our minds, I think we can see how good Hume's discussion is on this point. See his description of the people who welcome back their 'lawful prince' after the ejection of the usurper. The sort of relation exhibited in these examples of 'tacit consent' seems to me to be *presupposed* by explicit consent. (My criticisms of Hobbes largely revolved round an analogous point.)

Lecture 20

Interlude on Macpherson:[52]

- 'professedly written only to justify a particular constitutional revolution in late seventeenth-century England…' (p. vii)
- 'Locke's cause was decidedly the winner' (p. vii)
- 'Locke's case for the limited constitutional state is largely designed to support his argument for an individual natural right to unlimited private property.' (p. vii)
- 'Locke's fundamental ambiguity about human nature.'
- 'individuals must be understood to have agreed to give up their natural rights and powers[53] to an all-powerful civil society'
- but this society 'could not conceivably have delegated absolute or arbitrary power to any government…' (p. xiv)
- In a state of nature 'men's power is said to be limited to what they need to enforce the moral law of nature which is explicitly not arbitrary power.'
- But 'there are some men who do not obey the moral law, that is, who do exercise arbitrary power, so there is arbitrary power to be handed over.'[54] (p. xv)
- Property in the state of nature[55]
- 'extensive system of markets, commerce, wage-labour, and accumulation… attributed to the state of nature' (p. xviii)

---

51. Simone Weil, 'Are We Struggling for Justice?' trans. Marina Barabas, *Philosophical Investigations* 10, no. 1 (1987): 1–10; 'The Legitimacy of the Provisional Government', trans. Peter Winch, *Philosophical Investigations* 10, no. 2 (1987): 87–98.
52. Eds: Winch was responding to the students' questions by discussing this list of quotes from Macpherson. His line of thought is reconstructed in footnotes from Reid's notes.
53. Marginal note: N.B. 'rights' and 'powers'. [Eds: Presumably intended to highlight what he saw as the illicit inference from powers human beings possess in the state of nature to the right to exercise those powers.]
54. (!) (sic)
55. Marginal notes: Locke … 'tacit agreement' in value; 'by consent' right to 'larger possessions'. Labour: 'mixing [is the] source of private possessions; source of value. Labour → capital (→ power (Marx). (Ambiguity in Locke's use of 'property' (life, liberty, and property).)
[Cf. the 'Lectures on Locke on Property', above, Chapter 1.5.]

- Locke has 'read back into the state of nature a class division' (p. xviii)
- state of nature 'divided into two stages, before and after the introduction of money and inequality' (p. xix)[56]

Let us now turn to Hume's second 'more regular, at least... more philosophical, refutation'[57] of Locke. Allegiance to the state, Hume argues, is 'artificial', in the sense

---

56. Eds: According to Reid's notes from the time, the substance of the discussion was that Macpherson treats the whole of Locke's theory as a consequence of what Macpherson holds to be an ambiguity about human nature in Locke, and of Locke's account of property rights. Winch thought there was more to Locke than this, and in general he was attempting to get the class past the simple idea that a philosopher's assumptions about human psychology (what individuals happen to be like) determine their account of the state. Rather, his focus was on a question that is perhaps related, but importantly different. Namely, his focus was on an understanding of rational agency that makes the very idea of obedience unintelligible.

Winch set the stage by contextualizing Locke's 'almost metabolic' justification of natural property rights in a certain system of production and exchange (barter for sustenance). Locke's account is that the tendency of goods to spoil leads to the introduction of money (which doesn't spoil – obviously Locke was not considering inflation) and the growth of accumulation. This changes the whole picture: there is growth of a certain kind of power exercised by one group of people over another. (He mentioned in this context Marx, and Rousseau's essay 'On the Origins of Inequality in Society'.) The complexity of a moneyed system of exchange leads to concentrations of power to which people are subject but have not consented. Rousseau thought such power was illegitimate: the purpose of the state was to overcome that and legitimate this illegitimate power. Macpherson traces out the two stages in the state of nature – two states of nature – before and after inequality. On p. xv in particular, Macpherson tries to argue that Locke is inconsistent in appearing to offer a contractualist account of limited government while in fact requiring that the contractors hand over everything to an all-powerful civil society. Winch highlights that Macpherson invented the argument (found nowhere in Locke, hence Winch's exclamation point) that since some people don't respect the law of nature and do attempt to exercise arbitrary power over others, 'there is arbitrary power to be handed over'. Furthermore, that arbitrary power is characterized by Macpherson entirely in terms of the growth of inequality through the role that money plays in a society, which seems to conflate avariciousness – accumulating more than others have – with dominance and oppression. Winch thinks Macpherson doesn't get the crucial philosophical difference between predicting what would happen (given a certain psychological make-up of persons) and distinguishing what one does and does not have the conceptual resources to say in describing the situation. Winch emphasizes that what Locke is doing with private property and the blindness he shows to his own class assumptions are important matters, and the transformation between the two states of nature before and after inequality has been discussed by later authors – but Winch doesn't agree that the whole of Locke's argument flows from his views about how money can exist and accumulate in Locke's state of nature. He briefly commented on Rousseau's criticism – that you can't talk about property in the state of nature because you'd be talking about a form of power to which no consent would be given; and Marx's – that economic power *is* a reality and the political conferral of legitimacy is often nothing more than a show.

57. Eds: David Hume, 'Of the Original Contract', 54 ff.

that it is not something that people have a natural impulse towards, as they do, for instance, towards caring for their children, their mate, their friends.[58]

Lecture 21

Hume: Justice as an 'artificial' virtue.[59]

Positively, he characterises such 'duties' as springing from 'a sense of obligation, when we consider the necessities of human society and the impossibility of supporting it if these duties were neglected.' Let us leave aside the last bit, as involving a theory of Hume's that we need not try to evaluate at this point. The point we can work on is the idea that the 'sense of obligation' involved here is something that results from the peculiarities of life in society. We need not ask whether it arises from reflection on those peculiarities, or in a more immediate way.

What is striking about such 'obligations' is that when they are recognised, people will often act in a way which conflicts, perhaps quite radically, with their natural propensities. I.e. people will do things, under the influence of these 'obligations' which they would not do if they were simply rationally pursuing their own interests, *even if we include in those 'interests' concern for the welfare of (certain selected) others.*[60]

The notion of an 'original contract' or of 'consent', Hume argues, is introduced in order to explain why people *should* act like this, why they *should* acknowledge such 'obligations', and that means, in this context, why it is *rational* for them to do so. But, he continues, it cannot in principle provide such an explanation because it has exactly the same sort of puzzling character itself. If someone acts out of respect for an agreement he has committed himself to, that may involve him in neglecting the pursuit of his own concerns in just the same way as may respecting the authority of a sovereign. So the fundamental difficulty has not been addressed.

What is the fundamental difficulty? It is that of seeing how one's will, in the circumstances one is placed in at present can be 'bound', restricted in its exercise not in the sense of being constrained by circumstances, but in the sense that one somehow voluntarily accepts these constraints oneself. (Kant reacted to the same problem when he talked of the moral will as being 'self-legislating'.) The difficulty is in seeing how the will can bind itself.

It is a conceptual difficulty, not, as it were, one of envisaging a certain degree of mental agility. One might of course decide to go along with one's earlier decisions and keep to that decision; but how can one be 'bound' to it? All one needs to do, apparently,

---

58. Eds: Apparently students' interest in Macpherson and Winch's expansion on topics indicated in his marginalia took up more time than anticipated, as virtually all of the content of Lecture 21 was optimistically included in Lecture 20 (and then repeated for Lecture 21).
59. Eds: David Hume, *Treatise of Human Nature*, Book III, Part II, Section I.
60. Eds: The example in lecture was that justice might require protecting the property rights of one person against another who in fact has much greater need of what the first owns, and against one's own sense of benevolence that one would like to see the property given.

is to change one's mind. How can 'voluntary constraints' be counted as genuine constraints? Hobbes might have commented that we are dealing with fictions here. The trouble with that of course is that Hobbes himself needs something like the notion of being bound by one's word. (He tries to obtain it, you remember, through the analogy between 'injustice' and 'absurdity'.) That he can't get it is precisely the major difficulty in the way of accepting his 'covenant'.

What exactly, then, is the difference between Hume and Locke here? It lies in the fact that Locke recognises the difficulty only where someone is thus bound by the will of another; whereas Hume thinks the same difficulty exists where someone is bound by his or her own past will. The question now arises whether Hume is right to think these difficulties the same.

It's relevant to mention here – though we can't go into it properly – that Hume had distinctive ideas about personal identity. He could not see any genuine identity between the state of what we call 'the same person' at two different times.[61] This being the case, it is of course understandable that he should see the same sort of radical difficulty in the case of a person's being bound by his or her 'own' past will as in that of a person's being bound by someone else's will. Since, on his view, the past will is one's 'own' only by courtesy of a fiction.

Locke also struggled with the problem of personal identity and, relevantly to our problem, connected it intimately with our practices of assigning responsibility for actions. But he did not share Hume's rather radical scepticism about the notion. So it was natural for him to distinguish the two cases: in which one is 'bound' by someone else's, and one's own past, will respectively.

It is a curious situation. Hume, with his radical scepticism about personal identity: i.e. about the continuity between a person's present self and his or her past self (a scepticism which makes even that way of putting the position impossible!) stressed the historical character and the continuity involved in the notion of 'legitimacy'. Whereas Locke, seeking a strong sense of personal identity, wants to make the conception of legitimacy quite ahistorical: something generated anew by and for each generation. But Hume of course was very conscious of the (social and political) power of what he regarded as 'fictions'.

I say that Locke was 'seeking' a strong sense of personal identity. But he hardly found one. The sense of the notion as it occurs in discussions of rights and responsibilities, he seems to argue, is independent of any particular resolution of the metaphysical difficulties about identity with which both he and Hume wrestled. It is a 'forensic' notion; and maybe this is not so far from Hume's conception of it as a fiction, a product of the workings of the imagination. – For when Hume talks in this way, he does not regard those workings as random: they are conditioned and given direction by the exigencies of human life in society.

---

61. Cf. Derek Parfit. [Eds: Winch probably has in mind Parfit's theory in his *Reasons and Persons* (Oxford: Oxford University Press, 1984)]

Lecture 22

I am going to leave discussion of Locke and Hume now. We have been brought to a point which is a useful springboard for the next phase of the discussion. What has come to the fore is the problematic character of the conception of continuity; and the interplay between difficulties concerning what sort of continuity to ascribe to the life of a society, the institutions of a state, and the life of an individual. One great merit of the difficulties in what Locke and Hume say, it seems to me, is the way in which they bring these questions together, without, perhaps, getting very close to a satisfactory settlement of them.

The 'problem of continuity' rightly has a central place in Hart's discussion of the concept of law; and I want now to turn to this. I want to shift my main focus back to the concept of law now. I shall use Hart's book *The Concept of Law*[62] as my point of reference. And first I shall try to locate Hart's discussion in relation to my own preceding one.

As I have done, Hart takes the 'positivist' theory of law (Austin, derived from Hobbes via Bentham) as his starting point.[63] And his criticisms of positivism run parallel to my own for quite some distance. Hart's main objection to Austinianism is that the notion of a habit of obedience on the part of subjects to the commands of a sovereign who does not himself habitually obey anyone is inadequate to our understanding of what law is in various related ways; and that it has to be modified by giving a central place to the concept of a rule.

You remember that I distinguished what I called the 'sociological' and the 'philosophical' perspectives on these questions, characterising the first as an interest in power structures, the second as an interest in people's reasons for acting. My own foregoing discussion has been entirely from the 'philosophical' perspective. Hart makes a somewhat similar point, though with a different emphasis, when he says that the positivist interest is in description, explanation and prediction of what does and will happen; and that notions like that of a 'habit of obedience' are adapted to that interest; whereas the notion of a 'rule' introduces the idea of a justification or reason for what one does. It's important to this point that those whose behaviour is governed by rules themselves appeal to those rules in making their decisions, justifying what they do, criticising what others do, and so on.[64]

This is parallel to something I want to bring out in my own discussion, concerning the spontaneity of someone who accepts legitimate authority. This point applies both to state authority, and also, in a general way, to people's attitude to the law. When someone decides not to do something, or urges someone else not to do something, because it's 'against the law', the interest is not just in predicting what will happen if the forbidden act is nevertheless done; the law itself (the rule) is thought of as having

---

62. Eds: H. L. A. Hart, *The Concept of Law* (Oxford: Oxford University Press, 1961).
63. Eds: Winch once commented to Reid that while Ryle was his supervisor at Oxford, he was everyone's supervisor at that time; Hart was a greater influence.
64. Eds: In Reid's notes he emphasizes that there is not a hard and fast distinction between 'habit' and 'rule'.

authority. Similarly, someone may be criticised for having acted against the law; and an unpopular course of conduct may be justified as having been required by law. In such cases, the relation of the citizen to the law (or the state) is not that of someone being coerced by an external agency. He or she is, in a way, participating in the institution: by using in his or her own practical reasoning concepts or considerations which have their home in those institutions and draw their sense from them. Consequences (e.g. the imposition of sanctions) certainly constitute the normal background of these ways of thinking and speaking; but that is not what is being spoken or thought of – or at least it need not be.

With what I was saying last time as a background, I should like now to focus on what Hart says about the concept of obligation. Let me just run through this, before making my comments. Hart argues (I think rightly) that the Hobbes/Austin positivist account of law involves a confusion between the notions of 'being obliged' and 'being under an obligation'. If I say I am obliged to do something, I may mean the same as 'I am under an obligation to do it'; but I may also mean something quite different, namely that I am compelled to do it. 'I was obliged to hand over my money to him; he was holding a knife at my throat.' Here I am clearly not saying that I was under any obligation to hand the money over. (While, as I said, 'being obliged' is sometimes used in the sense of 'being under an obligation', the converse does not seem to be true. I do not say 'I am under an obligation to do such and such' meaning that I am being compelled to do it.) Austin's view is that being under a legal obligation consists in its being probable that I shall suffer sanctions if I don't do what the law requires. – But while I can say: 'I am obliged to do that; I shall be sent to prison if I don't'; it's odd to say; 'I am under a legal obligation to do that; I shall be sent to prison if I don't',[65] even though both parts of the statement may be true. For I am still under a legal obligation (if I am at all), even if there is no chance whatever of my being sent to prison. The way to determine whether I am under a legal obligation is not to calculate my chances of being sent to prison.

> The fundamental objection is that the predictive interpretation obscures the fact that, where rules exist, deviations from them are not merely grounds for a prediction that hostile reactions will follow or that a court will apply sanctions to those who break them, but are also a reason or justification for such reaction and for applying the sanctions.[66]

In line with what we've already discussed Hart argues (again, I think, rightly) that in order to make these notions of 'reason' and 'justification' intelligible, we need a notion of following a rule, which is absent from the positivist apparatus. But of course, as he notes:

> The statement that someone has or is under an obligation does indeed imply the existence of a rule; yet it is not always the case that where rules exist the standard of behaviour required

---

65. Eds: The implication here seems to be that it would be odd to say this if the clause after the semi-colon were to be taken (as Hart takes it) as glossing (in the sense of both explaining and justifying) the subject's being 'under a legal obligation'.
66. Hart, *The Concept of Law*, 82.

by them is conceived of in terms of obligation. 'He ought to have' and 'He had an obligation to' are not always interchangeable expressions, even though they are alike in carrying an implicit reference to existing standards of conduct or are used in drawing conclusions from a general rule.[67]

It is at this point that something seems to me to go wrong with Hart's account of obligations. Let me quote two paragraphs *in extenso*:

> Rules are conceived and spoken of as imposing obligations when the general demand for conformity is insistent and the social pressure brought to bear upon those who deviate or threaten to deviate is great. Such rules may be wholly customary in origin: there may be no centrally organised system of punishments for breach of the rules; the social pressure may take only the form of a general diffused hostile or critical reaction which may stop short of physical sanctions. It may be limited to verbal manifestations of disapproval or of appeals to the individual's respect for the rule violated; it may depend heavily on the operations of shame, remorse, and guilt. When the pressure is of this last-mentioned kind we may be inclined to classify the rules as part of the morality of the social group and the obligation under the rules as moral obligation. Conversely, when physical sanctions are prominent or usual among the forms of pressure, even though these are neither closely defined nor administered by officials but are left to the community at large we shall be inclined to classify the rules as a primitive or rudimentary form of law. We may, of course, find both these types of serious social pressure behind what is, in an obvious sense, the same rule of conduct; sometimes this may occur with no indication that one of them is peculiarly appropriate as primary and the other secondary, and then the question whether we are confronted with a rule of morality or rudimentary law may not be susceptible of an answer. But for the moment the possibility of drawing the line between law and morals need not detain us. What is important is that the insistence on importance or *seriousness* of social pressure behind the rules is the primary factor determining whether they are thought of as giving rise to obligations.
>
> Two other characteristics of obligation go naturally together with this primary one. The rules supported by this serious pressure are thought important because they are believed to be necessary to the maintenance of social life or some highly prized feature of it. Characteristically, rules so obviously essential as those which restrict the free use of violence are thought of in terms of obligation. So too rules which require honesty or truth or require the keeping of promises, or specify what is to be done by one who performs a distinctive role or function in the social group are thought of in terms of either 'obligation' or perhaps more often 'duty'. Secondly, it is generally recognised that the conduct required by these rules may, while benefiting others, conflict with what the person who owes the duty may wish to do. Hence obligations and duties are thought of as characteristically involving sacrifice or renunciation, and the standing possibility of conflict between obligation or duty and interest is, in all societies, among the truisms of both the lawyer and the moralist.[68]

---

67. Eds: Ibid., 85.
68. Eds: Ibid., 86–87.

Lecture 23

We were discussing Hart's attempt to elucidate the notion of obligation in terms of rules, compliance with which is enforced with 'serious' social pressure.

Of course, it's true that, in many cases, where there is a very widespread and very strong sense that certain actions are obligatory, that will be manifested in 'social pressure' of one form or another on individuals who are delinquent or who look as if they might become so. (I think it's a bit dangerous to lump so many things together under that rubric, but let that pass.) It's not, I think, the case that wherever there is strong social pressure the notion of obligation is prominent. Hart mentions etiquette, saying rightly, I think, that this is not characteristically a matter of obligation. But it may be subject to very strong social pressure all the same. More, sometimes, than in the case of matters involving morality. Sometimes people will care more about, say, the 'proper' dress for someone to wear than about his or her dishonesty or laxity about promises.

More importantly perhaps, what account will Hart give of those (not uncommon or outlandish) cases in which an individual will feel him or herself under an obligation in the face of a strongly critical social consensus? One of the most difficult of one's obligations may be to resist such pressure. (Cf. Plato's treatment of the 'perfectly just' man who everywhere has the reputation of injustice: *Republic*, Book II; also Christ.) This is connected with the way Hart treats notions like shame, remorse and guilt. He writes as though these are, as it were, instruments of social pressure. Of course they may be. That is more likely, maybe in the cases of shame and guilt – so it is often said anyway. But I don't think remorse will fit into this picture. One may feel remorse over something which the common run of mankind doesn't feel particularly strongly about; one may indeed be urged on all sides to 'snap out of it'. That's a not-uncommon situation.

There is in Hart's treatment of this topic too much of an air of the individual as the object of a pressure exerted by others. He does, it is true, pull back from one brink on page 85, when he warns us of the danger of being trapped into a misleading conception of obligation as essentially consisting in some feeling of pressure or compulsion experienced by those who have obligations.

But what he is here (rightly) resisting is the psychologising of the notion of being under an obligation – identifying it with feeling obliged – and that is not quite my point. More to the point is his emphasis on the 'internal aspect' of rules; i.e. the way they are actually appealed to by agents in justification of how they behave or propose to behave, etc. But it isn't altogether clear to me how precisely he thinks this is to be applied in the special case of being under an obligation. My thought that I am under an obligation is not, as he says, a feeling of being obliged by social pressure; nor, I take it, is it the thought that this is something people feel strongly about. (That last may of course be part of my reason for thinking I'm under an obligation, but is certainly not identical with it.)

I can't see that Hart gives any answer to the question how social pressure is related to the notion of obligation. And he seems to me to commit a *hysteron proteron* (or, less pompously, to put the cart before the horse). Where people think something is a matter of obligation they are likely to exert social pressure on its observance – though, as I've said, not always. But that pressure cannot be called on to elucidate the concept in the way Hart believes.

What is in general wrong here it seems to me is his conception of the relation between the individual and the community. I will say more about this.

Some of the discussions which take place of 'natural law theory' from the side of 'legal positivism'. There are two main points I want to make.

It shouldn't be assumed that the question: 'Does this or that have the force of law?' has an unambiguous sense. It is for instance different when addressed by a client to a lawyer and when raised by a citizen who feels that the legislation enacted by the regime has passed certain limits of acceptability. It does not quite make the position clear to say that the latter question amounts to: 'Am I morally bound to conform to this law?' It is possible to distinguish the case in hand from cases which could be described in that way.

It seriously undervalues the resources of the natural law tradition to suppose that all (or even the main thing) it has to say is that a law which contravenes morality is no law. It points to other important issues concerning the relation between the authority of law and morality which positivism tends to underplay.

Law as union of primary and secondary rules.

A. Exposition.
B. Hart's modified positivism: He still looks at the law very much from the point of view of a lawyer; but the law is what it is just as much because of the role it plays in the lives of *citizens* who are not lawyers. One might speak here of a 'system of tertiary rules' except that 'rule' is the wrong word to use here. The 'authority' of the law (cf. 'majesty') is a function of that authority.
C. Here we are wandering into the natural law camp.[69]

---

69. Eds: Reid's lecture notes fill out this outline as follows. Primary rules: rules or norms of conduct. E.g. moral rules and standards. They change over time. Try this: a natural historical process, slowly; or rapidly (in war and revolution). Nothing like an explicit mechanism for changing such rules. (Like there is for amendments of laws.) In a typical legal system, there is an authoritative way of discovering what the law actually is. This is important for continuity. This is an advance over Austin's primitive positivism. What exactly is Hart's relation to the traditional conflict between Austin and Aquinas (positivism and natural law)? 'Positivism and the separation of law and morals' – Hart comes down on the side of positivism. 'There is a sense in which the existence of a law is a matter of fact.' The question in legal practice of the relevance of moral questions or social policy. (Bork [whose nomination to the Supreme Court by Reagan was defeated in this period]: hostile to considerations of social policy; meanings of words and intentions of legislators... A sea plane violating the speed limit in a harbour. The courts have to decide if a sea plane is a vessel. Trying to determine what the legislature intended about sea planes is ridiculous (the law being passed before there were any). You have to raise general questions about the purpose of the law, and make a judgment about how best to further those purposes in the current context. Attitudes about what ought to be have played a role in the decisions of the SC. But those decisions have been made: that's what the law is. Questions can be raised about whether it's a good law or not. Whether it ought to have been passed. That's another question. Hart is partly emphasizing that. (American legal realists [neo-positivists] – you don't have a law until a judge has made a decision.) 'Rule skepticism.' Hart's discussion brings into the open the fact that the question of 'what the law is' is something that has a different significance in different contexts. 'What

Lecture 24

I want now to discuss another issue concerned with the relation of law to morality: to what extent is it the business of the law to enforce a generally accepted morality? This is certainly a question we ought to discuss; though I am suspicious of it. Suspicious, that is to say, of the extent to which its discussion properly belongs to philosophy. There are genuine divisions of opinion about this; and it is by no means that there is such a thing as a 'correct' resolution of those divisions discoverable by philosophical reasoning. What I think one can fairly expect from a philosophical discussion here is some clarification of the issues involved and a pointer towards characteristic muddles in argument about them.

It is obvious that not all laws are attempts to enforce what are regarded as moral principles. Many are there for the sake of practical expediency. An obvious example would be traffic regulation. Here, the content of the regulation has no moral weight at all. And the case for there being any sort of regulation is hardly a moral one. It is simply that there would be chaos, and heavy motorised traffic would be impossible, in the absence of regulation. Again, most taxation laws are without (obvious, at any rate) intrinsic moral force; they are there to serve the needs and expediencies of government. Many laws are enacted in the service of a particular political program or ideology. There may often be something that we should want to call a 'moral' impetus behind

---

is the right decision?' The judge asking it. Hart can draw this quasi-positivist distinction. Contrast that with the question asked when what is at stake is what sort of allegiance one has to a particular legal situation... Hart's allegiance to positivism was related to a German jurist who came to think positivism inadequate because of his experience with the Nazis. Hart's response was: however awful it is, it is still the law. Hart thinks that law is constituted by primary rules (which proscribe particular conduct) and secondary rules (for enforcing, applying, changing them). Winch suggests we could also speak of a tertiary level. Something that is missing in Hart's discussion. The law isn't merely of interest professionally, or insofar as one finds oneself in court. One's attitude to the law will be important to one's relation to the society one is living in. (Vietnam was discussed as an example.) The kind of role all this plays in the life of the community (*not* something that can be characterized in terms of rules). Natural law: it derives its validity because of its content. It deals with issues in which there is a particular importance. So Hart, in talking about the seriousness of sanctions, is nudging towards natural law. 'Is this law?' may mean different things in different contexts. Lawyer advising a client. Citizen of Germany deciding whether to harbour a Jewish person. Hart's take was: you're really asking if this system of law is morally tolerable. (Not if it's law.) In some contexts, recognizing something as the law *is* recognizing a moral force of the law – not just 'do I morally approve of it or not?' but 'is this the sort of entity I can accept as a reason for acting or not – when something says "but it's against the law"?' Legal positivism appeals to lawyers. It answers to the kind of interest lawyers have in the law. (Is my client going to be made to suffer a penalty or not?) But the law has significance beyond that. The relevance of what natural law theory says to the Nuremberg trials (where there is a dimension to our understanding that goes beyond whether they ought to have done it or not – the evil of it takes one beyond that) compared to its relevance to cases where there is serious question about 'what we ought to do' (e.g. flat tax). There's a difference.

the support of such programs; but it is pretty certain that such programs rest on many considerations that do not have much to do with morality.

Claims like these are hard to accept or reject without unease, partly because of the great unclarity as to what we are to count as deserving the epithet 'moral'. Closely connected with this is the fact that one needs to ask: '*Whose* morality?'

I think we need at this point to think about another point of general principle: what is the law up to when it declares certain kinds of conduct criminal? In raising this question we obviously have to bring into focus the law's *coercive* function: the function that is central to the legal positivist's position (with its emphasis on liability to sanctions) and to Hobbes's account of the state (with its emphasis on the power of the sword). And putting the matter like this again shows that we have to go back to consider the role of the state in all this — because it is, at least, through the power of the state that the law, in modern societies, is able to exercise a coercive function. (I ought to emphasise again that this is not an eternally necessary connection. Coercion can be exercised in certain contexts otherwise than through the power of the state. — Certain 'primitive' societies without state institutions; lynch law; vendetta. The question is not as to whether these are better or worse than enforcement by the state; the point is that they exist.)

Philosophers who have discussed the nature of the state's authority and the citizen's relation to it have of course always, and naturally, seen the state's coercive function as at least a central issue. The relation of this function to the law is multiform and has been given very different emphases. Some have seen law as a sort of emanation from the state's coercive function (Hobbes, Austin). Others have seen it as that which gives the state's coercive function its rationale (Locke). Sometimes the law has been seen as a framework within which the coercive power of the state can be tamed (Jefferson?). Maybe it's a mistake to suppose we have to make a final choice between these, or even to strike an eternally valid balance between them. These, and other, aspects will be more, or less, relevant according to the historical and sociological circumstances.

Let's consider Locke again. For him, the role of the state is essentially that of an 'umpire'. His account of the reasons for abandoning the state of nature is designed to make this point: the 'inconveniences' of that condition spring from the lack of any generally acknowledged authority to adjudicate in disputes between individuals; that becomes the role of the state.

For my present purposes at least the central feature of this account is that it makes the protection of the rights of individuals central. Indeed, Locke says that the purpose of government is to protect (individual) 'natural rights'. This is an account which seems, *prima facie*, to apply best to the role of the state in civil law. Here the disputes are between individual persons (sometimes of course, especially now, corporate 'individuals'). Action is initiated by individuals (not the state). The court adjudicates in the dispute according to the established law. The coercive power of the state stands in the background to enforce that adjudication. According to this picture the state has no interests of its own to protect. Or at least, such interests as it has are derivative from its function in protecting the lawful interests of private individuals.

This point draws attention to the fact that something like a criminal law has to stand behind the civil law seen in such terms. Because the state has to have the power to enforce the adjudication of the court. If that power is resisted, that seems to be an attack on the state itself (rather than on the interests of either of the individual disputing parties). And now of course the state will be expected to take action on its own behalf.

Locke of course also includes a function for the state in protecting its citizens against external attack. And here too the state itself must be thought to acquire derivative interests. For such protection is possible only if the citizens can be mobilised. If any citizen refuses to be thus mobilised the interests of the state (seen as deriving from this protective function) are themselves threatened and internal coercion could be justified on those grounds.

What we have here is a picture of what is these days called a 'minimalist' state. Some argue that this is the only sort of state that is actually justified. (Nozick: *Anarchy, State and Utopia*.[70]) It's important to realise, of course, that all modern states go far beyond this minimalist function in fact. Naturally, that in itself is not an objection to the minimalist position, which is self-consciously revisionary. I don't want to involve myself in general discussion of this – at least not now. But I do want to explore certain difficulties already inherent in the position as I have sketched it so far.

Now even many of those who would regard themselves as minimalists would not accept this. They would say that the criminal law itself has a more direct role in the protection of individuals. 'Crimes against the person': rape, murder, assault, fraud, theft, etc. (Not all: cf. the 'abolitionists'.) Although the state may be said to act to protect individuals, it cannot plausibly be said to be acting as an 'umpire'. It is the one that initiates action. And it will act even against the wishes of the (individual) injured party. It is almost as if it is itself the injured party. This does seem to give it 'interests' not explicable simply in terms of an 'umpiring' role.

Or is this too hasty? Perhaps it is a mistake to focus exclusively on the state's role as a court of appeal between individual conflicting parties. Because, after all, its role is essentially, even on Locke's view, a public one. We have to remember that he does think that the fact that people are judges in their own cause threatens a degeneration of the state of nature into a state of war. And the institution of civil society is supposed to prevent this. That is, civil society is not merely an agency for supporting the rights of individuals; it is also the guardian of public order. And this may be threatened even if individuals do not dispute about their respective rights. Thus the state, consistently with its Lockean purpose, may be regarded as entitled, and even duty bound, to act as itself the injured party when public order is threatened. Much of the criminal law can no doubt plausibly be regarded as having this sort of rationale.

This is still a pretty 'minimalist' conception. Modern states certainly claim far more of a role than this. E.g. in furthering political programs and social policies. (Redistributing income, providing social services, education, etc.) Of course minimalists are aware of this and would not regard it as an objection. Their case itself has the character of a reformist program. The Reagan administration is clearly influenced by such considerations: and hence seeks to change the current role of the state. However, it is one thing to pursue

---

70. Eds: Robert Nozick, *Anarchy, State and Utopia* (New York: Basic Books, 1974).

such a policy as a political program, in opposition to others. To do this is to work, as it were, within the framework of the state. It would be going a good deal further to claim that those who do not work within such a limiting framework cannot be regarded as exercising legitimate state authority at all, but as mere usurpers. (Such changes may be made as a matter of partisan political rhetoric. It would be something, very much something else, seriously to act on such a view.[71])

Lecture 25

Let's examine this notion of the 'the defense of public order' a bit more closely and also compare this rationale of criminal sanctions with others. (These two things can go together, since the nature of the public order case will be clearer if seen in contrast with the others.) There are two popular contenders in the field:

A. That the criminal law has the function of protecting people from harm done to them by others;
B. That the criminal law has the function of enforcing certain moral standards.

Obviously A is a good deal more restrictive than B, since not all moral standards have to do with inflicting harm on others. Where it stands in this regard in relation to the public order position I will consider shortly.

A differs from both B and from the public order case in being a much more individualistic perspective. It concentrates entirely on the relations between individual persons. Morality, as already noted, doesn't just concern interpersonal relations. (At least not all people think of morality that way.) And I did after all introduce the conception of public order (in connection with Locke's minimalist state) precisely to extend the law's scope beyond the mere regulation of individuals' relations with each other.

J.S. Mill states the classic, liberal, 'harm to others case.'

> The only purpose for which power can be rightfully exercised over any member of a civilized community, against his will, is to prevent harm to others.[72]

What does it mean? There are difficulties in determining the scope of 'harm to others'. In the first place it is not at all clear in many cases where the line is to be drawn between 'to oneself' and 'to others'. E.g. seat belt laws (compare the danger of rock-climbing, stunt aviation, etc.), smoking (especially in public places) and drug abuse.

---

71. Eds: According to Reid's lecture notes, Winch glossed this in the lecture by saying that these partisans 'do not, for instance, raise an army and march on Washington'. That the Republicans were embarking on a course towards this situation thirty years later was not readily apparent.
72. Eds: Mill, *On Liberty*, Chapter 1. We have supplied the quote Winch was presumably referring to with his placeholder '[quote]'.

Let's now consider whether this standard, or suggested criterion, does correspond with judgements we habitually make about criminal offences, or with our attitudes towards crimes. The clearest case of coincidence with this standard seems to be crimes against the person, such as various forms of physical assault – with murder, perhaps, at the top end of the scale. It would obviously be perverse to deny that such acts characteristically involve the infliction of serious harm on the victim; and it seems equally clear that the thought that this is so plays an important role in our attitudes towards the criminality of such acts.

Without wanting to weaken my acknowledgement of that in any way, I do all the same want to point out that there are complications; that the matter is not so altogether simple as might appear even in these clear-looking cases. One cannot, for example, make any very secure generalisations about the actual harm suffered in particular cases. There are e.g. 'blessings in disguise', sometimes in the most unlikely disguise. And not all cases of murder, e.g. do in any obvious sense involve harm to the victim. What about euthanasia, consented to and welcomed by an incurable sufferer? I put that in the form of a question, and not a rhetorical one, since people will certainly make radically different judgements about such cases. But that really reinforces my point: that the matter is not as simple as may appear.

What about property offences: theft, fraud, etc.? Again, it would be foolish to deny that, in very many cases, such acts do involve serious harm to the victim. But it's not at all clear that our attitude to the criminality of such acts follows at all closely our perceptions of harm. E.g. theft from the very rich, minor theft. Different attitudes to belongings – those who would shrug off a theft as an amusing inconvenience and those who would be shattered by it. Etc.

Of course it's open to anyone to say that the criminal law should be changed to accommodate these differences. That is an arguable position: though the sorts of changes that would be required aren't too easy to envisage at all concretely. Nor would it be at all easy to get a working agreement on what the changes should be. That at least shows that the proposed criterion is itself a controversial one, not one that can be appealed to in order to settle controversies.

Let's consider a rather different sort of difficulty about the notion of 'harm'. Many of one's actions do harm others in a sense, even though perfectly legal and morally acceptable. E.g. getting a job in competition with someone else. Almost any form of competition (e.g. in love). Etc. etc. Even where the doing of harm is deliberate, though it may be morally offensive, it isn't clear we should want to make it criminal. (E.g. cases of emotional cruelty of one sort or another.) It isn't clear that Mill would have so wanted either.

Thus, some restriction is needed. Mill suggests one such in the way he talks about people's 'interests'. This is important but itself not without its difficulties. Consider some of the things he says:

> What, then, is the rightful limit to the sovereignty of the individual over himself? Where does the authority of society begin? How much of human life should be assigned to individuality, and how much to society? Each will receive its proper share, if each has

that which more particularly concerns it. To individuality should belong the part of life in which it is chiefly the individual that is interested; to society, the part which chiefly interests society. Though society is not founded on a contract, and though no good purpose is answered by inventing a contract in order to deduce social obligations from it, every one who receives the protection of society owes a return for the benefit, and the fact of living in society renders it indispensable that each should be bound to observe a certain line of conduct towards the rest. This conduct consists first, in not injuring the interests of one another; or rather certain interests, which, either by express legal provision or by tacit understanding, ought to be considered as rights; and secondly, in each person's bearing his share (to be fixed on some equitable principle) of the labours and sacrifices incurred for defending the society or its members from injury and molestation. These conditions society is justified in enforcing at all costs to those who endeavour to withhold fulfilment. Nor is this all that society may do. The acts of an individual may be hurtful to others, or wanting in due consideration for their welfare, without going the length of violating any of their constituted rights. The offender may then be justly punished by opinion, though not by law. As soon as any part of a person's conduct affects prejudicially the interests of others, society has jurisdiction over it, and the question whether the general welfare will or will not be promoted by interfering with it, becomes open to discussion. But there is no room for entertaining any such question when a person's conduct affects the interests of no persons besides himself, or needs not affect them unless they like (all the persons concerned being of full age, and the ordinary amount of understanding). In all such cases there should be perfect freedom, legal and social, to do the action and stand the consequences... But neither one person, nor any number of persons, is warranted in saying to another human creature of ripe years, that he shall not do with his life for his own benefit what he chooses to do with it. He is the person most interested in his own well-being: the interest which any other person, except in cases of strong personal attachment, can have in it is trifling, compared with that which he himself has; the interest which society has in him individually (except as to his conduct to others) is fractional, and altogether indirect: while, with respect to his own feelings and circumstances, the most ordinary man or woman has means of knowledge immeasurably surpassing those that can be possessed by anyone else. The interference of society to overrule his judgement and purposes in what only regards himself, must be grounded on general presumptions; which may be altogether wrong, and even if right, are as like as not to misapplied in individual cases, by persons no better acquainted with the circumstances of such cases than those are who look at them merely from without.[73]

A complication in this passage that I won't dwell on but which deserves mention is that Mill discusses together (though he does distinguish) the right to make certain conduct illegal and subject it to criminal penalty and the right 'of society' to punish such conduct by public opinion. He's obviously right to take the latter seriously, as 'the tyranny of public opinion' is no mere phrase.

But on the other hand, it's not easy to make quite clear what one is talking about here. Presumably we're not just talking about a right to disapprove of conduct we find disgraceful. It would be quite against Mill's position to suggest restrictions on that – or

---

73. Feinberg and Gross (2nd ed.), 182 ff.

even on expressions of disapproval. He is speaking, one must assume, of behaviour which goes beyond the mere voicing of opinion; such as public ridicule, ostracism, the kind of excommunication said to be practised, e.g. by the Amish in dealing with those who stray from the faith. And of course there are many ways in which the expression of opinion itself may become very seriously oppressive. (Murdoch-style journalism.)

But the main trouble here is that in deciding what is and what is not a (legitimate) interest it looks as though one will already have made much of the important decision that this notion was supposed to provide a criterion for.

One important point that's been dealt with in the (comparatively) recent secondary literature on Mill is the way Mill passes to talking about a person's 'interests' (even his 'legitimate' interests; even those which 'ought to be considered as rights') from talking about what 'interests' him, what he is 'interested in'.

I'm not suggesting this notion of someone's interests is no good for anything, not at all. The question is whether it's any good for Mill's purposes. The difficulty is that (as Mill himself, perhaps unconsciously, brings out) it is a notion very close to that of 'rights' and as such already operates to draw distinctions between what is and what is not a matter for legal enforcement. – Courts will make very different rulings, based on precedents, on what interests of parties before it should be recognised. These may be established by law or Constitution. Think of the constitutional right to remain silent on grounds of possible self-incrimination.

The general direction of Mill's argument requires him, as it were, to go behind the notion of 'interests-cum-rights' to utilitarian considerations uninfected by what legally, or quasi-legally, has already been established. Because his question is: What *should* be established in this area?

Lecture 26

This brings me back to the relation between this approach and that which leans on the notion of 'public order'. You remember Locke's argument that the role of the state stems from the danger of degeneration into a state of war. Here the emphasis is not so much on the private rights of individuals as on a general interest in public order. Of course this 'general interest' does involve private interests too, but cannot, or so I believe, be reduced to them.

What are we to understand by 'public order'? When people talk about the maintenance of public order ('Law and order'), we think of quiet streets, no rioting, muggers, burglars, rapists, etc. O.K. Most of us think it appropriate for such behaviour to be dealt with through the penal law.

To think of it in this way is to think of the conduct as the responsibility of the individuals who indulge in it, something for which they are answerable, sometimes in the form of being liable to punishment for it. And there surely is an important place for this way of thinking about it. There are those who would like to eradicate it, on the grounds that notions of responsibility manifest a superstitious and 'unscientific' belief in free will (Barbara Wootton). But if one were really to take that seriously it is difficult to see what would become of our sense of our own identities.

I don't want to get involved in this free will controversy here, more than I can help. One thing I do want to say is that I don't see any good reason for thinking that to assign individual responsibility for actions and hold individuals accountable for them is incompatible with recognising that social patterns of certain sorts of behaviour have social conditions.

If there is considerable unemployment and poverty, there will be an increase in certain sorts of crime. It would be surprising if there were not. Again, certain sorts of economic conditions lead to unrest which in turn may give rise to rioting. We all understand, in a rough and ready way, mechanisms of this sort, even if we don't trace the detailed cause and may be wrong in a lot of our beliefs about such mechanisms. But it would be difficult to deny that they exist. Does this mean that someone who, say, in the course of a riot loots a store and injures the security guard cannot be held individually responsible for what he has done? Why on earth should it mean this?

But these considerations do point us in the general direction of something important. – Our image of 'public order' was a too-simple-minded one. Quiet streets, safety for travellers, security of property, may be the outward manifestation of a very wide range of different social orders. More especially, they may mask considerable injustice. The notion of justice cannot be kept out of our characterisation of public order.

This is of course implicit in Locke's account. The degeneration into a state of war is thought of as the outcome of injustice; and the role of the state is to enforce justice and thereby preserve public order. What is perhaps amiss in Locke is an over-individualistic account of justice itself. But what do I mean by that?

Perhaps it's more to the point to say that for Locke the reason why injustice is an evil – a social evil that is – is that it will be the cause of strife. Whereas perhaps one ought to say that it is injustice *simpliciter* that is the evil; and social strife is one of the outcomes of this evil. But social strife, as such, need perhaps not be regarded as an evil: not if it is the expression of a struggle against injustice (Beijing, June 1989). Consider the situation in South Africa (in the time of Botha). Tacitus: They (the Romans) make a desert and call it peace.

So perhaps really what I wanted to say all along was not that the rationale of the penal law is the preservation of public order, so much as the preservation of justice. The preservation, or attainment, of a *just social order.*

It is clear that some such conception is at work in Mill's argument. His conception of harm, as soon as it is made to depend on the notion of a person's legitimate interests, presupposes the notion of justice.

But this is of course contrary to his avowed intentions. For him justice is not a primitive notion. In *Utilitarianism* he tries to derive from utility. And he cannot afford to make it a primitive notion, since its application involves one in making precisely the kind of evaluative judgement for which he wanted to provide a criterion. As it were, one finds oneself out in the open sea again when one thought one was safely in harbour. One has to use the same rough and ready navigational aids one had all along.

How does this way of putting things relate to the 'enforcement of morality' position? It's important to notice that an important part of Devlin's case for this – perhaps the only part that involves argument – is that society is held together by commonly held moral principles and if these are flagrantly and frequently broken the social fabric is threatened. There are two sides to the argument here. On the one hand, such flagrant immorality will incite the man on the Clapham omnibus to such indignation that there will be a threat to public order. On the other hand, since society is in a sense constituted by its public morality, the disintegration of that morality *is* the disintegration of the social fabric.

It is important to note that these are different sorts of claim. The first sounds like an empirical prediction. There probably are situations of this sort; but as a general claim it does not seem to me very persuasive. But quite apart from that, it seems to close a question that surely ought to be left open: viz., ought 'public order' to be preserved at any case? (Think of South Africa and China, again. The banning of sexual contact between races through the Immorality Act(s?).[74]) An argument which represents itself as upholding morality could look, in some circumstances, uncommonly like a moral abdication: surrender to the lynch mob. The Nazis weren't at all bad at enforcing law and order: perhaps even at enforcing what was the dominant morality at the time. I don't know about that last; it seems to me not impossible.

The second is hardly an empirical claim at all. And it seems open to the charge of Hart that it identifies the destruction of 'society' with the destruction of a particular preferred form of society. To this extent it looks also as though it is open to the same charge as the first; it forecloses discussion on whether that form of society really is to be preferred.

These are surprising results – or is it naive to think that? It is noteworthy that all these attempts to provide a 'criterion' seem to lead to a sort of moral dereliction.

So – I find myself left with the notion of justice as central. (*That* perhaps is not so surprising.) Another way of arriving at the same result and, perhaps, deepening our understanding of that result, will also serve to introduce my last main topic: punishment.

Lecture 27

Let us look back at the form in which the notion of punishment has so far come into the argument. In positivist theory it comes in the form of the notion of 'sanctions': i.e. the threat of evil consequences to anyone who disregards the commands of the sovereign. As we saw, the whole positivist conception of a 'command' is made to depend on the existence of such sanctions. In Hobbes, punishment is the exercise of the power of 'the sword'. Thus, the leading idea here is that of a *threat*. And that is an essentially forward-looking notion; i.e. the notion of an incentive or disincentive to future action.

---

74. Eds: The singular/plural uncertainty perhaps relates to the history of the Immorality Act and/or the multiple pieces of legislation that constrained sexual relations. The 1927 Immorality Act was amended in 1950, extending its original ban on relations between white and black persons to a ban on relations between white and non-white persons (and these categories were legally defined and applied to the population by another act passed in 1950). A 1949 Prohibition of Mixed Marriages Act had preceded the revisions to the Immorality Act.

Looked at in this way, the actual infliction of the punishment is in a way incidental; I mean that it is of course required in order to make the threat a real one. But that is the only reason it is required. It is justified as a means of getting certain results.

Of course this is not the only way in which punishment can be thought of as 'forward-looking'. It may for instance put a potential criminal out of the way (in jail or dead). But in so far as punishment is seen as a sort of instrument of 'social engineering', the threat is surely by far the most important factor.

Now a similar emphasis runs right through the various viewpoints we have been examining. (I don't mean by this that the writers concerned have not also had important things to say about punishment of a different sort.) For instance, in Locke the infliction of punishment is, for the individual in a state of nature, a means of protecting his rights; for the state it is a means of preserving a just social order. In Mill, the point of punishment is to prevent people from inflicting harm on each other.

One might suppose that the idea of law as 'enforcing morality' involves a different, non-consequentialist emphasis, since it seems to require the punishment of certain kinds of action simply on account of their immorality rather than on consequences. But actually, for Devlin, its role is to enforce morality: i.e. to make sure that people do observe a basic morality by inflicting evil consequences on them if they do not. And furthermore, it turns out that there is a sort of consequentialist justification even for that: i.e. the danger of a 'breakdown of society' if 'morality' goes.

Of course, there is absolutely no doubt at all that punishment as we understand it does have this (consequentialist) dimension and that it is an extremely important one. There is also a temptation – but one that I shall argue should be resisted – to suppose that it is the only possible dimension. That there is no other way of making sense of it. That position is expressed very succinctly by Protagoras in Plato's *Protagoras*.

This approach is very widespread – and does indeed correspond with important ways in which we undoubtedly think about punishment in practice. E.g. when certain kinds of crime are prevalent, you will find the judiciary handing down severe sentences *pour encourager les autres*. (Voltaire: *Candide*: satiric comment on the British treatment of an unsuccessful admiral (Byng).)

But in philosophical discussions of punishment, the role of this forward-looking attitude is frequently treated not just as corresponding to one important strand in our actual practice; but as somehow constituting the only possible rational attitude to punishment – the only conception of it which makes rational sense. It was in this connection that I referred to Plato's *Protagoras*. Consider the following passage:

> Punishment is not inflicted by any rational man for the sake of the crime that has been committed – after all one cannot undo what is past – but for the sake of the future, to prevent either the same man, or, by the spectacle of his punishment, someone else, from doing wrong again. (324b)

'One cannot undo what is past.' That has the authentic ring of philosophy. One's natural response is: 'No of course one cannot'. But what we should ask is: what exactly is being said?

Consider the proverb: 'There's no use crying over spilt milk.' One would feel like crying over spilt milk in circumstances in which, for instance, an expensive and irreplaceable tablecloth had been ruined, or in which there was no more milk to replace what was spilt, or one was too poor to buy any, etc. But there wouldn't be any question of crying over what was spilt in other circumstances. One would simply have one's servant pour another glass.

These are not frivolous remarks. Their point is to bring out that in one common type of use of the expression, what has been done can sometimes be undone and sometimes not. But this is not what Protagoras wants to say. He says *the past* cannot be undone. He means that it makes no sense to speak of making something that has happened, or been done, not have happened, or been done. While the spilling of the milk may or may not matter, and any momentary inconvenience may or may not be easily rectified, it remains the case that the milk has been spilt. Perhaps one feels like saying it remains 'eternally' the case that...

This is closely connected with certain metaphysical ideas about time, perhaps. – That the past is fixed and unchangeable, the future still undetermined. One undoubted truth in this is that action, human action, is differently related to the past and future respectively. Though it is not at all easy to express this difference clearly and unobjectionably.

These ideas, if applicable to punishment, look as though they will have to be much more widely applicable also. I.e. the idea is really that any form of human action ultimately has to find its rationale in its relation to the future. This idea finds expression, for instance, in Alasdair MacIntyre's widely read book *After Virtue*.[75] In Chapter 15 MacIntyre considers the concept of 'the unity of a life' in relation to that of a 'tradition'. His idea, surely right, is that at least in many cases – and particularly in cases that raise important ethical issues – the significance of what a person does can be seen only in the context of his life, perhaps of his life 'as a whole'. (This is brought out all the time in serious novels.) He emphasises that what has happened in the past helps both to create and eliminate possibilities in the present. But he then goes on:

> [Along with a certain unpredictability there is] a second crucial characteristic of all lived narratives, a certain teleological character. We live out our lives, both individually and in our relationships with each other, in the light of certain conceptions of a possible shared future, a future in which certain possibilities beckon us forward and others repel us, some seem already foreclosed and others perhaps inevitable. There is no present which is not informed by some image of some future and an image of the future which always presents itself in the form of a telos – or of a variety of ends or goals – towards which we are either moving or failing to move in the present.[76]

What is it I am uneasy about here? There is a sense (at least there is a temptation to say there is a sense) in which one's actions are necessarily oriented towards the future:

---

75. Eds: Alasdair C. MacIntyre, *After Virtue: A Study in Moral Theory* (Notre Dame, IN: University of Notre Dame Press, 1984).
76. Ibid., 200–201.

the pattern of action, one feels like saying is deliberation (if any), act, consequences. And that is a temporal pattern. Of course it is also true that one's action may change the significance of something in the past. An important promise which I fail to keep becomes, in retrospect, part of an act of treachery. Even here, though, this 'becoming' has the temporal direction of present towards future. At the crucial moment where I betray my promise the treachery still lies in the future; can one say the character of my past promise as part of an act of treachery still lies in the future?

One can say all these things and there is a truth in them. But I am still suspicious of them. I don't think MacIntyre is sufficiently suspicious of them. In particular, it surely doesn't follow from them that one's acts are always informed by a telos in the sense of 'an image from the future'. One's eyes may, in certain cases, be fixed firmly on something in the past. In some cases this may make it impossible for us to think of any future. (Think of Raskolnikov in Dostoevsky's *Crime and Punishment*.) These considerations are particularly important in various ways when we are considering the nature of punishment and questions concerning its 'justification'.

Lecture 28

I want today to examine the notion of justification involved when people ask about 'the justification of punishment'. That is: I am not going to consider directly the justification of punishment. This is not because I want to evade any issue. On the contrary. It seems to me that certain issues are already being evaded, or at least passed by, if one assumes without question that one has a clear understanding of the questions being asked. It seems to me that there are issues here that are raised surprisingly infrequently in the literature. Sometimes apparently similar questions are asked; but they seldom go as deep as is necessary.

It will be well to remind ourselves here of a distinction made early on: that between a sociological examination of institutions and a philosophical examination of concepts. We have certain penal institutions: the machinery of courts, police, prison, etc.; and we also talk and think in terms of the notion of punishment. Of course, we apply this notion in administering, criticising and justifying our penal institutions. It may well be the case (it would be hard to deny that it is the case) that our penal institutions and the way they are administered in many ways fall short of what we should think ideal. Perhaps sometimes we may think they fall so far short as to 'more honoured in the breach than in the observance'. To think this, however, is not necessarily to think the whole concept of punishment discredited: for it may be the case that what our institutions fall short of is precisely what the concept of punishment itself, properly understood, requires.

Suppose, for example, that we come to the conclusion, as we probably shall, that in the main sending people to prison under actually prevailing conditions is more likely to brutalise them and their gaolers than to make them truly penitent for the error of their ways. That may be taken as a reason for radically modifying, even abolishing, the prison system. But that will be because that system is seen to fall short of what punishment properly requires. It is not, in itself, any reason for disillusionment with the idea of punishment. Of course, we may come to think that no institution could meet the required standard. And that would be a possible reason for thinking the standard impossible of application. (Though it might remain the case that we use it as a standard against which we measure what actually happens and is done.)

But much philosophical discussion of 'the justification of punishment' attacks the concept itself more directly. I.e. what we are supposed to have to 'justify' is not this or that practice, but a way of thinking about crime and its consequences. How does this work? It is tempting to suppose that the practice is just the totality of the individual acts, the individual cases of infliction of punishment. What may incline us to think that is, for instance, that if we are asked to display the practice to someone, all we can do is offer him examples of individual acts and say: these, and other acts like these, constitute the practice of punishment.

But what are these individual cases we shall display? They have to be cases of punishment. But if they are cases of punishment, they carry with them the whole range of concepts needed to characterise them as such cases; and that means they carry with them the range of possible 'justifications' which apply to them qua cases of punishment. – Understanding that what someone is doing is a case of punishment involves understanding what kinds of question can appropriately be asked about it and what kinds of answer are relevant to such questions.

It looks as though we were trying to ask: What is the justification of these justifications? And that sounds a weird kind of question. It is a weird kind of question. Weird or not, though, can we make sense of it? Can the kind of circularity suggested by the above be avoided as follows? (What follows is in fact the way in which the philosophical question is frequently posed.)

Let's consider an example. (Forgive its gruesome character.) Suppose someone is employed as an official executioner: a hangman, let's say. I see him engaged in his professional activities (unaware of his role and status) and ask what justifies his treating the man in his hands like this. He answers by appealing to the fact that he is an officer of the law, carrying out legal and constitutional duties in a conscientious and proper manner. The man he is executing, furthermore, has been properly convicted by courts performing in an exemplary manner the duties imposed on them by the law and constitution of the state.

Undoubtedly this man has provided a justification for what he is doing. This remains true whether we accept it as an adequate justification or not. The point is that if I had asked for a justification and received this answer I certainly would not be entitled to reject the answer as irrelevant to my question, even if I found it an unacceptable answer. – It's still an unacceptable *answer*. I might say: it's an answer that falls within the concept justification. But by the same token, we may say that the justification is one that falls within the concept of punishment. Let me explain.

I may say that what justifies taking this man out and hanging him is that he has committed, been convicted of, a certain crime (let's say murder). That is a perfectly intelligible statement, again whether one accepts the justification or not. – One couldn't say: What's that got to do with it? – But the justification amounts to saying: the hanging is a punishment for his crime. I.e. I am relying on the concept of punishment to provide the justification.

Take a slightly different case. I realise that what is happening is that an executioner is properly carrying out his public duties. But I ask: Why (= with what justification) is this man being punished like this? The answer is perhaps that he is a convicted murderer and the legal penalty for murder is death. Here again the whole exchange is carried on under the auspices, as it were, of the concept of punishment. Why is this important? The philosophical literature concerning the justification of punishment is of course in a way not concerned – not directly anyway – with justifications like these. It is concerned not with the justification of this or that infliction of punishment, but with the justification of punishment. Its question is: Is the practice of punishment in general justified and if so how? But how is this question related to those I have so far been considering?

Lecture 29

Punishment involves an act of wrongdoing and an infliction of pain or unpleasantness on the wrongdoer. Let us ask: what justifies the infliction of pain on a wrongdoer? Or: in what way, if any, does the commission of a wrong justify the infliction of pain on the perpetrator?

If you are alert, you will have noticed that I did not formulate the question as: What justifies the infliction of pain on someone for his wrongdoing. The reason is, of course, that this would be to reintroduce the concept of punishment into the case by the back door. The natural way to read the phrase 'inflicting pain on someone for his wrongdoing' is as 'punishing him for his wrongdoing'. But to do this is already to beckon forward the ranges of 'justification' which are already involved in the concept of punishment.

But if we leave out this notion of 'for his wrongdoing' the question we are trying to ask seems to become hopelessly vague and unanswerable in general terms. I may justify my infliction of pain on someone who has done wrong by saying that I made a bet with someone that I would do this; or that somebody promised to pay me for doing it; or that I like making people suffer and that this is the only sort of occasion I can get away with it without myself being stopped or hurt by other people in some way.

You may of course well say that you would not in most circumstances accept anything like these as valid justifications. O.K. But there are many cases in which you would not accept justifications in terms of, e.g. desert, as valid justifications; other cases in which you would. To recognise something as a possible justification for a type of case does not involve accepting all possible instances of it as a valid justification. Before I can raise the question whether something is a valid or invalid justification, I must first recognise it as falling under the concept justification.

The main difficulty I want to highlight is the way in which most of our understanding of justifications here presupposes the notion of punishment. It is the conception of punishment that provides the appropriate notions of justification. The central idea which the difficulty is that of punishment's being inflicted *for* an act of wrongdoing. How are we to construe 'for' in this context?

Compare the notion of 'laughing at', say, a joke. This doesn't mean that one laughs on the occasion of hearing the joke; not even that one's laughter is caused by the joke. 'Laughing at' brings in the idea of the comic or funny – see my 'Text and Context' for a discussion of this.[77] The problem of how the funniness of a joke explains my laughter is analogous to the problem of how desert justifies my punishment.

Obviously 'for' comes quite close to the notion of 'desert' here. I say it comes close, not that they are identical. One may be punished for something that one does not deserve. Nevertheless, unless the question of desert were in the offing, I do not think that 'for' would mean quite what it in fact does. To say that someone does not deserve the punishment inflicted on him, perhaps because he did not commit the alleged offence, or because the penalty is disproportionate to the offence, or because there were mitigating circumstances dictating leniency, is to say the person was unjustly punished for that offence. That is to say, his relation to the offence is not of the sort to warrant that punishment. I emphasise 'unjustly' there. Here, as always, it is extremely important to distinguish criticisms on grounds of injustice from criticisms on grounds of one or other kind of expediency. – Which is not at all to say that arguments on grounds of expediency have no place. They often do have a very important place. But I think it is the considerations relating to justice which take us closest to the difficulties at the heart of the concept of punishment. (Remember how Socrates's discussion of punishment in *Gorgias* starts from, and turns on, the notion of justice.)

Let's now, from this perspective, look sketchily at the traditional 'justifications' of punishment on offer: on the one hand there are those that appeal to desert ('retribution'); and on the other hand are those which appeal to results to be achieved by punishment (consequentialism: e.g. deterrence, reform, release of hostile energy, etc.). It's evident that only the former address themselves directly to the relation between the offence and the penalty. If we are simply concerned with consequences, the fact that the person punished has committed an offence seems to be at best contingently relevant. We might get the same result by inflicting punishment on an innocent man – at least as far as deterrence is concerned. Though one should notice that there are difficulties here too: since it is hard to see how the imposition of those penalties is going to have the desired deterrent effect if it is not generally thought that they have been imposed for the commission of a crime. However, perhaps there need not be any notion of desert involved here. In that case the difficulty is going to be in reconciling the infliction of penalties with justice. The notion of retribution, on the other hand, does address itself to the question of justice and also directly to the relation between the offence and the penalty. This prompts one to ask whether these two issues may not be closely related. I will return to that in a moment.

There is another matter I want to deal with first. It has been said (e.g. by Quinton) that the notion of retribution concerns a different issue to that of consequences: namely to the issue of definition rather than justification.[78] I.e. if pain is inflicted on someone, it just will not count as 'punishment' unless it is inflicted on account of an (at least supposed) offence. The commission of the offence then, and the relation of the inflicted pain to

---

77. *Philosophical Investigations* 5, no. 2 (Jan 1982). [Eds: reprinted in *Trying to Make Sense* (Oxford: Basil Blackwell, 1987), 18–32.]
78. Eds: Anthony M. Quinton, 'On Punishment', *Analysis* 14, no. 6 (1954): 1933–1942.

that, serves to constitute what is happening as a case of punishment. Consideration of consequences, on the other hand, serves to justify the infliction of punishment.

Perhaps there is something in this; but it does not help too much as it stands. One of the objections to pure consequentialism is that while it may take us some way towards justification, it does not address itself to the justice of inflicting punishment. Pain inflicted simply for the sake of future consequences looks likely to be severely unjust. But now it is said, justice is preserved if the pain inflicted really counts as punishment; if, that is, it is inflicted because it is deserved by the offender. But this of course is to assume that the notion of 'being deserved by the offender' itself provides a justification. Or perhaps better: it assumes that pain inflicted simply on account of an offence having been committed really is deserved, i.e. justified. The mere definition of the word 'punishment' will not in itself provide such a justification.

What was being looked for was some justification of this: of the infliction of a penalty for an offence. The notion of 'desert' was supposed to furnish this. But the notion of 'desert' itself belongs to the concept of punishment. It cannot provide an independent justification.

2.2

ILLINOIS SEMINAR ON POLITICAL AUTHORITY [1990][1]

From Wittgenstein's *Culture and Value*, page 17e:

> Ramsey was a bourgeois thinker. I.e. he thought with the aim of clearing up the affairs of a particular community. He did not reflect on the essence of the state – or at least he did not like doing so – but on how *this* state might reasonably be organized. The idea that this state might not be the only possible one in part disquieted him and in part bored him. He wanted to get down as quickly as possible to reflecting on the foundations – of *this* state. This was what he was good at and what really interested him; whereas real philosophical reflection disturbed him until he put its result (if it had one) to one side and declared it trivial. (1931)[2]

Wittgenstein was using this political language as a metaphor for Ramsey's attitude to questions in the philosophy of mathematics and logic. But what he says applies marvellously to much work, both contemporary and earlier, in political philosophy proper.

The distinction drawn is very important to me in the context of the seminar; and I want to start by considering some of its ramifications. At the same time I want to sketch two issues which are pivotal to the problems I should like this seminar to concern itself with.

What, first, did Wittgenstein have in mind in relation to mathematics? I can only guess, but my guess would be he had in mind the attitude of most philosophers of mathematics: that their problems are internal to the practice of mathematicians. Now with regard to this: Questions [that] it's natural to think of as 'philosophical' certainly do arise in the context of fundamental work in mathematics (and other sciences). Cf. Einstein's problems about simultaneity in connection with the Special Theory of Relativity. More strongly, probably the most interesting questions *do* arise in this way.

An important question is: are these questions to be put aside as settled, when the position is reached that mathematical work can continue unimpeded? or is something else required? I think it's the latter attitude that Wittgenstein had in mind when he spoke of 'real philosophical reflection'.

---

1. Eds: Computer printout; lecture notes; 8 pp., Peter Winch Archives (GB 0100 KCLCA K/PP171, Box 25), King's College London.
2. Ludwig Wittgenstein, *Culture and Value*, eds. G. H. von Wright and Heikki Nyman, trans. Peter Winch (Oxford: Basil Blackwell, 1989), 17e.

How are these considerations to be applied to political philosophy? Questions and difficulties arise in the interpretation of institutions and concepts peculiar to particular kinds of state: 'democracy', 'representation', 'monarchy'. *These* pretty plainly only have application in particular states.

There are also concepts which have a more general, perhaps a much more general, application: e.g. the term 'state' itself, 'society', 'community'; 'citizen', 'legitimacy', 'authority', 'obligation' and 'law'. Difficulties may arise about these too.

These difficulties too may be quite explicitly focussed on such questions as the application and interrelation between such concepts within the context of the workings of a particular state or type of state. E.g. the questions discussed by Carol Pateman about 'democracy', 'representation' and 'obligation', within the confines of what she calls a 'liberal democratic' state (i.e. one like this) (*The Problem of Political Obligation*[3]).

This case seems to correspond roughly to the sort of question Wittgenstein said Ramsey was solely interested in. One feature of such cases is that one has certain paradigms, or landmarks, in relation to which one can orient oneself. These landmarks are features of the kind of political tradition to which the particular state one is interested in (probably one's own) belongs.

This is important. I think here of Wittgenstein's remark in *Philosophical Investigations*[4] that the philosopher is not a citizen of any intellectual community. This is of course a feature of *many* of the concepts we are concerned with here that they have a very much wider application than to any particular state, kind of state, or even tradition. (Though admittedly that's a claim one must be careful about.) E.g. 'state' itself, 'authority', 'law', 'obligation'.

There are in fact difficulties and issues of interest concerning the nature and possibility of such concepts arising, at least in large part, from complexities and obscurities about their relation to other aspects of human life. *It is such issues that I am mainly interested in and which I should like to keep in focus as far as possible in this seminar.* I think they correspond to the questions we can see are designated as 'philosophical' in the quoted remark about Ramsey.

One of the difficulties inherent dealing with such questions is the lack of paradigms or landmarks. Perhaps this is partly responsible for the disquietude noted by Wittgenstein in Ramsey when such questions were raised. There is also the liability to boredom, also noted by Wittgenstein in relation to Ramsey.

But there is a much more serious and insidious danger, and one with which I think political philosophy is riddled, not least at the present time. It arises from supposing the considerations which may have a certain force *within* the confines of particular institutions or a particular tradition have some universal validity.

---

3. Eds: Carol Pateman, *The Problem of Political Obligation: A Critique of Liberal Theory* (Berkeley: University of California Press, 1985).

4. Eds: This is an error on Winch's part – the relevant remark is in fact to be found in Ludwig Wittgenstein, *Zettel*, eds. G. E. M. Anscombe and G. H. von Wright, trans. G. E. M. Anscombe (Oxford: Basil Blackwell, 1967), §455.

Locke is a good example of this. So is Pateman; and Carol C. Gould's *Rethinking Democracy* (with her idea that democracy can be justified by reference to a 'social ontology').[5]

The confusion is brought out beautifully and Simone Weil's paper: 'The Legitimacy of the Provisional Government':

> Legitimacy is one of those beautiful words which the human mind cannot link with any conception but which, considered simply as words, have a power infinitely greater than any human conception.
>
> If we try to define any such word by means of a human conception, it loses its virtue and becomes a cause of evil.
>
> 'Truth', 'justice' are such words. 'God' is the main one. These words are alive. 'The word of God is living and active, sharper than any two-edged sword, and it discriminates amongst the thoughts and feelings of the heart'.
>
> Even though we cannot answer Pontius Pilate's question; 'What is truth?', we have to be absolutely certain that we prefer truth to falsity, whatever each may be. When we have so chosen in respect of everything without exception, unconditionally, definitively and irrevocably, for all eternity, our thinking comes closer to the truth with each effort of attention. That is completely certain.
>
> *But if by contrast we assimilate truth to an established system of opinions, as does the Catholic idea of orthodoxy, of which the Inquisition is the direct consequence, we plunge ourselves into darkness. This holds whatever the system of beliefs in question.*
>
> *Exactly the same is true of legitimacy. This beautiful word draws marvellous power from its ability to direct intention, desire, will. It generates evil if we want to define it by a human conception, through forms of government.*
>
> *A king can be legitimate. So can a parliamentary head of government. A king can be illegitimate; so can a parliamentary head of government, no matter how regular the forms which have been observed.*
>
> *A head of government governs a country legitimately if he wants above all else to be a legitimate head and if nearly all the people regard him as a legitimate head and feel that he wants to remain so.*
>
> *The first objective of forms of political institutions is to allow the head of government and the people to express their feelings. They are analogous to love letters, exchanges of rings, and other tokens between lovers. In some circles a woman would not consider herself truly married if she did not wear a gold ring. Of course, the conjugal bond does not consist in the ring. It is all the same needful for women who feel like this to wear a ring.*[6]

This is, incidentally, a beautiful example of something I said at the start.

4 September 1990

Last week we discussed a difficulty about what one is doing in raising 'philosophical' questions about authority. The difficulty concerned the apparent absence of any specific political context to such questions and the consequent lack of any landmarks, models or

---

5. Carol C. Gould, *Rethinking Democracy: Freedom and Social Cooperation in Politics, Economy, and Society* (Cambridge: Cambridge University Press, 1990).
6. Eds: Emphasis Winch's; Simone Weil, 'The Legitimacy of the Provisional Government', trans. Peter Winch, *Philosophical Investigations* 10, no. 2 (1987): 87–98 (87–88).

political standards to appeal to. Though I did also say – without perhaps emphasising it sufficiently – that such questions are typically raised with reference to particular political situations and that their 'philosophical' character depends rather more on the spirit in which they are discussed and what it takes to resolve them, rather than on what initiates them.

I spoke also of the temptation of falling into a mythology here: inventing some universal, as it were context-less, context. I said I was susceptible to such temptations myself. Perhaps what I am going to say is evidence for that. I will consider that point towards the end of my introduction.

Let's consider some typical features of questions about authority.

The notion is connected with that of *legitimacy*. Not all authority is necessarily legitimate. That doesn't correspond to the way we talk. But to use the term 'authority' (rather than, say, 'power') does seem at least to raise the question of legitimacy.

To regard someone as having authority seems to involve a willingness to *accept* this person's decisions, at least in a certain area. The 'acceptance' that's in question is more than the sort of resignation involved when one recognises that someone else has a power over one that one cannot evade. – But I don't by any means want to suggest that there is any clear dividing line here. And no doubt that there's a certain sort of attitude of resignation which is compatible with its being authority (rather than power) which is being accepted. Example: the ambivalent attitude of many (most?) people towards paying taxes. Clearly such an acceptance is, at least, closely connected with a recognition of legitimacy.

This notion of acceptance again introduces some action of the subordinate's *active will* as an essential feature of the relationship. Again, this is very difficult to articulate. Because there is some sense in which this is true even in a quite naked power relationship. If I'm forced to do something at the point of a gun, it is still, nevertheless, something that I do (if, for example, the contrast is with a case in which someone moves my arms for me). Clearly the notion of *will* is a difficult, slippery one. But it is hard to dispense with it. Perhaps a way to put the important point would be this. – When I resign myself to someone else's power this is provisional, in the sense that I am ready to evade it if the opportunity arises. If I recognise someone's authority, that is not so. There's a sense in which I may be said to be on the same side as the one having authority. But again, there are no sharp dividing lines here.

The exercise of *reason* by the subordinate comes in too in an important way which is, again, very hard to characterise. It can't be said that the exercise of reason as such differentiates subjection to authority from subjection to power. One subject to power may exercise reason both in recognising the power to which he is subject and in the way he or she deals with the situation. Conversely, one subject to authority needn't respond as he or she does on the basis of reasons for doing so. Though perhaps such a person may be expected to try to give reasons, if asked.

Perhaps more to the point is that reasons are addressed to a different question in the two cases. In the one case someone, if challenged, may say he or she has no choice to obey, or that it's in his or her best interests to obey. And in the other case the reason will be designed to show, roughly, why one 'ought' to comply, or why the other has a 'right' to make the demands. Of course, the reasons will have to take a particular form…[7]

My main interest is focussed on these twin notions of *will* and *reason*, on the relations between them, and on the difficulties in their application.

Harking back to last week: these difficulties may be expected to be of two sorts, some of them peculiar to particular political contexts and traditions, others of a more general character. In what I've already said, I have suggested a fairly intimate connection between will and reason. The character of an agent's will is closely bound up with the kinds of reasons that are appropriate in the explanation of what he or she does. I.e. if we want to explicate the agent's relation to the action his or her reasons (or lack of reasons) will be an important part of that explication.

Let's look at the notion of reasons (for an action). A few elementary points first:

1. One may have a reason for doing something without doing it.
2. There may be a reason for doing something without my being aware of it or without my accepting it.
3. One may have (and accept) a reason without having thought about it in advance (or at all).
4. Very often at least (*perhaps* always) my reasons will relate to my *beliefs*.
5. Again very often, my *reasons* will relate to things that I *want*.

The above points are nothing more than notes on various aspects of our linguistic usage. (When I say 'merely', I don't want to suggest they have to be unimportant – certainly not. I mean they are not, as it were, theoretical points.)

But of course many philosophers do think it their business to construct a theory of practical rationality. And points like those I mentioned play an important role in such a theory. For instance, the role of *desires* and *beliefs* is given a certain slant. It may suggest an account of, as it were, the point of acting for reasons. To act is to initiate a change. Or, where we are dealing with inaction, if that is not to initiate a change in circumstances where it would be possible to do so.

I will of course have some ideas about what sorts of change my actions are likely to initiate and what kinds of further consequence may be expected. I.e. some *beliefs* about such matters. These beliefs may be expected to affect the choices of action I make. E.g. I will not get in my car in order to drive to the University if I believe that my car is not functioning mechanically. I will also have preferences. Some outcomes are more welcome to me than others. I.e. I have certain *desires*. These too may be expected to affect my choices. I will probably not get in my car to drive to the University unless my being at the University is a situation I prefer.

---

7. 'I did that because the law says…': that can be a matter of fearing being punished; or the law in itself can be a reason.

You'll notice I am expressing myself circumspectly. Though still not circumspectly enough.

We are on the verge of a theory (throwing circumspection to the wind): to act for a reason is to do something that one *believes* will satisfy, or lead to the satisfaction of, one's *desires*. (Obviously a lot of refinement is going to be necessary to make that acceptable. But that is the sort of thing philosophers who go this way love best.) Perhaps we even think that we have a causal theory. (Such being the best sort.)

Let's discuss this.[8]

---

8. Eds: Reid's notes from the seminar suggest that this session stayed focused on the question of the relationship between legitimate authority and the exercise of power, following through on questions students raised about the 'Stockholm syndrome'. Winch resisted the idea that one should treat legitimacy as merely one end point on a scale of coercion. Consider 'a case where duress is there at the outset but it develops into true consent vs. a case where it develops only into something even enthusiastically accepted but with what one would call false consciousness.' Winch discussed Simone Weil's factory diary. In Reid's notes: 'Life is full of coercion and inevitably so. The coercion in the factory is sometimes a matter of the bloody-mindedness of the people and sometimes of the situation itself: the production could hardly go on otherwise. As in family life. Coercion is hardly an independent variable to which one can appeal: recognizing it involves many of the same considerations that a judgment of legitimacy involves.'

The seminar from this point forward consisted in student presentations. Reid's notes suggest that Winch took the last session of the seminar and led a discussion about the idea of logic as a normative science, along the lines of his unpublished TS 'Persuasion and Reason.'

2.3

PLATO'S *GORGIAS* [1996][1]

Lecture 1

...The dialogue form. Why? At issue are the terms in which human life can be, and is best, discussed. The dialogue represents different approaches to such discussion in action. The *Gorgias* is not a philosophical treatise as is, say Hume's *Enquiry* or Kant's *Grundlegung*.

The ways of arguing are given embodiment in actual characters, which are expressed in the arguments used. Gorgias, Polus, Callicles – and, of course, Socrates. These characters are represented as in a dialectical struggle, a struggle to *persuade*. And the subject at issue in the dialogue is at first, and in a sense remains, the nature of persuasion and its different forms.

Lecture 2

'Persuasion'
Gorgias, when pressed as to the nature of his 'art' (rhetoric, oratory) would like to content himself with saying it's persuasion: i.e. the art of getting other people to change their opinion in a direction which suits you. Socrates keeps insisting that this isn't enough, since *many* forms of talk do this. Hence Gorgias's definition doesn't differentiate rhetoric; doesn't show that it is indeed a distinctive art. He gets Gorgias to admit that different kinds of discourse are distinguished by their *subject matter*. Gorgias submits but (understandably) with reluctance, since this seems to rob rhetoric of its predominant splendour over other forms of discourse. He says that the subject matter of the sophist's art is 'right and wrong'. (He is thinking of advocacy in law courts and politics.)

One might at this point expect that Socrates would want to say that the kind of discourse he admires and engages in ('philosophy') is not a matter or persuasion at all, but is simply a concern with discovering truth. But interestingly, he doesn't do this.

(454 C–455A) Let's consider this. 'Two kinds of persuasion': one leading to belief, the other to knowledge. What difference is Socrates pointing to here? Incidentally, the issue isn't of merely antiquarian interest. Cf. Rorty.[2]

---

1. Eds: These notes are excerpted from a longer lecture course, called 'Ethics and Value Theory', which Winch gave to undergraduate students in Illinois. 1996. Typescript; lecture notes; 25 pp., Peter Winch Archives (GB 0100 KCLCA K/PP171, Box VIII/X), King's College London.
2. Eds: Elsewhere Winch references Rorty, *Philosophy and the Mirror of Nature (Princeton NJ: Princeton University Press, 1979)*.

Knowledge and belief are both related to the idea of truth, but differently. It's harder to state the position clearly than you may imagine. Someone who believes something, thinks it true. But what he thinks is true may nevertheless be false. One who knows something also thinks it true. And if he really does know it, it must *be* true. This is not to state some mysterious power that knowledge has. (It's, as it were, agnostic with regard to that.) Nor is it to say that human beings are infallible – about anything whatever. (It's agnostic with regard to that too.) It makes a purely linguistic or, as I shall say, *grammatical* point. It says that I cannot say of someone that he knows a certain thing but that the thing he knows is not true. This would be a sort of contradiction. I.e. if I find out that what he claimed to know is *not* true, I cannot accept his claim to know.

However, this linguistic point is already powerful enough as far as the statement of Socrates's case is concerned. The persuasion of one who aims to 'instruct', to produce knowledge, is not directed simply at the hearer's state of mind. It is guided, and limited, by a relation to truth. Given that my aim is to instruct, if I persuade someone to accept a view which turns out to be false, I have failed – however intensely I have persuaded my interlocutor to believe it.

On the other hand, if my aim is not instruction but 'mere' persuasion, then it is irrelevant whether what I am peddling is true or not. I have succeeded if I get my hearer to believe it. Of course it may be well as a tactical matter not to base my persuasion on obvious falsehoods – since it's unlikely then to be successful. (Even that has been denied – e.g. by Hitler: the Big Lie. Senator Joseph McCarthy is also a relevant case.)

In these initial exchanges with Gorgias Socrates is intent to insist on this distinction and to prepare the ground for arguing that there is something incoherent in Gorgias's idea that there could be an 'art of persuasion' which involved no concern for truth at all. This is the point of his repeated insistence on 'subject matter'.

I want to 'digress' here to consider this distinction more closely. (It's not really a digression of course.) It's a distinction which has always been central to philosophy – at least since Plato, but probably earlier too. Aristotle, Plato's great pupil, disciple (at first) and successor more or less created the subject of logic in order to clarify the distinction. Importance of the idea of *validity*.

Lecture 3

The development of this subject by Aristotle – *and also by most of his successors down to the present day* – has, by and large, focussed attention on the importance of certain linguistic forms and tried to work out systematic relations between these. (Aristotle's syllogism; but also Frege's *Begriffschrift*.) Thus, logic has been seen as closely analogous to *mathematics*. Indeed, in recent times they've been seen as identical. (Frege again; and Russell.) We might call this the 'algorithmic' conception of reasoning: its reduction to a calculation the nature of which is quite independent of the reasoner.

The question then arises: whence do these canonical forms derive their authority. In Aristotle and his successors (e.g. Russell) there is an appeal to 'metaphysics' – 'the fundamental structure of reality'. This is connected with a certain conception of the 'compulsion' we seem to feel to think in certain ways. Lewis Carroll: 'What the Tortoise Said to Achilles'.

Plato, who in a sense gave the impetus for all this, *had a quite different conception*. It's a conception which is made to appear in the dramatic role Socrates plays in certain dialogues (amongst which I should say the *Gorgias* is pre-eminent.) According to this *sound, healthy thinking* is itself an essentially *moral* phenomenon. Its nature can be brought out only by our paying attention to the fundamentally diverse, even opposing, characters of different ways in which human beings may live and conduct themselves. In a sense, I am saying, the depiction of the character of Socrates is, for Plato, itself a contribution to logic. The appeal of Socrates: also a contribution to logic. [As is] ambivalence [towards him]: even Callicles; but par excellence Alcibiades. (Another example of this: Primo Levi in *The Periodic Table*.)

Note especially Socrates's opposition to long speeches (by others at least!); his emphasis on the importance of a 'dialectic', of which the most fundamental requirement is that each participant shall give honest expression to what he really thinks. – Socrates's exchanges with his interlocutors display the unexpected difficulty of this.

In recent times this conception has been spectacularly reactivated in the work of *Wittgenstein*. Logic is to be displayed in the description of 'language games'.

In what I have been saying I have wanted to *contrast* Plato's conception of 'instructive' persuasion with that which underlies the *logic* derived from Aristotle. And I do want to emphasise the contrast. Still, it would be one-sided of me not to note that Plato's own conception – as expressed here too – contains elements which can easily be thought to lead to the 'impersonal', 'algorithmic' Aristotelian conception.

I am thinking of Socrates's emphasis on the *subject matter* of one's discourse. It might easily be thought that the point here is that the independent facts one is talking about determine the form of one's argument, what is valid and what invalid. But I think it could equally well, indeed better, be said that on Socrates's view what determines the form of the argument is the speaker's (one's own) relation, attitude to the subject matter. There's even a sense in which it may be said that two people, two lawyers say, one of whom is out to win the case at all costs, while the other is out for justice, even though they are in a sense talking about the same facts are actually concerned with something different. I.e. we do take the speaker's attitude to be relevant to the question what he or she is talking about. And if we read Socrates's emphasis on 'subject matter' in the context of his insistence on honesty in argument, willingness to face refutation, concern above all for truth, we can see that this is what he is saying too. I.e. it is a mistake to think of him as a precursor of 'Aristotelianism'.

I was talking about the distinction between knowledge and belief, the way this distinction enters into Socrates's discussion of 'two sorts of persuasion'. I touched on his idea that sophistic rhetoric is a 'semblance (an imitation) of the art of politics'. The idea is that it feeds on and exploits a *genuine* inquiry into justice (right and wrong): i.e. one which is concerned to get at the 'truth of the matter'. It's only in so far as people have *some* inkling of such an inquiry that rhetoric can be effective, since that is required for them to understand what it is for a claim about justice to be 'true'; and if they don't have that, how can they be persuaded of the truth of the sophist's claims?

This is connected with a further point about the distinction between knowledge and belief that we touched on last time: that I only *know* something if I've arrived at [it] in a way appropriate to what it is. E.g. a geometrical proof. In relation to 'knowledge of right and wrong', I think we are to take the representation of Socrates in action as an indication of the 'way appropriate to what that distinction is'. And here Socrates's insistence on a rigorous self-examination, on people 'saying what they really think', is very important.

Of course this notion of saying what you really think is not as simple as it may sound. Cf. Socrates's claim about what Polus (and everyone else!) 'really thinks concerning the preferability of suffering over doing wrong' (473E–474C). Here again Socrates's *example* is important for our understanding of what this comes to. (There are too strong connections here with Kierkegaard's ruthless rooting out of forms of 'doublemindedness'.) *Self-deception*. The words of the Delphic oracle to Socrates: 'Know thyself'.

But this is running ahead. Let us now prepare the ground for Socrates's discussion of the 'will' (461–468). This comes in the discussion with Polus, who had taken over because Gorgias had got into difficulties about the responsibility of a teacher of rhetoric for any evil use his pupils might make of the teaching.

Polus thinks that Gorgias has simply been trapped by Socrates because 'Gorgias did not like not to agree with you that the orator must know what is right and honorable and good, and asserted that if a pupil came to him ignorant of these things he would teach him himself.' It is this which led him into inconsistency. It is clear, I think, that on Polus's view the skill which the sophists teach has nothing to do with 'what is right and honorable', though this question is not pursued directly straight off. In what ensues the roles of questioner and answerer are, at least initially, reversed, Polus asking Socrates about what he takes oratory to be. Socrates's answers circle round the previous question, as it were, and eventually approach it again from behind.

Socrates's first move is to dispute whether oratory is, as Gorgias and Polus both claim, a genuine 'art'. It is rather, he says, 'a sort of knack gained by experience' of 'producing a kind of gratification and pleasure'. He says: '(T)he whole of which oratory is a branch seems to me to be a pursuit which has nothing to do with art, but which requires in its practitioners a shrewd and bold spirit together with a natural aptitude for dealing with men. The generic name that I should give it is pandering: it has many subdivisions, one of which is cookery, an occupation that masquerades as an art but in my opinion is no more than a knack acquired by routine. I should classify oratory and beauty-culture and popular lecturing as species of the same genus ....'

The idea running through this is that oratory involves no genuine understanding on the part of its practitioners. Specifically, the orator does not understand *how* the desired effect is produced in the audience; it's simply a knack acquired by experience; nor does the orator understand to what end he or she is working. It's simply a matter of gratifying tastes. If these change, so does the direction of the orator's efforts. There is no end which is, as it were, the orator's own (except acquiring personal power – and hence the importance of understanding rightly what this *is*).

Lecture 4

We were discussing Socrates's contention that the skill of the sophist is not an art but a mere 'knack'. This point is obviously closely connected with an issue raised between Socrates and Gorgias that I have so far neglected and that I must go back to: Socrates's suggested analogy between 'knowledge of right and wrong' and knowledge of a 'craft', like carpentry or medicine. Socrates argues: someone who has learnt medicine properly preserves health; a properly trained carpenter produces good furniture and someone properly trained in right and wrong will act rightly. Most people feel uneasy with this analogy – probably rightly. But there is more to Socrates's argument than is frequently allowed.

One common argument turns on the distinction between means and ends and assumes that an art concerns only the means. Gorgias heads this way when he tries at first to maintain that it is entirely up to his pupils what they do with their skill. But this account does not really fit even acknowledged 'crafts'. The standards inherent in them are by no means universally instrumental or utilitarian.[3] In any case the objection doesn't strike at the root of Socrates's case. He is mainly concerned with the claim of the sophists, including Gorgias, that possession of oratorical skill is necessarily a benefit. Socrates thinks that the 'beneficial' goes hand in hand with acting rightly. *This* is what he is mainly leading up to.

The same point underlies Socrates's dispute with Polus as to whether the 'successful' orator really does possess great power. The nub of Socrates's argument is that somebody who has the ability so to act that he *does himself serious harm* is not someone who has great power.

The way the argument seems to be presented may cause you difficulty. Socrates almost seems to be saying that it would be *false* to say that someone who can do what 'seems best to him' is very powerful when he is *wrong* in what he thinks best. Now, as a matter of linguistic usage, that is probably untenable; pretty certainly in English and, I am willing to bet, in Attic Greek too.[4] Socrates's argument with Polus turns on a distinction between 'doing what you will' and 'doing what seems best to you'. Power is doing what you will. You may do something that seems best to you at the time but later, for one reason or another (and of course there is a multitude of different kinds of possible reason), come to wish you hadn't done this.

I say there's a variety of different cases, though Socrates forces them all into one mould: where you act for the sake of some end and your action doesn't achieve this end. His argument proceeds through three fundamental claims.

1. To act for a purpose involves the will, and the object of our will is the purpose rather than our act.
2. The purpose for the sake of which we act is *always the good.*
3. The good for which we act is *our own advantage.*

---

3. Marginal handwritten note: N.B. that 'ethics' is part of medical learning.
4. Handwritten addition: But this doesn't affect the main point: whether oratorical skill is necessarily beneficial.

Let's consider these in order.

1. 'If a man acts with some purpose, he does not will the act, but the purpose of the act.' (Socrates, 467) The nerve of this point, I think, is that in cases where I act for a purpose, I would not do the act but for the prospect of achieving the purpose. If that either becomes impossible, or is already achieved, or is abandoned, then I will not so act. – This seems to me a perfectly good *stipulation* of a use of the verb 'to will', though I very much doubt whether it corresponds to actual usage. But no matter.

   Socrates does not actually say here (though I seem to recall that he does elsewhere) that all action is performed for the sake of some purpose. But he obviously thinks this so in the vast majority of cases. (Other cases might be where the action is performed 'for its own sake', but I do not think Socrates would regard these as significantly different from the point of view of the argument now to come.) You may think this qualification hardly worth making. But I shall later try to persuade you to the contrary.
2. Socrates then divides everything there is in the world into good, bad and indifferent. And he claims: 'we will the good, not what is neither good nor evil, nor what is evil' (468). If we translate this in the way I first suggested, it becomes something like: we would not do any of the things we do, were it not for the expectation of some good to be attained by doing so.
3. The claim is pushed a stage further, though Socrates does not make it explicit that a new claim is being made (as is in fact the case). 'Then when we slaughter, or banish from the city or deprive of property, we do not thus simply will these acts: but if they are advantageous to us, we will them; if harmful, we do not: for as you say, we will the good, not what is neither good nor evil, nor what is evil'. Here, 'willing the good' is equated with 'willing what is advantageous to us'.

I turn to criticism.

1. Since Socrates's argument concerns 'the will', I qualified the claim that we always act for a purpose by inserting 'when we will'. I must say it seems to me quite clear that we do not always 'act for a purpose' in any natural sense. I know this will strike you as outrageous, but let me just say a bit more before you explode.

What difference does the introduction of 'the will' make? It is pretty clear from the total context in the dialogue that its importance for Socrates lies in its connection with the potentiality of our acts for good and evil. It's also a term that emphasises the importance of deliberation, choice, decision. It is connected with his stand about 'the unexamined life'. Clearly these two points are connected. Socrates seems to think that the acts which are significant from the point of view of good and evil are acts coming within the scope of decision, etc. Many have thought this: above all Kant. (On this question I think Hume was closer to the mark than Kant perhaps.)

But is it true? [Continues in handwriting:] Cf. Caleb Garth [in George Eliot's Middlemarch; the passage is quoted in Chapter 3.3 below] (p. 224). It would be stretching things to think that 'will' comes into these mannerisms – at least in the sense of ideas. (Though we may say – as George Eliot nearly does – that they express what Caleb *is*.)

Consequences – these turn out badly. (Explain.) Perhaps we will think this is down to some sort of 'weakness' in Caleb. But it's possible to regard this almost as a component of Caleb's 'goodness'. Would I call him a 'weak man'?

Where purpose does come in. – Different cases.

1. An athlete's training so as to win a match.
2. Medical treatment – health (a favourite of Socrates).
3. Visiting a sick friend. Cf. *Culture and Value*, p. 58 (Goal/Context).
4. Philosophical discussion. The kind of clarity sought is a kind internally related to the kind of discussion.
5. And Caleb Garth – Weil's woman sewing layette.[5]

Lecture 5

I was discussing the claim that when we do act for a purpose, what we aim at is always the good. There's more than one point to disentangle here. Remember that the 'purpose' may be related to the 'act' in quite different ways. Consider going for a walk:

* to deliver some goods to someone
** to visit a friend
*** for pleasure

And note this marvellous passage from Wittgenstein: 'When I pay someone a visit, I don't just want to make him have feelings of such and such a sort: what I mainly want is to visit him, though of course I should like to be well received too' (*Culture and Value*, p. 58).[6]

When Socrates says that the purpose for which we act is always the good, which sort of relationship does he have in mind? I don't know the answer to this. I suspect there is none. But the impression sometimes given in Plato's dialogues (perhaps notably in *The Symposium*) is that it's (at least in certain respects) conceived to be like the first case (*). And actually the way the argument is presented to Polus makes it look rather like that. (We do indifferent acts for the sake of something else. Walking is indifferent, but delivering the goods is good.)

A somewhat parallel difficulty concerns the relation between that for the sake of which we would normally say we act (which would be many, many different things in different cases) and 'the good'. Is 'the good' something further we hope to achieve over and above the particular object? In Plato, it is very often made to seem so – again

---

5. Eds: Simone, Weil, *The Need for Roots: Prelude to a Declaration of Duties Toward Mankind*, trans. Arthur Wills (New York: G. P. Putnam's Sons, 1952), 91–92.
6. Ludwig Wittgenstein, *Culture and Value*, eds. G. H. von Wright and Heikki Nyman, trans. Peter Winch (Oxford: Basil Blackwell, 1989).

especially in *The Symposium*. (And I don't want categorically to deny that this is ever so.) But it quite evidently cannot be agreed to be so, just like that, in every case. Suppose I am taking food to a sick person. And suppose it isn't because the sick person is my friend and all I want to do is help him. I take the food to a stranger, 'because I think it is good to do so'; or because I think that doing so will be good. Here it is the action that I think of as good. The good will be achieved by the action in that way, because that is the action's own character; not as something further that the action 'brings about'.

Two points: There's a sense in which a person's 'will' can be focussed on the good even though it doesn't explicitly enter his or her thoughts at all. For example, consider George Eliot's description of Caleb Garth in *Middlemarch*. This suggests a quite different dimension for the connection between our presence in the world and good and evil. Simone Weil's example of the father playing with his child.[7] Simone Weil's contrast between the free expectant mother sewing her baby's layette and a woman performing the 'same' operation as a prisoner in jail. But do all actions that are performed for a purpose aim at the good in any of these ways? (Consider Weil's comparison between the persecution of the weak and the behaviour of hens attacking one of their number who is wounded.[8]) A 'quasi-mechanical' reaction. – But no less evil for that.

Lecture 6

Let me turn to the last of the three claims I said were involved in Socrates's argument: that the 'good' at which one always, necessarily, aims is something *to one's own advantage*. He seems to take this for granted. Look at the following abrupt transition (at 468).

> SOCRATES...As you say yourself, we will what is good; we do not will what is indifferent, still less what is bad. Am I right, Polus, or not? Why don't you answer?
> POLUS. You are right.
> SOC. Then, if that is granted, when a dictator or an orator kills or banishes or confiscates because he believes it to be to his advantage, and it turns out to be to his disadvantage, we must allow that he does what he pleases, mustn't we?
> POL. Yes.
> SOC. But does he do what he wills, when what he does turns out to be bad? Why don't you answer?
> POL. I agree that he doesn't do what he wills.
> SOC. How can one say then that such a man has great power in the state, when by your own admission great power is an advantage to its possessor.
> POL. One can't.

---

7. Eds: See Winch's 'Moral Integrity', in *Ethics and Action* (London: Routledge and Kegan Paul, 1972), 171–192 (181).
8. Eds: Simone Weil, *Waiting for God*, trans. Emma Craufurd (New York: Harper and Row, 1973), 91.

Notice Polus's reluctance. He suspects, rightly, that Socrates has something up his sleeve that he is not going to like. But as things stand at present, what Socrates is saying might seem quite to Polus's taste. He after all thinks that the most reasonable way to behave is to pursue what is in one's own interest.

Two ways of interpreting the claim that what is good = what is to one's advantage.

1. We find out what is to our advantage and conclude that it would be good to act in that way. (Polus's view)
2. We find out how it would be good to act and conclude that acting like that would be to one's advantage. (Socrates's view – as I think.)

This point is extremely important. It relates to something I had intended to discuss right at the end of my treatment of this dialogue: the story of the judgement of the soul before the gods after death. But I think it will be better to say something about this now. Socrates describes in great detail what awaits 'the soul' of someone who dies. He or she appears before the gods to be judged. Both the dead one and the gods are 'naked'. Those who have lived evil lives are punished. I should like to discuss the details, which are interesting, but there isn't time.

It is tempting to read this myth in the following way. (I know it is tempting since students nearly always succumb to the temptation and seem little moved by arguments of the sort I shall now try to give!) – Socrates, in his discussion with Polus, has introduced his argument by getting Polus to accept that human beings do not just have a body, but there is such a thing as the soul too. He goes on to argue that what is good for the soul is different from what is good for the body and is much more important to the person concerned than what is good for the body. Now clearly (and I accept it): the story about judgement hangs together with this. The temptation I referred to is to think that the reason this is so is that while someone may escape punishment on earth, he or she can't escape it after death, and the post-mortem punishments are more terrible and last longer than the earthly ones; and will be all the more terrible if the wrongdoer has escaped punishment on earth.

There are, however, difficulties about this. If it is asked: *what* harm then is supposed to come to the soul of an evil doer, the story of judgement seems to give the answer. As though I should say: don't commit a robbery as otherwise you will spend a long time in jail. And obviously that analogy does play *some* role here. But don't be too hasty in judging *what*.

The nudity of the soul and of the judges (And don't forget that the judges are *gods*.) The role of these is to secure absolute justice. (Certainty, impartiality.) *Don't overlook the strangeness of this conception.* Suppose someone were to propose that we could ensure absolute justice in our courts if all participants were naked! Obviously this is a figure to remind us that we are not now dealing with appearances, but with justice itself.

Some last remarks about the judgement myth. I was considering some difficulties with the 'literal' interpretation. But one might ask what 'literal' is supposed to mean here.

After all we are talking of the 'soul' and of the 'gods'. What is the 'literal' interpretation of such talk?[9]

A couple of further points. The account is presented as a 'story', but one which Socrates is convinced is 'true'. What does this mean. If it's a matter of believing that 'yes, that's what's going to happen', isn't it weird that someone so anxious for 'proof' should be so easily satisfied?! And furthermore, in life, things go in the opposite direction. If you want to make more certain of justice and impartiality, you, as it were, make the empirical network denser. You don't abolish it altogether.

And a connected point here is that, however great your precautions, there's always the 'theoretical' possibility of someone's slipping through the net. *But I don't think this is supposed to make sense in the last judgment.* But how can it not make sense? Doesn't such a possibility help to characterise our understanding of such matters. *The analogy with geometry.* (N.B. that Socrates chides Callicles with 'forgetting geometry': though in a different connection.)

The question of motivation. One considerable difficulty about this way of looking at it is that Socrates, after all, has argued that just punishment is a good and not an evil to the person on whom it's inflicted. The 'suffering' of the evil soul after death is not, as is earthly punishment, medicinal. It's too late for that. The person has died in an evil state. No more choices. No more chance of redemption. This was the person's life; and this is his or her misfortune. Remember that this is an argument addressed to the living. Its challenge is: do you want this to have been your life? Cf. Dickens's *A Christmas Carol*. The Ghosts of Christmas Past and Present show Scrooge what he has made of his life. The Ghost of Christmas Yet to Come shows him what his life will have been, unless he repents. *What is at issue here is not some theory about 'what will happen if...'.* It is a question of the *possibility of a different type of judgment on a life.*

Before we begin with the argument proper note (what I think) a very important interpolation by Socrates in which he describes and says he will give Polus 'a taste of the sort of proof that I believe in'. We must take this seriously if we want to understand what is going on and what sorts of criticism are appropriate to Socrates's argument. The interpolation is a riposte to Polus who has appealed, as it were, to public opinion to support his case: 'Do you suppose that reasons are needed, Socrates, when you say things that no one else in the world would say? Ask any of our friends here.' To this Socrates replies that he is 'no politician' and that he is interested only in the opinions of 'the man I am arguing with ...; the rest of the world are nothing to me; I am not talking to them.' Although this is a position that Socrates takes quite generally, I think it is of particular importance to the present issue; and I think that is why Plato has interpolated it at this point in the dialogue.

Notice how this undercuts the supposed opposition between 'absolutism' and 'relativism'. Socrates is certainly not advocating adherence to the accepted opinions of

---

9. Eds: Cf. Winch's critique in 'Understanding a Primitive Society' (*Ethics and Action* [London: Routledge and Kegan Paul, 1972], 8–49) and in various papers on religious belief of the view that religious language and spiritual practices can be given (and criticized) in their literal meaning.

one's time and place. But neither is he interested in teaching his interlocutor some as it were revealed 'universal truth'. He is interested in arriving at what his interlocutor really does think about the issue in hand.

At the same time there is something strange about Socrates's attitude to his interlocutor. (By which I do not necessarily mean that it is suspect and certainly not that it invalidates his procedure.) He does not take what his partner says at its face value as necessarily expressing his or her true opinion. I don't mean that he suspects (e.g.) Polus of lying; rather of being confused about what he really thinks.

In what I think an astounding (and too little attended to) exchange Socrates thinks he can say in advance: 'that you and the world in general, as well as I, consider doing wrong worse than suffering wrong and not being punished worse than being punished.'

> POLUS. And I say that neither I nor anyone else believes such a thing. Would you rather suffer wrong than do wrong?
> SOCRATES. Yes, and so would you and so would everybody.
> POLUS. On the contrary, neither you nor I nor anybody would make that choice.
> SOCRATES. Well, will you answer my questions?

A question to consider is what sort of claim this is Socrates is making (empirical, necessary truth… or something else)? But we need to think about the nature of his argument for the claim first. I hope I shall remember to return to the question.

Socrates's argument hinges on getting Polus to agree that doing wrong is more 'base' (shameful) and perhaps, too, 'ugly', than suffering wrong. See the important footnote by the translator on p. 62 of Penguin (aischron [αἰσχρόν], kalon [καλόν] ('fine'): obviously in some measure aesthetic terms). He then introduces a *criterion* of fineness and baseness; viz. either pleasant, or useful or both; and either painful, or harmful or both. – I'll return to this criterion in a moment.

So, if doing wrong is baser than suffering wrong, it must be either more painful, more harmful, or both. It is not more painful, so it must be more harmful: hence 'a worse evil'. Here comes the crucial move (as is evidenced by the serious way Socrates exhorts Polus to answer honestly):

> SOCRATES. *Would you then prefer* a greater degree of evil and baseness to a lesser? Don't be afraid to answer, Polus. Be a man and submit to the argument as you would to a doctor, and answer 'yes' or 'no' to my question.

Polus's answer is 'no'; and they also agree that 'according to this argument' *nobody* would prefer it. Though Socrates shortly afterwards says that if he can get Polus's 'vote', he cares 'nothing for those of the rest of the world'. The point being, I take it that the process would have to be gone through afresh with each individual. It cannot be 'proved' once [and] for all time. Someone has to *accept* the argument before anything is proved.

Why is this? The clue lies in Socrates's question: '*Would you … prefer ….*' Polus is not *asked to draw a conclusion; he is asked to state an attitude.* To state it *honestly*: therein lies the difficulty. How do we recognise an honest answer when we see it?

Don't try to answer this question too quickly! Perhaps one antidote against answering it too quickly is to ask yourself: how you know *of yourself* that you are answering honestly or not. Once Polus has answered no, of course the argument is lost. Because it amounts to an admission that he *does* think it *worse* to do than to suffer wrong.

Lecture 7

Socrates's crucial move has been to replace the impersonal 'Which is better?' with the direct personal challenge 'Which would you prefer?', having prepared the ground by presenting the choice in a certain light and emphasising certain things about it that Polus wanted to suppress. (Like: if I do choose evil over good, *what does that make me?*)

The argument about *punishment*. The need for this is obvious. Socrates has argued that someone who commits evil is worse off than one who suffers evil and his argument seems to hinge in some way on the *consequences* of an evil-doer's action to the agent.

This is one reason why it is so important to be clear about the precise sense of 'consequence' here. Cf. 'What does that make me?' One at least of Socrates's examples (the man who runs berserk with a knife) might be thought to concern the likelihood of *punishment* for the evil deed. Socrates wants to guard against a misinterpretation and he argues, against Polus, that, if you have done something wrong, then you are *better*, not worse, off if you are punished. So this is not the sort of 'consequence' that his previous argument had relied on.

The argument is an extension of the first one and relies again on Polus's *preference* for what is 'fine' – in *this* case justice. But there's an important new move – which may look sophistical. It turns on the relation between the active and the passive voice in verbs. If A *x*'s B, then B is *x*'d.

> SOCRATES.... what the object has done to it correspond[s] in nature and quality to the act of the agent' (476). So with burning, striking, kicking and... doing something just to. Hence if I justly punish you, you are justly punished; I do something just to you and you receive something just. But if justice is something fine, then you receive something fine. And if you prefer what is fine to what is base then you prefer receiving justice to not receiving it, hence you prefer to be justly punished to not being justly punished. I.e. you think it *better* to be justly punished for a wrong you have committed to not being so punished.

You will be uneasy about this argument. But what the argument at least does is to draw attention to what you must give up if you want to reject the conclusion. Perhaps the best way to think of it is in terms of examples. What does someone look like who thinks in these terms. – Raskolnikov[10] –

A last qualification. It's important that Socrates's method of argument puts all the weight on the first person. (Polus must say what *he* thinks.) Hence we must beware of

---

10. In Dostoyevsky, *Crime and Punishment*. See Peter Winch, 'The Universalizability of Moral Judgements', in *Ethics and Action* (London: Routledge and Kegan Paul, 1972), 151–170 (174–176).

trying to use the argument in connection with any actual penal system. Justice: the offender must him or herself understand and accept the justice of what is being done. I don't think Socrates provides an argument which logically compels one to think in the way described. What he does is present a certain way of thinking. We must decide on our attitude to it.

Socrates and Callicles (481–522)

Callicles is Socrates's most formidable opponent. A man of affairs, involved in Athenian political life (see 481), obviously with some taste for the intellectual life, but who wants to keep this firmly 'in its place'. Particularly when it threatens his conception of himself. Familiar enough. The contrast with Socrates is very skilfully conveyed in the opening exchanges: Socrates insisting that he wants only to know the truth and that if Callicles can refute him and show him wrong he will take this as a true favour from a friend. (Irony? A very complex irony.) Callicles brutally dismissing all this as 'claptrap' and accusing Socrates of using the tricks of a 'catchpenny speaker'. (Turning against Socrates his [more politely phrased] charges against Gorgias.)

Callicles correctly identifies the reason for Polus's downfall as the same as that of Gorgias, viz. *shame*: in Gorgias's case this made him say that he would, if necessary, teach his pupils the difference between right and wrong; in Polus's case it made him admit that doing wrong is 'baser' than suffering wrong.

Callicles adds that this is '*false* shame':

> The fact is, Socrates, that under pretense of pursuing the truth, you are passing off upon your audience a low, *popular* notion of what is fine, a notion which has its foundation merely in convention and not in nature.

Nature and Convention

This is itself, and still, a very *popular* distinction. (We'll find it strongly operative in Hume at a crucial point in his argument.) Convention as what is instilled by education, indoctrination, brainwashing. I've listed those in descending order of respectability. Everyone would agree that brainwashing is a bad thing, which takes one *away* from the truth; but education? Callicles himself certainly connects convention with falsehood, nature with truth.

There's a quite powerful theory behind this (which Socrates at a later stage brilliantly turns *against* Callicles). The theory is: Naturally, the strong dominate the weak. This can almost be made to look like a tautology, or necessary truth. Thrasymachus in *The Republic*. The Greek ambassadors to Melos in Thucydides *Peloponnesian War*. Hobbes. Nietzsche. Freud. The weak combine together in order to defend themselves against the strong. Their defences consist largely of institutions which curb the depredations of the strong: police, law courts, prisons, executioners. And, more especially and relevantly, *education*. Education is, as it were, a pre-emptive or prophylactic measure. It instils a sense of shame in people so that they come to refrain from exercising their power of their own accord. One result of this mechanism is that everyone (the potentially strong included) come to think that the values of the weak are better than those of the strong. But that is a merely *conventional* judgement. Naturally, *in nature*, the strong and the values of the strong, are better than the weak and *their* values.

Lecture 8

The first part of Socrates's counter-argument is largely directed at this last point and at what he sees as a confusion in Callicles's thinking about the relations between 'stronger' and 'better'. Callicles's first response to Socrates's questions about this is that the terms are 'synonymous' (488). But his emphasis is clearly on the former: better because stronger. It's here that, as I said Socrates turns Callicles's own theory against him. The many in combination are clearly stronger than individuals who would one-to-one be stronger. Hence the majority must be 'better' than the minority and 'the laws which they establish are by nature good'.

These laws involve or are based on, the belief that it is 'baser' to do than to suffer wrong, which therefore 'appears to be founded in nature as well as in convention' (489). Callicles, angry, backtracks and now reverses the relations between 'stronger' and 'better'. Not 'better insofar as stronger' but 'stronger in so far as better'. By 'better', it turns out, Callicles means 'wiser', 'more intelligent'. Callicles accepts Socrates's characterisation of his view, as follows: 'Then on your theory it must often happen that one wise man is stronger than ten thousand fools, and that he ought to rule over them as subjects and have the lion's share of everything' (490).

There are two points that need to be taken up here. The introduction of 'ought': that was of course always involved in Callicles's position, though it was kept in the background. It is not taken up by Socrates here (at least explicitly). There's obviously a difference between saying that the wise *will* exercise power and saying they *ought* to. It may of course be argued that if they inevitably will, there's no point in fighting it. But Callicles clearly does *not* think they inevitably will. He is complaining that they often *don't*. I think Callicles confusedly thinks that the values he espouses are somehow embedded in the nature of things. *This is certainly not peculiar to him.* It's against this sort of view that *Hume* is protesting when he says that you can't derive an 'ought' from an 'is'. Cf. The confirmation hearings on Judge Thomas: 'natural law'.

The second point in Callicles's position that Socrates does take up concerns the view that the wise and intelligent should 'have the lion's share of everything'. Socrates gently ridicules Callicles by spelling this out in terms of food and drink, clothes, shoes. (If you think this far-fetched, remember Imelda Marcos!) Callicles is angry; but has he any right to be? I think Socrates's point is that Callicles has little right to reject this, since what he would like to say is that the stronger should be able to satisfy their desires and he has offered no principle by which to *discriminate* between desires.

This leads Socrates back to more serious argument. He raises the question of the ruler's *self* control, as distinct from control over *others*. The connection with the earlier argument is that otherwise they will simply flutter from one pleasure to another, which is not the sort of life that Callicles really has in mind – nor perhaps, is it consistent with the idea of a wise strong ruler. He takes the opportunity to take another thrust at Callicles in this connection: pointing out how inconsistent Callicles himself is in his arguments: constantly shifting his ground according to what he thinks will have the greatest effect. (Contrasting the attitude of the philosopher who 'always says the same thing': i.e. who is guided by the argument and is hence much more in control of himself.) I am sure this is all a deliberate dramatic illustration on Plato's part of the content of the dialogue – one finds such devices right through.

But Callicles at first angrily rejects the suggestion that the rulers must exercise self-control.

> CALLICLES. What a funny fellow you are, Socrates. The people that you call moderate are the half-witted.
> For how can a man be happy that is in subjection to anyone whatever? I tell you frankly that natural good and right consist in this, that the man who is going to live as a man ought should encourage his appetites to be as strong as possible, instead of repressing them, and be able by means of his courage and intelligence to satisfy them in all their intensity by providing them with whatever they happen to desire. (491 f.)

This should be related to Callicles's characterisation of the 'better' as the 'wiser', 'more intelligent'. It's clear that he is assuming a purely *instrumental* conception of intelligence. One's desires are given and the function of intelligence is to devise means of satisfying them. Socrates, on the other hand, is going to stress that intelligence and wisdom are *also* needed for deciding which desires are *worthy* of satisfaction.

There follows (493–500) a series of arguments directed at the heart of Callicles's position that the main aim of the wise man should be to seek out pleasures; it attacks that position by insisting that there is a distinction between good and pleasure and that pleasure should be sought only insofar as it is a means to good, not vice versa. The argument is in two parts. The first (also divisible into two sub-sections) aims at appealing to Callicles's sense of shame (which was what brought down Gorgias and Polus). The second is more technical – though it eventually culminates in the same sort of *elenchos*.[11] Socrates tries to characterise the life that Callicles is in fact advocating in terms of analogies which he thinks will be unacceptable.

'A pitcher with holes in it because it cannot be filled up' (493). He develops this analogy through a contrast with someone with sound casks which he fills with wholesome food so that he need not worry about where his supplies are to come from. Callicles gets the better of that round claiming – plausibly – that what Socrates is describing is 'the existence of a stone', whereas 'the pleasure of life consists precisely in this, that there should be as much running in as possible'. Socrates counters that Callicles is describing 'the existence of a greedy and dirty bird'. This is knockabout stuff: really preliminary sparring. The next point is more serious.

---

11. Eds: This is Winch's slightly untypical spelling of elenchus (which itself is a latinisation of the Ancient Greek ἔλεγχος).

Socrates aims at a central feature of Callicles's position: since pleasure is the criterion of what someone should aim at, he is unable to discriminate between pleasures as more or less worth pursuing. Hence he asks: 'can a man who itches and wants to scratch and whose opportunities of scratching are unbounded be said to lead a happy life continually scratching?' Callicles is shocked at how 'thoroughly vulgar' Socrates is becoming – even more so when Socrates raises the ante by supposing that the context is that of what Callicles will take to be low sexual pleasures. But of course the vulgarity is deliberate on Socrates's part: and he makes clear that he wants to 'shock' Callicles and make him feel shame as he did with Gorgias and Polus: his point is that these vulgarities are in fact consequences of Callicles's own position: viz. 'that pleasure is identical with good'.

From (495) to (497) there is a rather technical argument which seems to try to show directly that good and evil cannot be respectively identical with pleasure and pain. (It seems to me not to come off. – For what that's worth.) The argument turns on the idea that good and evil cannot both be present (as it were at the same place or in the same way) at the same time; whereas this is not true of pleasure and pain. Socrates argues that pleasure comes from satisfying desire, but desire itself is painful. (Does that sound quite right?) So when one satisfies a desire (which is pleasant) one experiences pleasure and pain at the same time 'and in the same part of something which you may equally well, I think, call body or soul'. Pains and pleasures, unlike good and evil, come to an end together.

Callicles is exasperated with these 'quibbles' – perhaps with *some* justification? – though he is certainly over-impatient. There is *something* in the previous argument, though I think the next more telling (497–500). It is directed immediately at what seems to me the crucial point: namely that we need to make room for an assessment of pleasures themselves as being better or worse. Callicles has to agree with Socrates that some people whom he would judge 'better' than some others nevertheless feel pleasure and pain to roughly the same degree in similar circumstances. Perhaps the balance is even unfavourable to Callicles's position. The coward feels as much, perhaps more, fear than the brave man and as much perhaps more, pleasure when the danger is over. Socrates: 'Then the good and bad feel joy and pain in about the same degree.'

The way the argument concludes sounds a bit odd, but I think in the context it's O.K. Socrates shows that on Callicles's position, 'whoever feels joy is good and whoever feels pain is bad'. Put like that of course it's implausible: but I think it really is Callicles's position. And of course it is now easy for Socrates to show that Callicles has admitted things incompatible with that. Maybe the position would be more naturally stated if we said that it is good to feel pleasure, bad to feel pain and that the good life is one containing much pleasure and little pain. If it is put like that, I think Socrates's argument will still go through. Callicles here tries to mend his fences. (He realises that his position is badly damaged.) But his attempt just makes matters worse, as far as that position is concerned.

> CALLICLES. I've been listening to you and expressing agreement for a long time, Socrates, with the thought in my mind all along that if one gives in to you on any point even in jest, you seize on the admission triumphantly with all the eagerness of a child. *As if you didn't know that like everybody else I distinguish between better and worse pleasure.*

It's true, of course, that Socrates did know this. But up to now Callicles hadn't wanted to admit it. And with this admission Callicles is virtually finished. He does his best to get out of the argument but remains, very grudgingly, at the behest of the prestigious Gorgias – who is depicted as really caring about the issues Socrates is raising.

One can divide what remains into two parts (500–522) Application of argument to relation between rhetoric and politics (522 – end) Myth of soul's judgement. This we have already discussed.

From now on Callicles, apart from a couple of minor recoveries becomes something of a cipher; indeed, for a long stretch he leaves Socrates to conduct the dialogue all by himself: giving the answers to his own questions! I think this doesn't improve either the dramatic impact or, connectedly, the intellectual content, of the work. Socrates becomes much more dogmatic and hounds Callicles mercilessly. It's hard not to agree sometimes with Callicles's complaint that Socrates is a 'bully'. Worse, from the point of view of the philosophical content, Socrates is now much more prone to speak of the positions he favours as having been 'proved' in a sense which seems no longer dependent on eliciting the actual agreement of one's dialogic partner.

Socrates also launches a savage attack on respected contemporary statesmen: Pericles, Themistocles, Cimon. Of course there is nothing wrong with this as such. It's good to deflate the exaggerations endemic to politics. But doesn't Plato err in the same way in the opposite direction? There's something important behind this, to which I will return. There is also an intemperate and, though interesting, very one-sided attack on art – music and dramatic poetry, which is depicted as mere entertainment (and hence 'pandering') with which Plato/Socrates contrasts philosophy. Plato's ambivalent relation to art. His own artistry (*Gorgias, Apology, Crito, Symposium*). Surely Plato must have been quite aware of the instructive/educational dimension of art.

Let's turn to the main topic here: the relation between philosophy, rhetoric and politics. Plato seems sometimes almost to be identifying the first and last: and this is where the trouble lies. His main objection to the sophistic 'semblance' of the art of politics is that it's a 'pandering' to the whims, prejudices and opinions of the demos; hence not concerned with their good. Such concern demands philosophical inquiry.

The 'philosopher king': brings down his knowledge of the good from the cave '*von oben herab*'.[12] If necessary this must be *imposed* on the demos (*Republic*). The trouble, one trouble, with this is that, as exemplified by Socrates, the 'good' in question is inextricably linked with the means of attaining it: it emerges from a life of inquiry. (Sometimes: it seems to *consist* in such a life.) It is hard to see that the demos can be educated philosophically. And Plato hardly believes this. See Callicles at (513). And compare Alcibiades. And actually, Socrates himself has almost just made the same point – in telling Callicles that the only way he can gain the sort of power he wants to live the kind of life he admires, is to become 'like' those over whom he wants to exercise power (and whom he despises) (513).

---

12. Eds: This is German for 'from above'.

The big question is whether there is any *other* way of exercising political power. Or better, should one think of the political good as something that can be understood independently of actual immersion in dealings with the demos and which can then, as it were, be brought to them. Political difficulties (out of which understanding of this good must develop) *are* in large part difficulties in dealing with the demos. Perhaps one needs to think in terms of a division of function: as between President Roman Herzog and Chancellor [Helmut] Kohl?

2.4

REASON, WILL AND REPRESENTATION IN ROUSSEAU [1993][1]

Hume's essay 'Of the Original Contract' makes two criticisms of Locke's theory that political authority is based on *consent*.[2] Both of them are relevant to understanding Rousseau's position.

No one seriously believes that authority is founded on contract; Governments would not accept it as a let-out; Subjects themselves do not believe it (the deposed prince); and talk about 'tacit consent' is ludicrous (the press-ganged mariner).

The 'more philosophical' objection. To derive the obligation to obey the state from a *promise* gets one nowhere, since the obligation to obey a promise is just as problematic, and in just the same way, as the obligation of allegiance. The point is something like this. What is problematic about accepting the authority of the state is that I regard my will in the *present* situation as 'bound' by something external to it (the will of the Sovereign perhaps). But this is unintelligible. Something is either subject to my will or it is not. If it is, then that is as much as to say that I am able to do as *I* think fit within the limits of what is possible.[3] What the appeal to *consent* does is to say that my present will is bound, not by someone else's decision, but by my own *past* decision; but this is no more intelligible than what it is supposed to explain. If I can will, I can will.

Where does Rousseau stand with regard to these points? In a sense he accepts them both (without mentioning Hume[4]), but draws diametrically opposed inferences. With respect to the first point, he argues that it is true that no states in fact are based on such principles. But instead of concluding that the source of their legitimacy lies elsewhere, as does Hume,[5] he infers that no existing states are, or perhaps ever have been, legitimate; so that maybe there has never been such a thing as a genuine state! Hume would certainly have regarded this as at least equally ludicrous as Locke's position (and not without some justice). But we mustn't be too hasty. Rousseau is presenting what he regards as an ideal; what Wittgenstein would have called 'an object of comparison'. (Analogy with geometry again.)

---

1. TS distributed to students at Åbo, September 1993. Source: Olli Lagerspetz.
2. Eds: David Hume, 'Of the Original Contract', in *Political Essays*, ed. Charles W. Handel (Bobbs Merrill, The Library of Liberal Arts, 1953), 43–63.
3. Descartes's conception of the will as essentially unlimited is perhaps similar.
4. By whom he was materially helped and whom he treated with paranoia.
5. Hume has a quasi-utilitarian account with interesting idiosyncrasies, but I shall not be discussing this.

The second point: 'Will cannot be represented', says Rousseau: *'La volonté ne se représente point: elle est la même, ou elle est autre; il n'y a point de milieu.'*[6] ['The will cannot be represented: it is the same, or it is different; there is no middle ground.'] And this comes to much the same; he also has much the same reasons as Hume. Rousseau concludes that laws cannot be valid unless they really do express the present will of those subject to them; nobody can legislate on anyone else's behalf.[7] Rousseau draws an acid conclusion concerning the English system of government:

> *Le peuple Anglais pense être libre, il se trompe fort; il ne l'est que durant l'élection des membres du parlement: sitôt qu'ils sont élus, il est esclave, il n'est rien. Dans les courts moments de sa liberté, l'usage qu'il en fait mérite bien qu'il la perd.*[8]
>
> [The people of England regards itself as free; but it is grossly mistaken; it is free only during the election of members of parliament. As soon as they are elected, slavery overtakes it, and it is nothing. The use it makes of the short moments of liberty it enjoys shows indeed that it deserves to lose them.]

That seems to me a very characteristic mixture of penetration and silliness.[9]

What Rousseau needs then is a form of society in which laws express the will of all those subject to them *in the present*. (I am not sure whether this should be expressed as a continuous present or timelessly.) Or, as he puts it, in which a citizen, in obeying the laws, obeys only himself.

Let's try to see the problems about this and the way Rousseau tries to overcome them through comparison with Hobbes. One obvious point of positive analogy is the central role played for them both by the notion of *sovereignty*. For both the sovereign is the sole source of political authority and the sole source of law. Perhaps more important still is the fact that for both the existence of sovereignty is what constitutes civil society; and what constitutes the *unity* of a civil society.

---

6. *Du contrat social*, Book III, Chapter XV.
7. If this is reminiscent of Kant's distinction between heteronomy and autonomy, this is no accident. Kant acknowledged his debt to Rousseau.
8. Ibid.
9. Cf. Wittgenstein, *Culture and Value*. *'In den Tälern der Dummheit wächst für den Philosophen noch immer mehr Gras, als auf den kahlen Höhen der Gescheitheit.'* (*Vermischte Bemerkungen*, §564). [*Culture and Value*, ed. G. H. von Wright and Heikki Nyman, trans. Peter Winch (Oxford: Basil Blackwell, 1989), 80.] [The valleys of foolishness have more grass growing in them for the philosopher than do the barren heights of cleverness.] There are several other remarks to similar effect. Rousseau's remark, though, is careless as well as silly. On his view, it isn't at all clear why one should be regarded free in the election of members of parliament. It is the law itself which is supposed to be an emanation of the will: so, if Rousseau really wanted to find some particular political act or episode which gave expressions to the citizen's freedom, it would apparently need to be something more like a referendum. But, as I shall shortly argue, this is not perhaps the most fruitful way to look at what Rousseau's point really is.

Their conceptions of what this unity consists in, though, are very different. Hobbes writes:

> A multitude of men, are made one person, when they are by one man, or one person, represented; so that it be done with the consent of every one of that multitude in particular.[10] For it is the unity of the representer, not the unity of the represented, that maketh the person one. And unity is not otherwise to be understood in multitude.
>
> And because the multitude naturally is not one, but many; they cannot be understood for one; but many authors, of everything their representative saith, or doth in their name; every many giving their common representer, authority from himself in particular.[11]

Rousseau, on the other hand:

> *A l'instant, au lieu de la personne particulière de chaque contractant, cet acte d'association produit un corps moral et collectif, composé d'autant de membres que l'assemblée a de voix, lequel reçoit de ce même acte son unité, son moi commun, sa vie et sa volonté.*[12]
>
> [At once, in place of the individual personality of each contracting party, this act of association creates a moral and collective body, composed of as many members as the assembly contains votes, and receiving from this act its unity, its common identity, its life and its will.]

Hobbes's reasons for his view are both metaphysical – his atomism – and political – his conception of the 'natural condition of mankind': that it is impossible for there to be any genuine mutual understanding unless the conditions for this are imposed from without. In both respects he is dogmatic. Rousseau, perhaps surprisingly, is much more pragmatic. On the one hand (I am thinking especially of his *Discourse on the Origins of Inequality*) he gives a much more realistic looking picture of social development which lacks Hobbes's dogmatic atomism; and on the other hand he gives proper weight to the natural ties of affection, relatedness and cooperation that can exist prior to the formation of his state. *Because* he allows for all this he can also give some weight to the existence of conceptions of justice and injustice in such a state. The state, for Rousseau, does not bring justice and injustice into being; it is introduced in order to combat an existing condition in which injustice is rife.

Closely connected with the last point is the fact that whereas for Hobbes people sign away absolutely their right to decide for themselves to the sovereign, whom they undertake to obey in everything, this for Rousseau is an impossibility:

> *Si donc le peuple promet simplement d'obéir, il se dissout par cet acte, il perd sa qualité de peuple; à l'instant qu'il y a un maître, il n'y a plus de souverain, et dès lors le corps politique est détruit.*
>
> [If then the people promise simply to obey, by that very act it dissolves itself and loses what makes it a people; the moment a master exists, there is no longer a Sovereign, and from that moment the body politic has ceased to exist.]

---

10. N.B.!
11. *Leviathan*, Part 1, Chapter XVI.
12. *Du contrat social*, Book I, Chapter VI.

The reason why it is an impossibility takes us back to Hume's point again. My will can only be 'bound' insofar as I myself now *will* it to be bound. Hence, if my will is bound by the sovereign's command, the sovereign's command must be *my* command.

This for Hobbes would be a mere playing with words. I can't bind my own will, because my own will can unbind me at any time I choose. There is here no *constraint*. What is the issue between Hobbes and Rousseau at this point? One way to put it is that they mean different things by 'will'. For Hobbes it is the last appetite in a series of conflicting appetites constituting a 'deliberation' immediately preceding action. For Rousseau, on the other hand, it appears that there is, properly speaking, no will prior to the institution of the sovereign *general* will. Up to that point Rousseau's conception of what a human being is seems not so different from that of Hobbes: one is simply governed by 'appetite' or 'desire'. The difference being that Rousseau, unlike Hobbes, does not wish to dignify this with the name 'will':

> *C'est alors seulement que, la voix du devoir succédant à l'impulsion physique et le droit à l'appétit. L'homme, qui jusque-là n'avait regardé que lui-même, se voit forcé d'agir sur d'autres principes, et de consulter sa raison avant d'écouter ses penchants.*[13]
>
> [Then only, when the voice of duty takes the place of physical impulses and right of appetite, does man, who so far had considered only himself, find that he is forced to act on different principles, and to consult his reason before listening to his inclinations.]

Here one sees even more strongly, perhaps, Rousseau's influence on Kant. But it may be more helpful to us to notice too the similarity to Plato: I mean Socrates's distinction between 'doing as you please' and 'doing what you will' in *Gorgias*.

The question we need to consider is: how far is Rousseau's difference from Hobbes 'merely verbal'? Is it simply that they are using the word 'will' in a different way? – The trouble is with the word 'simply'. Yes they *are* using 'will' differently, but that difference is a manifestation of a quite deep-seated difference in the way they conceive human beings.

Rousseau thinks that considerations of the sort that Plato discusses under the heading of 'doing what you will' are possible only where there is a *general* will in which they participate. This is, I think, because if we simply consider an individual human being in isolation, we have nothing with which to *contrast* his/her present desires. It is only where there is a social setting which provides for the possibility of *discussion* of what someone really wants, within which there is room for the question whether someone is *right* about this or making a mistake, that such a distinction is intelligible.

Here there is another difference, or another aspect of the difference, between Rousseau and Hobbes. Reasoning about what is really good for one is possible only for a human being in society; it is not, as Hobbes thought, attributable to someone considered simply as an isolated individual.

In this regard I am sure Rousseau has the superior view. But he exaggerates in speaking of it as though it is a sudden transition. *Either* the individual is *simply* an isolated

---

13. *Du contrat social*, Book I, Chapter VIII.

individual with no genuine relations with others, *or* a member of a society ruled by a general will. This sounds parallel with Hobbes, who also thought in such an all-or-nothing way: either full-blown sovereignty or a *bellum omnium contra omnes* in which human beings are 'solitary'.[14]

I think the quasi-'historical' way in which Rousseau expresses himself does real damage (as it does with others before and since). On the one hand (as I remarked earlier) Rousseau does at times offer a much more historically, or anthropologically, plausible suggestion about the first human societies: especially in the *Discourse on the Origins of Inequality*. But even more important in this connection is that the 'general will', as Rousseau speaks of it, is not the same as 'the will of all'; but a sort of ideal construction. And this means that the kind of society Rousseau is talking about here is also an ideal construction (as indeed is the 'nasty, brutish' condition he is contrasting with it).[15] Such constructions are what Wittgenstein speaks of as 'objects of comparison'; they serve to help us bring out aspects we consider important for one reason or another of real situations and states of affairs.

But in this case we cannot say that there can be no genuine discussion of what is good for an individual except in a society ruled by a general will as Rousseau conceives it. Rather, we must say (insofar as we go along with the whole line of thinking), such a discussion requires a social context in which there are *some* common conceptions of what is good for a human being. But if it requires that there must be the kind of agreement presupposed by Rousseau's general will – well, then we shall have to wait a long time for such a discussion to become possible.

---

14. '...and the life of man solitary, poor, nasty, brutish, and short'.
15. As he acknowledges in *Émile*, towards the end. I want to speak next week, or the following, about some remarks of Wittgenstein's, important in this connection, concerning the notion of the 'ideal'.

Part 3

'THE LAST BOOK OUTLINE' [C. 1995]

3.1

THE PARADOX OF AUTHORITY[1]

The Genesis of the Book

The paradox of authority [is that] it must be, yet apparently cannot be, compatible with reason. By and large the classical social contract tradition (Hobbes, Locke, Rousseau) has tried to show that authority is, or can be made, compatible with reason; Hume is the most formidable critic of this tradition.

Hume (nearly) sees that the reaction to authority is something primitive. I initially concentrated on developing this insight, e.g. in the early *Aristotelian Society* paper.[2]

This did involve seeing the social contract account of the relations between authority and reason as back to front; and I did try to develop this ('Authority and Rationality' in *The Human World* and 'Certainty and Authority' in *Wittgenstein Centennial Essays*).[3] But I still didn't see clearly enough how radically a proper understanding of these relations undermines not merely certain orthodox conceptions of the authority of the state but also certain orthodox conceptions of reason and logic.

In this way I get from political philosophy to the philosophy of logic. If we think that reason must be the source of authority we must ask *what is the authority of reason*. This is now my more fundamental concern.

Socrates, Plato, Hobbes, Locke, Hume, Rousseau, Wittgenstein are the writers I shall *mainly* be referring to: Hobbes, Locke and Rousseau as representing the social contract tradition; Hume as a critic of that tradition; and Socrates, Plato and Wittgenstein as offering a wholly different conception of reason and its relation to authority.

---

1. Eds: Computer printout; book outline; 24 pp., Peter Winch Archives (GB 0100 KCLCA K/PP171, Box 16), King's College London.
2. R. S. Peters, Peter Winch, and A. E. Duncan-Jones, 'Symposium: Authority', *Proceedings of the Aristotelian Society* Supplementary Volume 32 (1958): 207–260.
3. Peter Winch, 'Authority and Rationality', *The Human World* 8 (1972): 11–21; Peter Winch, 'Certainty and Authority', in *Wittgenstein Centenary Essays*, ed. A. Phillips Griffiths (Cambridge: Cambridge University Press, 1991), 223–238.

3.2

EMPIRICAL AND CONCEPTUAL QUESTIONS[1]

> Nothing appears more surprising to those who consider human affairs with a philosophical eye than the easiness with which the many are governed by the few and the implicit submission with which men resign their own sentiments and passions to those of their rulers.[2]

Hume's puzzlement could be expressed in the form 'How is political authority possible?' How should the question be construed? As empirical (sociological) or conceptual/grammatical (philosophical)?

It may seem anachronistic to impose these distinctions on philosophers who did not think in terms of them. But many have got into difficulties through not noticing them. This is particularly true of Hobbes (as we shall see later in more detail), but Hume himself raises both sorts of question without seeing any difference between them. And anyway confusion about the distinctions is as rampant now as ever. ('Political science'/'political philosophy')

The (deliberately) Kantian tone of my formulation shows clearly that it is intended as a conceptual/philosophical/'grammatical' one. But it also points towards the reasons why such a conceptual investigation is needed and towards the parallel between this central question in political philosophy and philosophical questions from quite other areas. The suggestion clearly is that there is some internal difficulty in the notion of political authority; that it is a concept which, as it were, claims to be something that cannot possibly exist.

Consider a parallel with the concept of memory. This presents itself, as it were, as the concept of an awareness of something past. (I confine myself for my present very limited purposes to memory as recollection of past events.) But now, it is reasoned, I can only be aware of something which is present: a past event is, *ex hypothesi*, not present. One may even be inclined to say it has no real existence (Augustine). So what I am aware of in memory can only be something present (an image perhaps). And if we try to say that the image represents a past event, we simply push the question back a bit: what account are

---

1. Eds: Computer printout; book outline; 24 pp., Peter Winch Archives (GB 0100 KCLCA K/PP171, Box 16), King's College London. Corresponding Sessions of the Åbo Seminar on Political Authority are indicated in the footnotes.
2. Hume, 'Of the First Principles of Government', in *Political Essays*, ed. Charles W. Handel (Bobbs Merrill, The Library of Liberal Arts, 1953), 24–27 (24).

we to give of our awareness of the relation between the present image and that in the past that it is supposed to represent? So, we conclude, memory cannot possibly exist in the form it is commonly supposed to take.[3]

The question about the possibility of political authority, then, may be understood as analogous in form. There seems to be something about this concept which makes a somehow absurd claim.

What is this claim? Well, that really is the subject of this book. But a preliminary hint is this: I appeal to the decision of someone else as a reason for what *I* do.

Hobbes catches this beautifully in his definition of 'command'.

> COMMAND is where a man saith, *do this*, or *do not this* without expecting other reason than the will of him that says it.[4]

I shall come back to this later.[5] At present, sketchily, I want to say that the underlying question here is, how can I possibly take someone else's will as a reason for what I do? At the very least, surely, this can only be because I *want* to do his will; and that relocates the reason for my action in my *own* will.

Remember that at the present time the canonical account of 'reasons for action' is that they are a certain combination of desires and beliefs.[6] (I.e. the agent's desires and beliefs.)[7]

Let's take a preliminary look at Hobbes in connection with the distinction between empirical and conceptual questions. Maybe it's wrong to say Hobbes 'doesn't notice' the distinction.[8] Perhaps rather he thinks it unreal – itself based on a confusion: 'Covenants without the sword' are just 'air'.[9] He seems to suppose that there's no such thing as a self-discipline that would give one's words a meaning through committing us somehow. Discipline has to be something imposed. And hence for Hobbes there can only be settled concepts within an institutional framework. So Hobbes cannot be disposed of quickly. One needs to be able to show that this view of his itself involves confusions.

The distinction I tried to draw between conceptual and empirical questions is, then, closely bound up with the question whether we mean by the word 'authority' certain institutions or a certain concept/set of concepts. In Hobbes again these tend to be confused. His account of the contract, which is seen as an instrument for

---

3. Eds: See Winch's discussion of memory in his 'Ceasing to Exist', in *Trying to Make Sense* (Oxford: Basil Blackwell, 1987), 81–106.
4. Eds: Hobbes, *Leviathan*, Part 2, Chapter XXV.
5. Eds: Chapter 3.4 below.
6. Eds: As an example, Winch would typically give Davidson's psychologistic desire-belief model of the explanation/motivation of action.
7. Eds: Up to this point, the Chapter 2 outline is identical to the notes for the first session of the 1990 Åbo Seminar on Political Authority. In the Åbo notes, he ends with 'And there we have it. But it is going to take me quite a time to work back towards this question in its political context.'
8. Eds: As Winch said above, in Chapter 3.1.
9. Eds: Hobbes, *Leviathan*, Part 2, Chapter XVII.

creating the institution of the state, also has to be a device for generating the concept of political authority.

The distinction is complicated by the interdependence of our having these concepts and living within these institutions. For instance the working of the institutions requires that people apply the requisite concepts in the ways they behave/live. Democratic institutions, for instance, require that people understand what voting is and this requires that they act in certain ways in the context of elections.

Consider too Hume's description of behaviour in the context of hereditary monarchy in his wonderful essay, 'Of the Original Contract'. I add this example in order to emphasise – for reasons the importance of which may emerge later – that it's not only democratic institutions that work through the exercise of concepts by those subject to them.[10]

And again part of applying the requisite concepts is having appropriate attitudes towards the institutions.

There's a connection here with Rousseau's point that in order to have free institutions you must create citizens who are not slaves. And with the paradox that men become free only in the context of free institutions. This is at least one reason why Rousseau's treatment of education is of such importance to his political philosophy. *Émile* is a story of the education of a free citizen. It ends with the theory of the social contract – which Rousseau clearly thinks would be useless to someone not thus educated.

Contrast Hobbes's quite explicitly stated view in *Behemoth*:

> You may perhaps think a man has need of nothing else to know the duty he owes his governor, and what right he has to order him, but a good natural wit; but it is otherwise. For it is a science,[11] and built upon sure and clear principles, and to be learned by deep and careful study, or from masters that have deeply studied it. And who was there in the Parliament or in the nation, that could find out those evident principles, and derive from them the necessary rules of justice, and the necessary connection of justice and peace?[12]

Part of the contrast lies in the fact that whereas Rousseau has in mind a training in concepts, for Hobbes what is at issue is the inculcation of a certain *theory*.

But there's another, or at least consequential, contrast that perhaps isn't so evident. In Hobbes the relation between subject and sovereign is seen in the first instance in *institutional* terms. First one understands who is one's 'governor', then one learns what duty one owes him. (Of course I'm putting this more starkly and crudely than does Hobbes.) For Rousseau, on the other hand, the upbringing which results in the mastery of certain concepts is what *brings about* that peculiar relation between

---

10. Eds: David Hume, 'Of the Original Contract', in *Political Essays*, ed. Charles W. Handel (Bobbs Merrill, The Library of Liberal Arts, 1953), 43–63 (53). He will return to discuss this passage from Hume in Chapter 3.5 below.
11. Note that Hobbes seems hardly to consider my alternative: that what is required is neither just 'natural wit' nor 'science'; it's 'a question of upbringing'.
12. Hobbes, *Behemoth*, Dialogue IV.

citizen and sovereign. For the exercise of those concepts is precisely *constitutive* of that institutional relation.[13]

In a sense the theory of the social contract which Émile is taught at the end of the book is redundant, doesn't add anything new, it's a summing up of the grammar of what Émile has been taught throughout his education by Jean-Jacques.

In connection with this issue compare too Wittgenstein's repeated discussions of how we *learn* the concepts he is trying to elucidate. This belongs with his insistence that concepts are what they are by virtue of their place in the lives we lead: we come to lead the lives we do lead by virtue of the way we are educated. (It's not to be assumed of course that everyone is going to respond to his or her upbringing in just the same way.)

This was a point Rush Rhees made in 'Wittgenstein's Builders'.[14] The mistake he there ascribes to Wittgenstein in what Wittgenstein says about Language Game Two is *in one respect* quite analogous to what I am saying about Hobbes.

Vico wrote of Hobbes that he described 'the original condition of mankind' as if people in that condition were already developed philosophers. What exactly is the force of this criticism? It is not, I think, that he treats them as though they have already undertaken the kind of 'study' of the 'science'[15] of living in society under a sovereign that Hobbes speaks of in *Behemoth*. It is rather that he treats them as having the ability to think in a sense that applies only to those who have had a certain sort of upbringing: an *upbringing*, of course, into the concepts and thought habits of [a] particular culture and historical epoch.[16]

---

13. Eds: Marginal handwritten note in the Åbo Seminar notes: *Help me to express this better!*
14. Eds: Rush Rhees. 'Wittgenstein's Builders', *Proceedings of the Aristotelian Society* 60 (1959–1960): 171–186. Winch discusses the paper in his 'Understanding a Primitive Society', in *Ethics and Action* (Routledge and Kegan Paul, 1972), 8–49 (40–41). Phillips discusses the influence Rhees's paper had on Winch in his 'Winch and Romanticism', *Philosophy* 77, no. 2 (2002): 261–279 and 'Beyond Rules', *History of the Human Sciences* 13, no. 2 (2000): 17–36.
15. Vico's 'new science' is not simply a variation on the old science (of which Hobbes's philosophy is an example). It is intended as an entirely new conception of what a 'science' of society must be.
16. Eds: Up to this point, the Chapter 2 outline is identical to Session 2 of the 1993 Åbo Authority Seminar, except that 'What follows…' is instead: 'His point, I take it, was precisely that the concepts which are essential if people are to act in the way described by Hobbes can be used only by people living precisely the kind of life which the 'original condition' designedly rules out. And people can come to lead such a life only as the result of a certain childhood training.'
Session 3 of the Åbo Authority Seminar consists in:
   I ended last time with a reference to Vico's criticisms of Hobbes. I connected it with the fact that Hobbes makes no room for the role of education in concept formation: he thinks what is needed is a theory (a 'science'). There is a connected issue in Plato's *Republic*, however different a philosopher he may be. The prisoners in the cave cannot understand what the enlightened one wants to persuade them of; argument, reasoning, are useless. He himself had to be taken into the light 'by force'. We can take this to mean that his concepts, his whole way of thinking, has to be changed. And this raises a serious question concerning the relevance of

It is of course noteworthy, negatively, that the participants in Hobbes's 'covenant' are fully formed adults and there is no account of how they became such; and, positively, that he gives an account of human rational capacities which precisely emphasises that they belong to human beings as *individuals*, not as members of a society.

In Rousseau on the other hand education is set squarely in the centre. He writes in *Du contrat social* that you cannot have free institutions unless you first have free citizens. Of course, the well-known paradox in this is that you cannot, perhaps, have free citizens unless you first have free institutions. In *Émile* Rousseau has Jean-Jacques try to overcome this by shielding Émile from the influence of social institutions until his education shall sufficiently have protected him. This too has its problems, however. It's not clear how feasible this insulation really is; and, a connected point, it is not clear how Jean-Jacques, the tutor, comes to be untainted.

---

philosophy, considered as a process of argument, to politics. See Blumenberg's *Höhlenausgänge* [which Winch had reviewed: 'In and Out of the Cave: Review of *Höhlenausgänge* By Hans Blumenberg', *The Times Literary Supplement* 4515 (1989): 1127]. And *Gorgias*, where Callicles raises this question in its most brutal form. In *Gorgias* too Polus, in his discussion with Socrates, is a case study of the limited utility of argument with someone who does not have the requisite concepts; and the contrast between Polus and Socrates brings out the connection between 'having concepts' and living in a certain way.

That is, in the seminar, he turns directly to concept formation, which is discussed in Chapter 10 of the 'Last Book Outline' (Chapter 3.10).

3.3

SOCRATES AND POLITICS[1]

Gorgias: stage-setting (everything I want to discuss except the authority of the state! For that we must go to *Crito* – and *Republic*?)[2]

We must distinguish between the (dramatic) form and the content. The relation between these must be understood if we are to get a proper picture of what the dialogue is saying. The content might be expressed as the place of language in human life. This, with its many and surprising manifestations, is *discussed* by the participants. But it is also *exemplified* by the participants in the dialogue. Socrates's way of using language, along with the manner of life with which this belongs is contrasted with those of his interlocutors. [I.A.1. and I.A.2]]

What is rhetoric? In fact this is soon widened by Socrates (Plato) to something like: what is discourse? [I.B.–I.B.1.]

[There are] two sorts of persuasion: Philosophy and politics. What is the authority of these two kinds of persuasion? [I.C.1.–2.]

The Importance of This Topic for 'How Is Political Authority Possible?'[3]

The root of the problem about political authority lies in the question what sort of reason have the edicts of an acknowledged organ of political authority. The question, one might say, concerns how the notion of political authority fits under the general category of

---

1. Eds: Computer printout; 24 pp.; Peter Winch Archives (GB 0100 KCLCA K/PP171, Box 16), King's College London, supplemented with two TSS, 'Action, Reason and Will' and 'Limits of Argument', both in the same archive collection (box location not recorded). The relation of the TSS to the outline is given in square brackets in the text. Corresponding Sessions of the Åbo Seminar on Political Authority are indicated in the footnotes.
2. Eds: In the Åbo Seminar, he discussed the distinction between reasons and causes first (in Seminar 4) before turning to Socrates's argument that that for the sake of which an agent acts is always something the agent sees as good. In this book outline, a discussion of two kinds of persuasion frames the arguments about action being aimed at some good to the agent, which in turn is discussed in the first instance through Plato's version of this view, and not through Hobbes's version, as he approached it in the 1992 Lecture Notes above and earlier – where starting with Hobbes he would present his own discussion of the difference between reasons and causes, briefly mentioning Plato's version of the view. In this present book outline, the discussion of reason and cause in Hobbes follows (Chapter 3.4).
3. Eds: The remaining text of this chapter is the TSS 'Action, Reason and Will' and 'Limits of Argument'. The progress of these TSS match the bullet point Chapter 3 outline, with some variations that will be noted in footnotes. The section titles in this chapter are those of the 'Action, Reason and Will' TS (these differ from the Chapter 3 outline).

rationality. In his representation of the figure of Socrates, Plato tries to depict, as it were, reason in action; and he does this in large part by contrasting Socrates's demeanour and procedures with those of the other protagonists in the dialogues. [I.A.2.] But his interest also has a deeply political dimension. He is concerned with the question how far the rational procedures of Socrates can be used in the conduct of public human affairs. Historically, biographically speaking, Plato's worry about this question clearly stems in large part from the shock of what Socrates's activities actually led to, namely his trial and execution.

In the *Republic* the myth of the prisoners in the cave provides a focus for the representation of these difficulties.[4] In *Gorgias* the difficulties are hinted at in the problems Socrates has in convincing Polus by argument and the somewhat different problems he has with Callicles. In this latter case Callicles actually argues for the irrelevance (or worse) of Socratic discussion when one is dealing with public affairs. I'll come back to this general question of relevance at the end. For now, I will concentrate on the positive account of action, will and reason which Socrates develops early in the discussion with Polus.

Socrates's Argument in *Gorgias*

Socrates's Method of Inquiry

The intellectual core of Socrates's case is perhaps the conception of action, will, and reason that he develops in his discussion with Polus. Let us recall how this discussion is introduced. [I.C.2.a–c]

The dialogue starts with Socrates questioning Gorgias about what it is he teaches. Gorgias replies by saying it is a technique for using words in order to persuade; and he also claims that this ability to persuade gives great power to its possessor. His responses to Socrates's questioning make it clear that he wants to think of this 'power' as ethically neutral in the sense that it lies outside any consideration of whether the orator's persuasion is directed towards good or evil. Under pressure from Socrates, however, he is forced to give up this important part of his position. His pupil Polus, however, undertakes to defend it. Socrates questions whether the ability to persuade people that Gorgias claims to teach is really a form of power. Polus is incredulous that this should be doubted: is it not power to be able to make people do what you will? Perhaps, replies Socrates, but do Gorgias's pupils really learn this? Is there not a distinction between 'doing what you will' and 'doing what seems best to you'; and is it not the latter that Gorgias's pupils

---

4. Eds: In the Åbo Seminar Winch considers Hobbes and Plato as embroiled in a similar point here despite their differences, as follows:

> there is available a point of view from which reason recommends a just political order, but that point of view is not available to the citizens. In Hobbes, the Leviathan has to arrange the power of the sword over their heads to secure their obedience (though perhaps some may learn the science he himself has discovered). In Plato, metaphorically, the prisoner has to be dragged from the cave to achieve the perspective granted by the (painful) light of the sun.

learn to do? This leads into the important discussion on the question 'What is it to do what you will?' or, as we may say, 'What is the object of the will in action?'

I will distinguish four elements in Socrates's case [I.D.: 'Reason, Purpose, Will']:

1. All actions (at least in so far as to be considered interesting in connection with questions about how a person should live) are performed for some purpose;
2. The reason why a person acts is never provided by the action itself, but only by the purpose for which it is to be performed;
3. The purpose behind an action is always something (seen as) good. This is of course the main premise for Socrates's argument that only out of ignorance do people act contrary to the good;
4. The good a person aims at is always to that person's advantage, i.e. it is good for that person. This is of course essential for Socrates's view that it is always worse to do than to suffer evil.[5,6]

[Let us discuss these points. If we are lucky, the discussion will bring out how very little Socrates's argument relies on 'looking' at how we actually do speak of acting.[7]]

Action and Purpose

There is a difference between the role of point (1) in the argument and that of the rest. Whereas points (2)–(4) are explicitly argued for, or at least stated, (1) is not. But I think it is clearly presupposed by Socrates; without it his argument would have a major gap. Let me examine it.

[I.D.1.a] Understood as generally as I have stated it, the point seems easily refuted by the fact that we have an application for the concept of a purposeless action.[8] Purposeless actions are not all of the same type and for some purposes it would be important to categorise them. I do not think, however, that it will be necessary to attempt this for my purposes, since I think Socrates errs, not so much in confusing different types of purposeless action, as in assuming that only actions which are rightly said to be 'done for a purpose' are of interest in the context of his discussion with Polus. This discussion may be described, in very broad terms, as concerned with what is a good life for human beings; or with what it is for a person to be oriented towards the good. Socrates is not discussing the criteria for right action and though, at this point, he does make Polus focus on the nature of individual actions, it must not be forgotten

---

5. Eds: This last sentence is an addition in the Åbo Seminar notes. We have amended Winch's formulation of this point which he had put the wrong way around ('it is always worse to suffer than to do evil'). This was certainly a typo.
6. Eds: Introducing these four elements is the second half of Session 4 of the Åbo seminar.
7. Eds: We have interpolated this sentence from another MS of Winch's discussing Socrates.
8. Eds: See Winch's 'Moral Integrity' (pp. 171–192) and 'Can a Good Man Be Harmed?' (193–209) in *Ethics and Action* (London: Routledge and Kegan Paul, 1972).

that his interest in these is the kind of significance such actions have in the life of a good human being. We may therefore take his assumption about the purposiveness of actions to be directed mainly at those actions which do have significance in making someone's life a good life. So the question we need to ask is whether it is true that only actions done for a purpose have such a significance; or, somewhat more strongly, whether it is only the purposes for which people act, rather than their acts themselves, that have such significance.

Consider a passage from George Eliot's *Middlemarch*. [I.D.1.a.1] Fred Quincy, an amiable but somewhat feckless young man, has got into a scrape because of imprudent transactions concerning a horse. He goes to a family friend, Caleb Garth, for help. Caleb

> was one of those rare men who are rigid to themselves and indulgent to others. He had a certain shame about his neighbours' errors, and never spoke of them willingly; hence he was not likely to divert his mind from the best mode of hardening timber and other ingenious devices in order to preconceive those errors. If he had to blame anyone, it was necessary for him to move all diagrams with his stick, or make calculations with the odd money in his pocket, before he could begin; and he would rather do other men's work than find fault with their doing. I fear he was a bad disciplinarian.
>
> When Fred stated the circumstances of his debt, his wish to meet it without troubling his father and the certainty that the money would be forthcoming so as to cause no one any inconvenience, Caleb pushed his spectacles upward, listened, looked into his young favourite's clear young eyes, and believed him, not distinguishing confidence about the future from veracity about the past; but he felt it was an occasion for a friendly hint as to conduct, and that before giving his signature he must give a rather strong admonition. Accordingly, he took the paper and lowered his spectacles, measured the space at his command, reached his pen and examined it, dipped it in the ink and examined it again, then pushed the paper a little way from him, lifted up his spectacles again, showed a deepened depression in the outer angle of his bushy eyebrows, which gave his face a peculiar mildness (pardon these details for once – you would have learned to love them if you had known Caleb Garth), and said, in a comfortable tone, 'it was a misfortune, eh, that breaking the horse's knees? And then, these exchanges, they don't answer when you have 'cute jockeys to deal with. You'll be wiser another time, my boy.'
>
> Whereupon Caleb drew down his spectacles, and proceeded to write his signature with the care which he always gave to that performance; for whatever he did in the way of business he did well.

Of course the irony of the passage is critical, if gently so, of Caleb Garth; and indeed, in the further development of the plot his (over-?)trusting nature has fairly disastrous consequences. But this does not alter the fact that George Eliot here clearly wants to depict a character which is, in the phrase I used a little way back, oriented towards the good. After all, in life, and indeed in the rest of *Middlemarch*, there are characters enough who avoid Garth's kind of over-trustingness at a much greater cost, both to themselves and others.

The point I want to focus on here is the role of the descriptions of the numerous mannerisms surrounding Caleb Garth's underwriting of Fred Vincy's debt: his pushing around of the papers on his desk, constantly raising and lowering his spectacles and so on. One would – at least I would – hardly want to call these 'actions performed with a purpose'; for one thing he was clearly hardly aware of doing them; and George Eliot's description seems to emphasise this in contrasting them with the way Caleb signed the paper, 'with the care which he always gave to that performance; for whatever he did in the way of business he did well'. None of this is to deny that those mannerisms may properly be said to have played a role in the general economy of Garth's behaviour, the role perhaps of serving to conceal his embarrassment. But that does not mean that Garth did them 'in order to' conceal his embarrassment: that would have been a different sort of case. And anyway, leaving this aside, such a purpose as wanting to conceal his embarrassment would not be what one would wish to focus on in order to bring out the importance of this behaviour for the ethical assessment of Caleb Garth's character. That he was embarrassed in that way is indeed relevant to such an assessment, in showing his goodwill and lack of censoriousness. But the point is that this orientation of his will does not lie in any 'purpose for which he acted'.

For reasons of this sort I think Socrates goes off the track, before his explicit discussion with Polus even begins, in trying to characterise a person's will in terms of the purposes for which he or she acts.

Purpose, Reason and Will [I.D.1.b 'Will and Purpose']

The first point for which Socrates explicitly argues is point (2); that what one wills in acting is not the action itself but always the purpose for which one acts, that for the sake of which one acts, that which provides the reason for one's action.

The talk about 'will' in this context should be freed, it seems to me, from the accretions that have attached themselves to this notion in more recent philosophy. It is not the notion of some special causal factor which brings actions about. Rather, a person wills that on the expected attaining of which his or her act depends. So, a person will probably give up the plan to undergo a painful operation on learning that it is unlikely to improve his or her health.

A major difficulty with his position is that he makes no distinction between different forms of purpose, so that the precise import of what he is claiming remains unclear. One of his preferred examples – one that does a great many different jobs for him – is that of medical treatment. People do not seek unpleasant medical treatment he says, without fear of contradiction, for the sake of having that treatment, but for the sake of the improved state of health they expect to result from it. In this example the end to be attained by the action is a distinct state of affairs which one expects to be brought about by the action. Whether one achieves improved health as a result of one's treatment depends on the course of events: one must wait and see.

The limitations of this model are clear in one of the principal applications Socrates makes of it: at a later stage of his argument with Polus he compares punishment with medical treatment. Punishment is to be accepted in the same spirit as one accepts, say, a surgical operation; it will heal one's sick soul. The difficulty with the analogy is that a surgical operation may or may not heal one's sick body, whereas just punishment[9] cannot fail to 'heal one's sick soul'. For Socrates this is clearly a conceptual matter. Just as, if I kick someone, he receives a kick, so, if I punish someone justly, he receives a piece of justice; the injustice in his soul is thus removed.

Now, whatever may be the merits or demerits of insisting on this sort of conceptual connection between punishment and the soul of the offender, it must, I think, be clear that within this way of speaking, the end to be achieved by the act of punishing is not a distinct state of affairs from the act of punishing itself. We may say that the soul of the person punished becomes just *as a result of* the punishment and this sounds superficially like saying that the body of the person operated upon becomes healthy *as a result of* the operation, but the italicised phrase is used quite differently in the two contexts.[10] The difference is such that one might want to say that whereas medical treatment is to be valued for what it may bring about, punishment, as understood by Socrates at least, is to be valued for what it is.

Not everyone will be willing to accept Socrates's way of thinking about punishment, but it is important to realise that the relation between purpose and action when we speak of the purpose with which one acts is frequently of that sort. Examples come readily enough to mind and abound in the philosophical literature. If somebody looks through the window and wants to know why, for what purpose, I am holding forth before a roomful of people, the answer may be given that I am conducting a seminar. That is indeed the purpose of my holding forth like this. But clearly enough the conducting of a seminar is not some further state of affairs brought about by my holding forth; that is what my holding forth under these circumstances amounts to, is.

(I want now to discuss step (3) in Socrates's argument with Polus.)

Purpose and Good [I.D.c][11]

Socrates's next claim is that the end for the sake of which an agent acts is always something that the agent sees as good. Elizabeth Anscombe argues at some length for a somewhat similar claim in *Intention*:[12] she thinks that any claim that represents the achievement of a certain end as the reason for one's action must display the end in question under a 'desirability characterization'. In this form the case looks strong. We will, after all, not accept just any state of affairs as constituting an intelligible end such as would provide (even a rather bad) reason for acting. One needs to be shown, as it were, what it might be like to see something in it worth having.

---

9. I think it is clear that in the context of Socrates's argument, 'punishment' = 'just punishment'. I shall not here discuss the merits and demerits of this usage. A bit more is said in my ancient pieces 'Ethical Reward and Punishment' and 'Can a Good Man Be Harmed?' in *Ethics and Action* (London: Routledge and Kegan Paul, 1972), 193–209 and 210–228.
10. Eds: The text itself does not contain italics. We have italicised 'as a result of' as that seems clearly to be Winch's intention.
11. Eds: From here to 'see my "Notes on the Limits of Argument"' is the same as two-thirds of the Åbo Seminar Session 5.
12. Eds: G. E. M. Anscombe, *Intention* (Oxford: Basil Blackwell, 1957).

[I.D.1.c.1.] It is not too difficult to think of cases that seem to support Socrates's claim. But are there examples which do not fit? In Benjamin Britten's operatic version of Herman Melville's story 'Billy Budd',[13] Claggart, the Master-at-Arms of the warship Indomitable, who is bent on Billy's destruction, sings a powerful aria, as it were explaining his motivation, after the failure of his attempt to lure Billy into mutiny.[14] Claggart reflects on the squalor and evil of the conditions in which he had grown up and how he had adapted himself by carving out for himself a tolerable mode of living within this hell, without either rejecting it or ceasing to understand that it is indeed a hell. The extraordinary innocence and goodness so evident in Billy threatens this vulnerable equilibrium, by manifesting the rejected possibility of things being different. In a savage blasphemy Claggart parodies St. John's Gospel. 'The light shone in the darkness and the darkness comprehended it, and suffered.' The world with Billy in it is intolerable to him; he has no alternative but to wipe him off the face of the earth, so that it will be as though he had never been.

Is this a counterexample to Socrates's claim or not? It is hard to know what to answer. As far as Anscombe's very much weaker claim is concerned, we may of course perfectly well say that Claggart offers an intelligible 'desirability characterization' of his aim: he shows how, from his perspective, the death of Billy can appear as desirable, and even perhaps desirable on account of Billy's goodness. There are some who will want to say that Claggart cannot really take Billy's goodness seriously, that what enrages him is the way in which Billy appears good in the eyes of the world; but I do not think this will wash. The force of Claggart's despair will be lost if we do not realise that it is his recognition and acknowledgement of Billy's goodness that causes it.

'Good' and 'Desirable'[15]

In the above argument I have reconstructed Claggart's thinking in a way that involves a distinction between what he finds 'desirable' and what he recognises as 'good'. There are difficulties here. Let me approach them by trying to apply R. M. Hare's account of the meaning of 'good'. For Hare, if this word is used without explicit or

---

13. Librettists E. M. Forster and Eric Crozier.
14. I don't have the text with me in Finland, but it begins, approximately: 'Handsomely done, my lad, handsome indeed! And handsome is handsome does.' (Then, as Billy exits:) 'Oh beauty, handsomeness, goodness, would that I ne'er had found you'. [Eds: The libretto has 'O beauty, o handsomeness, goodness! Would that I never encountered you!' The line 'And handsome is as handsome did it, too' appears earlier than Winch recalls here.]
15. Eds: The Chapter 3 outline has a section entitled 'Good and advantage' instead, which is reflected in the 'Ethics and Value Theory' notes (Chapter 2.3 above) that go into detail as Socrates engages with Polus's claim about acting to one's own advantage. But the Claggart discussion here leads Winch deeper into purpose and good, and this section instead prepares the idea of a paradigm that consists in something concrete and real, but that is nonetheless in some sense 'indestructible' – though it is vulnerable to falling out of use. The direction the Claggart discussion takes him in – unity and diversity in conceptions of the good – is not clearly part of the Chapter 3 outline.

implicit inverted commas, it has a prescriptive meaning, both expressing the speaker's own practical attitudes and enjoining others to share those attitudes. I have said that Claggart's monologue does show how, from his perspective, Billy Budd's destruction can be seen as desirable. Does this mean simply 'desired by Claggart'? Again it is hard to answer this. Yes, it is an expression of Claggart's desires. But there is also something universal involved. As I noted, it is not just Billy Claggart needs to destroy, but the very goodness exemplified by Billy. For Claggart, the world must not be allowed to contain the possibility of such goodness. One can hardly get much more universal than that! Furthermore, I have said, Claggart really does mean goodness, not just people's opinions about goodness. I.e. the goodness Claggart wishes to destroy has no inverted commas round it.

Does any of this make sense? I am reminded of Wittgenstein:

> 'Something red can be destroyed, but red cannot be destroyed; and that is why the meaning of the word 'red' is independent of the existence of a red thing.' – Certainly it makes no sense to say that the colour red is torn up or pounded to bits. But don't we say 'The red is vanishing'? And don't clutch at the idea of our always being able to bring red before our mind's eye even when there is nothing red any more. That is just as if you chose to say that there will still always be a chemical reaction producing a red flame. For suppose you cannot remember the colour any more? – When we forget which colour this is the name of, it loses its meaning for us; that is, we are no longer able to play a particular language-game with it. And the situation then is comparable with that in which we have lost a paradigm which was an instrument of our language.[16]

And that in turn reminds me of Simone Weil's repeated insistence that values can be destroyed – when civilisations that embody them are annihilated (Troy, *Langue d'Oc*).[17] So let's not take false comfort. Perhaps what Claggart wants is not so senseless as it might appear. If Billy is dead and forgotten, in what sense is the possibility of his peculiar goodness still a reality?

But there's a further difficulty. What's the use of talking about 'goodness' like this until we have reached agreement on what goodness is, i.e. on what things are good, or on what the good life consists in?

It is true that there is great diversity in the ways people live, in what they try to emulate in others, even in what they admire in others. And while this diversity may be modified in some cases as a result of discussion, there is really no prospect of its being eliminated – the diversity may even be intensified – and anyway, why should increasing uniformity in these dimensions be thought desirable? There will be considerable diversity about that judgement too.

We need to notice as well, as far as Socrates is concerned, that his discussions do not typically try to arrive at agreement on whether, for instance, military or religious values

---

16. [Ludwig Wittgenstein,] *Philosophical Investigations* [eds. G. E. M. Anscombe and Rush Rhees, trans. G. E. M. Anscombe (Oxford: Basil Blackwell, 1953)], §57.
17. Eds: Simone Weil. 'The Iliad, or the Poem of Force', trans. Mary McCarthy; published in many places since 1945, including *Chicago Review* 18, no. 2 (1965): 5–30.

are the right ones to embrace. They are focussed on the role played in life, in whatever sphere, by such embracing notions as good and evil, justice and injustice, beauty and ugliness. And when interlocutors such as Meno refer to the great diversity of values characteristic of different walks of life, Socrates does not deny this diversity, nor does he condemn it; his only complaint is that reference to the diversity as such does not answer the kind of question he is interested in. The unity he hopes to find is a unity within such diversity, not a unity to replace it.

People may differ in what they find good without meaning something different by 'good'. If there were not a sense in which they meant the same by 'good', they could, indeed, hardly be meaningfully said to differ in what they found good. They would simply be talking about something entirely different.

'Good' and 'to my advantage'[18]

Plato and Socrates: The Limits of Argument

The Cave[19]

Everyone is initially imprisoned in the cave. Even the eventually enlightened Socrates-figure is removed as it were against his will. And when he returns (this time voluntarily but again in a sense unwillingly) he cannot reach his former fellow prisoners by argument.[20] In other words, philosophy is not a possible method of government.[21] The kind of training a philosopher needs, and the kinds of condition necessary for the pursuit of philosophy, are not to be found in the context of ordinary social life.

Blumenberg points out that the philosopher's obligation to return to the cave – to engage in politics – is derived from the understanding he has acquired outside the cave. There seems to be a deep paradox here. His disinclination to return into the cave cannot be regarded as simply a result of personal distaste. The life necessary to the cultivation of understanding is itself antithetic to the practical life of politics or 'affairs'. So the problem cannot be merely that the philosopher will be unable to communicate his understanding to those living in the midst of practical affairs – though that [is] a

---

18. See my 'Notes on the Limits of Argument' on this. Eds: Therefore we have reproduced here that argument. That TS does not specifically address 'good' and 'to my advantage'; for that discussion (see previous footnote), see the 'Ethics and Value Theory' lecture notes (Chapter 2.3 above).
19. Acknowledgements to Hans Blumenberg, *Höhlenausgänge*. Eds: See Peter Winch, 'In and Out of the Cave: Review of *Höhlenausgänge* by Hans Blumenberg', *The Times Literary Supplement* 4515 (1989): 1127.
20. Eds: In Session 3 of the Åbo Seminar, he compares the fact that those in the cave cannot be reached by reason with the fact that Hobbes makes no room for the kind of education Rousseau describes – concept formation. (His thought is somewhat elliptical in the outline but is clearer in the lecture materials of Part 2: Hobbes says there is a science but the science is the science of how to arrange the disincentives to disobedience in such a way that the sword makes the covenant something more than mere 'air'.)
21. Eds: Chapter 3 outline I.C.1. listed two sorts of persuasion as 'philosophy' and 'politics' (not rhetoric and philosophy) and this MS seems to pick up that point.

real enough problem. It is also that the philosopher himself is going to have to struggle to retain his understanding in the conditions in which (his understanding dictates to him!) he must live.

I don't believe that Plato ever reached a solution of these difficulties, even (perhaps especially) one that satisfied him. But I think they were difficulties that were never far from the forefront of his mind throughout his work.

Theaetetus *and Simone Weil*

That last point is important to bear in mind in thinking about, for instance, *Theaetetus*. The so-called 'Digression' is in fact, I would say, the fulcrum round which the argument of the dialogue revolves. (Ryle thought it without philosophical interest![22]) It deals with the contrast between the relation to time of the philosopher and the man of practical affairs respectively.[23] I think it's important not to regard the point as simply a 'psychological' one. I.e. it's not just that it's almost impossible to think satisfactorily about philosophical questions unless you are freed from the temporal pressures of practical affairs; rather, you just are not thinking about philosophical questions unless you think about them in a way that's not dictated by the temporal pressures of practical affairs.

What Plato is writing about here is evidently (and not at all accidentally) very closely related to what Simone Weil writes about attention. In the essay on school studies in *Waiting on God* she, like Plato/Socrates is talking about apparently 'purely intellectual' questions; while in 'Are we Struggling for Justice?'[24] she writes about what it is to understand the reality of another human being. But it is obvious in both writers that these themes are interwoven. In Socrates, for instance, thinking about philosophical questions is – and once again this is a conceptual, grammatical point rather than a psychological, contingent one – something which takes place in the context of a special sort of discussion between a very few, ideally two, individuals in which each a) says what he really thinks, or at least really thinks he thinks!, and b) attends to what the other person actually says and tries to understand it through critical attention.

In 'Are we Struggling for Justice?' she makes the same sort of point about temporal pressures as does Plato in *Theaetetus*, but with a different emphasis. She writes of the way the need to 'get things done' (since 'otherwise we will perish') leads to 'sacrilege' in that we have to treat other human beings in ways which do not answer to their real needs (and therefore do not respect their reality). This is precisely what 'injustice', for her, consists in. So it looks as though human affairs for her are antithetical to justice in the same way as, for Plato, they are antithetical to philosophy. But of course this is

---

22. Eds: Gilbert Ryle, *Plato's Progress (Cambridge: Cambridge University Press, 1966)*. Ryle's exact phrasing is that the digression is 'long and philosophically quite pointless' (158).
23. Eds: see Marina Barabas, 'The Strangeness of Socrates', *Philosophical Investigations* 9, no. 2 (1986): 89–110.
24. Eds: Simone Weil, 'Are We Struggling for Justice?', trans. Marina Barabas, *Philosophical Investigations* 10, no. 1 (1987): 1–10.

only a difference in emphasis, insofar as the nature of justice is one of the most central concerns of philosophy, as understood by Plato.

Gorgias: *Socrates, Polus and Callicles [I.G.]*

The survivors in the cave do not understand what the returning philosopher is talking about. It is useless for him to try to reach them by argument, as Socrates understands this. Let me consider this. The only presupposition for entering into discussion on which Socrates insists, remember, is that his partner shall say what he really (thinks he) believes and not speak 'just for the sake of argument'. This fact must be given a central place if one is to understand the character of Socratic argument. Socrates is not in the business of simply testing philosophical 'positions', considered abstractly, for their consistency. He is trying to get his partner to become clear about what he, the partner, 'really thinks'.

At the height of his discussion with Polus on whether it is better for a person to do or to suffer wrong, he does not, as perhaps one might expect, say to Polus: when you have considered the matter in the light in which I shall present it to you, you will change your mind and think as I do. No, in an astounding passage that seems to receive all too little attention from commentators, he says: 'I think that you yourself Polus think as I do; indeed I think that everybody else thinks as I do too.' So the object of the discussion is not to get Polus to change his mind, but rather to get him to understand what his mind really is.

The first question we have to consider is why Socrates's remark should seem so outrageous. Clearly one important part of the answer is this. In countless cases we regard the best possible method of finding out what someone thinks about a certain matter to be asking him. And in countless cases we accept what that person says as settling the matter. An example of such a case would be my asking a friend when he thinks the train that we want to catch is due to leave. I may of course be prepared for his being mistaken about the time of departure, but I would not make much sense of the suggestion that he was mistaken about what he thinks to be the time of departure. If a third party were to tell me that my friend did not really believe what he had told me, the natural way to take that would be as an accusation that he had lied to me.

Taking the speaker as authoritative in this way concerning what he thinks is, we may say, an important feature of the grammar of speaking about thoughts of a certain sort. If we take Polus's thoughts concerning whether it is better to do or to suffer a wrong to be of this sort, then it is natural for us to think that Socrates, in refusing to accept what Polus says he thinks must be accusing him of lying. In philosophising about the situation a certain sort of explanation of this grammatical situation comes naturally to us. (I will not here go into the reasons why this is so.) A person's thought, we may think, are mental processes necessarily transparent to, and only to, the person who has them. Another person can only guess at what someone else thinks; but the person concerned cannot but know what he thinks.

These facts then: first, the grammatical peculiarities of the way we – in some contexts – speak of what we think; and second, the explanatory gloss we find it natural, when philosophising, to put on this grammar, combine to make Socrates's suggestion that Polus and everyone else do not know what they think not merely gratuitously offensive, but almost unintelligible.

I have tried to be careful to qualify the application of what I have just written to certain kinds of case. For it must be clear that not all cases of 'saying what one thinks' are alike. Indeed, as soon as this possibility is raised, it is obvious that the case of saying what you think about the relative desirability of doing and suffering wrong is most unlike the case of saying what you think concerning the time of the train's departure. But before turning to the case of Polus let me consider a case of a different sort again. It is common in the context of certain sorts of personal relationship for one person to ask another, after a period of silence, what he or she is thinking. I imagine I am not alone in finding myself embarrassed when asked such a question; I do not mean because of the contents of my thoughts – though that too of course is a possibility – but because I may well not know what to answer. Anything definite that I might say would be a falsification: whether I say that I am not thinking anything at all, or that I am thinking about such and such a topic, or that such and such definite images, sentences, words, are before my mind. A somewhat similar case is that of having to stop to think what to say next in the course, say, of giving a lecture. The interval may indeed enable me to go on in a way that satisfies me, but I may be totally incapable of giving a definite answer to the question what went on in my mind during the interval.

This sketchy sampling of cases suggests how indeterminate is the concept of saying what one thinks, and in a variety of dimensions. The kind of thing someone wants to know of another in raising this question varies from case to case, as does the natural expectation whether or not the person asked will be able to give a definite answer; and in some cases it may be unclear whether there really is a definite answer to be given. In cases of this last sort, incidentally, one should beware of supposing that this sort of radical indeterminateness makes the question meaningless, or even uninteresting. The fact that thinking about the question is not going to result in an 'answer' does not mean that the thinking must be unproductive.[25]

Consider now the application of these remarks to the confrontation between Socrates and Polus. Apparently the application cannot be very direct, since the grammar of 'thinking that it is better to do than to suffer wrong' (or vice versa) is likely to turn out very different from any of the examples I have just been considering. What are some of the most important features of this sort of case?[26]

First, it is not a question that will ever have occurred to many, perhaps most, people at least in explicit terms, prior to becoming acquainted with Socrates's arguments. It is a question one will probably have to 'make up one's mind about'. This phrase, as used in the present context, deserves examination. It is important that I had to add the italicised qualification above when I wrote that most people will probably not have considered the question previously. If I am reading Socrates's discussion with Polus in the *Gorgias* for the first time I am not like one learning chemistry for the first time who is asked

---

25. I take it that some such thought as this underlies the title of Rush Rhees's volume, *Without Answers* [(London: Routledge and Kegan Paul, 1969)].
26. Handwritten marginal note: Political relevance: *Crito* and *Apology*.

what he thinks, say, is the specific gravity of mercury and has to look up the answer in a textbook. What I shall need to do is to reflect on my own attitudes, which will involve, for example, remembering situations I have encountered in the past, how I have acted, how I have reacted to others' actions, how I have reacted subsequently to my own actions, and so on. I may, as a result of such reflection, feel that there is a clear answer, implicit in all this material, to the question 'what I think' about Socrates's question – and this answer may go in either direction. Alternatively, and perhaps more probably, I may feel that my reflection yields no determinate answer, that my diverse actions and reactions show that I am 'in conflict with myself'. It is in such a case that I may have to make up my mind, but again this may take a variety of forms. It may be that I shall feel my past attitudes point in no direction and that I need to make a decision that will be a pure act of will; on the other hand I may also feel that the conclusion I come to is more or less dictated by attitudes I already possessed.[27] And it is perfectly possible that I shall be surprised by the answer too. I think it may well be this sort of situation Socrates has in mind when he makes his claim about what Polus – and everybody else – really think: but this, so I am suggesting, is by no means the only possible sort of case.[28]

So, interpreting Socrates as I have hitherto done, my conclusion must be that he may be right in what he says about Polus; that will remain to be seen from the way the discussion goes. But there is no warrant thus far for the further extraordinarily universal claim, that he does in fact go on to make in the dialogue, namely that everybody believes it worse to do than to suffer wrong. However, there is still more to be said. I said just now that Socrates may be shown to be right about Polus by the way the discussion goes. But of course, even in cases where the evidence does not seem ambiguous, there is plenty of room for disagreement about what a discussion of this sort actually shows. Different onlookers may, without either of them making anything like a mistake, interpret the outcome in quite conflicting ways. Moreover, quite often the evidence is ambiguous. Even with a hard case like Callicles for instance we have the important passage in which he confesses to the attraction Socrates's view of things has for him, even though he is unable or unwilling to commit himself to it.

Faced with such a situation of ambiguous, conflicting evidence, shifting moods, possibilities of conflicting interpretations, there is nothing to stop someone like Socrates from holding to a determination not to give up, but to go on arguing and trying to show his interlocutor that, in spite of what he thinks, he actually does share Socrates's view. For many of us there will come a time when we feel that enough is enough and that further argument is futile. But someone who does not take this view is not making any obvious mistake; and many of us whose patience is not limitless may have an uneasy feeling sometimes that this is a fault in us rather than evidence of superior rationality. In other words the issue at this point is not so much who is right about the facts, but who has the greater faith in the power of argument.

---

27. I am reminded here of George Eliot's depiction of Gwendoline's 'decision' to marry Harcourt in *Daniel Deronda*.
28. Handwritten marginal note: What prevents Polus and Callicles from going along with Socrates isn't lack of intelligence. (A certain sort of courage?)

Socrates and Polus [I.F.1.][29]

Let us now look at how Socrates does in fact deal with Polus. His procedure is to confront him with his initial statement of what he believes and get him to draw certain conclusions from this, step by painful step. But this sort of argumentation cannot not, by itself, generate any radical challenge to the way Polus understands himself, since inevitably he interprets, understands the conclusions he is induced to draw from his original statement of position in terms of the very same mode of thinking which is expressed in that original statement itself.

It is Polus who introduces the example of the tyrant Archelaus into the argument. He is supposed to be an example of someone who has derived maximum advantage from the injustices by which he has lived and who has never had to face any penalty.

Socrates cannot and does not try to challenge the facts of the case as Polus presents them: that Archelaus has seized power in the state by tricking and murdering his enemies, enriched himself, behaved in any way he pleased, and with impunity, in order to achieve what he wanted, etc. For this reason Polus is not just incredulous but bewildered when Socrates refuses to accept the conclusion: that Archelaus has profited from his injustice.

The way the gap between Socrates and Polus is presented at this point makes it plain that it is not a gap which can be bridged by any formal logical steps, although Socrates does indeed sometimes give the impression of thinking that if only the argument went on long enough a chain of logical steps might be produced that would lead Polus to the same conclusion as he, Socrates, has reached.

Polus thinks that Socrates must have some additional facts up his sleeve, but Socrates of course never claims anything of the sort. This is why it is so perverse, in reading the dialogue for us to suppose that the myth of the soul's judgement after death with which Socrates ends the dialogue, is such an additional set of facts. As though he were saying: Hold on Polus, up to now things are indeed as you say they are; what you do not know [is] that waiting round the corner is a new set of events which will decisively tip the balance in favour of my conclusion. As far as Socrates is concerned, things never were as Polus said they were. What was wrong with Polus was not that he overlooked some important additional facts but that his way of thinking completely distorted his reading of the facts.

Hence the role of the judgement story cannot be to provide some additional premises in the foregoing argument to make it possible for Polus to draw a new conclusion. It is not an expansion of the argument but an attempt to get Polus – and presumably us – to understand the purport of the argument differently, by changing the way we think.[30]

---

29. Eds: The Chapter 3 outline has also I.F.2.: 'Is it that they mean something different by *advantage*? Or what?' The order of discussing the lack of communication between Socrates and Polus and the appeal to shame and saying what one really believes is reversed in the 'Limits of Reason' TS compared to the Chapter 3 outline.

30. This still does not quite put the matter properly. I shall try to qualify it shortly.

It attempts this by presenting us with a certain picture[31] in terms of which we can see ourselves, and our place in the world, from a different perspective.

I shall come back to this very shortly, but first I must look at another aspect of Socrates's mode of arguing with Gorgias, Polus and Callicles, that I think very fundamental – it is striking that at the climax of the discussion with each of these three dialogue partners, Socrates appeals to their sense of shame. [I.F.3.][32] In the case of Gorgias this is the way Socrates gets him to acknowledge that he cannot be indifferent to whether his pupils have a proper understanding of right and wrong and must teach them better if they lack it. In the case of Polus, Socrates puts him in the position of having to say that doing evil is more shameful than suffering evil, so that he has to acknowledge that his argument is an expression of preference for the shameful over the honourable: and this he is ashamed to persist in. Only Callicles tries to challenge this whole procedure by claiming that a sense of shame is a purely 'conventional' attitude induced in the weak by the strong in order for their own purposes to veil the way things really are.[33] Socrates is able to undermine this position by argument and then returns to the attack, trying to get Callicles to acknowledge that he would actually be ashamed of living in ways which his own ostensible position should lead him to approve. I almost feel inclined to say that the appeal to his opponents' sense of shame plays the [same] role in Socrates's arguments [that the] … the forcible wrenching of the chosen one out of the Cave [does] in *The Republic*.

How does this feature of Socrates' procedure relate to the myths: to the myth of judgement in the first instance but also to his appeals to myths more generally?

The Story of the Soul's Judgement and Socrates's Argument [I.1. Argument and Myth]

'Literal' *and* 'Metaphorical'

I have said that it is perverse to regard the myth of the soul's judgement after death narrated by Socrates at the end of *Gorgias* as the introduction of a new set of facts to bridge the gap between acknowledged premises and desired conclusion. For one thing the details of the mythical story would be just too fantastic and indeed irrelevant if interpreted in that way. I think for instance of the detail that both the judges and the soul of the deceased appear naked in court in order to ensure impartiality. Imagine

---

31. In speaking this way I very consciously lean on what Wittgenstein says about the use of 'pictures', e.g. in religion, in the Lectures and Conversations and elsewhere. Eds: *Lectures and Conversations on Aesthetics, Psychology and Religious Belief: Compiled from Notes taken by Yorick Smythies, Rush Rhees, and James Taylor*, ed. Cyril Barrett (Oxford: Basil Blackwell, 1966).
32. Eds: See also 'Plato's *Gorgias*', Chapter 2.3 above.
33. Eds: In the Chapter 3 outline at I.H., Winch indicates that he intends to go in some detail through Callicles's challenge to Socrates and the theme of nature and convention (I.H.1.) and how Socrates replies and Callicles himself succumbs to shaming (I.H.2.). For this, see the lectures reproduced above ('Plato's *Gorgias*', Chapter 2.3). And he indicates that he will go on to discuss the limits of argument in relation to each of Polus, Callicles, and Alcibiades (Chapter 3 outline I.H.3.a–c), when the materials we have focus on the limits of Socrates's argument with Polus.

someone suggesting the introduction of such a technique into our human system of judgement! Well, why not? If the gods find it a good idea, surely it ought to be worth a try by us! Everybody would agree that this is absurd; and I take it that few would want to accuse Socrates or Plato of that sort of childishness.

But if we are clearly not meant to take such details with that kind of 'literalness', why on earth should we suppose that the myth in broad outlines is meant to be taken in that way? But in what way? My scare quotes round 'literalness' were not a piece of academic archness, but had a serious purpose. I understand what would be the literal meaning of saying that human judges and a human accused appeared naked in court; and I can think of circumstances in which that might be said metaphorically too. But here we are talking about the soul of a dead person and about the gods. If I am told that I have to apply the distinction between 'literal' and 'metaphorical' in the same way in this context as in the other, then I do not as yet understand what it is that I am supposed to do. Where am I to suppose the soul and the gods left their clothes before entering the court? Who took their measurements when the clothes were made for them? And so on. The questions are obviously laughable, but they are questions which go with interpreting the story 'literally' where this is understood as interpreting it in the same way as I interpret the story about the human trial.

Anyone who reads the *Gorgias* judgement story with the barest minimum of understanding takes it for granted that the talk about nakedness in the story is an emphasising of the necessary impartiality and justice of this divine court's proceedings. Of course this is not at all incompatible with readers' having before them a picture illustrating the story (for all I know, such a picture has been painted). But what is important for their understanding of the story is not their having such a picture but how, if they do have it, they apply it.

If, then, I am told I ought to take the story literally, I am inclined to reply that taking it as a story about impartiality and real justice *is* 'taking it literally'. The idea that it is metaphorical is based on an illusion: the illusion that there is a genuine literal meaning with which such a metaphorical meaning can be contrasted.

To all this it may be objected that Socrates does after all introduce the story of the soul's judgement by saying he believes it to be true! But this is a problem only if it is – absurdly – supposed that Socrates is using the word 'true' to carry all the theoretical baggage with which a modern philosophical 'realist' tries to load it. It is much more natural, however, to take Socrates to mean what anyone might mean in such a context, namely that he himself holds by this story in the sense that it is fundamental to his own thinking about life. This of course still leaves it entirely open what role the story plays in his thinking about life. As Wittgenstein says, 'p is true' is equivalent to 'p', but this still leaves it entirely open what the decision for or against p looks like in any particular case.

The Conclusion of the Argument

Suppose that, waiving for a moment these considerations, we pretend that we understand talk about 'taking the judgment story literally' and that we then try to apply it in the suggested way: i.e. as providing further facts which will enable Socrates to get to the conclusion he wants concerning the preferability of suffering over doing injustice. Let us now ask what conclusion such an argument would actually yield.

The conclusion would be that the rational way to behave would be that which ensures the best, or the least bad, future consequences for oneself and that, since suffering everlasting pains after death would be the worst possible outcome for oneself and since this would be the inevitable outcome of living by inflicting injustices on others, it is rational not to live like that. But can this be the conclusion that Socrates wants? There are at least three reasons why the answer to this must be no.

Firstly, the attitude described would be that graphically described by Rush Rhees in the following passage.

> Is the reason for not worshipping the devil instead of God that God is stronger than the devil? God will get you in the end, the devil will not be able to save you from his fury, and then you will be *for* it. 'Think of the future, boy, and don't throw away your chances.' What a creeping and vile sort of thing religion must be.[34]

Does this really describe the attitude to life of the Socrates depicted by Plato?

Second, an important segment of Socrates's argument with Polus concerns the object of a person's will which is, Socrates suggests, the purpose for the sake of which someone acts. Anything which is just a means to the achievement of that purpose is not the object of the agent's will. The assumption we are considering in the present context is that the purpose for which someone acts in avoiding doing evil to another person is the avoidance of some unpleasantness to him or herself. The avoidance of doing evil to another person is thus not the object of the agent's will, not what the agent understands to be good.

It is true that Socrates does argue that doing good rather than evil to another is necessarily good for oneself. But his argument is not that this is what makes it good not to harm another; on the contrary, his argument is that because not harming another is good, it is necessarily good for the agent. But this good for the agent comes about only if the agent genuinely wills what is good, i.e. the avoidance of harm to the other. But, as we have seen, this is not what is willed by the agent who acts to avoid punishment for himself.

And finally, in any case, one of the most prominent, most explicit, pieces of argument in Socrates's exchanges with Polus is directed at showing that, for one who has committed injustice, punishment is something to be welcomed, not shunned as an evil. It would be odd if, in the end, Socrates should be found to be assuming that, after all, in the end the main thing to do is to avoid being punished.

There is, of course, a genuine difficulty here. The punishments discussed in the body of Socrates's exchanges with Polus are punishments inflicted by living human beings on living human beings. Such punishments Socrates tries to interpret as analogous to medical treatment, unpleasant in themselves, but worth tolerating for the sake of the ultimate good they bring about. The punishments suffered by the soul after a person's

---

34. Rush Rhees, *Without Answers* (London: Routledge and Kegan Paul, 1969), 113.

death are not like that, however. It is too late for the dead person to regain spiritual 'health' (he is after all dead!); and so the punishments he suffers cannot be thought of as medicinal in character; medicine can only be administered to the living.

Part of the trouble here lies, I think, in the fact that the medical analogy limps and in the end does more harm than good. The relation between medicine and cure is a contingent, causal one; whereas the relation between punishment and spiritual recovery of which Socrates speaks has to be understood as an internal, conceptual relation. Leaving that aside, however, it is clear that much of the incoherence pointed out in the last paragraph comes precisely from interpreting the myth of the soul's punishment as a further set of premises on all fours with the other premises involved in Socrates's argument with Polus. 'Punishment' (just as much as 'nakedness') in the context of the myth has to be understood in a different way from that in which it is understood in living human contexts.[35]

The Role of the Myths [Outline I.I.]

The Soul's Judgement in Gorgias

To regard the myth of judgement in the way I have been criticising is to see it as filling out in an explanatory way what Socrates had meant in arguing that it is better for someone to suffer than to do injustice. My criticisms involve seeing the logical relations the other way round. I have argued that the myth cannot be understood in the way proposed since to do so would be at odds with what Socrates is clearly aiming at in his argument. But this still leaves open the question what the point of introducing the myth actually is. I can do no more than make a suggestion about this.

We should remind ourselves first that neither Polus nor Callicles are actually persuaded by Socrates' arguments. Instead of offering them, and us, his vicarious interlocutors, yet more of the same, what Socrates does in introducing the myth is offer us a point of view from which, if we respond to it as he hopes, the arguments may after all gain a foothold. It is a point of view from which the terms in which the argument is couched may be understood in a different way. I am offered a view of my life from the point of view of my own death; as Wittgenstein puts it in the *Tractatus*, it is a view of my life as 'a limited whole'.[36] Knowing that one day I shall die, I know that one day my life will be such a limited whole; while, living, I can never actually have such a view of my life, I can nevertheless try to live that life in the knowledge that one day it will be possible to speak of it, to speak of me, thus. 'This is what he was.' And I can, now, ask myself what I would like it to be possible to say of me from that point of view, which means also asking what difference the ways in which I now act and propose to act will

---

35. Eds: In the Chapter 3 outline, he goes on to Callicles, with a reference to nature and convention. He may have had in mind his own much earlier paper, but perhaps not; see above, Chapter 2.3.
36. Eds: *Tractatus Logico-Philosophicus*, trans. David Pears and Brian McGuinness (London: Routledge and Kegan Paul, 1961), 5.6s.

make to that possibility. If I am now, for instance, proposing an act of great injustice, I will now ask myself not just, or even mainly, how I am likely to reckon its advantages to me while living, but rather: what difference is such an action going to make to what I have been, indeed to what I am, at a time when I shall no longer be alive. Is it going to make of me an unrepentant liar, cheat and murderer, for example? And is that the sort of person I admire? If not, can I admire myself if I live like this? The appeal here is obviously very closely related to Socrates's appeals to his interlocutors' sense of shame, to which I have already drawn attention.

Now all this does not constitute an argument in the sense in which the main body of what Socrates says in the dialogue consists of arguments. And there is no guarantee that anyone reading the myth actually will ask him or herself these kinds of question, nor what answer he or she will give them if they are asked. Nevertheless someone may be persuaded and may feel, not without reason, that in being thus persuaded he or she has been shown something, has learnt something. If not, no harm will have been done and there is no reason in principle why anyone has to feel tricked by such tactics. Whether such a reaction is appropriate or not will depend on the particular case.

The Cave

The myth of the prisoners in the cave in *The Republic* in a sense goes philosophically deeper in that it is precisely a way of representing the limits of conventional philosophical argument. It shows one that there are ways of failing to understand the force of an argument which are not a result of lack of logical acumen or attention to the detailed steps of the argument. One may systematically fail to understand in the appropriate way what is being said and it may be only by being persuaded to take up another point of view, or even by being jolted into another point of view, that one can come to understand. The Cave myth is an invitation to the reader to take seriously the possibility that this is the situation he or she is in.[37]

The Political Relevance of All This[38]

A first thought might be that, insofar as the foregoing represents an application, however fumbling, of a Socratic type of deliberation, it is indeed hard to see how that is going to have much place in anything we would naturally describe as 'the conduct of political affairs'. But this does not take us far.

Perhaps the following would be more to the point. I have yet to discuss in any sort of useful detail the kind of difficulty it is easy to see in reconciling recognition of the authority of the state with what we understand by 'practical reason'. But I have tried to sketch the problem: to act for a reason, one might think, is to act in furtherance of what concerns one in the light of one's own best assessment of the situation one finds one in.

---

37. Eds: 'Limits of Argument' TS ends here and is 'signed' and dated: Peter Winch 04.10.93; 4:44 pm. The following turns back now to the 'Action, Reason and Will' TS.
38. Eds: Not in the Chapter 3 outline.

To accept the authority of another, however, seems to be precisely to forego the possibility of doing this, insofar as one is now going to act in the light of someone else's assessment of the situation. Put like this, acceptance of another's authority seems to be to renounce the most fundamental principle of practical rationality. But perhaps what we ought to have been more suspicious of is the idea that there is any such thing as the most fundamental principle of practical rationality. Suppose for instance that one compares Socrates and Claggart, their 'fundamental principles' seem to be diametrically opposed. Whereas reason, in Socrates's practice, necessarily directed towards the good, Claggart conceives it to be his mission to protect evil against the threat of good! Maybe someone will want to contest the claim that Claggart is 'exercising reason', pointing out how obsessional he clearly is. Well yes, but if we are to be fair, perhaps we must admit that Socrates is pretty obsessional too. Once we have conceded that, we shall not be too far away from the thought that reason is always exercised within parameters set by a person's overall perspective on life. At that point we shall find it difficult to rule out the possibility that acknowledgement of an authority may be one such parameter.

Is all this too 'relativistic'? Does it amount to saying that there is nothing to choose between Socrates and Claggart? By no means! But why should the choice have to be made according to the criterion of who is the most 'rational'? Why should that be the overriding consideration? I intend that by the way as a genuine, not just rhetorical, question.

3.4

REASONS AND CAUSES[1]

[Recall Hobbes in the *Behemoth* [I.A.]]

> You may perhaps think a man has need of nothing else to know the duty he owes his governor, and what right he has to order him, but a good natural wit; but it is otherwise. For it is a science[2], and built upon sure and clear principles, and to be learned by deep and careful study, or from masters that have deeply studied it. And who was there in the Parliament or in the nation, that could find out those evident principles, and derive from them the necessary rules of justice, and the necessary connection of justice and peace?

Hobbes is trying to persuade his readers. But what sort of 'persuasion'? (Is he giving them reasons for actions, or trying to cause them to behave differently?) Are reasons causes?

The promiscuous uses of 'reason': e.g. [I.B.]

1. What is the reason why my car won't start? (Perhaps the fuel line is frozen.)
2. What is the reason why she has not come to the lecture today? (Perhaps she is unconscious as the result of a traffic accident.)
3. Or perhaps she feels a bit feverish and thinks she had better stay at home and rest in case her condition should worsen.

[The first] concerns an inanimate object, [the second] a human being. But (1) and (2) are similar in form when contrasted with (3), which we can re-express: '*her reason for* not coming'. This, in the present context, is one of the most important distinctions we have to keep our eye on.

In cases like (3) we can often ask whether someone's reason for doing or not doing something was a *good* or *bad* reason. This is of course different from asking whether such and such really was someone's reason or whether he actually acted for some quite different reason. People may act for bad reasons and they may fail to act when they

---

1. Eds: Computer printout; 24 pp.; Peter Winch Archives (GB 0100 KCLCA K/PP171, Box 16), King's College London, supplemented with TS 'Reasons and Causes' from the same archive collection (box location not recorded). We have indicated in square brackets where the 'Reasons and Causes' text corresponds with the Chapter 4 outline.
2. Note that Hobbes seems hardly to consider my alternative: that what is required is neither just 'natural wit' nor 'science'; it's 'a question of upbringing'.

have good reasons for doing so.[3] This dimension is lacking from case (1). If we *should* ask whether the frozen fuel line was a good reason for the car not to start, this can only mean: was that actually the reason for its not starting. The same goes for case (2). If I said that being unconscious in bed as the result of an accident were no good reason for her not coming to the lecture, that could only be a bad and callous joke.

Let's, for convenience, follow precedent in calling cases like (1) and (2) *causes*, and those like (3) *reasons*, not forgetting that this is really legislative because of the promiscuity with which we actually use these words. [1.B.2.; I.B.2.a]

However, I don't want to give the impression that the distinction is entirely unproblematic. By this I do not mean to say that it is unproblematic whether there is such a distinction; it is real enough and of great significance. I mean that its application is problematic by way of being indeterminate in certain situations. [III. Indeterminacies in application; III.A.]

Consider e.g. someone who betrays his friends under torture. There are cases where we (some of us) would probably want to say that 'his reason for .... etc.' was to avoid further torture. That implies that he 'had a choice' (careful!). But in some cases some may think he 'had no choice'; that the disclosure was 'wrung', 'forced' from him. (As water may be wrung out of a wet cloth.) [III.B.]

It is quite normal for such judgements to be matter for disputes, which are not always resolvable. The possible roots of such disputes are various.

They may depend for instance on how one judges the gravity of the situation. Thus, for instance, someone tells me she could not come to my lecture because she was lying in bed with a high fever; 'I meant to come, but I had no choice, I couldn't get out of bed'. Normally, I would certainly accept that. If, however, the appointment she did not keep was that of appearing as a witness able to prove the innocence of someone on trial for a serious crime, the situation would not be so clear. I might think that in this extremity she ought to have dragged herself out of bed however great the difficulty.

Of course there will be some cases in which this would be absurd; if, for instance, she was lying unconscious at death's door; but in other cases there will be disagreement about where absurdity begins.

Apart from cases like those just mentioned where the disagreements involve differing assessments of the importance of the particular act omitted, there are also disagreements based on the varying standards to which one thinks people must be held. Such variation may be based on a person's particular interests. E.g. a military commander may be unwilling to condone any breach of security, even under the severest torture. (Others may think he is being unreasonable...) But the variation may also be an expression of more or less rigorous moral or religious outlooks. [III.C.1.–3.]

One is perhaps tempted to say that such disagreements are not truly 'factual' disputes. This may be in order for certain purposes. But we should be careful, perhaps,

---

3. It need not be the case that they have better reasons for not doing so. They may for instance be lazy, or cowardly.

not to overestimate the firmness of our grip on this distinction between what is and what is not 'a matter of fact'. [III.D.]

Which concept is Hobbes using in my quotation from *Behemoth*? It seems clear that he was speaking of reasons in the sense sketched. He believed that the English people had behaved foolishly in rebelling against the King and he wanted to give them good reasons for changing their attitude in the future. [I.A.2.a/I.B.1.a]

I am sure this is the right answer, but there is an embarrassment about putting the matter in these terms; for Hobbes did not acknowledge any such distinction. In Part 1 of *Leviathan* he argues at some length that a person's reasons for acting are the causes of his action in roughly the sense in which I have explained the word 'cause' above. Human beings are mechanical systems like any other; they behave according to certain general causal principles; one's aim in discovering those principles is to be able to influence their behaviour in ways that will be advantageous to oneself. According to Hobbes, the underlying causal principles are self-interest and, especially, fear of death and disorder. The purpose of discovering this is to be able to exploit it for one's own ends. That is, as it were, Hobbes's official account. But of course in his actual practice he makes similar kinds of distinction to the rest of us – distinctions like those above for instance.[4] [I.B.2.b]

Hobbes and the nineteenth century jurist John Austin, author of *The Province of Jurisprudence Determined*, were separated by two centuries. The major immediate influence on Austin was Jeremy Bentham; and in a sense Austin represents the juristic wing of Benthamite Utilitarianism. Still, it is noteworthy that the conceptual, or at least terminological, framework of Austin's account of law is pretty much that of Hobbes. [I.B.1.a]

Law is a 'command of the sovereign' and a command is what it is by virtue of being backed by sanctions. Because of this striking similarity it's instructive to compare the two writers: their differences bring what they were respectively doing into relief.

Which concept is Hobbes using in my quotation from *Behemoth*? It seems clear that he was speaking of reasons in the sense sketched. He believed that the English people had behaved foolishly in rebelling against the King and he wanted to give them good reasons for changing their attitude in the future.

John Austin too wanted to found a science of law, but in a very different sense from that of Hobbes. Austin's aim was to give a clear and distinct account of the limits of what a jurist studies and he took this to be a matter of knowing how to recognise a certain empirical phenomenon and to distinguish it from other empirical phenomena. What we have to do, he says, is observe carefully how a given society is structured in terms of who commands and who obeys. If there is someone (human being or corporate body) whom everyone else habitually obeys and who does not habitually obey anyone else, then he, she or it is the 'sovereign' and his/her/its commands have the force of law.

---

4. For a very useful discussion of the distinction see Grete Hermann, *Die Überwindung des Zufalls*. [Greta Henry-Hermann, 'Conquering Chance: Critical Reflections on Leonard Nelson's Establishment of Ethics as a Science', trans. Peter Winch, *Philosophical Investigations*, 14, no. 1 (1991): 1–80.]

It was important to Austin's programme that command and obedience should also be empirical concepts in the sense that one could recognise simply by careful observation when someone was obeying and when commanding. Now while of course it is in a sense true that one can do this, much depends on what one is going to count as 'observation' in this context. Austin's approach to this (to speak anachronistically) was a 'behaviouristic' one.

We might say that Austin was not much interested in people's reasons for obeying the law in the sense of case 3. discussed in my previous sections. He thought probably, as I think many jurists still do, that this is something 'subjective' and hence(?) undiscoverable. He was interested in what explains why people in general obey the law, perhaps in the sense of a sort of cause. Though he had not, I think, thought much about the distinctions between different 'Why?' questions discussed in the previous sections.

He certainly wouldn't have welcomed the suggestions I made earlier that the applicability of causal explanation in certain circumstances will depend on one's own ethical attitudes. One of his main aims was precisely to free the concept of law from the dependence on ethical concepts emphasised in the rival 'natural law' juristic tradition.

For Austin, a certain sort of causal explanation is built into the definition of law in a rather curious, discreet way. I mean by this that his definition of 'law' involves the idea of people in general being influenced in their behaviour by the threat of sanctions; but that he does not of course make any requirement about how any individual must have been motivated on any particular occasion. Any distinction like Kant's between 'in accordance with' and 'for the sake of' would have been quite foreign to him.

Austin's idea is that law is a sort of sociological concept (my terminology, not his); it rests on the assumption that we can observe certain general patterns of behaviour in society. In particular we can observe that there are certain people who habitually obey and certain others who habitually command without habitually obeying anyone else. These latter constitute the 'sovereign'.[5] [V.A.1.–7.]

We have already seen that Hobbes's emphasis is quite different. His definition of command is based precisely on considerations about the reasons the one who obeys has for what he or she does.[6]

> COMMAND is, where a man saith, *do this*, or *do not this* without expecting other reason than the will of him that says it. From this it follows manifestly, that he that commandeth, pretendeth thereby his own benefit: for the reason of his command is his own will only, and the proper object of every man's will, is some good to himself.
>
> COUNSEL, is where a man saith, *do*, or *do not this*, and deduceth his reasons from the benefit that arriveth by it to him to whom, he saith it. And from this it is evident, that he that giveth counsel, pretendeth only, whatsoever he intendeth, the good of him, to whom he giveth it.

---

5. Of course there are all kinds of difficulties concerning the application of this schema to the case of any actual society which is at all complex. But I shan't go into this side of the matter here.
6. As I remarked earlier, although Hobbes himself does not (officially, as it were) recognise any distinction between reasons and causes, his practice belies his official doctrine.

There is a big difference between the direction he is pointing in and that suggested by Austin's definition of 'law' in terms of a habit of obedience. Whereas Austin's question is a sort of 'sociological' one – how can we identify the laws of a society – Hobbes's concern with definition here is a means to a wider end. He is not interested in the fact that a majority of people does habitually obey someone identified as sovereign. He is interested in bringing it about that they do so obey. He is interested in the reasons they might have for obeying; and again, not simply as a matter of detached theoretical interest. – He wants to give reasons for obeying. He cannot, therefore, take 'a habit of obedience' as a datum. [V.B.–C.]

[I. of the Chapter 4 Outline indicates Winch will fill out this chapter with the following.]

C. What can Hobbes 'science' persuade one of?
  1. Self-interest
  2. Trust
  3. Loyalty
D. 'Science' versus education
  1. Hobbes and Rousseau
  2. Connection with 'The Limits of Argument'
     a. different sorts of persuasion
  3. In what way is a 'reason' *persuasive*

[IV. of the Chapter 4 outline contains the following, which roughly maps to I.C.A. but does not carry on through the rest of I.C.]

Although Hobbes himself would no doubt have vigorously and indignantly disputed this, I think there is a sense in which one can say that his political attitudes are not so much based on his 'science' as his science is based on his political attitudes. What I mean is that the way in which Hobbes applies certain key notions in his argument (like that of 'reason' for instance) already presuppose certain quasi-political judgements. There are points at which this peeps through.

Consider, for instance, the remarkable passage in which he speaks of the rare few great-hearted individuals who have 'a glory, or pride in appearing not to need to break (their word). This latter is a generosity too rarely found to be presumed on…'[7]

Hobbes clearly admires such individuals; whereas, it seems, he ought, on his own theory of rationality, to condemn them as fundamentally irrational, since force and fraud are precisely the instruments of rationality where there is no power to enforce performance of contracts.

There is a better, less *ad hominem* argument. The 'generosity' of which Hobbes writes here itself defines a way of reasoning. The generous hearted individual will reason in a different way and respond to different kinds of argument from those of the mass. This indicates that our judgements of what is and what is not rational behaviour is not always 'value neutral'.

---

7. Hobbes, *Leviathan*, Part 1, Chapter XIII.

190   POLITICAL AUTHORITY

Notice the difference in spirit between Hobbes and Socrates: 'a generosity too rarely found to be presumed on'. Hobbes is here following his hated Aristotle in taking human nature as a given; he does not see that the spectacle of generosity can change people. Is this argument? It's certainly an attempt to get people to reason in different way (as opposed to getting them to draw conclusions according to their familiar way of reasoning).

1. For example, the film 'Lacombe, Lucien'[8]
2. The influence of a great teacher[9]
3. The impact of literature
4. The influence of a great orator...

---

8. Eds: In this 1974 Louis Malle film (co-written with Patrick Modiano), the 17-year-old Lucien, after a chance series of events, joins the French auxiliaries of the Gestapo towards the end of World War Two, when the Allies are already fighting in Normandy.
9. Eds: In lectures, Winch would reflect on the interchange attributed to Thomas More and Richard Rich by Robert Bolt in 'A Man for All Seasons' (first performed on BBC Radio in the 1950s and later on stage and in film):

> Sir Thomas More: Why not be a teacher? You'd be a fine teacher; perhaps a great one.
> Richard Rich: If I was, who would know it?
> Sir Thomas More: You; your pupils; your friends; God. Not a bad public, that.

3.5

THE HISTORICITY OF POLITICAL PHILOSOPHY[1]

[I.] Given that the thinkers we will consider are (as we all are) historical beings, how far do the points they make have a general relevance, rather than just a limited historical bearing? This is a more complex issue than may appear.

We must not assume that everyone who talks of 'the nature of political authority' will be raising the same issue. The question must be understood in the context within which it is being asked. No doubt this is true of any question whatever, but it may be more urgent that we keep it in mind in some cases than in others. It is particularly urgent when philosophy is in the air, since a large part of the puzzlement generated by many philosophical questions arises from the fact that they are treated as if they had a sense independent of any particular context.[2]

[I.A.] One important consideration in this connection may be brought out by considering the following reflections by Wittgenstein on the peculiar cast of Frank Ramsey's thinking:

> Ramsey was a bourgeois thinker. I.e. the purpose of his thoughts was to put in order the affairs of a given/particular community. He didn't reflect on the essence of the state – or he didn't like doing so – but on how this state might be reasonably organised. The thought that this state might not be the only possible one partly disturbed him, partly bored him.

---

1. Eds: Computer printout; 24 pp.; Peter Winch Archives (GB 0100 KCLCA K/PP171, Box 16), King's College London, supplemented with TS 'Authority: General and Particular' from the same archive collection (box location not recorded) from the beginning of this chapter to '... agreements underlying the Hannoverian settlement'. We have indicated in square brackets where the 'Reasons and Causes' text corresponds with the Chapter 5 outline. This TS has the same content as the Åbo Seminar session 7. We provide in footnotes materials in the Åbo Seminar notes that are not in the 'Authority: General and Particular' TS; where the Chapter 5 outline has sections not covered in the TS, we include the text of the outline. Section numbers in square brackets in the text indicate the relation of the 'Authority: General and Particular' text to the corresponding Chapter 5 outline.
2. Contrast, for instance, Wittgenstein's treatment of the relationship between 'simple' and 'complex' early in the *Philosophical Investigations* [eds. G. E. M. Anscombe and Rush Rhees, trans. G. E. M. Anscombe (Oxford: Basil Blackwell, 1953)] and in *Tractatus* [trans. David Pears and Brian McGuinness (London: Routledge and Kegan Paul, 1961)].

He wanted to get on as quickly as possible with thinking about the foundations – of this state. This was what he could do and what he was really interested in; whereas really philosophical reflection made him uncomfortable until he set its result (if any) aside as trivial.³

Wittgenstein was here of course using talk about the state as a figure for Ramsey's work on the foundations of mathematics. But I want to take literally his description of different approaches to questions about 'the nature/essence of the state'.

Those who raise such questions will, of course, come from quite particular historico-political contexts and will tend to have institutions of a particular form in the forefront of their minds. They will perhaps be familiar in the first instance with the presidential-cum- congressional system of the USA, or with the British parliamentary system, or with a communist people's democracy, or a non-constitutional monarchy. The particular starting point will tend naturally to dictate the use of certain kinds of example rather than others in the discussion.

A writer may, in the style attributed by Wittgenstein to Ramsey, be interested in the peculiarities of particular political systems. From this point of view it may well be important to contrast the authority exercised, say, by an American president with that exercised by a French president; and both of these again with that exercised by a British Prime Minister.

Contrast this with Locke's statement of purpose as expressed early in his *Second Treatise of Government*: 'To understand political power right and derive it from its original....'⁴ The formulation is completely general; and despite M[a]cpherson and other commentators, I think it is clear from the general lines of Locke's argument that it is *meant* to be so.⁵

---

3. *Vermischte Bemerkungen* (1931), S. 473. [The reference is to the Suhrkamp Werkausgabe, Band 8.] Handwritten marginal note: C&V, p. 17. [*Culture and Value*, ed. G. H. von Wright and Heikki Nyman, trans. Peter Winch (Oxford: Basil Blackwell, 1989).]
4. John Locke, *The Second Treatise of Government*, Chapter II, Section 4.
5. Eds: Åbo Seminar Session 7 includes a repetition of the second paragraph above at this point, and the following:

> The treatment of this sort of puzzlement will consist in large part of pointing out the different contexts in which such questions may naturally arise and noting that in philosophy, such differences of context are characteristically forgotten. This will belong to what Wittgenstein often called the dissolution of the original problem (rather than its solution) the sign of which is that one ceases to ask the original question.

The following is the continuation of the previous paragraph the Åbo Seminar Notes and in the 'Authority: General and Particular' TS, but is crossed out in the latter.

> Now all this may seem to justify Ramsey's boredom or impatience with such questions. How, then, does Wittgenstein's attitude differ from Ramsey's? I think he is ambivalent. On the one hand the remark about Ramsey suggests that he does indeed attach a kind of importance to the philosophical questions that Ramsey misses. On the other hand we have:

Locke's Difficulties with Consent [I.B.3 Locke and 'Consent']⁶

However, there are serious difficulties in understanding what the object of a 'philosophical' interest in issues of political authority could actually be. They are difficulties that arise with any attempt to raise general philosophical questions of this kind, but I will stay with Locke for a moment. It is clear that he, the professed generality of his interest notwithstanding, has the particular circumstances and problems characteristic of his own time and place, namely the aftermath of the 'English Revolution of 1688' very much at the forefront of his mind. As Professor Thomas F. Peardon says in the introduction to his edition of the *Second Treatise*,⁷ he has for this reason often been called 'the theorist' of this revolution.

Without any doubt it is perfectly legitimate to treat Locke in this way: one can indeed learn much about the nature and problems of the English political scene in the late seventeenth century by studying Locke. Moreover, like most other serious writers on questions of political philosophy, his interest in such questions was to a large extent stimulated by the political questions thrown up by events in his own time. However, I think it is a serious distortion of Locke to claim that this was 'really' what he was studying. At the same time, I must give due weight to the difficulties that lie in the way of explaining what *else* he could have been studying.⁸

We may get an idea about what these difficulties are by noticing a paradox, into which Locke – like others, Rousseau for instance – is driven. Locke tries to differentiate 'political power' from other sorts of power by specifying certain conditions that must hold as between rulers and ruled. These conditions are spelled out in terms of consent, and what Locke writes about consent can certainly be seen as in part an attempt to spell

---

> Philosophy has made no progress? – If someone scratches himself where he has an itch, must he make progress? Isn't it genuine scratching otherwise, or a real itch? And cannot this reaction to the irritation go on for a long time, before a way of dealing with the itch is found? [*Culture and Value*, ed. G. H. von Wright and Heikki Nyman, trans. Peter Winch (Oxford: Basil Blackwell, 1989), 86–7]
>
> I tend to prefer the first attitude to the second. But it's hardly necessary to decide between them; after all, if one has an itch, one must scratch! Ramsey, perhaps Wittgenstein is saying, didn't have it.

6. Eds: The Chapter 5 outline indicates an intention to discuss also Plato and Post-Bellum Athens (Socrates) and Hobbes and the Civil War [I.B.1.-2.], alongside the discussion here of Locke and the 1688 Settlement.
7. New York, Liberal Arts Press, 1952.
8. It is important of course that the general form of the difficulty is not specific to the details of any particular account. It would for instance apply equally to accounts which see political power as something divinely instituted. Political communities differ enormously in their histories and structures and the hope of finding anything common to them all and differentiating them from non-political communities seems doomed to disappointment or destined to end in arbitrariness.

out the agreements underlying the Hannoverian Settlement.⁹ [I.C.1. His method and the historian's; a) 'a difference in grammar'] The verification of what he says, interpreted thus, would be the business of a historian.¹⁰ What sort of case would a historian need to make? No doubt there were plenty of actual negotiations the course and outcome of which would need documenting and analysing. Compromise will have been reached, promises made. But of course there will also have been larger scale – and much less explicit adjustments in the interrelations between different groups and interests in the population at large, changes in people's expectations and hopes, the forging of new alliances and the disintegration of old ones.¹¹ Serious historical inquiry demands that hypotheses about such events shall be as specific and as precise as possible; otherwise there can be no worthwhile 'verification'.

But of course, however much what Locke writes may be inspired by his reading of the Hannoverian Settlement, he does not himself write as a historian, and he does not invite his readers to 'verify' what he writes after the manner of historians. This is clearly connected with the fact that *it is not the Hannoverian Settlement as such in which he is interested, but, simply, 'political power' – however much his conception of political power was in fact shaped by his experience of the Hannoverian Settlement.*¹²

There is a danger at this point in supposing that the difference between these interests is, as it were, a difference in degree. One thinks perhaps that any agreements

---

9. Eds: In Åbo Seminar 7, he continues:

> Now questions that certainly deserve to be taken seriously have been raised concerning whether such conditions are ever satisfied: by Hume for instance in his great essay 'Of the Original Contract'. For the present I want to leave such doubts on one side and to focus on the fact that, if we accept Locke's account, we seem committed to saying that any society in which such conditions are not exemplified cannot be one in which it is proper to speak of the exercise of political power or one that can properly be said to constitute a state. This seems preposterous, as indeed Locke himself seems to have recognised in so watering down his notion of consent that consent is to be deemed as having been given on the basis of the mere fact that the person concerned finds himself within the territory on which power is exercised.
>
> I shall be discussing the crux in Locke's thinking in more detail later on. At present I want to point out that the general form of the difficulty is not specific to the details of any particular account. It would for instance apply equally to accounts which see political histories and structures and the hope of finding anything common to them all and differentiating them from non-political communities seems doomed to failure or destined to end in arbitrariness.

10. Eds: From this point to '...over whom it is exercised' below is the same as the beginning of Åbo Seminar 8.
11. A lively sense of the beginnings of some of these changes can be gained from Samuel Pepys's Diary, which is illuminating because written, as it were at the intersection of public and private life.
12. [Åbo Seminar 8] What I am interested in is the relation between these: how far the fact that his conception was thus 'shaped' is compatible with his being able to say anything of wider validity. (Not very well expressed.)

underlying the institution of political power must have been made very much longer ago and be much more difficult to determine. But, as I noted, Locke does not 'write after the manner of historians' at all. The difference between what he is investigating and what historians investigate is, one might say – following Wittgenstein – 'a difference in grammar'.[13] What counts as establishing what Locke wants to establish is different from what counts as establishing, e.g. that two politicians struck a deal on such and such a date. Locke's arguments are based on his conception of *the nature of political power*.

Because, his thought is, the exercise of authority over a rational adult, involves a renunciation on the latter's part of his prerogative of deciding for himself what it best for him to do, it *can only* come about as a result of his or her consent since each person has to make such a renunciation for him or herself. The 'has to' in that sentence must be understood as having quasi-logical force. To adapt a remark of Wittgenstein's from another context, it is like doffing your hat; you can only do this yourself.[14] Whatever anyone else may do will not count as being that. Similarly, whatever anyone else may do it will not count as my renouncing my prerogative of deciding for myself.[15] Hence, Locke thinks, if there really is such a thing as political authority there must be a real consent to that power on the part of each of those over whom it is exercised.[16]

[I.C. Cases where this relationship holds (voluntary associations, co-operative ventures)]

With many kinds of authority something like this is no doubt true. I am subject to the authority of the president of the local Angler's Association only insofar as I am a member of that Association and such membership requires my voluntary agreement.

---

13. If anyone finds this phrase incomprehensible or repulsive for any reason, I am quite willing to substitute 'conceptual difference' – though I do not think this points to the specifics of the difference nearly as well.
14. *Vermischte Bemerkungen*, S.452: '*Niemand kann einen Gedanken für mich denken, wie niemand also ich den Hut aufsetzen kann.*' [*Culture and Value*, ed. G. H. von Wright and Heikki Nyman, trans. Peter Winch (Oxford: Basil Blackwell, 1989), 2.] This remark is from 1929: interestingly early, as it has all the marks of Wittgenstein's maturity. It's a 'whole cloud of philosophy condensed into a drop of grammar'! (Cf. *Philosophical Investigations*, Part 2, 222.) What is interesting about the analogy is that it prompts one to think of the point of our speaking in this way.
15. [Åbo Seminar 8] Cf. again Rousseau's 'Power may be delegated, but not will' (or words to that effect).
16. Eds: The Chapter 5 outline indicates a discussion of 'Authority, rationality, freedom, consent' at this point. It may correspond to the discussion of Locke's 'we are born free as we are born rational' in the following (Chapter 3.6), which relates rationality and freedom. The Åbo Authority seminar notes from Session 8 continue at this point with a discussion that seems pertinent to the topic:

> We discussed last time what led Locke to think that consent in this case must be a tacit consent and I considered some of the difficulties in this notion (though without, like some, wanting to get rid of it). They both have to do with what I called the 'grammatical difference' between Locke's investigation and a historian's. Locke treats tacit consent as something theoretically, conceptually required by political authority, not as something accepted on the basis of empirical evidence. Indeed, he maintains it in the face of the empirical evidence – as Hume beautifully brings out in 'Of the Original Contract'.

Here too it is easy enough to specify what behaviour of mine it is that has constituted giving such voluntary agreement – perhaps I filled in and signed an application for membership on a certain date, in which I expressed my agreement to abide by the rules of the Association and to accept the decisions of its properly appointed officers in matters falling within their stated field of competence.

[I.F. The difficulty with political authority.] But being subject to political authority is not like that. If I am presented with a tax demand I cannot escape it by complaining that I have never agreed to join this club. By 'I cannot' I mean both that of course such a riposte will not be accepted by the tax authorities or the courts, but also that it is a riposte that would for most be incomprehensible, except perhaps as a feeble joke. Some states may have ceremonies in which adolescents pledge their allegiance, but most have nothing like this. Anyway, pledging your allegiance is itself most unlikely to be a voluntary matter. You are certainly not going to escape the obligations of citizenship by refusing to do it. And again, even if there were at some historical moment an explicit founding of the state in which all prospective members pledged their allegiance to a constitution, there will – as Locke himself emphasises – still be a story that needs telling about how that probably remote historical event is supposed to bind *my* will *now*.

Tacit Consent [I.F.-I.F.1. Why Is Locke Forced in This Direction]

Considerations of this sort leave Locke to say that the consent on which political allegiance is based is for the most part given 'tacitly', not explicitly formulated but rather to be inferred from some features of the relevant individual's situation of behaviour. Notoriously, he waters down the specifications of these features to such an extent – so that it is sufficient for someone merely to be within the boundaries of a state for him or her to be deemed to have consented to its authority – that the notion of consent seems to be drained of all content; or, to change the metaphor, to become an idle wheel. In fact Locke's attempt does show something, but the reverse of what he wanted to show. Because the voluntariness of allegiance can be maintained only by draining it of content, it is not voluntary, at least not in the sense understood by Locke!

There is another, somewhat subtler, difficulty in this point, consideration of which points in the same direction. Locke himself insists that *in the first instance* there has to be *unanimity*[17] on the part of the people who are to become citizens. I have been suggesting that the reason for this is Locke's assumption that the original source of any genuine authority over an individual has to be the will of that individual. But Locke's description of the situation of a foreigner in a strange land gives the impression that the source of authority in that land will be a simple matter of fact, which can be established by observation and the testimony of others just like any other simple matter of fact. He does not ask whether there are not certain prerequisites for the possibility of the kind of observation and comprehension that will be necessary. But is a consequence of Locke's own account of the nature of authority that no individual can, as it were, get from

---

17. Eds: Emphasis is added in handwriting.

anyone else information about where authority lies. It isn't for Locke a question of 'getting information'; it is a question of a personal disposition of the will. Clearly this is why he tries to interpolate 'tacit consent' between physical presence and duty to obey.

I have stated this narrowly, as a problem for Locke, as indeed it is. But it's actually a problem for anyone. – What [is] involved here is a very fundamental and difficult set of questions about the nature of an individual's membership of a human community. All the difficulties we have encountered seem to spring from regarding that as simply a relation 'to an environment' – I mean in the sense of a stage on which the individual is placed and on which there are other things and people the behaviour of which he has to take into account. But it's becoming clear that this image does not adequately render what we understand by 'living in a human community'. Some further reflections on the notion of tacit consent may help to take us deeper into this issue.

[I.F.2. Is there such a thing? a) Yes.] Some influential writers[18] have maintained that Locke's mistake lay in introducing the notion of 'tacit consent' at all, claiming that there is no such thing, that all genuine consent is explicit. This seems to me a bad mistake. I want to show first – what should perhaps hardly need showing – that the notion of tacit consent does indeed have perfectly good applications; and second – more strongly and more controversially perhaps – that tacit consent (or something like it) is a prerequisite of there being such a thing as explicit consent.

Consider two people living together. Let us suppose this has come about without any explicit agreements between them and that they live in such a way that each person's possessions are used as matter of course and at need by the other, again without any explicit agreement. If this has gone on over a period of time it would be perfectly natural to say that A consents to the use of his things by B and B to the use by A of hers.

When would it be natural to say this? I suppose if this practice were challenged by someone: by either one of the parties, or an outsider. There are different sorts of case of course. An outsider, C, who knows A, sees B driving his car and being ignorant of her relations with A, challenges her. She replies by saying she has the car with A's consent. Would she be lying? A challenge to B from A, however, must have a different significance; A is clearly not speaking from ignorance of the relationship. In so far as his challenge could be made intelligible at all, it would have to be read as a signal that for him the relationship is disintegrating or that he intends to break it up. If his challenge takes the form of saying that he 'never consented' to B's use of his belongings he would at the very least be speaking disingenuously – a charge that would not be countered, but rather confirmed, by any insistence on his part that no explicit consent was ever given, however true that might be.

What these complications show, perhaps, is that the notion of consent becomes applicable only in the context of some challenge, or at least in the context of some challenge, or at least in the context of some potential challenge. It is not quite right to

---

18. E.g. John Plamenatz *in Consent, Freedom and Political Obligation* [(Oxford: Oxford University Press, 1968)]. See also Carol Pateman for something similar [presumably *The Problem of Political Obligation: A Critique of Liberal Theory* (Berkeley: University of California Press, 1985)].

say that 'tacit consent has been given' simply as part of a description of the relationship between A and B, where no suggestion of a possible challenge is in the offing.

[I.F.3. Is it less fundamental than explicit consent? (a) Nein.] My second, stronger, claim was that the existence of situations like that which I have just been discussing is a prerequisite of our being able to apply any notion of explicit consent. We can see this by considering one of the big difficulties faced by Hobbes's account of his 'Covenant'.[19] It has to be remembered that the Covenant which creates the sovereign is in a very special position; it is presupposed by all other covenants. This is because covenants are binding only where there is a system of enforcing compliance; and Hobbes thinks of his Covenant as the only way of setting up such a system. This Covenant therefore, cannot derive its bindingness from any pre-existing system of enforcement.

[I.F.3.b Hobbes: obligation *in foro externo* and *interno*] Hobbes tries to meet this difficulty by distinguishing a bindingness '*in foro interno*' from one '*in foro externo*'.

> The laws of nature oblige *in foro interno*; that is to say, they bind to a desire they should take place: but *in foro externo*; that is, to the putting them in act, not always – For he that should be modest, and tractable, and perform all he promises, in such time, and place, where no man should desire to do so, should but make himself a prey to others, and procure his own certain ruin, contrary to the ground of all laws of nature, which tend to nature's preservation.

It will be helpful here to remind oneself of Wittgenstein's discussion of the relation between talking to oneself and talking to others, or between mental arithmetic and arithmetic performed in writing. You could not learn mental arithmetic unless you had already learnt to do sums aloud or in writing. So you could not wish that there should be such a thing as written or spoken arithmetic on the basis of your familiarity with mental arithmetic. Is it not analogous with learning what it means for a covenant to be binding *in foro interno*? The notion of *bindingness* here belongs to the description of a certain language game. I cannot wish that there should be binding covenants if I have no experience of such things; and since the concept of a covenant is internally connected with that of bindingness, this is as much as to say that I cannot have the notion of a covenant unless I am familiar – familiar in action, as it were – with the phenomenon *of being bound*.

Hobbes's mistake lies in his construing being bound '*in foro interno*' too much as though it were just the same as being bound '*in foro externo*' except for being internal rather than external. And this is connected with the legalistic terms in which he states the problem – in terms of the 'laws of nature' and of the 'keeping of covenants'.[20] Being

---

19. In what follows I use upper case 'C' when referring to the creation of a 'Commonwealth' and lower case 'c' for more run-of-the-mill agreements.
20. Locke does not face quite the same difficulties as does Hobbes, insofar as his 'state of nature' is far less asocial than is Hobbes's 'natural condition of mankind'; hence for him the original contract does not have to bear the same intolerable conceptual weight as does Hobbes's Covenant. But Locke also obscures much by expressing the sociality of the state of nature in legalistic and intellectualistic terms. The state of nature has a 'law' to govern it and 'reason' is that law.

bound, however, is not something that exists only in the context of covenants or explicit agreements; perhaps not even primarily so. We have to remember that covenants do not take place in a vacuum, but in the context of multifarious human activities and relationships; and the forms they take vary with the forms of these activities and relationships.[21]

I suggested earlier that questions about consent arise characteristically when someone's behaviour in the context of a given relationship or activity or institution, etc. is for some reason challenged. In other words, what gives such questions their sense is that certain sorts of behaviour are accepted as normal in given contexts. It is a corollary of this point that the form consent takes, or what counts as 'consent', will also depend on this sort of context. If I am selling my soul to the Devil I may have to sign on parchment with my blood and have my signature witnessed by a Justice of the Peace; if I am licensing a friend to take a short cut through my back garden a wave and a grin will suffice. Such differences will of course be connected with the kind of actual trust that is characteristic of the relationship in question. In cases like the first of these two examples it may be appropriate to say that what is taken as an expression of consent is a matter of *convention* – sometimes very solemn convention. In cases like the second, such language is hardly appropriate; here the ways in which consent is expressed and acknowledged are on the same level as what I called the 'sorts of behaviour accepted as normal' against the background of which questions as to whether someone has consented or not themselves come to have sense.

[I.F.4. Living together in a community] I have been describing examples of what we understand by 'living in a human community'. My relation to fellow members of such a community is not – or not exclusively, nor even mainly – that of an observer. I do not merely note that certain kinds of behaviour are accepted as normal; indeed for the most part I do not even take note of that fact at all. I simply react to those kinds of behaviour as to something normal and, for the most part, the ways in which I react are in their turn responded to by others as to something normal.

[I.F.4.a. the political dimension of all this – I.F.4.a. (1) Rush Rhees 'all facing in the same direction'] This holds good as much for the 'political' as for other aspects of our lives together. There are normal ways of reacting towards someone in a policeman's uniform or to the receipt of an income tax form. I do not mean by this that everyone will always – or even normally! – react in the same way; that would be obviously false. I mean rather that most of us can tell from the way someone reacts whether he or she has indeed recognised this as, say, a policeman's uniform, or an income tax form, or a court of law, and understands what these things are. There will be a good deal that is more concrete too. Those who live together in the same political community by and large have

---

21. See A. I. Melden's *Rights and Persons* [(Oxford: Basil Blackwell, 1977)] for discussion of this sort of point. Of the classical writers I discuss it seems to me that Rousseau, especially in his *Discourse on the Origin of Inequality*, understands best the importance of natural quasi [Eds: fn. incomplete]

access to the same selection of newspapers, radio and television programmes, etc. and thus acquire a relation to the personalities, events and issues involved in the country's political life. Their relation to these things is at the same time partially constitutive of their own relations with each other. It enters into their discussions, jokes, friendships, quarrels, and so on in countless different ways. Rush Rhees once[22] described this sort of relation as 'all facing in the same direction', a phrase which, if not pressed too hard, seems to me not a bad image.

How do these considerations bear upon Locke's account of tacit consent as being implied by one's barely being within the territorial bounds of a given state? The individualistic way in which he talks about authority and consent makes it difficult to state in his terms. It is as though for him each individual is alone, face to face with a source of power the authority of which he or she has to consent to; until that consent has been given the source of power is for the individual concerned just that, something purely external. Its authoritative nature is bestowed solely by this voluntary act of the individual. What is missing here is any appreciation of the state as a public phenomenon; it is what it is by virtue of its place in the life of the community, a 'place' that cannot be reduced to a series of relations between a sovereign and a particular individual. [I.F.4.a. (2) Wittgenstein: 'a community bound together by science and education'] Wittgenstein makes a similar point in an epistemological context:

> 'We are quite sure of it' does not mean just that every single person is certain of it, but that we belong to a community which is bound together by science and education.[23]

Adapting this to the issue before us, we may say: We acknowledge the same authority, does not mean just that every single person acknowledges it, but that we belong to a community bound together by certain political institutions.

[I.F.4.c. locating the source of authority] If, then, I find myself in a foreign land, I must, if I am to recognise a source of authority, have the requisite relation to the life of the community. Locke is presumably assuming that the foreign land in question will be recognisably similar to that with which I am already familiar. Recognising that this is a state in whose territory I find myself will already involve my positioning myself in a certain way vis-a-vis its citizens; I shall bring with me the predispositions to the kinds of attitude which are normal in my mother country and this will enable me to recognise – to a greater or less degree – 'the direction in which they are facing.' Of course if the life here is extremely different from what I am already familiar with, there will indeed be difficulties (to which I shall return).

---

22. In a lecture at King's College, London in the lateish seventies.
23. Eds: A footnote is indicated but missing. *On Certainty*, ed. G. E. M. Anscombe and G. H. von Wright; trans. Denis Paul and G. E. M. Anscombe (Oxford: Basil Blackwell, 1969), §298.

G. Hume's twofold critique[24]

1. The quasi-empirical (but this is really about the application of Locke's theory)
   a. 'They consent, because they already perceive him to be by birth their lawful sovereign'[25]
   b. Hume is here pointing to the public character of the state
      (1) something that is commonly accepted in the community
      (2) but also something the power of which transcends that of private associations
2. The 'more philosophical' objection[26]

H. Hume's own account of politics

1. His emphasis on custom
   a. allows for historicity
   b. rejects the idea that political obligation is accepted for reasons
2. But his utilitarian tendencies seem to suggest again a more universal and more 'rational' foundation
3. Parallel with Anscombe?
4. Say more about Hume in last chapter[27]

---

24. Eds: The Chapter 5 outline continues as follows, with no TS to match it. Consider the 1992 Lectures, Lecture 19 ff. in Chapter 2.1 above; see also the posthumous Winch paper (edited by Phillips): 'How Is Political Authority Possible?', *Philosophical Investigations* 25, no. 1 (2002): 20–32 (26–30 for a discussion of Locke and Hume). The reference is to Hume, 'Of the Original Contract', in *Political Essays*, ed. Charles W. Handel (Bobbs Merrill, The Library of Liberal Arts, 1953), 43–63.
25. Eds: Ibid., 53.
26. Eds: Ibid., 54 ff.
27. Eds: Perhaps he meant Chapter 3.9, 'The Habit of Obedience'.

3.6

CONSENT AND RATIONALITY[1]

I want now to return to the large question I started with: the difference, and the relation, between what someone may say in characterising the 'agreements' which underlie a particular historical regime, such as the Hannoverian Settlement, and the 'agreements' thought to underlie political authority as such. It was discussion of this question which led me into consideration of Locke's use of the notion of consent and Hobbes's of Covenant.[2] I started by saying that Locke's aim: 'to understand political power right and derive it from its original' should not be thought of as simply a (much) more general inquiry of the same sort as an inquiry into the origins of the Hannoverian Settlement. I said the two inquiries differed in 'grammar' – or conceptually. The intervening discussion (of Locke on tacit consent and of Hobbes on Covenant) should have given some indication of my reasons for saying this. The kinds of consideration these two writers adduced, as well as the kinds of consideration I have adduced in discussing them, are totally different from what a historian could recognise as a contribution to his inquiry. But now – how are we to characterise this difference?

[I.A.] Locke treats tacit consent as something theoretically, conceptually, *required* by political authority, not as something accepted on the basis of empirical evidence. Indeed, he maintains it in the face of the empirical evidence – as Hume beautifully brings out in 'Of the Original Contract'.

[I. B. Remember that even radically innovative states have a pre-existing political and intellectual background.] We need to call to mind that, even in cases where a new state has been founded, as it were from scratch – like the USA after the War of Independence – there was still a good deal of history behind it of both a very practical political sort (there had after all been a War of Independence!) and also of an intellectual sort. As a matter of fact one of the intellectual roots of the US Constitution was precisely Locke's *Second Treatise*! What I am getting at is that the Founding Fathers may have invented a new constitution, but they did not invent the concepts of the state

---

1. Eds: This is a continuation of the 'Authority: General and Particular' TS (also identical to the second half of the Åbo Authority Seminar Session 8), which fits the Chapters 5 and 6 outline. This (Chapter 6) outline is a mix of bullet point and narrative form. We have not marked whether text is repeated in each source. We have indicated in square brackets in the text the number and text in the Chapter 6 outline to which this text from 'Authority: General and Particular' corresponds.
2. Eds: In the Chapter 6 outline, Hobbes on the covenant precedes the discussion he is summarizing here rather than appearing alongside the discussion of Locke.

and of political allegiance. One can go further and note that the ways in which they understood these concepts were in terms of their own times. For instance the 'right to bear arms' enshrined in the Constitution was introduced as a means of ensuring the availability of a reserve militia and thus obviating the need for a standing army; and the reluctance to allow a standing army stemmed directly from the experience of such armies taking political sides in Europe. There is no question here of political and constitutional principles being worked out de novo. [I.C.] Locke himself distinguishes between the 'contract' that creates civil society from the decisions and agreements which lead to a particular form of government. [I.D.] And in both Hobbes and Rousseau it is even clearer that we have to deal in the first instance with the introduction of a new concept. Hobbes plainly thinks that the Covenant brings into being for the first time concepts of justice and injustice and of obligation. Rousseau emphasises particularly strongly that once a true political community is formed the position of individuals changes completely; their relations with each other and with the society as a whole [and] also their conception of themselves and of their own interests. (He speaks of the individual becoming for the first time 'a man'.)

[I.E. 'We are born free as we are born rational'.] I want to try to characterise more precisely what I have called the 'grammatical' peculiarity of this kind of inquiry. Locke's account of the way political authority rests on the consent of the governed is closely connected with his conception of rationality; 'we are born free as we are born rational', he writes. 'Freedom' means precisely not being subject to the authority of another. I think it is clear that these two concepts are not, for Locke, contingently connected. The life of a rational being *is* a life in which one decides for oneself what course of action to follow. Insofar as one's actions are decided by someone else, one is not acting as a rational being. It follows that any genuine exercise of authority by one adult over another must be made consistent with the latter's rationality and hence freedom. This can only be the case if it has been *freely and rationally accepted, i.e. consented to.*

Now this account thus far is not the account of any historical process by which authority, or a certain form of authority, has come into being. It is an attempt to characterise what the concept of authority is and to locate it in relation to other concepts used in the description of human life; in this sense it is completely abstract. The next stage of the argument is to infer that insofar as there do exist cases of legitimate authority exercised over adults, these must derive from the free consent of those over whom it is exercised. As I remarked earlier, there are of course many, many cases in which it is easy enough to identify acts of giving consent; but the case of political authority is not one of these. [I.F.] And so Locke introduced the notion of tacit consent in order to fill the gap. [I.F.1.] His procedure at this point is reminiscent of moves familiar in other areas of philosophy: for instance, of our inclination to postulate unconscious, inconceivably rapid, mental processes underlying our use of language in order to allay our bewilderment about how this use can be seen as possible. In those cases too the postulated process usually turns out to be an idle wheel, incapable of performing the function for which it is introduced.

Relativism?

I don't want to dwell any further at present on this particular defect in Locke's argument. The main question under consideration is a different one; [II.A.] is it possible to give any sort of account, having the generality Locke requires, of the relations between notions like 'rationality', 'authority' and 'consent'? The generality required, it must be remembered, is one that transcends the history, institutions, customs and ways of thinking of any particular time and place.

This is not an easy question to answer. [II.A.1.] On the one hand, one is perhaps inclined to think that notions like this must be applicable to any sort of life that one would be able to recognise as human. And if this is so, must we not understand these concepts in a way which is *not* confined to particular cultures and epochs? [II.A.2.] But on the other hand it is difficult to see what such an understanding can amount to. Let us allow, for the sake of argument, that an analysis in completely formal terms could be given of these concepts, which would be universally applicable across cultures and epochs. (I will refrain from asking how we could possibly know such a thing in advance!) We still face the problem of knowing how these formal schemata are to be applied. Suppose for instance that I have been brought up by lawyers and have learnt to use the notion of consent only in contexts where everything is written down and signatures witnessed. And suppose I now come across people who seem to regulate their mutual relations simply with casual-looking gestures and facial expressions. What can show me that the notion of consent is to be applied here too? It will be no help to say, e.g. well the signed witnessed agreement is a manifestation of the author's free rational decision to allow the other party certain rights; so all I have to do is to determine whether that is what these gestures and facial expressions also do! Obviously another idle wheel is being introduced here; if I am in a position to determine that, then of course I am in a position to determine whether the party has consented. But the one determination is as difficult as the other; indeed, they are virtually indistinguishable.

[II.B.] I think we must recognise that there is nothing that determines in advance how such notions are going to be applicable. We can only wait on familiarity with the details of particular cases and then see what we want to say. Sometimes we shall not hesitate; at other times we shall hardly know what to say; and of course there are many cases in between these extremes. Often the realisation of what we want to say may come as a surprise and a discovery; and such a realisation may be very salutary in the loosening of prejudices. But perhaps it is more common for one's prejudices to distort one's responses. I do not know of any general method of detecting when this is happening.

3.7

THE ROLE OF AUTHORITY IN OUR LIVES[1]

A. The education of children
   1. Overlooked (catastrophically) by Locke in his discussion of the relation between rationality and freedom (and *a fortiori* between rationality and authority)[2]
   2. Rousseau
      a) Sees the relation between education, rationality and freedom[3]
      b) But misses (or rather rejects) the role of authority in the growth of reason[4]
   3. Something on Anscombe again here perhaps on 'the practices of reason'?

---

1. Eds: Computer printout; 24 pp.; Peter Winch Archives (GB 0100 KCLCA K/PP171, Box 16), King's College London.
2. Eds: Winch mentions this briefly in Lecture 15 (1992 Lectures, Chapter 2.1 above) and in Peter Winch, 'How is Political Authority Possible?' *Philosophical Investigations* 25, no. 1 (2002): 20–32; he cites Anscombe's 'practices of reason' in p. 31n., but does not develop the discussion. He ties Locke's neglect of education to his empiricist epistemology and refers the reader to R. F. Holland's 'Epistemology and Education' in his *Against Empiricism* (London: Routledge and Kegan Paul, 1980).
3. Eds: A TS on Rousseau ('Reason, Will and Representation in Rousseau') was distributed to participants in the 1993 Åbo Authority Seminar (Chapter 2.5 above) but it discusses the general will rather than education.
4. Eds: See his earlier 'Man and Society in Hobbes and Rousseau', in *Ethics and Action* (London: Routledge and Kegan Paul, 1972), 90–109, for a substantial discussion. Winch concludes the latter paper with a statement of the importance of Rousseau's account of education and its role in what he calls in this 'Last Book Outline' 'concept formation':

   …we cannot make sense of an immediate Hobbesist transition from a state of nature in which considerations of justice make no sense at all to a civil society in which all justice is embodied in a concrete set of factual political arrangements. Conceptions of justice are only developed through discussions of injustices. Men capable of becoming citizens must then receive an education which enables them to understand what those injustices are, an education which consists not merely in inculcating a 'science' of what human relationships necessarily are, but rather in creating human beings of a sort who will be capable of discerning qualitative distinctions between different types of human relationships and who will therefore be capable of entering into such relationships. (pp. 108–109)

    4. Mainly of course Wittgenstein: *On Certainty*[5]
       a) and, trailing behind, my 'Certainty and Authority'![6]
B. The continuing role of authority in adult life
    1. *On Certainty*
    2. 'Certainty and Authority'
    3. The political dimension of this to be further explored in next chapter

---

5. Eds: Ludwig Wittgenstein, *On Certainty*, ed. G. E. M. Anscombe and G. H. von Wright, trans. Denis Paul and G. E. M. Anscombe (Oxford: Basil Blackwell, 1969). For other discussions of *On Certainty* in Winch's papers, see Peter Winch, 'True or False?', *Inquiry* 31, no. 3 (1988): 265–276 and 'Judgement: Propositions and Practices', *Philosophical Investigations* 21, no. 3 (1998): 189–202. In addition, he published a translation of Wittgenstein's notes on causality: Ludwig Wittgenstein, 'Cause and Effect: Intuitive Awareness', trans. Peter Winch, *Philosophia* 6, no. 3 (1976): 409–425. He discussed these as a prefiguration of *On Certainty* in 'Im Anfang War Die Tat', in *Trying to Make Sense* (Oxford: Basil Blackwell, 1987), 33–53.
6. Eds: Peter Winch. 'Certainty and Authority', in *Wittgenstein Centenary Essays*, ed. A. Phillips Griffiths (Cambridge: Cambridge University Press, 1991), 223–238.

3.8

THE AUTHORITY OF REASON[1]

Discussion of my question 'How is political authority possible?' should have brought out that it is akin to the question: 'How is political authority compatible with reason?'. The assumption has been that the acknowledgement of such authority must somehow be *based on reason*. And some of the difficulties we have encountered have suggested that this may not be the right question to ask. I want now to turn the question round: instead of asking for the reason of authority, let's ask: *what is the authority of reason?*

This is one important aspect of what is under discussion in Plato's *Gorgias*. So let's return briefly to that.[2] The question the dialogue opens with concerns the nature of the skill Gorgias claims to teach. It is a technique of *persuasion* and Socrates is critical of the claims Gorgias makes on its behalf. In developing his criticisms he distinguishes Gorgias's rhetoric from a form of discourse based on a contrasting principle, a discourse which obviously Socrates's own practice is supposed to exemplify.[3]

The difference is that Socratic dialogue is said to be informed by a genuine logos in a way rhetoric is not. Socrates aims at knowledge, not just belief, at truth and not just changing his interlocutor's mind. What interests me most here is that Socrates does not describe the difference in the way most of us probably expect him to. He does not say that Gorgias aims merely at persuasion, [and] Socrates at something else. He says that there are *two sorts of persuasion* that [are] practiced by Gorgias and Socrates respectively.

It seems to me that the dialogue as a whole can be read both as a discursive treatment and at the same time an exemplification of what the difference between these 'sorts of persuasion' consists in. The content and the form of the dialogue go hand in hand and reinforce each other.

Why my emphasis on this particular way of putting it? My interest isn't really philological. (Indeed, since I know no Greek, I may be relying too much on an

---

1. Eds: Computer printout; 24 pp.; Peter Winch Archives (GB 0100 KCLCA K/PP171, Box 16), King's College London, supplemented with TS 'Authority of Reason', distributed to seminar participants at Åbo. It is the same as session 10 in the Åbo Seminar on Political Authority. We present it here as continuous text, as in the 'Authority of Reason' TS.
2. This marks a return to the discussion of Chapter 3.
3. See Peter Winch, 'Persuasion' (*Midwest Studies in Philosophy* 17, no. 1 (1992): 123–137) for a more extended discussion of the contrast between Wittgenstein's conception of logic and 'Aristotelian' logic (broadly, formalization as an approach to the normative evaluation of practices of reason). Winch distributed a TS in this era (not in the archives), 'Persuasion and Reason', that repeats some of the discussion of the TS here.

idiosyncratic translation!⁴) Let me try to make my point by contrasting Plato/Socrates with Aristotle, who, I believe, would never have made the contrast in such terms. *Aristotle* regards logic as a *science*. (I hope some bells ring: remember *Behemoth* and Hobbes's 'science' of politics.) The science consists in an exposition of relations which hold between propositions by virtue of their form: relations which in their turn derive from the structure of reality. Behind the logic stands a metaphysics of substance and attribute, individuals and classes, etc.

On the Aristotelian view, the difference between Gorgian sophistry and rational discourse is that the latter is guided, as the former is not, by the rails mapped out in this metaphysically based logic. The former is arbitrary, subject to the whim, the will, of the speaker: the latter is subject to the constraints of *how things are*. The mainstream conception of logic has followed this Aristotelian picture ever since.

Wittgenstein, so Rhees says, used the term 'Aristotelian logic' (with which he contrasted his own way of treating logic) to *include Frege and Russell*! I believe that Wittgenstein was following a more Socratic tradition (hard as he usually is on Socrates when he happens to refer to him). This picture is beautifully lampooned in that profound *jeu d'esprit* by Lewis Carroll, 'What the Tortoise said to Achilles'.

> 'Now that you accept A and B and C and D, of course you accept Z.'
>
> 'Do I?' said the Tortoise innocently. 'Let's make that quite clear. I accept A and B and C and D. Suppose I *still* refuse to accept Z?'
>
> 'Then Logic would take you by the throat, and *force* you to do it!' Achilles triumphantly replied. 'Logic would tell you "You can't help yourself. Now that you've accepted A and B and C and D, you *must* accept Z". So you've no choice, you see.'
>
> 'Whatever *Logic* is good enough to tell me is worth *writing down*', said the Tortoise. So enter it into your book, please. We will call it (E) If A and B and C and D are true, Z must be true. Until I've granted that, of course, I needn't grant Z. So it's quite a *necessary* step, you see?'
>
> 'I see', said Achilles; and there was a touch of sadness in his tone.⁵

It is Aristotelian logic of which Achilles speaks. I think the moral of this is usually misunderstood. It certainly is by those who try to find a formal *refutation* of the Tortoise's argument. The point is not to show that *modus ponens* is invalid, but to undermine a certain conception of what logical validity is.

Before I take this further, let me get back briefly to Socrates, before I forget him. He and Plato are often said, somewhat condescendingly, to have anticipated Aristotle but without having the logical acumen to set things out as Aristotle eventually did. One's attitude to this must depend in large part, it seems to me, on what one makes of

---

4. Eds: In his final lecture courses on Classical Ancient Philosophers, Winch begins to introduce Ancient Greek terms (in the original alphabet) and gives some discussion of their linguistic significance.

5. 'What the Tortoise Said to Achilles', Lewis Carroll, *Complete Works*. [*Mind* 4, no. 14 (1895): 278–280.]

dialogues like *The Sophist* and *The Statesman* which form the later part of the series to which *Gorgias* belongs. These do indeed seem to be going in an Aristotelian direction, but it's important to note that Socrates has been replaced by a 'Stranger', who is indeed strange when compared with Socrates. Can it be that he was a lampoon by Plato of his uppity junior, Aristotle?[6]

In *Gorgias* the *authority* carried by Socrates's arguments is *the authority of Socrates, the man*. And this is emphasised in the dramatic structure of the dialogue. Or rather, it is the *authority carried by the spectacle of a certain type of life, which Socrates both exemplifies and describes*.[7] This is connected with the fact which (I think) I drew attention to before: that Socrates's appeal to all three of his interlocutors is, at the most crucial point, an appeal to their sense of shame. It is as though he says to them: 'Disagree with me if you can, or *dare*!'[8]

Now, back to Wittgenstein, and to another quotation relating to Ramsey:

> F. P. Ramsey once emphasized in conversation with me that logic was a 'normative science'. I do not know exactly what he had in mind, but it was doubtless closely related to what only dawned on me later: namely, that in philosophy we often compare the use of words with games and calculi which have fixed rules, but cannot say that someone who is using language must be playing such a game. – But if you say that our languages only approximate to such calculi you are standing on the very brink of a misunderstanding. For then it may look as if what we were talking about were an ideal language. As if our logic were, so to speak, a logic for a vacuum. – Whereas logic does not treat of language – or of thought – in the sense in which a natural science treats of a natural phenomenon, and the most that can be said is that we construct ideal languages. But here the word 'ideal' is liable to mislead, for it sounds as if these languages were better, more perfect, than our everyday language; and as if it took the logician to shew people at last what a proper sentence looked like.
>
> But all this can only appear in the right light when one has attained greater clarity about the concepts of understanding, meaning, and thinking. For it will then also become clear what can lead us (and did lead me) to think that if anyone utters a sentence and means or understands it he is operating a calculus according to definite rules.[9]

Let me consider 'logic does not treat of languages in the sense in which a natural science treats of a natural phenomenon'. This can be read in two ways:

1. As a contrast between logic and empirical studies like the psychology, or sociology, or physiology of speaking and thinking. This is perhaps the more obvious reading.
2. As a warning against thinking of logic as the natural science of the ideal, as it were. Consider, e.g. Wittgenstein's criticisms of Hardy's conception of mathematics as a sort

---

6. Cf. Lynette Reid's beautiful paper and, alas, the earlier book by [Stanley] Rosen. Eds: *Plato's Sophist* (New Haven: Yale University Press, 1983).
7. Eds: See the lecture notes included in Chapter 2.3, 'Plato's *Gorgias*'.
8. Handwritten marginal comment: Or: 'Can you face yourself if you disagree with me?'
9. [Ludwig Wittgenstein,] *Philosophical Investigations*, [eds. G. E. M. Anscombe and Rush Rhees, trans. G. E. M. Anscombe (Oxford: Basil Blackwell, 1953)] §81.

of super-physics of mathematical objects. But in a sense *all* Wittgenstein's arguments are directed against conceptions of this sort. (That's a bit of an exaggeration perhaps, but not much. In any event I think §81 absolutely central to *Philosophical Investigations*.)

This is of course the 'Aristotelian' conception that he is criticising. Let me repeat that this has two aspects:

1. A conversion of what we say into 'canonical form' – which is supposed to express the *real* form of our thought, a form which is supposed to take its authority from its mirroring the structure of reality;
2. The idea that this structure exercises a special sort of *constraint* on our thinking. (This is the aspect picked up by Lewis Carroll's Achilles and exposed as hollow by the Tortoise.)

What is Wittgenstein's alternative to this conception? In §81 he says that 'we *construct* ideal languages'. But he is disturbed by the possibly misleading implications of the word 'ideal'; misleading because it seems to bestow a kind of authority on our constructions that Wittgenstein thinks spurious. And here is another, perhaps even more emphatic quotation:

> For we can avoid distortion, or emptiness, in what we assert only insofar as we present the prototype as what it is, an object of comparison – a measuring rod, so to speak; not as a prejudice to which reality has to correspond. (The dogmatism into which we so easily fall when we philosophize.)[10]

But at this point there seems to arise a serious dilemma: if we do not accord our constructions a special status, what is their point? Why should we, or anyone else, take any particular note of them? *What is their authority?* In a sense this is the Tortoise's challenge to Achilles: one that Achilles is not in a position to meet.

The analogy of the measuring rod in my last quotation gives a hint where we should look. What is the authority of a measuring rod? – After all, it is in a certain sense arbitrary; what is taken as the unit of measurement is *conventional*. ('It's just a bit of wood, with certain marks' etc.) Yes, but it is also deeply embedded in our practices and in the lives we lead. We need to ask ourselves: *what else should we be giving up, were we to give this up?* This is a question that Wittgenstein's investigative procedures constantly force on us.

We don't *have* to think like this, but first let's be clear what we should be losing and what gaining, were we to give it up, and second, let's be clear about what we think, as a result of philosophising in a certain way, is *wrong* with the way we at present think.

The connection of these points with the claims often made that Wittgenstein is a 'conservative'. It's true that, in the face of certain kinds of *a priori* philosophical argument, Wittgenstein constantly calls us back to the way we *do* at present think. 'Don't think, look'. It's also true that the upshot of this 'looking' is the realisation that our

---

10. Wittgenstein, *Philosophical Investigations*, §131.

present way of thinking is not tainted in the way the philosophical picture suggested. But Wittgenstein does not say: 'You *cannot* give this up' nor even: 'Do not give this up'. Rather he asks the question: '*Do you really want to give this up?*' Moreover, Wittgenstein does not expect, or even want, the answer to such a question to go only one ('conservative') way. By no means! Cf. the following exchange with Turing.

Turing, contrary to Wittgenstein, wants to say that mathematical calculations are really experiments. He does not say he is going to prove Turing wrong. Rather, he insists on the *persuasive* character of what he is about to attempt:

> ... I think that if I could make myself quite clear, then Turing would give up saying that in mathematics we make experiments.[11]

He then asks how it is that the misunderstanding between him and Turing is so difficult to clear up and compares the issue between them to the way in which he, Wittgenstein, would respond to a remark of Hilbert's: 'No one is going to turn us out of the paradise which Cantor has created':

> I would say: 'I wouldn't dream of trying to drive anyone out of this paradise'. I would try to do something quite different: I would try to show you that it is not a paradise – so that you'll leave of your own accord. I would say, 'you're welcome to this; just look about you'.[12]

Wittgenstein had in mind here the kind of talk about infinity that often went with set theory. I believe he thought that a great deal of the appeal of set theory lay with confusions in this talk. His aim was not to disprove anything in mathematics and to this extent he was not in conflict with his remark that 'Philosophy leaves everything as it is'. On the other hand he not only allowed for the possibility that people would talk and act differently if their minds were cleared of confusions, he hoped and, perhaps, expected they would. See also this remark from *Culture and Value*:

> The solution of philosophical problems compared with the gift in a fairy tale which looks magical in the enchanted castle and, if one examines it outside in daylight, is nothing but an ordinary lump of iron (or something of the sort).[13]

---

11. Ludwig Wittgenstein, *Lectures on the Foundations of Mathematics 1939*, ed. Cora Diamond (Chicago: University of Chicago Press, 1989), 102.
12. Ibid., 103.
13. Wittgenstein, *Vermischte Bemergkingen*, 1931 (Suhrkamp Band 8), 466. Eds: *Culture and Value*, ed. G. H. von Wright and Heikki Nyman, trans. Peter Winch (Oxford: Basil Blackwell, 1989), 11.

3.9

THE HABIT OF OBEDIENCE[1]

In the classical social contract tradition in the philosophy of the state (roughly Hobbes, Locke, Rousseau), there is a tendency to make everything too explicit, as it were. This is connected with the fact that their central concern is the citizen's 'reasons for obeying'. It comes out in more than one way:

A. [I.A.3.a] At the receiving (citizen's) end it comes naturally to talk in terms of deliberations, leading to decisions or choices. (Of course, I am not endorsing this, simply recognising it for a fact.)
B. [I.A.3.b] At the dishing out (state's) end, it comes naturally to describe that which the citizen 'obeys' as a command. This holds more for Hobbes and Rousseau than it does for Locke.[2]

More attention is paid to the citizen's relation to the highest organs of the state [I.A.] than to his relation to subsidiary state organs (police, magistrate's courts, employment offices, national insurance offices, etc.)

This list is indeterminate in two respects: firstly, of time and place; secondly, in respect of doubt as to what is to count as 'state' function (e.g. schools, money). [I.B.2.] State and society often come to be confusedly identified, e.g. in the regulation of professional training. The distinction between social control and political power thus may be elided.

---

1. Eds: Computer printout; 24 pp.; Peter Winch Archives (GB 0100 KCLCA K/PP171, Box 16), King's College London. This is supplemented with a TS entitled 'Habit of Obedience' (from the archives, box not recorded). This TS roughly follows the bullet point of the Chapter 9 outline and the following chapter, with some discussions missing. We have given the 'Habit of Obedience' TS, indicating in square brackets where it corresponds to the Chapter 9 outline. In footnotes, we quote the Chapter 9 outline where there is no corresponding content in the TS. The last half of this chapter is in outline form alone and is given here in the body of the Chapter.
2. Eds: The Chapter 9 outline has: 'I.A.1. In Hobbes, Rousseau, reasons for this evident: only the sovereign has authority; everything else derivative. I.A.2. Locke does not have the same reasons for this; but nevertheless a similar emphasis is there. I.A.2.a Though the central discussion of property introduces a somewhat different emphasis'.

On schools J.M. Coetzee [I.C.1.], reviewing an autobiographical work by Helen Suzman, writes of the destabilising effect of gangs of young black teenagers, who have refused to attend school:

> There is a strong argument to be made that, from 1976 to the present, the engine of history has been driven by young black teenagers, with their elders left puffing behind, trying to look as if they are in charge. In a stagnant economy, with black unemployment, even among high-school graduates, at alarming levels, it will be hard to persuade children to give up the tumultuous and in many ways exciting life they have led on the streets to return to the drudgery of the class room, in the charge of demoralised and often ill-educated teachers teaching sterile curricula.
>
> Until schooling and the discipline that goes with schooling – a discipline which, not to put too fine a point on it, amounts to *social control* – have taken firmer root in South Africa, Suzman's vision of the triumph of moderation will remain unpersuasive.[3,4]

A very large question looms behind this: concerning the relation between 'social control' and political power. [I.C.] How is the power of the state related to that of other social institutions, organisations etc.? There won't be any single answer to that: the answer will differ from case to case and from time to time. It does seem clear that there will be no stable political regime without some stability in social life; and also that the quality of the regime – its relative freedom or oppressiveness, for instance – will be related to that of the life of the society. In that relation different social formations will have diverse kinds of relevance, and no doubt this is something which will also change from one time to another. It is fairly certain that the relations here will be very difficult indeed to establish with any certainty, and perhaps there will be a good deal of genuinely ineradicable indeterminacy in the matter too.[5]

[At this point the Habit of Obedience TS continues with materials that match the Chapter 10 outline and are reproduced below in Chapter 3.10 before rejoining this outline with the following.]

---

3. J. M. Coetzee, 'Resisters', *The New York Review of Books* XL, no. 20 (December 2, 1993). The italics are mine. In the same issue of the *The New York Review of Books*, 'Supergirls', a piece on children's, especially girls', literature by Diane Johnstone is relevant.
    Eds: The latter (a review of the Joyce Carol Oates's novel *Foxfire: Confessions of a Girl Gang*) includes the relevant passage:

    > In the Fifties there were fewer words for oppression. The girls have the sense that they are victimized, but nobody has told them so, and people like the congressman tell them the opposite. Without buzz words, all they can feel is that the men are 'assholes.'...

    The quasi-political rebellion of the young women in this novel is continuous with – perhaps difficult to disentangle from – the criminal nature of their activities.
4. Eds: The Chapter 9 outline indicates that Winch intended to discuss other examples, missing in the 'Habit of Obedience' TS: 'I.C. 2–3 money; regulation of professional training, e.g. lawyers'.
5. Eds: In the Chapter 9 outline, PW comments here: 'I.C.4 One sees here how state and society come to be (confusedly) identified'.

Somewhere I must make room for a discussion of Hume on this topic of 'the habit of obedience' (his phrase?).[6] [I.D., I.D.1.] What needs clarifying here is the relation between his treating custom and habit as, almost, primitive concepts and his looking for an underlying utilitarian-type justification.[7]

One has to locate the attitude in question within the whole complex of relationships, attitudes, power relationships, loyalties, etc. that I am trying to sketch. [cf. I.D.2–3.][8]

---

6. In 'Of the Origin of Government', Hume says 'habit consolidates what other principles of nature had imperfectly founded, and men, once accustomed to obedience, never think of departing from that path...' (*Political Essays*, ed. Charles W. Handel [Bobbs Merrill, The Library of Liberal Arts, 1953], 39–42 [40–41]). In 'Of the Original Contract' (43–63), he speaks of a habitual 'acquiescence' (45).
7. Eds: In the Chapter 9 outline, Winch turns to how framing the issue in terms of obeying the commands of a state authority is distorting the discussion (see below, D.2.).
In the 'Habit of Obedience' TS, he continues:

> Maybe this should be combined with a discussion of the difference between the attitude of the prince's subjects to 'their lawful sovereign' in Hume's examples and their attitude to the usurper.
>
> They have a reason for obeying the usurper – namely the sanctions that he can impose. One might say that their relation to the usurper is, as it were, an 'external' relation – it might just as well have been someone else who wielded the power; whereas their relation to the lawful prince is an internal one: they obey him because of who he is.
>
> But this of course cannot be generalised. It cannot in this form be applied, for instance, to an elected government. Here too it is only because it is they who happen to have been elected that... How then should one put the point? The safest formulation perhaps is a negative one: to acquiesce in the authority of a government because it is the legitimate one is to be prepared to go along with it even if there is no danger of sanctions. (But of course this would apply to other sorts of case too.)
>
> Is it perhaps a mistake to look for a simple formulation?

This discussion in the 'Habit of Obedience' TS diverges from the Chapter 9 outline. In the book outline, the Hume passage about the Prince ('Of the Original Contract', 53–54) has come up for discussion in Chapter 3.5 (and is foreshadowed in Chapter 3.2), and is not mentioned in the Chapter 9 outline. Instead of taking on Hume's quasi-justification of the Prince's authority by the habit of obedience (a statement of the fact of the habit of obedience – which attracts Winch – combined with a quasi-utilitarian justification of the existence of such habits – which Winch rejects), in this Chapter 9 outline, Winch turns to a much more distributed picture of how the legitimacy or illegitimacy of the state is expressed in many different relationships between citizens and between citizens and subsidiary bodies and functions of the state.
8. Eds: In the 'Habit of Obedience' TS, Winch has introduced this point through a discussion of Hume's acknowledgement of the Prince's legitimacy, he continues with the following, which diverges from the Chapter 9 outline:

> It is important that I should regard it as my government, my prince. But what is the force of this possessive pronoun? I may feel a peculiar obligation to criticise it for its errors or wrongful acts. I may feel ashamed, or proud of what it does. I feel committed to support it, perhaps, in time of war, even if I do not approve of its policy.
>
> The distinction between concepts and institutions is important again here. For instance the fact that state institutions exercise power (through police forces, penal systems and

D. Hume and the habit of obedience. How far are these attitudes based on reasons?[9]
   1. The question is necessary because of Hume's tendency to bolster up the habit with 'usefulness to society' or 'because society could not otherwise subsist'.
   2. The first thing to say is of course that the complex of attitudes is very misleadingly expressed under the generic label 'obedience'.
      a. A readiness to obey certainly belongs here, in some contexts.
      b. Equally important, perhaps more fundamental, is the acknowledgement of the authority of someone to do certain things.
      c. In some important cases even that is rather remote: e.g. the use of money.
   3. *Within* such a complex of attitudes reasons of course often enough have a place.
   4. But often enough any specification of reasons would be more or less mythical.
      a. Cf. Wittgenstein's question: why do parents educate their children?
      b. Do we use money because we find it useful to do so? Do we have any choice? Our life is like that.
      c. Hume's 'because society could not otherwise subsist'.
         (1) That is often enough not true (insofar as one can what it means, if taken quite generally).
         (2) It may be that this (sort of) could not subsist; but that may be largely tautological, since this society is here characterised as one having these and these institutions.
            (a) Cf. Devlin on the Wolfenden Report and Hart's criticisms.[10]

---

the like) provides me with plenty of reasons for acting of an obvious sort. On the other hand if I support the constitutional government (say at a time of unrest) because it is the constitutional government that is a 'reason' of a different sort. If I do what the Mafia tells me because I recognise its power to do things that I would find unwelcome if I should refuse, my reason [is] in a way not, because the mafia order it, but because I want to avoid the unpleasantness that the Mafia would cause me. Of course it's important not to suppose that the distinction is clear-cut and mixed cases will be characteristic; and it often won't be possible to decide whether a given case is the one or the other. But all this need not rob the distinction of usefulness.

9. Eds: The remainder of the 'Habit of Obedience' TS matches the Chapter 10 outline and is presented in Chapter 3.10 below; the remainder of the Chapter 9 outline reproduced here has no corresponding TS text.

10. Eds: The 1957 *Report of the Departmental Committee on Homosexual Offences and Prostitution* (the 'Wolfenden Report') recommended decriminalization of male same sex sexual relations. Lord Devlin, in a lecture later published as *The Enforcement of Morals,* argued against the Wolfenden report that the law should be used to achieve social cohesion and bolster common 'moral' feelings like indignation and disgust (Patrick Devlin, *The Enforcement of Morals* (Oxford: Oxford University Press, 1968)). Hart took to the BBC to criticise Devlin's arguments. Hart had a number of criticisms of Devlin from the perspective of legal positivism. However, the specific criticism that Winch took up was Hart's criticism of the 'disintegration thesis'. Hart points out that it is tautological to justify a law by its role in the maintenance of public order: to label social change as 'social disintegration' is to ignore the fact that the changed society is equally a society with its own ideas and norms. H. L. A. Hart, 'Social Solidarity and the Enforcement of Morality', *University of Chicago Law Review* 35, no. 1 (1967): 1–13. See Lectures 26 and 27 in 'Philosophy of Law and the State', Chapter 2.1 above.

3.10

FORMATION OF THE CONCEPT OF THE STATE[1]

A. How does this topic fit into my overall argument?
   1. I wrote earlier: 'what reason is in any particular context is revealed by the shape of the form of life in question'.
      a. (having argued that the authority of reason derives from the authority of the form of life it shapes)
   2. But the 'shape' of a form of life is marked precisely by the concepts involved in it.
   3. 'Reason' is not something that stands above the particular concepts of our discourse; it's a function of those concepts.
      a. This seems to lead to the conclusion that there are as many 'reasons' as there are forms of life, well, perhaps that's an exaggeration, but it's an exaggeration of a truth.
B. The constitutional direction of authority derivation is quite different from that of concept formation.[2]
   1. E.g. the policeman's authority (something a child learns pretty early, I imagine)
   2. Something like what Wittgenstein says of the formation of a world picture applies here. 'Light dawns gradually over the whole.'[3]
      a. Insofar as it does! It is possible – even usual – to get by with a pretty primitive picture of the world of authority, I imagine.
   3. The relation between the applications in the context [in] which a concept is learnt and what is thereby learnt – which may include the ability to question those original applications.

---

1. Eds: Computer printout; 24 pp.; Peter Winch Archives (GB 0100 KCLCA K/PP171, Box 16), King's College London. Some paragraphs of the 'Habit of Obedience' TS from the Archives (box number not recorded) fit this Chapter 10 outline, but they do not treat these points in the same order as the outline. We have reproduced the Chapter 10 outline in full and given the text that can be matched to that outline from 'Habit of Obedience' below. The outline is relatively wordy, and the corresponding TS text relatively sparse, so that integrating them is not feasible. As a result, the text of this chapter is repetitive. If one wants to follow the 'Habit of Obedience' TS as such, this can be done by reading Chapters 3.9 and 3.10 together: the 'Habit of Obedience' TS begins with Chapter 3.9, turns to Chapter 3.10, and returns to Chapter 3.9. Note that some of the TS text is in a footnote: Chapter 3.9, n. 6 and n. 7.
2. Eds: See excerpt below from the 'Habit of Obedience' TS that ends this Chapter.
3. Eds: Ludwig Wittgenstein, *On Certainty*, ed. G. E. M. Anscombe and G. H. von Wright, trans. Denis Paul and G. E. M. Anscombe (Oxford: Basil Blackwell, 1969), §141.

a. This is why Wittgenstein's philosophy is not constitutionally 'conservative' (not to say reactionary).
      i. 'Philosophy leaves everything as it is' – including the possibility of criticism!
   b. Not 'sociology of knowledge' (in any deterministic sense)
C. But we must also recognise that these more primitive applications represent a dimension to the concept that in a sense endures.
   1. I mean that the concept of state authority is never going to be exhausted by the account a constitutional lawyer might give of it. His account will say very little about the ground-level applications of the concept by the citizen. And without those ground-level applications the concept is going to be quite empty.
   2. This is important to the notion of the legitimacy of an authority.
   3. Remember too that the legitimacy of a regime may be just as much damaged through corruption at this ground level as through corruption at the top, in the government.[4]
      a. Of course, given notions of the responsibility of a government for the behaviour of its subordinate organs, these are likely to go hand in hand – to a large extent anyway.
   4. Not to forget that it can also work in the reverse direction.
      a. E.g. attitudes towards the police, towards schools, towards the press may be influenced by the perception that they are supportive of a corrupt regime.
D. It's also important that 'state concepts' inform not only citizens' relation to authorities of one sort and another, but also their relations with each other.
   1. E.g. marriage, contract, military life
   2. Also, more amorphously, but very importantly, the relation of *fellow-citizen*
   3. Of course this relation may be undermined through the activities of state organs.
      a. E.g. secret police informers[5]
      b. Encouragement of hatred towards minorities

---

4. Eds: Winch would discuss Weil's contention that the French government before the war had lost its legitimacy not through actions of the state but through the indifference of citizens as an example of a failure of what might be called tacit consent; corruption at the 'ground level' may mean on the part of the citizenry. Simone Weil, 'The Legitimacy of the Provisional Government', trans. Peter Winch, *Philosophical Investigations* 10, no. 2 (1987): 87–98.
5. Eds: Winch would also discuss examples from the Soviet bloc at this time. He had taken part in at least one clandestine meeting between Eastern and Western European intellectuals before the fall of the wall in 1989 and was involved in the activities of the *Institut fur die Wissenschaften vom Menschen* to foster intellectual interchange through these years of transition. He was interested in Vaclav Havel's example of the greengrocer required to put a sign, 'Workers of the world, Unite' in this shop window as illustrating the way that the exercise of political authority could corrupt the citizen's relation to one another and to truth. (V. Havel, 'The Power of the Powerless', in *Living in the Truth*, ed. J. Vladislav (London: Faber and Faber, 1990), 36–122; Olli Lagerspetz, 'Peter Winch on Political Authority and Political Culture', *Philosophical Investigations* 35, no. 3–4 (2012): 277–302; also Reid personal recollection). The discussion was not just about the way that the process of surveillance corrupts citizens' relations with one another, but also (as Havel describes) the way that the state exercises its power through requiring a corrupted relationship to truth on the part of its citizens; this becomes a vulnerability of state power to a particular kind of moral rebellion on the part of citizens.

FORMATION OF THE CONCEPT OF THE STATE 221

    c. Look at Rush Rhees's discussion of *Mario und der Zauberer* ('The Tree of Nebuchadnezzar').[6]
E. The state to be distinguished from particular regimes
  1. A regime of course *wields* the authority of the state.
    a. Though how far it's necessary for one subject to it to have a picture of that is unclear (see B.2.a).
    b. Read [Simone Weil] '*La légitimité du gouvernement provisoire*'[7] on this.
  2. The case of the civil servant leaking secrets to her M.P.[8]
  3. The judge in that case and Hobbes's 'unity of the representer'[9]

On a theory of sovereignty, like that of Hobbes (or Austin) the authority of a local official, say, derives from that of the central government. For Hobbes this is *a priori*: there can be no ultimate authority that is independent of that of the sovereign. I don't know what constitutional lawyers would say, but no doubt they would more or less agree. But in any event, I think it must be clear that concept formation goes in the other direction. [I.B.] One does not learn of the policeman's authority by way of understanding the precise position it occupies in the constitutional chain of authority! And most people probably never know this very precisely. [I.B.1.–2.]

In relatively stable and law-abiding communities a child will learn very early that the power of the policeman is different from that of a neighbourhood bully. What does such a child come precisely to understand? [I.B.3.] (Naturally in other sorts of community

---

6. Eds: Rhees's discussion of *Marie und der Zauberer* is actually in a follow-up letter to his 'Tree of Nebuchadnezzar' (*The Human World*, 4 (1971): 23–26), published two volumes later (*The Human World*, 6 (February 1972): 51–54). In the Thomas Mann story, an itinerant hypnotist in an Italian resort town in 1930 forces out of the waiter Mario an enactment of his love for his girlfriend; Mario responds to the humiliation of this by murdering the hypnotist. The story is in part a depiction of the growth of fascism in Italy and Germany and how it is re-shaping the society – the lives of children and of adults. Rhees's discussion here centres around the idea that what is profoundly expressive of the inner self and entirely without wrong-doing or shame can be subject to a powerful form of degradation when (whether by the influence of politics or of hypnotism), a 'division of labour' (the term Mann puts in his character's mouth) is forced on the agent: the doing and the willing are separated.
7. Eds: Simone Weil, 'The Legitimacy of the Provisional Government', trans. Peter Winch, *Philosophical Investigations* 10, no. 2 (1987): 87–98.
8. Eds: There are two candidates for what Winch might have had in mind, neither of which perfectly matches what he says here: in 1983, Sarah Tisdall, a junior civil servant (a clerk), leaked to the *Guardian* newspaper the imminent arrival at Greenham Common of American nuclear cruise missiles and the intention of the Minister of Defence to keep this secret. She was convicted and jailed under the Official Secrets Act after the *Guardian* (controversially) handed over the evidence that it had received anonymously. In 1985, Clive Ponting, a senior civil servant, leaked to a Labour MP that the government was misleading parliament about the sinking of the General Belgrano in the Falklands War; he was acquitted by jury despite the recommendation of the presiding judge to convict. See Richard Norton-Taylor, *The State of Secrecy: Spies and the Media in Britain* (London: Bloomsbury, 2023).
9. Eds: The following paragraphs are the last sections of the 'Habit of Obedience' TS, which fit the Chapter 10 outline here.

no such difference may be recognised; and this may indeed be a realistic attitude in many cases.)

This must be connected with what Lars [Hertzberg] pointed out: that people who reject the legitimacy of a government (perhaps in a pre-revolutionary situation) may nevertheless continue to call in the police to protect their property or defend them. (Is this quite right though?)

Here it will be very important to distinguish between the power of the state and that of particular regimes and/or governments: another very unstable, but nonetheless important, distinction. Cf. the case (in the middle 1980s) of the civil servant who sent classified documents relating to an alleged abuse of power to her M.P., claiming that her duty to the state overrode her duty to the government of the day. The judge, unfortunately, held that such a distinction could not be recognised and that the state was embodied in the government of the day. I am sure the judge was confused about this. [I.E.2.] The state comprises so very much more. That judge's attitude was close to Hobbes's ('the unity of the representer, not the unity of the represented'). [I.E.3.] Unlike Locke and even unlike Rousseau who, although he has a theory of absolute sovereignty, distinguishes between the government and the sovereign.

[...]

What exactly is the force of the point about concept formation? We must of course recognise that our concepts may develop far beyond the applications in which we originally learn them. They may indeed develop in such a way that we come to question those original applications. What we learn is a way of thinking. We can do so of course only in the context of certain applications: but what we learn is not in the end tied to those particular applications.

But we must also recognise that these more primitive applications represent a dimension to the concept that in a sense endures. I mean that the concept of state authority is never going to be exhausted by the account a constitutional lawyer might give of it. His account will say very little about the ground-level applications of the concept by the citizen. And without those ground-level applications the concept is going to be quite empty. [I.C.1–2.]

This is important to the notion of the *legitimacy* of an authority. Remember too that the legitimacy of a regime may be just as much damaged through corruption at this ground level as through corruption at the top, in the government. Of course, given notions of the responsibility of a government for the behaviour of its subordinate organs, these are likely to go hand in hand – to a large extent anyway. [I.C.3]

It's also important that 'state concepts' inform not only citizens' relation to authorities of one sort and another, but also their relations with each other. E.g. marriage, contract, military life. [I.D., I.D.1] Also, more amorphously, but very importantly, the relation of *fellow-citizen*. [I.D.2]

APPENDICES

4.1

AUTHORITY, CONSENT AND PRACTICAL REASON [1990][1]

1. Introduction

A. Different kinds of question
  1. The problem of how to discriminate
  2. Wording not infallible guide
  3. Look at how people look for the answer and what implications they see in that answer.
     (a) This works O.K. in some cases.
        1. Examples.
     (b) But not in others.
        1. People may have been confused about what they are asking.
           a. Examples
  4. There is no formula: judgement necessary. But one can be self-conscious about one's own inquiry.
  5. Such inquiries not necessarily trivial, peripheral or merely preliminary; they may uncover quite substantive issues.
     (a) Examples.
B. Application to 'what is political authority'?
  1. Consider Hume's 'Of the First Principles of Government',[2] which opens with the well-known observation:

  Nothing appears more surprising to those who consider human affairs with a philosophical eye than the easiness with which the many are governed by the few and the implicit submission with which men resign their own sentiments and passions to those of their rulers.

  2. This may be understood
     a. Sociologically
     b. Morally [?]

---

1. Eds: Dated February 12. Source: Typescript; 4 pp., Peter Winch Archives (GB 0100 KCLCA K/PP171, Box 6), King's College London.
2. David Hume, *Political Essays*, ed. Charles W. Hendel (Indianapolis: Bobbs-Merrill, 1953), 24–27 (24).

    c. Philosophically [conceptually]³
  3. These (and other) aspects may be combined.
    a. Such combinations *may* be symptom of, or lead to, confusion
    b. But we should not *assume* this must be so in all cases.
  4. Example: their combination in Hume
C. Conceptual questions
  1. Their relation to philosophical puzzlement
  2. 'Grammar'
    a. Wittgenstein's use of this term
    b. Don't assume it's trivial
      1. Cf. Guess's irritation about my speaking thus of St. John in the SW book.⁴
      2. N.B. the mingling with 'ethics'

II. Reason and Will

A. Whose action?
  1. When is this naturally asked?
  2. Responsibility
    a. Different uses
      1. Who did it?
      2. Who's to blame? (etc.)
B. Action and event
  1. Questions of 'criteria'
    a. Davidson
C. 'The will'
D. Will and reason
  1. Belief and desire
  2. Thought and action
    a. Hume
    b. Kant
    c. Simone Weil

III. Authority and Agency

A. Political and other forms of authority
B. Representation
  1. Hobbes
  2. Rousseau

---

3. Handwritten marginal note:
   L1: Reasons and coercion
   L2–3: Austin
   L4: Reason and coercion
   L5: Hobbes
4. Peter Winch, *Simone Weil: 'The Just Balance'* (Cambridge: Cambridge University Press, 1989).

C. Consent
    1. Tacit consent
        a. Locke
        b. Hume
        c. Plamenatz
        d. Pateman
        e. Simone Weil

IV. Social Contract

A. State and government
B. Legitimacy and democracy
    1. Pateman[5]
    2. Gould[6]
    3. Simone Weil
C. Practical reason

V. *On Certainty*

A. Reason and authority
B. Individual and community

VI. State and Citizen

---

5. Carol Pateman, *The Problem of Political Obligation: A Critique of Liberal Theory* (Berkeley: University of California Press, 1985) or *The Sexual Contract* (Stanford: Stanford University Press, 1988).
6. Carol C. Gould, *Rethinking Democracy: Freedom and Social Cooperation in Politics, Economy, and Society* (Cambridge: Cambridge University Press, 1990).

4.2

REASONS FOR ACTION/WITTGENSTEIN ON AUTHORITY [N.D.][1]

INTRODUCTION

1. REASONS FOR BELIEF/ACTION
   Wittgenstein, *On Certainty*[2]
   P. Winch, 'Certainty and Authority'[3]
2. THE PHILOSOPHICAL TRADITION OF THE 'AUTHORITATIVE INDIVIDUAL'
3. HOW IS POLITICAL AUTHORITY POSSIBLE

MAIN SECTION

4. REASONS FOR ACTION
   4.1 BELIEF AND ACTION
      4.11 FOUNDATIONALISM
         (1) NO GROUNDS FOR BELIEF
         (2) EXCEPT ACTION
         R. Rorty, *The Linguistic Turn*, 'Introduction'[4]
         R. Rorty, Philosophy and the Mirror of Nature[5]
      4.12 HOLISM
         (1) A SYSTEM OF THOUGHT,
         (2) AS A FRAMEWORK
         D. Davidson, *Inquiries into Truth and Interpretation*
         'Radical interpretation'[6]
         'The Very Idea of a Conceptual Scheme'[7]

---

1. Source: Typescript; 1 p., Peter Winch Archives (GB 0100 KCLCA K/PP171, Box 25), King's College London.
2. Eds: Ludwig Wittgenstein, *On Certainty*, trans. Denis Paul and G. E. M. Anscombe, ed. G. E. M. Anscombe and G. H. von Wright (Oxford: Basil Blackwell, 1969).
3. Eds: Peter Winch, 'Certainty and Authority', in *Wittgenstein Centenary Essays*, ed. A. P. Griffiths (Cambridge: Cambridge University Press, 1991), 223–238.
4. Eds: Richard Rorty, 'Introduction: Metaphilosophical Difficulties of Linguistic Philosophy', in *The Linguistic Turn: Essays in Philosophical Method*, ed. Richard Rorty (Chicago: Chicago University Press, 1967), 1–39.
5. Eds: Richard Rorty, *Philosophy and the Mirror of Nature* (Princeton, NJ: Princeton University Press, 1979).

4.2 RULES AND ACTION
4.21 INDETERMINACY OF RULES
4.22 SYSTEM OF JUDGEMENTS, NOT RULES[8]
4.23 THE NOTION OF A MISTAKE
4.24 BEING BOUND BY A COMMUNITY
4.3 WILL AND ACTION
4.31 WILL AS PHENOMENON AND AS TRANSCENDENTAL EGO
4.32 ETHICS IS EXTERNAL TO THE WORLD
4.33 WILL AS ACTION ITSELF

Wittgenstein, *Notebooks 1914–1916*, 4 November 1916[9]
Wittgenstein, *Tractatus* 6.373, 6.4–6.5[10]
Wittgenstein, 'A Lecture on Ethics', *The Phil Rev*, 74 (Jan 65)[11]
Wittgenstein, *Philosophical Investigations* §630–[ff.][12]
P. Winch, 'Wittgenstein's Treatment of the Will', *Ethics and Action*[13]
R. Bernstein, *Praxis and Action*, pp. 245–247, 254–[ff.][14]

CONCLUSION

5. QUESTIONS
5.1 REASON?
5.2 INDIVIDUALISM?
5.3 AUTHORITY?

---

6. Eds: Donald Davidson, 'Radical Interpretation', originally published in *Dialectica* 27, no 1 (1973): 314–328, reprinted in *Inquiries into Truth and Interpretation* (Oxford: Oxford University Press, 1984).
7. Eds: Donald Davidson, 'On the Very Idea of a Conceptual Scheme', originally published in *Proceedings and Addresses of the American Philosophical Association* 47 (1973): 5–20; reprinted in *Inquiries into Truth and Interpretation* (Oxford: Oxford University Press, 1984).
8. Eds: See Peter Winch, 'Judgement: Propositions and practices', *Philosophical Investigations* 2, no. 3 (1998): 189–202.
9. Eds: Ludwig Wittgenstein, *Notebooks, 1914–1916*, eds. G. H. von Wright and G. E. M. Anscombe, trans. G. E. M. Anscombe (Chicago: University of Chicago Press, 1961), pp. 86–88.
10. Eds: *Tractatus Logico-Philosophicus*, trans. David Pears and Brian McGuinness (London: Routledge and Kegan Paul, 1961).
11. Eds: Ludwig Wittgenstein, 'A lecture on ethics', *Philosophical Review* 74, no. 1 (1965): 3–12.
12. Eds: Ludwig Wittgenstein, *Philosophical Investigations*, eds. G. E. M. Anscombe and Rush Rhees, trans. G. E. M. Anscombe. (Oxford: Basil Blackwell, 1953).
13. Eds: Peter Winch, 'Wittgenstein's Treatment of the Will', in *Ethics and Action* (London: Routledge and Kegan Paul, 1972), 110–129.
14. Eds: Richard J. Bernstein, *Praxis and Action* (London: Duckworth, 1971).

4.3

SESSION 9 OF ÅBO SEMINAR ON POLITICAL AUTHORITY [1993][1]

1. Let me put together the topics we have discussed, and chart a course.
    a. The distinction between conceptual/grammatical questions and questions about the functioning of institutions. [Session 1; Chapter 3.2]
    b. More about that distinction in relation to Hobbes and Rousseau. Hobbes's idea that understanding one's political obligations requires knowledge of a 'science' versus Rousseau's emphasis on education/upbringing. [Session 6; Chapter 3.4]
    c. More on that last contrast. The limits of 'argument'; the cave in Plato's *Republic*; Polus's failure to understand Socrates in the *Gorgias*. [Sessions 4 and 5; Chapter 3.3]
    d. Authority as a reason for acting: the importance of the distinction between concepts and institutions once more; what counts as a reason for acting? – Socrates and Polus. The good and what is to one's 'advantage'. [Session 5; Chapters 2.3 and 3.3]
    e. Do human beings always seek what they take to be good? Claggart and Britten's opera *Billy Budd*. Relevance of this issue to politics: the assumption that rational action requires deciding what it is best to do according to one's own lights seems incompatible with doing something just because someone else says so. [Session 5; Chapter 3.3]
    f. 'Reason' and 'cause'. More about Hobbes from this point of view; contrast with Austin. [Session 4; Chapter 3.4]
    g. The difference between an inquiry into the nature of authority in a particular state at a particular period and philosophical inquiry into 'the nature of political authority'. Locke on the 1688 Settlement versus his claim to speak about 'political power' as such. [Sessions 7 and 8; Chapter 3.5] Locke on consent express and tacit. [Chapter 3.6]

---

1. Eds: The lecture notes for the 1993 Åbo Authority Seminar are almost completely contained in the 'Last Book Outline' (Part 3), with the exception of this Session 9 (of 10), which outlines the materials covered to that point and how he might take them forward. Source: Typescript; lecture notes; 2 of 26 pp., Peter Winch Archives (GB 0100 KCLCA K/PP171, Box 16), King's College London.

h. More about consent. [Chapter 3.6] His claims about the internal relations between freedom, rationality, authority and consent. [Chapter 3.5] Does rationality transcend history and cultures? [Chapter 3.6]
2. This looks something of a kaleidoscope. In the time that remains I want first to put the issues discussed into some sort of intelligible arrangement. Then I want to state more sharply the general issue: How is Political Authority Possible?[2] Then to consider how we should deal with this question.
3. The notion of a reason for acting has been central throughout.[3]
   a. All the writers we have considered (Plato, Hobbes, Locke, Rousseau (of whom more later) have assumed that a quite general account can be given of this notion).
   b. I think they have also considered (and this of course is connected) that the force of reason is quite universal in the sense that it transcends particular circumstances of culture, time and place.
   c. Plato's discussion (*Gorgias*) is typical in focussing on the idea that action is guided by a conception of the good. You find the same idea in others – it's very prominent in Hobbes for instance, and implicit, possibly, in Locke and Rousseau.
   d. Having a reason for acting is thought of as having two aspects: (1) It motivates to action; (2) It is a basis for justification and/or criticism.
   e. These last two aspects are evident in Hobbes's conception of what his 'science' of politics might achieve.
   f. So we have a picture here of what a political philosophy might be and ought to be: a systematic exposition, accessible to and valid for, any rational person (anywhere and anywhen) of reasons for maintaining a certain political attitude: out of respect for and allegiance to any authority which meets certain conditions laid down in the theory.
   g. Rousseau is interestingly anomalous as far as this picture is concerned.
      1. On the one hand his rationalism is possibly the tightest of any of those we've considered.
      2. On the other hand he, more than any of the others, emphasises that this sort of rationality comes into being only as a result of a certain kind of education.

---

2. Eds: The capitalization may suggest a relationship to the MS of this name published posthumously, *Philosophical Investigations* 25, no. 1 (2002): 20–32.
3. Eds: This observation is consistent with two earlier brief draft book outlines ('Reasons for Action' (Appendix 4.2) and 'Authority, consent and practical reason' (Appendix 4.1)). These MSS indicate that attacking misconceptions about the nature of practical reason/reasons for action is his approach to criticizing the contract tradition; the 'Last Book Outline' (Part 3 above) announces in its introduction that the book coalesced for him as ready to be written when he realised that the question of the 'authority of reason' is in fact the central vulnerability of consent theory. The critique of the universalism of the belief/desire theory of practical reason sketched below is not absent from the 'Last Book Outline', but the question of the authority of reason is made central.

3. These two ideas, which seem to be in tension with each other, are resolved insofar as the education that Rousseau sets out to describe or depict is one that is supposed not to impose anything on the child, but to provide conditions in which the child's own potential rationality can properly develop.
4. Fundamental difficulties about the applicability of such a picture, that I have tried to develop, are:
   a. It is by no means clear that, as far as internal structure goes, practical reason does have the sort of internal uniformity supposed. Two points here:
      1. The case of Claggart. [Chapter 3.3]
      2. The difficulty about applying any such picture. It is here that the real 'considerations that move to action' will be found. And here we can hardly expect to find uniformity. (If we do think we've found it, the same difficulty will arise at the next level.)
      3. An example: the two patients' attitude to reading the gospel in Solzhenitzyn's *Cancer Ward*?[4]
   b. Somewhat connected with the last point: what people regard as rational changes remarkably in different historical epochs (alchemy, astrology, psychoanalysis) and differs from culture to culture (Azande).[5]
   c. These considerations suggest the possibility that the original difficulty arises out of a confused apprehension of what reason is.
5. In what follows:
   a. Rousseau.[6]
   b. Rationality and persuasion: the authority of reason. [Chapters 3.3 and 3.8][7]
   c. Authority and rationality. [Chapter 3.7][8]

---

4. *Trying to Make Sense*, p. 30. ['Text and Context', in *Trying to Make Sense* (Oxford: Blackwell, 1987), 18–32].
5. Cf. Charles Taylor, *Collected Papers, Vol. 1* [New York: Cambridge University Press, 1985]; Winch, 'Understanding a Primitive Society' in *Ethics and Action* [(London: Routledge and Kegan Paul, 1972), 8–49].
6. *Du contrat social*.
7. 'Persuasion', *Midwest Studies in Philosophy* [17, no. 1 (1992): 123–37].
8. 'Certainty and Authority' in *Wittgenstein: Centenary Essays* [ed. A. Phillips Griffiths (Cambridge: Cambridge University Press, 1991), 223–38].

BIBLIOGRAPHY

Unpublished Material by Peter Winch

Peter Winch. (1966). 'Laws of Thought and Forms of Life' [TS; 14 pp.], GB 0100 KCLCA K/PP171, Box 5. Peter Winch Archives, King's College London.

———.(1969–1970). 'Intercollegiate Lectures on Political Philosophy' [TS; lectures; 16 pp.], GB 0100 KCLCA K/PP171, Folder 'Politics IV', Box 7; also in Box 20, Peter Winch Archives, King's College London.

———. (1977). 'Other people' [TS; book chapter draft; 19 pp.], GB 0100 KCLCA K/PP171, Folder 'Politics IV', Box 7, Peter Winch Archives, King's College London.

———. (1984). 'Four Lectures on Consent' [Computer printout; lectures; 24 pp.], GB 0100 KCLCA K/PP171, Box 35, Peter Winch Archives, King's College London.

———. (1990). 'Authority, Consent and Practical Reason' [TS; book outline; 4 pp.], GB 0100 KCLCA K/PP171, Box 6, Peter Winch Archives, King's College London.

———.(1990). 'Illinois Seminar on Political Authority' [Computer printout; lectures; 8 pp.], GB 0100 KCLCA K/PP171, Box 25, Peter Winch Archives, King's College London.

———.(1991). 'Persuasion and Reason' [TS; lecture delivered at Brooklyn College; 20 pp.], GB 0100 KCLCA K/PP171, Box 28, Peter Winch Archives, King's College, London.

———.(1992). 'Philosophy of Law and the State' [Computer printout; lecture notes; 61 pp.], GB 0100 KCLCA K/PP171, Box 16, Peter Winch Archives, King's College London.

———.(1993). 'Åbo Seminar on Political Authority' [Computer printout; lectures; 24 pp.], GB 0100 KCLCA K/PP171, Box 16, Peter Winch Archives, King's College London.

———.(1993). 'Notes on the Limits of Argument' [Computer printout, 22 pp.], GB 0100 KCLCA K/PP171, Peter Winch Archives, King's College London.

———. (1993). 'Political Authority' [Computer printout; seminar notes; 24 pp.], GB 0100 KCLCA K/PP171, Box 16, Peter Winch Archives, King's College London.

———.(1993). 'Reasons and Causes' [Computer printout; 10 pp.], GB 0100 KCLCA K/PP171, Peter Winch Archives, King's College London.

———.(1996). 'Plato's *Gorgias*'; a selection from 'Ethics and Value Theory' [Computer printout; lectures; 23 of 25 pp.], GB 0100 KCLCA K/PP171, Box 8, Peter Winch Archives, King's College London.

———.(N.D.). [No title; 'The Last Book Outline'] [Computer printout; book outline; 22 pp.], GB 0100 KCLCA K/PP171, Box 16, Peter Winch Archives, King's College London.

———. (N.D.). 'Action, Reason and Will' [Computer printout; 16 pp.], GB 0100 KCLCA K/PP171, Box 10, Peter Winch Archives, King's College London.

———. (N.D.). 'Authority [Freedom and Servility]' [TS, 6 pp.], GB 0100 KCLCA K/PP171, Folder 'Politics VII', Box 21, Peter Winch Archives, King's College London.

———. (N.D.). 'Authority, Consent and Practical Reason' [Computer print-out; book outline; 4 pp.], Box 16, GB 0100 KCLCA K/PP171, Peter Winch Archives, King's College London.

———. (N.D.). 'Authority of Reason' [Computer printout; 7 pp.], distributed to students in Finland, September 1993; Olli Lagerspetz.

———. (N.D.). 'Authority, Society and the State' [TS; lectures; 8 pp.], GB 0100 KCLCA K/PP171, Folder 'Politics I', Box 16 and Folder 'Politics IV', Box 7, Peter Winch Archives, King's College London.

———.(N.D. [1993]). 'Authority: General and Particular' [Computer printout; 23 pp.], GB 0100 KCLCA K/PP171, Box 10, Peter Winch Archives, King's College London.

———. (N.D.). 'Habit of Obedience' [Computer printout; 4 pp.], GB 0100 KCLCA K/PP171, Box 10, Peter Winch Archives, King's College London.

———.(N.D.). 'Locke on Property' [Handwritten; lectures; 22 pp.], GB 0100 KCLCA K/PP171, Folder 'Politics IV', Box 7, Peter Winch Archives, King's College London.

———. (N.D.). 'Reason, Will and Representation in Rousseau' [Computer printout; 5 pp], distributed to students in Finland, September 1993; Olli Lagerspetz.

———. (N.D.). 'Reasons for Action/Wittgenstein on Authority' [TS; book outline; 1 p.], GB 0100 KCLCA K/PP171, Box 25, Peter Winch Archives, King's College London.

Secondary Sources

Anscombe, G. E. M. *Ethics, Religion and Politics: Collected Philosophical Papers, Vol. III.* Oxford: Basil Blackwell, 1991.

Austin, John. *The Province of Jurisprudence Determined*, edited by H. L. A. Hart. London: Weidenfeld and Nicolson, 1954.

Austin, J. L. 'A Plea for Excuses'. In *Philosophical Papers*, edited by J. O. Urmson and G. J. Warnock. Oxford: Oxford University Press, 1961.

Barabas, Marina. 'The Strangeness of Socrates'. *Philosophical Investigations* 9, no. 2 (1986): 89–110.

Barker, Ernest. *Social Contract. Essays by Locke, Hume and Rousseau.* Oxford: Oxford University Press, 1948.

Bernstein, Richard J. *Praxis and Action*. London: Duckworth, 1971.

Blumenberg, Hans. *Höhlenausgänge*. Frankfurt am Main: Suhrkamp, 1996.

Campbell, Michael and Lynette Reid, eds. *Ethics, Society and Politics: Themes from the Philosophy of Peter Winch*. Cham: Springer International Publishing, 2020.

Carroll, Lewis. 'What the Tortoise Said to Achilles'. *Mind* 4, no. 14 (1895): 278–280.

Cockburn, David. 'In the Beginning Was the Deed'. *Philosophical Investigations* 36, no. 4 (2013): 303–319.

Coetzee, J. M. 'Resisters'. *The New York Review of Books* XL, no. 20 (December 2, 1993).

Crary, Alice. 'Wittgenstein Goes to Frankfurt (and Finds Something Useful to Say)'. *Nordic Wittgenstein Review* 7, no. 1 (2018): 7–41.

Devlin, Patrick. *The Enforcement of Morals*. Oxford: Oxford University Press, 1968.

Davidson, Donald. 'Radical Interpretation'. *Dialectica* 27, no. 1 (1973): 314–328.

———. 'On the Very Idea of a Conceptual Scheme'. *Proceedings and Addresses of the American Philosophical Association* 47 (1973): 5–20.

de Juvenal, Bernard. *On Power: Its Nature and the History of its Growth*. New York: Viking Press, 1948.

Diamond, Cora. *The Realistic Spirit: Wittgenstein, Philosophy, and the Mind*. Cambridge, MA: MIT Press, 1991.

———. 'Truth: Defenders, Debunkers, Despisers'. In *Commitment in Reflection: Essays in Literature and Moral Philosophy*, edited by L. Toker, 195–222. New York: Garland, 1994.

Durkheim, Émile. *The Division of Labour*, translated by George Simpson. Glencoe Illinois: Free Press, 1933.

Feinberg, Joel and Hyman Gross, eds. *Philosophy of Law*. Encino, CA: Dickenson Publishing Company, 1975.

Fodor, Jerry A. *The Language of Thought*. Cambridge, MA: Harvard University Press, 1975.

Gaita, Raimond. *A Common Humanity: Thinking about Love and Truth and Justice*. Abingdon: Routledge, 2000.

Gould, Carol C. *Rethinking Democracy : Freedom and Social Cooperation in Politics, Economy, and Society*. Cambridge: Cambridge University Press, 1990.

Habermas, Jurgen. 'Towards a Theory of Communicative Competence'. *Inquiry* 13 (1970): 205–218.

———. *On the Logic of the Social Sciences*, translated by Shierry Weber Nicholsen and Jerry A. Stark. Cambridge: Polity Press, 1988.

Hare, R. M. 'Lawful Government'. In *Philosophy, Politics and Society, Third Series: A Collection*, edited by Peter Laslett and W. G. Runciman. Oxford: Basil Blackwell, 1967.

Hart, H. L. A. *The Concept of Law*. Oxford: Oxford University Press, 1961.

———. 'Social Solidarity and the Enforcement of Morality'. *University of Chicago Law Review* 35, no. 1 (1967): 1–13.

Havel, Vácav. 'The Power of the Powerless'. In *Living in the Truth*, edited by J. Vladislav, 36–122. London: Faber and Faber, 1990.

Hutchinson, Phil, Rupert Read and Wes Sharrock. *There Is No Such Thing as a Social Science: In Defence of Peter Winch*. Aldershot: Ashgate, 2008.

Henry-Hermann, Greta. 'Conquering Chance: Critical Reflections on Leonard Nelson's Establishment of Ethics as a Science', translated by Peter Winch. *Philosophical Investigations* 14, no. 1 (1991): 1–80.

Hertzberg, Lars. 'On the Attitude of Trust'. *Inquiry* 31, no. 3 (1988): 307–322.

———. 'Legitimacy and the Political Community'. In *Legitimacy: The Treasure of Politics*, edited by Tage Kurtén and Lars Hertzberg, 15–32. Frankfurt am Main: Peter Lang, 2011.

———. '"What Justifies the Justifications?" Winch on Punishment and Justice'. In *Ethics, Society and Politics: Themes From the Philosophy of Peter Winch*, edited by Michael Campbell and Lynette Reid, 41–55. Cham: Springer International Publishing, 2020.

Hobbes, Thomas. *Leviathan*. Edited by C. B. Macpherson. Harmondsworth: Penguin Books, [1651] 1966.

———. *Behemoth or the Long Parliament*. Chicago, IL: University of Chicago Press, [1681] 1990.

Holland, R. F. (ed.). 'Epistemology and Education'. In *Against Empiricism*. London: Routledge and Kegan Paul, 1980.

———. *Against Empiricism*. London: Routledge and Kegan Paul, 1980.

Horton, John. 'Peter Winch and Political Authority'. *Philosophical Investigations* 28, no. 3 (2005): 235–252.

Hume, David. *Political Essays*, edited by Charles W. Handel. Indianapolis: The Library of Liberal Arts, 1953.

Hume, David. *A Treatise of Human Nature*, edited by L. A. Selby-Bigge and P. H. Nidditch. Oxford: Oxford University Press, 1978.

Kant, Immanuel. *Grundlegung zur Metaphysik der Sitten*, edited by Rudolf Otto. Gotha: Leopold Klotz, [1785] 1967.

Lagerspetz, Olli. 'Legitimacy and Trust'. *Philosophical Investigations* 15, no. 1 (1992): 1–21.

———. 'Peter Winch on Political Authority and Political Culture'. *Philosophical Investigations* 35, no. 3–4 (2012): 277–302.

———. 'Political Philosophy and the Primacy of Agency'. In *Ethics, Society and Politics: Themes From the Philosophy of Peter Winch*, edited by Michael Campbell and Lynette Reid, 85–102. Cham: Springer International Publishing, 2020.

Levi, Primo. 'The Periodic Table'. In *The Complete Works of Primo Levi*, Volume 2, edited and translated by Ann Goldstein, 761–966. New York: W. W. Norton and Company, 2015.

Levy, D. K. 'What Is la force in Simone Weil's Iliad?' *Philosophical Investigations* 43, no. 1–2 (2020): 19–39.

Locke, John. *Second Treatise of Government*, edited by C. B. Macpherson. Indianapolis: Hackett, 1980.

MacIntyre, Alasdair C. *After Virtue: A Study in Moral Theory*. Notre Dame, IN: University of Notre Dame Press, 1984.

Macpherson, C. B. 'Introduction'. In *John Locke, Second Treatise of Government*, edited by C. B. Macpherson, vii–xii. Indianapolis: Hackett, 1980.

Marcel, Gabriel. *The Mystery of Being, Vol. 1, Reflection and Mystery*. London: The Harvill Press, 1951.
Norton-Taylor, Richard. *The State of Secrecy: Spies and the Media in Britain*. London: Bloomsbury Press, 2023.
Pateman, Carole. *The Problem of Political Obligation: A Critique of Liberal Theory*. Cambridge: Polity Press, 1985.
———. *The Sexual Contract*. Stanford, CA: Stanford University Press, 1988.
Parfit, Derek. *Reasons and Persons*. Oxford: Oxford University Press, 1984.
Peters, R. S., Peter Winch and A. E. Duncan-Jones. 'Symposium: Authority'. *Proceedings of the Aristotelian Society* Supplementary Volume 32 (1958): 207–260.
Plamenatz, J. P. *Consent, Freedom and Political Obligation*. Oxford: Oxford University Press, 1968.
———. *Man and Society*. London: Longman. 1975.
Plato, *Gorgias*, translated by W. Hamilton. Harmondsworth: Penguin Books, 1959.
———. *Republic*, translated by H. D. P. Lee. Harmondsworth: Penguin, 1974.
———. *The Theaetetus of Plato*, commentary by Myles Burnyeat, translated by M. J. Levett. Indianapolis: Hackett, 1990.
Quinton, Alan, ed. *Political Philosophy*. Oxford: Oxford University Press, 1967.
Reid, Lynette. 'The Ethical and the Political in the Dilemma of Winch's Vere'. In *Ethics in the Wake of Wittgenstein*, edited by Benjamin de Mesel and Oskari Kuusela, 256–276. NY: Routledge, 2019.
———. 'Winch on Punishment: Contested Concepts, Justification, and Primitive Reactions'. In *Ethics, Society and Politics: Themes From the Philosophy of Peter Winch*, edited by Michael Campbell and Lynette Reid, 57–83. Cham: Springer International Publishing, 2020.
Rosen, Stanley. *Plato's Sophist*. New Haven: Yale University Press, 1983.
Rhees, Rhees. 'Wittgenstein's Builders'. *Proceedings of the Aristotelian Society* 60, no. 1 (1960): 171–186.
———. *Without Answers*. London: Routledge and Kegan Paul, 1969.
———. 'Tree of Nebuchadnezzar'. *The Human World* 4 (August 1971): 23–26 and 6 (February 1972): 51–54. Reprinted in *Moral Questions*.
———. *Moral Questions*. Edited by D. Z. Phillips. New York: St. Martin's Press, 1999.
Riches, David, ed. *The Anthropology of Violence*. Oxford: Basil Blackwell, 1986.
Rorty, Richard. 'Introduction: Metaphilosophical Difficulties of Linguistic Philosophy'. In *The Linguistic Turn: Essays in Philosophical Method*, edited by Richard Rorty, 1–39. Chicago: Chicago University Press, 1967.
———. *Philosophy and the Mirror of Nature*. Princeton, NJ: Princeton University Press, 1979.
Rousseau, Jean-Jacques. *Émile*, translated by Barbara Foxley. London: J. M. Dent and Sons, 1972.
———. *Of the Social Contract and Discourses*, translated by G. D. H. Cole. London: J. M. Dent and Sons, 1973.
Ryle, Gilbert. *Plato's Progress*. Cambridge: Cambridge University Press, 1966.
Strauss, Leo. 'On Locke's Doctrine of Natural Right'. *The Philosophical Review* 61, no. 4 (1952): 475–502.
Tawney, Richard Henry. *Religion and the Rise of Capitalism: A Historical Study*. London: Penguin Books, 1984.
Taylor, Charles. *Philosophical Papers: Vol. 1, Human Agency and Language*. New York: Cambridge University Press, 1985.
Weil, Simone. *The Need for Roots: Prelude to a Declaration of Duties Toward Mankind*, translated by Arthur Wills. New York: G. P. Putnam's Sons, 1952.
———. *Écrits de Londres et dernières lettres*. Paris: Gallimard, 1957.
———. *Oppression and Liberty*, translated by Arthur Wills and John Petrie. London: Routledge and Kegan Paul, 1958.
———. *Waiting for God*, translated by Emma Crauford. New York: Harper and Row, 1973.
———. 'The Iliad, or the Poem of Force'. *Chicago Review* 18, no.2 (1965): 5–30.

———. 'Are We Struggling for Justice?', translated by Marina Barabas. *Philosophical Investigations* 10, no. 1 (1987): 1–10.
———. 'The Legitimacy of the Provisional Government', translated by Peter Winch. *Philosophical Investigations* 10, no. 2 (1987): 87–98.
———. 'Essay on the Notion of Reading', translated by Rebecca Fine Rose and Timothy Tessin. *Philosophical Investigations* 13, no. 4 (1990): 297–303.
Weldon, T. D. *The Vocabulary of Politics*. Harmondsworth: Penguin, 1953.
Winch, Peter. 'Understanding a Primitive Society'. *American Philosophical Quarterly* 1, no. 4 (1964): 307–324; *Ethics and Action*, 8–49. London: Routledge and Kegan Paul, 1972.
——— 'Introduction: The Unity of Wittgenstein's Philosophy'. In *Studies in the Philosophy of Wittgenstein*, edited by Peter Winch, 1–19. London: Routledge and Kegan Paul, 1969.
———. 'Authority and Rationality'. *The Human World* 8 (1972): 11–21.
———. 'Can a Good Man Be Harmed?' In *Ethics and Action*, 193–209. London: Routledge and Kegan Paul, 1972.
———. 'Ethical Reward and Punishment'. In *Ethics and Action*, 210–228. London: Routledge and Kegan Paul, 1972.
———. 'Human Nature'. In *Ethics and Action*, 73–89. London: Routledge and Kegan Paul, 1972.
———. 'Man and Society in Hobbes and Rousseau'. In *Ethics and Action*, 90–109. London: Routledge and Kegan Paul, 1972.
———. 'Moral Integrity'. In *Ethics and Action*, 171–192. London: Routledge and Kegan Paul, 1972.
———. 'Nature and Convention'. In *Ethics and Action*, 50–72. London: Routledge and Kegan Paul, 1972.
———. 'Trying'. In *Ethics and Action*, 131–150. London: Routledge and Kegan Paul, 1972.
———. 'The Universalizability of Moral Judgments'. In *Ethics and Action*, 151–170. London: Routledge and Kegan Paul, 1972.
———. 'Wittgenstein's Treatment of the Will'. In *Ethics and Action*, 110–129. London: Routledge and Kegan Paul, 1972.
———. 'Apel's "Transcendental Pragmatics"'. In *Philosophical Disputes in the Social Sciences*, edited by S. C. Brown, 51–73. Sussex: Harvester Press, 1979.
———. 'Ceasing to Exist'. In *Trying to Make Sense*, 81–106. Oxford: Basil Blackwell, 1987.
———. 'Darwin, Genesis, and Contradiction'. In *Trying to Make Sense*, 132–139. Oxford: Basil Blackwell, 1987.
———. '*Eine Einstellung Zur Seele*'. In *Trying to Make Sense*, 140–153. Oxford: Basil Blackwell, 1987.
———. 'Ethical Relativism'. In *Trying to Make Sense*, 181–193. Oxford: Basil Blackwell, 1987.
———. 'Facts and Superfacts'. In *Trying to Make Sense*, 54–63. Oxford: Basil Blackwell, 1987.
———. '*Im Anfang War Die Tat*'. In *Trying to Make Sense*, 33–53. Oxford: Basil Blackwell, 1987.
———. 'Language, Belief and Relativism'. In *Trying to Make Sense*, 194–207. Oxford: Basil Blackwell, 1987.
———. 'Particularity and Morals'. In *Trying to Make Sense*, 167–180. Oxford: Basil Blackwell, 1987.
———. 'Text and Context'. In *Trying to Make Sense*, 18–32. Oxford: Basil Blackwell, 1987.
———. 'True or false?' *Inquiry* 3, no. 3 (1988): 265–276.
———. 'He's to Blame!' In *Wittgenstein: Attention to Particulars: Essays in Honour of Rush Rhees*, edited by Dewi Z. Philips and Peter Winch, 151–164. Palgrave Macmillan, 1989.
———. 'In and Out of the Cave: Review of *Höhlenausgänge* by Hans Blumenberg'. *The Times Literary Supplement* 4515 (1989): 1127.
———. *Simone Weil: 'The Just Balance'*. Cambridge: Cambridge University Press, 1989.
———. 'Introduction'. In *The Political Responsibility of Intellectuals*, edited by Ian Maclean, Alan Montefiore, and Peter Winch, 1–16. Cambridge: Cambridge University Press, 1990.

———. *The Idea of a Social Science and Its Relation to Philosophy*. London: Routledge and Kegan Paul, [1958] 1990.

———. 'Certainty and Authority'. In *Wittgenstein Centenary Essays*, edited by A. Phillips Griffiths, 223–238. Cambridge: Cambridge University Press, 1991.

———. 'Persuasion'. *Midwest Studies in Philosophy* 17, no. 1 (1992): 123–137.

———. 'The Expression of Belief'. *Proceedings and Addresses of the American Philosophical Association* 70, no. 2 (1996): 7–23.

———. 'Can We Understand Ourselves?' *Philosophical Investigations* 20, no. 3 (1997): 193–204.

———. 'Professor Anscombe's Moral Philosophy'. In *Commonality and Particularity in Ethics*, edited by L. Alanen, S. Heinämaa and T. Wallgren, 177–196. London: Palgrave Macmillan, 1997.

———. 'Judgement: Propositions and Practices'. *Philosophical Investigations* 21, no. 3 (1998): 189–202.

———. 'How Is Political Authority Possible?' *Philosophical Investigations* 25, no. 1 (2002): 20–32.

———. *Spinoza: Ethics and Understanding*, edited by Campbell and Tropper. London: Anthem Press. 2021.

Wittgenstein, Ludwig. *Philosophical Investigations*, edited by G. E. M. Anscombe and Rush Rhees, translated by G. E. M. Anscombe. Oxford: Basil Blackwell, 1953.

———. *Tractatus Logico-Philosophicus*, translated by David Pears and Brian McGuinness. London: Routledge and Kegan Paul, 1961.

———. *Notebooks, 1914–1916*, edited by G. H. von Wright and G. E. M. Anscombe, translated by G. E. M. Anscombe. Chicago: University of Chicago Press, 1961.

———. 'A Lecture on Ethics'. *Philosophical Review* 74, no. 1 (1965): 3–12.

———. *Zettel*, edited by G. E. M. Anscombe and G. H. von Wright, translated by G. E. M. Anscombe. Oxford: Basil Blackwell, 1967.

———. *On Certainty*, edited by G. E. M. Anscombe and G. H. von Wright, translated by Denis Paul and G. E. M. Anscombe. Oxford: Basil Blackwell, 1969.

———. 'Cause and Effect: Intuitive Awareness'. *Philosophia* 6, no. 3 (1976): 409–425.

———. *Vermischte Bemerkungen*, edited by G. H. von Wright and Heikki Nyman. Frankfurt am Main: Suhrkamp, 1977.

———. *Last Writings on the Philosophy of Psychology, Vol. I*, edited by G. H. von Wright and Heikki Nyman, translated by C. G. Luckhardt and M. A. E. Aue. Oxford: Blackwell, 1982.

———. *Culture and Value*, edited by G. H. von Wright and Heikki Nyman, translated by Peter Winch. Oxford: Basil Blackwell, 1989.

———. *Lectures on the Foundations of Mathematics, 1939, from the notes of R. G. Bosanquet, Norman Malcolm, Rush Rhees, and Yorick Smythies*, edited by Cora Diamond. Chicago: University of Chicago Press, 1989.

INDEX

action
  nature of 20, 39, 226
  reasons for 229
  and thought 226
  and will 21, 44
agency 45, 226
anarchism 43, 62, 74
Anscombe, G. E. M. 41–44, 171, 201, 207
anthropology 8–10
argument
  and attitude 133, 141–43
  limits of 162n16, 189
  standards of 30
Aristotle 5, 132, 190
  human nature 10
  on logic 5–6, 132–33, 210–11
association, voluntary 19, 45–46
attitude
  and exercise of concepts 161
Augustine 159
Austin, J. L. 14, 38
Austin, John 187–88, 221, 226n3
authoritative individual 229
authority
  application of concept 220
  and consent 41, 45–51
  forms of 33
  and legitimacy 38–39, 43
  of logic 133
  as not natural 11
  obedience to 21
  paradox of 157, 159, 229
  philosophical questions concerning 127
  as primitive 157
  and reasons 225–30, 233
  of reason 157, 219
  role in our lives 207
  and will 16

Ayer, A. J. 12
Azande 9, 233

Bentham, Jeremy 104, 187
Bernstein, Richard 230

Carroll, Lewis 133, 210, 212
citizenship 220, 227
  in Locke 48–49
  in Rousseau 17, 21, 22, 25
  in Weil 26
coercion 49, 226n3
Cohen, G. A. xiii, 14, 16
community
  relation of individual to 227
concept formation 219, 222
consent 25, 41, 49, 51, 204
  and its expression 49
  tacit 19, 47–49
  voluntary 45–46
contract xviii, 47, 51
  contractarianism 11, 157
  social 14, 23, 92, 160–62, 204, 227.
    See also Hobbes, Thomas, covenant
contractarianism 64
contractualism 101n56
corruption 49, 222
critique 30–31, 219

Davidson, Donald 160n6, 226–30
de Juvenal, Bernard 38n15
deception 37
Dickens, Charles 140
divine right 47
domination and subordination 11, 15–16, 143–45
Dostoyevsky, Fyodor
  Crime and Punishment 142
Durkheim, Émile 51

education 161–63, 162n16, 189, 207
Eliot, George
  Caleb Garth 137, 138, 168–69

Filmer, Robert 16, 47, 94
force 24, 39
  as background to rationality 35
  versus duty 15
  relations of (versus political) 17
  versus right 16–17
  in state of nature 37
foundationalism 229
freedom 18, 31, 204
Frege, Gottlob 132, 210

generality 8
  and particularity 4
good, the
  and pleasure 145–47
Gould, Carol 127, 227

Habermas, Jurgen 27
habit
  habitual behaviour 49
  of obedience 189
  versus rules 25
Hare, R. M. 18, 95, 172
Hart, H. L. A. xxi, 3n1, 25
Hermann, Grete 187n4
Hertzberg, Lars 222
historical context 16
Hobbes, Thomas 12, 34
  command and counsel 19–21, 43–45, 160, 188
  contrasted with Rousseau 21–22, 29–30, 38–40, 150–53, 162
  covenant 22–24, 35, 36, 39, 44, 160, 163, 203
  deliberation 36, 152
  good and evil 29, 30, 36
  historical context 16, 157
  human nature 28, 38
  language 30, 36, 37
  limits to state authority 31, 39
  magnanimous man 39n19, 189
  materialism 35, 38, 151, 187
  passions 35
  person (natural and artificial) 22
  representation 24, 222, 226
  right of nature 22
  science of duty 161, 185

sovereign 19, 39, 44–45, 150, 221
state of nature 24, 36, 37, 46, 151
war 37
holism 229
Holland, R. F. 37, 37n8, 207
human nature 190
Hume, David 143
  apprehension of lawful sovereign 25, 41, 51, 161
  binding of the will 136, 152, 226
  'more philosophical objection' 51–52, 149, 157
  personal identity 52
  problem of obedience 15, 27, 41–42, 159, 225
  on tacit consent 19, 50, 149, 203, 227

ideal, the 17, 28, 149
geometry 17, 140
individual. See society, relation of individuals to
institutions 35
  based on force 17
  and concepts 160–63
  and grammar 30
  of particular states 126
  versus society 33
  and the state 33, 38

judgments
  versus rules 230
justice 25, 31, 36, 133, 143, 204

Kant, Immanuel 3, 6, 13, 18, 62, 131, 136, 150, 152, 188, 226
Kierkegaard, Søren 134

language
  and generality 5
law
  explanation of obedience to 187–89
  generality, explanation and understanding 4–5, 7–8
learning 219
legitimacy 11, 18, 25–28, 42, 128, 220
  of a regime in exile 27
Levi, Primo xxi, 133
lions 3
Locke, John
  consent and legitimacy 39, 41, 46, 49, 149, 157, 204
  historical context 16

state and government 222
state of nature 48, 207
   on tacit consent 47–49, 227
logic 3, 5–10, 57, 132–34, 157, 178, 182, 183, 210–13
loyalty 39, 189

MacIntyre, Alasdair 30, 119
Mafia 42–44, 72, 74, 217
Malle, Louis 190n8
Marx, Karl xiii, 12, 16, 27, 53, 55, 59, 100
   historical context 16
memory 35, 81, 159
More, Thomas 190n9

natural law 40, 144
nature
   and convention 11, 143–44
   human 30

Oakeshott, Michael 39n19
obedience
   versus duty 15
   versus prudence 21
   as reason for action 44
oratory. *See* sophistry

Pateman, Carol 126, 227
patriotism 31
persuasion 130n8, 131–33, 165, 185, 189, 209, 233
Peters, R. S. 39
philosophy
   versus behavioural sciences 42
   versus 'bourgeois' thinking 125–26
   conceptual versus empirical 34–35, 159
   dialogue form 131
   historicity of 204
   versus history 203
   interdependence of its questions 34, 35
   of mind 41
   versus practical political questions 16
   versus sociology 159, 225
   thought about the nature of thought 4, 12–15
Plamenatz, John 41, 48, 99, 197n18, 227
Plato
   and art 147
   cave analogy 147
   and the demos 39n19, 147
   forms 9

Gorgias 77, 123, 131–48, 152
   historical context 16
   judgment myth 139–40
   justice 107
   methodology 12, 157
   philosopher king 147
   Protagoras 118–19
   sophistry 5
positivism xxi, 16, 108
   legal 25, 72–77, 187–88
power 18
   versus authority 39, 128
   versus legitimacy 22, 26–28, 42–43, 49
   required to enforce obligation 21, 28, 45, 160, 189
   of the sovereign 25
   transmission of 21–22, 39
property 51
punishment 139, 142–43

Ramsey, Frank 125
rationality 35
   and authority 204, 207, 233
   and freedom 204, 207
reactions
   condition for rationality 38
reality 5–8
reason
   for action 43, 128–30, 160, 229
   and authority 227
   and cause 187
   versus cause 44
   growth of 207
   and morality 189
   practical 227
   practices of 207
reductionism. *See* positivism
relativism 5, 8, 40, 140, 205, 219
representation 226
responsibility 220, 226
   in Hobbes 45–46
Rhees, Rush 14, 25, 34n2, 162, 221
rhetoric. *See* sophistry
Rorty, Richard 131, 229
Rousseau, Jean-Jacques 17
   contrasted with Hobbes 21–22, 29–30, 38–40, 150–53, 162
   Émile 17, 29, 161, 207
   flattery 29
   force 16–17
   general will 14, 45, 151–53

Rousseau, Jean-Jacques (*Continued*)
  justice in the state of nature 151
  legitimacy 12, 149, 157
  no transmission of will 18–22, 149, 226
  on power 15, 27, 29–30
  representation of will impossible 150
  sinister interests 38
  state and government 222
  two capacities 38
rules 230
  indeterminacy of 230
Russell, Bertrand 133

self-deception 134
shame 143
social change 10
social practices 7–9
society 24, 33
  and rationality 35
  relation of individuals to 28, 33
sociology 24, 39, 189
Socrates
  authority of 18, 133, 157
  better to suffer than to do wrong 141–42
  and Callicles 143–47
  contrasted with Hobbes 190
  and Gorgias 135
  and Polus 134–42
  unity of virtues 40n23
solipsism 36
sophistry 3–5, 8, 131, 133
  as 'knack' 134–35
sovereign 22–24
  limits of 39
sovereignty 45, 150–53, 221
state, the 15
  actual versus ideal 18
  complexity and sovereignty 19
  concept formation 31, 219
  construed as a voluntary organization 19
  contrasted with mafia 42–43
  founding of 203
  legitimacy, authority, obedience 17, 22, 27, 46–52, 149, 157, 221
  versus particular states 125–26, 221
  relation of citizen's will to 19
  relation of subject to 27
  and society 33, 38

Thucydides
  ambassadors to Melos 143
trust 36
truth 37, 131–33

unity 23, 25, 38
utilitarianism 3n1, 116, 187

Vico, Giambattista 162

war 37
Weber, Max 8, 12
Weil, Simone
  consent 41, 49, 227
  legitimacy 12, 18, 26–28, 31, 41, 42, 49, 127, 221, 227
  loyalty 39
  will 137, 138, 226
Weldon, T. D. 34
Will, the
  active 128
  and action 226, 230
  in Hobbes (proper object is good to self) 20, 44
  in Hume (binding of the will) 52, 149
  in Plato (good as object of) 135–39
  and reason 226
  in Rousseau 149–53
  of the sovereign 19, 25
  subservience vs. authority 50
Winch, Peter
  'Certainty and Authority' 208, 229
  The Idea of a Social Science 30n31
  'Man and Society in Hobbes and Rousseau' xx, 207n4
  'Nature and Convention' 30n31, 36, 37
  'Understanding a Primitive Society' 9n4, 30, 30n31
  'Wittgenstein's Treatment of the Will' 230
Wisdom, John 3
Wittgenstein, Ludwig
  attitude towards a soul 38
  craving for generality 14
  Culture and Value 125, 137
  description not explanation 7
  forms of life 8, 10n5, 219
  friction 38

grammar 9, 30, 203, 226
ideal as object of comparison 153
language games 133
learning 162
Lecture on ethics 230
light dawns gradually 219
Notebooks 1914–1916 230
On Certainty 208, 227, 229

paradigms 8–10
Philosophical Investigations 126, 191n2, 211–13, 230
reason 157
rule-following 7–8, 36, 37
Tractatus Logico-Philosophicus 13, 182, 191n2, 230

www.ingramcontent.com/pod-product-compliance
Lightning Source LLC
Jackson TN
JSHW021904080625
85732JS00001B/4